Text, Speech and Language Technology

VOLUME 31

FWF Der Wissenschaftsfonds.

Veröffentlicht mit Unterstützung des Fonds zur Förderung der wissentschaftlichen Forschung.

Contributions to the Science of Text and Language

Word Length Studies and Related Issues

Edited by

Peter Grzybek
University of Graz, Austria

Springer

A C.I.P. Catalogue record for this book is available from the Library of Congress.

ISBN-10 1-4020-4067-9 (HB)
ISBN-13 978-1-4020-4067-2 (HB)
ISBN-10 1-4020-4068-7 (e-book)
ISBN-13 978-1-4020-4068-9 (e-book)

Published by Springer,
P.O. Box 17, 3300 AA Dordrecht, The Netherlands.

www.springeronline.com

Printed on acid-free paper

Printed in the Netherlands

Dedicated to all those pioneers in the field of quantitative linguistics and text analysis, who have understood that quantifying is not the aim, but a means to understanding the structures and processes of text and language, and who have thus paved the way for a theory and science of language

Contents

Preface

The studies represented in this volume have been collected in the interest of bringing together contributions from three fields which are all important for a comprehensive approach to the quantitative study of text and language, in general, and of word length studies, in particular: first, scholars from linguistics and text analysis, second, mathematicians and statisticians working on related issues, and third, experts in text corpus and text data bank design.

A scientific research project initiated in spring 2002 provided the perfect opportunity for this endeavor. Financially supported by the Austrian Research Fund (*FWF*), this three-year project, headed by Peter Grzybek (Graz University) and Ernst Stadlober (Technical University Graz) concentrates on the study of word length and word length frequencies, with particular emphasis on Slavic languages. Specifically, factors influencing word length are systematically studied.

The majority of contributions to be found in this volume go back to a conference held in Austria at the very beginning of the project, at Graz University and the nearby Schloss Seggau in June, 2002.[1] Experts from all over Europe were invited to contribute, with a particular emphasis on the participation of scholars from East European countries whose valuable work continues to remain ignored, be it due to language barriers, or to difficulties in the accessibility of their publications. It is the aim of this volume to contribute to a better mutual exchange of ideas.

Generally speaking, the aim of the conference was to diagnose and to discuss the state of the art in word length studies, with experts from the above-mentioned disciplines. Moreover, the above-mentioned project and the guiding ideas behind it should be presented to renowned experts from the scientific community, with three major intentions: first, to present the basic ideas as to the problem outlined, and to have them discussed from an external perspective in order to

[1] For a conference report see Grzybek/Stadlober (2003), for further details see `http://www-gewi.uni-graz.at/quanta`.

profit from differing approaches; second, to raise possible critical points as to the envisioned methodology, and to discuss foreseeable problems which might arise during the project; and third, to discuss, at the very beginning, options to prepare data, and analytical procedures, in such a way that they might be publicly useful and available not only during the project, but afterwards, as well.

Since, with the exception of the introductory essay, the articles appear in alphabetical order, they shall be briefly commented upon here in relation to their thematic relevance.

The introductory contribution by **Peter Grzybek** on the *History and Methodology of Word Length Studies* attempts to offer a general starting point and, in fact, provides an extensive survey on the state of the art. This contribution concentrates on theoretical approaches to the question, from the 19th century up to the present, and it offers an extensive overview not only of the development of word length studies, but of contemporary approaches, as well.

The contributions by **Gejza Wimmer** from Slovakia and **Gabriel Altmann** from Germany, as well as the one by **Victor Kromer** from Russia, follow this line of research, in so far as they are predominantly theory-oriented. Whereas Wimmer and Altmann try to achieve an all-encompassing *Unified Derivation of Some Linguistic Laws*, Kromer's contribution *About Word Length Distribution* is more specific, concentrating on a particular model of word length frequency distribution.

As compared to such theory-oriented studies, a number of contributions are located at the other end of the research spectrum: concentrating less on mere theoretical aspects of word length, they are related to the authors' work on text corpora. Whereas **Reinhard Köhler** from Germany, understanding a *Text Corpus As an Abstract Data Structure*, tries to generally outline *The Architecture Of a Universal Corpus Interface*, the contributions by **Primož Jakopin** from Slovenia, **Marko Tadić** from Croatia, and **Duško Vitas, Gordana Pavlović-Lažetić**, & **Cvetana Krstev** from Belgrade concentrate on the specifics of Croatian, Serbian, and Slovenian corpora, with particular reference to word-length studies. Jakopin's contribution *On Text Corpora, Word Lengths, and Word Frequencies in Slovenian*, Tadić's report on *Developing the Croatian National Corpus and Beyond*, as well as the study *About Word Length Counting in Serbian* by Vitas, Pavlović-Lažetić, and Krstev primarily intend to discuss the availability and form of linguistic material from different text corpora, and the usefulness of the underlying data structure of their corpora for quantitative analyses. From this point of view their publications show the efficiency of co-operations between the different fields.

Another block of contributions represent concrete analyses, though from differing perspectives, and with different objectives. The first of these is the analysis by **Andrew Wilson** from Great Britain of *Word-Length Distribution* *in Present-Day Lower Sorbian.* Applying the theoretical framework outlined by Altmann, Wimmer, and their colleagues, this is one example of theoretically modelling word length frequencies in a number of texts of a given language, Lower Sorbian in this case. **Gordana Antić, Emmerich Kelih, & Peter Grzybek** from Austria, discuss methodological problems of word length studies, concentrating on *Zero-syllable Words in Determining Word Length.* Whereas this problem, which is not only relevant for Slavic studies, usually is "solved" by way of an authoritative decision, the authors attempt to describe the concrete consequences arising from such linguistic decisions. Two further contributions by **Ernst Stadlober & Mario Djuzelic** from Graz, and by **Otto A. Rottmann** from Germany, attempt to apply word length analysis for typological purposes: thus, Stadlober & Djuzelic, in their article on *Multivariate Statistical Methods in Quantitative Text Analyses*, reflect their results with regard to quantitative text typology, whereas Rottmann discusses *Aspects of the Typology of Slavic Languages Exemplified on Word Length.*

A number of further contributions discuss the relevance of word length studies within a broader linguistic context. Thus, **Simone Andersen & Gabriel Altmann** (Germany) analyze *Information Content of Words in Texts*, and **August Fenk & Gertraud Fenk-Oczlon** (Austria), study *Within-Sentence Distribution and Retention of Content Words and Function Words.*

The remaining three contributions have the common aim of shedding light on the interdependence between word length and other linguistic units. Thus, both **Werner Lehfeldt** from Germany, and **Anatolij A. Polikarpov** from Russia, place their word length studies within a Menzerathian framework: in doing so, Lehfeldt, in his analysis of *The Fall of the Jers in the Light of Menzerath's Law*, introduces a diachronic perspective, Polikarpov, in his attempt at *Explaining Basic Menzerathian Regularity*, focuses the *Dependence of Affix Length on the Ordinal Number of their Positions within Words.* Finally, **Udo Strauss, Peter Grzybek, & Gabriel Altmann** re-analyze the well-known problem of *Word Length and Word Frequency*; on the basis of their study, the authors arrive at the conclusion that sometimes, in describing linguistic phenomena, less complex models are sufficient, as long as the principle of data homogeneity is obeyed.

The volume thus offering a broad spectrum of word length studies, should be of interest not only to experts in general linguistics and text scholarship, but in related fields as well. Only a closer co-operation between experts from the above-mentioned fields will provide an adequate basis for further insight into what is actually going on in language(s) and text(s), and it is the hope of this volume to make a significant contribution to these efforts.

This volume would not have seen the light of day without the invaluable help and support of many individuals and institutions. First and foremost, my thanks goes to Gabriel Altmann, who has accompanied the whole project from its very beginnings, and who has nurtured it with his competence and enthusiasm throughout the duration. Also, without the help of the Graz team, mainly my friends and colleagues Gordana Antić, Emmerich Kelih, Rudi Schlatte, and of course Ernst Stadlober, this book could not have taken its present shape.

Furthermore, it is my pleasure and duty to express my gratitude to the following for their financial support: first of all, thanks goes to the Austrian Science Fund (FWF) in Vienna for funding both research project # P15485 («Word Length Frequencies in Slavic Language Texts»), and the present volume. Sincere thanks as well goes to various institutions which have repeatedly sponsored academic meetings related to this volume, among others: Graz University (Vice Rector for Research and Knowledge Transfer, Vice Rector and Office for International Relations, Faculty for Cultural Studies, Department for Slavic Studies), Technical University Graz (Department for Statistics), Office for the Government of the Province of Styria (Department for Science), Office of the Mayor of the City of Graz.

Finally, my thanks goes to Wolfgang Eismann for his help in interpreting some Polish texts, and to Bríd Ní Mhaoileoin for her careful editing of the texts in this volume.

Preparing the layout of this volume myself, using TEXor LATEX 2_ε, respectively, I have done what I could to put all articles into an atrtractive shape; any remaining flaws are my responsibility.

PETER GRZYBEK

1

INTRODUCTORY REMARKS: ON THE SCIENCE OF LANGUAGE IN LIGHT OF THE LANGUAGE OF SCIENCE

Peter Grzybek

The seemingly innocent formulation as to a *science of language* in light of the *language of science* is more than a mere play on words: rather, this formulation may turn out to be relatively demanding, depending on the concrete understanding of the terms involved – particularly, placing the term 'science' into a framework of a general theory of science. No doubt, there is more than one theory of science, and it is not the place here to discuss the philosophical implications of this field in detail. Furthermore, it has become commonplace to refuse the concept of a unique theory of science, and to distinguish between a general theory of science and specific theories of science, relevant for individual sciences (or branches of science). This tendency is particularly strong in the humanities, where 19th century ideas as to the irreconcilable antagony of human and natural, of weak and hard sciences, etc., are perpetuated, though sophisticatedly updated in one way or another.

The basic problem thus is that the understanding of 'science' (and, consequently, the far-reaching implications of the understanding of the term) is not the same all across the disciplines. As far as linguistics, which is at stake here, is concerned, the self-evaluation of this discipline clearly is that it fulfills the requirements of being a science, as Smith (1989: 26) correctly puts it:

> Linguistics likes to think of itself as a science in the sense that it makes testable, i.e. potentially falsifiable, statements or predictions.

The relevant question is not, however, to which extent linguistics considers itself to be a science; rather, the question must be, to which extent does linguistics satisfy the needs of a general theory of science. And the same holds true, of course, for related disciplines focusing on specific language products and processes, starting from subfields such as psycholinguistics, up to the area of text scholarship, in general.

Generally speaking, it is commonplace to say that there can be no science without theory, or theories. And there will be no doubt that theories are usually

P. Grzybek (ed.), Contributions to the Science of Text and Language, 1-14.

conceived of as models for the interpretation or explanation of the phenomena to be understood or explained. More often than not, however, linguistic understandings of the term 'theory' are less "ambitious" than postulates from the philosophy of science: linguistic "theories" rather tend to confine themselves to being conceptual systems covering a particular aspect of language. Terms like 'word formation theory' (understood as a set of rules with which words are composed from morphemes), 'syntax theory' (understood as a set of rules with which sentences are formed), or 'text theory' (understood as a set of rules with which sentences are combined) are quite characteristic in this respect (cf. Altmann 1985: 1). In each of these cases, we are concerned with not more and not less than a system of concepts whose function it is to provide a consistent description of the object under study. 'Theory' thus is understood in the descriptive meaning; ultimately, it boils down to an intrinsically plausible, coherent descriptive system, cf. Smith (1989: 14)

> But the hallmark of a (scientific) theory is that it gives rise to hypotheses which can be the object of rational argumentation.

Now, it goes without saying that the existence of a system of concepts is necessary for the construction of a theory: yet, it is a necessary, but not sufficient condition (cf. Altmann 1985: 2):

> One should not have the illusion that one constructs a theory when one classifies linguistic phenomena and develops sophisticated conceptual systems, or discovers universals, or formulates linguistic rules. Though this predominantly descriptive work is essential and stands at the beginning of any research, nothing more can be gained but the definition of the research object [...]

What is necessary then, for science, is the existence of a theory, or of theories, which are systems of specific hypotheses, which are not only plausible, but must be both deduced or deducible from the theory, and tested, or in principle be testable (cf. Altmann 1978: 3):

> The main part of a theory consists of a system of hypotheses. Some of them are empirical (= tenable), i.e. they are corroborated by data; others are theoretical or (deductively) valid, i.e. they are derived from the axioms or theorems of a (not necessarily identical) theory with the aid of permitted operations. A scientific theory is a system in which some valid hypotheses are tenable and (almost) no hypotheses untenable.

Thus, theories pre-suppose the existence of specific hypotheses the formulation of which, following Bunge (1967: 229), implies the three main requisites:

(i) the hypothesis must be *well formed* (formally correct) and *meaningful* (semantically nonempty) in some scientific context;

(ii) the hypothesis must be *grounded* to some extent on previous knowledge, i.e. it must be related to definite grounds other than the data it covers; if entirely novel it must be compatible with the bulk of scientific knowledge;

(iii) the hypothesis must be empirically testable by the objective procedures of science, i.e. by confrontation with empirical data controlled in turn by scientific techniques and theories.

In a next step, therefore, different levels in conjecture making may thus be distinguished, depending on the relation between hypothesis (h), antecedent knowledge (A), and empirical evidence (e); Figure1.1 illustrates the four levels.

(i) *Guesses* are unfounded and untested hypotheses, which characterize speculation, pseudoscience, and possibly the earlier stages of theoretical work.

(ii) *Empirical hypotheses* are ungrounded but empirically corroborated conjectures; they are rather isolated and lack empirical validation, since they have no support other than the one offered by the fact(s) they cover.

(iii) *Plausible hypotheses* are founded but untested hypotheses; they lack an empirical justification but are, in principle, testable.

(iv) *Corroborated hypotheses* are well-grounded and empirically confirmed; ultimately, only hypotheses of this level characterize theoretical knowledge and are the hallmark of mature science.

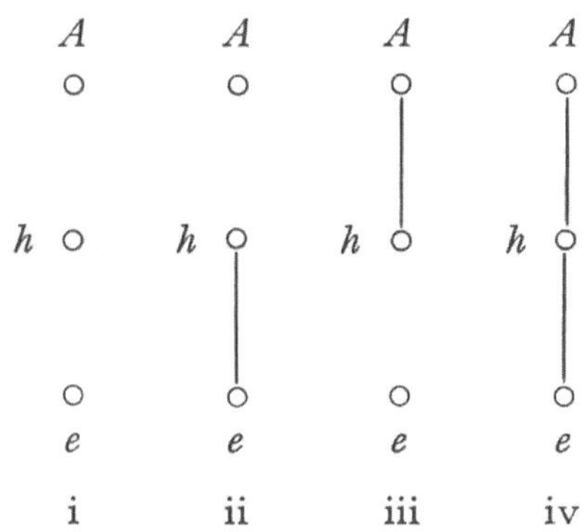

Figure 1.1: Levels of Conjecture Making and Validation

If, and only if, a corroborated hypothesis is, in addition to being well-grounded and empirically confirmed, general and systemic, then it may be termed a 'law'. Now, given that the "chief goal of scientific research is the discovery of patterns" (Bunge 1967: 305), a law is a confirmed hypothesis that is supposed to depict such a pattern.

Without a doubt, use of the term 'law' will arouse skepticism and refusal in linguists' ears and hearts.[1] In a way, this is no wonder, since the term 'law' has a specific connotation in the linguistic tradition (cf. Kovács 1971, Collinge 1985): basically, this tradition refers to 19th century studies of sound laws, attempts to describe sound changes in the history of (a) language.

In the beginnings of this tradition, predominantly in the Neogrammarian approach to Indo-European language history, these laws – though of descriptive rather than explanative nature – allowed no exceptions to the rules, and they were indeed understood as deterministic laws. It goes without saying that up to that time, determinism in nature had hardly ever been called into question, and the formation of the concept of 'law' still stood in the tradition of Newtonian classical physics, even in Darwin's time, he himself largely ignoring probability as an important category in science.

The term 'sound law', or 'phonetic law' [Lautgesetz] had been originally coined as a technical term by German linguist Franz Bopp (1791–1867) in the 1820s. Interestingly enough, his view on language included a natural-scientific perspective, understanding language as an organic physical body [organischer Naturkörper]. At this stage, the phonetic law was not considered to be a law of nature [Naturgesetz], as yet; rather, we are concerned with metaphorical comparisons, which nonetheless signify a clear tendency towards scientific exactness in linguistics. The first militant "naturalist-linguist" was August Schleicher (1821–1868). Deeply influenced by evolutionary theorists, mainly Charles Darwin and Ernst Häckel, he understood languages to be a 'product of nature' in the strict sense of this word, i.e., as a 'natural organism' [Naturorganismus] which, according to his opinion, came into being and developed according to specific laws, as he claimed in the 1860s. Consequently, for Schleicher, the science of language must be a natural science, and its method must by and large be the same as that of the other natural sciences. Many a scholar in the second half of the 19th century would elaborate on these ideas: if linguistics belonged to the natural sciences, or at least worked with equivalent methods, then linguistic laws should be identical with the natural laws. Natural laws, however, were considered mechanistic and deterministic, and partly continue to be even today. Consequently, in the mid-1870s, scholars such as August Leskien (1840–1916), Hermann Osthoff (1847–1909), and Karl Brugmann (1849–1919) repeatedly emphasized the sound laws they studied to be exceptionless. Every scholar admitting exceptions was condemned to be addicted to subjectivism and arbitrariness. The rigor of these claims began to be heavily discussed from the 1880s on, mainly by scholars such as Berthold G.G. Delbrück (1842–1922), Mikołai Kruszewski

[1] Quite characteristically, Collinge (1985), for example, though listing some dozens of *Laws of Indo-European*, avoids the discussion of what 'law' actually means; for him, these "are issues better left to philosophers of language history" (ibd., 1)

(1851–87), and Hugo Schuchardt (1842–1927). Now, 'laws' first began to be distinguished from 'regularities' (the latter even being sub-divided into 'absolute' and 'relative' regularities), and they were soon reduced to analogies or uniformities [Gleichmäßigkeiten]. Finally, it was generally doubted whether the term 'law' is applicable to language; specifically, linguistic laws were refuted as natural laws, allegedly having no similarity at all with chemical or physical laws.

If irregularities were observed, linguists would attempt to find a "regulation for the irregularity", as linguist Karl A. Verner (1846–96) put it in 1876. Curiously enough, this was almost the very same year that Austrian physicist Ludwig Boltzmann (1844–1906) re-defined one of the established natural laws, the second law of thermodynamics, in terms of probability.

As will be remembered, the first law of thermodynamics implies the statement that the energy of a given system remains constant without external influence. No claim is made as to the question, which of various possible states, all having the same energy, is at stake, i.e. which of them is the most probable one. As to this point, the term 'entropy' had been introduced as a specific measure of systemic disorder, and the claim was that entropy cannot decrease in case processes taking place in closed systems. Now, Boltzmann's statistical re-definition of the concept of entropy implies the postulate that entropy is, after all, a function of a system's state. In fact, this idea may be regarded to be the foundation of statistical mechanics, as it was later called, describing thermodynamic systems by reference to the statistical behavior of their constituents.

What Boltzmann thus succeeded to do was in fact not less than deliver proof that the second law of thermodynamics is not a natural law in the deterministic understanding of the term, as was believed in his time, and is still often mistakenly believed, even today. Ultimately, the notion of 'law' thus generally was supplied with a completely different meaning: it was no longer to be understood as a deterministic law, allowing for no exceptions for individual singularities; rather, the behavior of some totality was to be described in terms of statistical probability. In fact, Boltzmann's ideas were so radically innovative and important that almost half a century later, in the 1920s, physicist Erwin Schrödinger (1922) would raise the question, whether not all natural laws might generally be statistical in nature. In fact, this question is of utmost relevance in theoretical physics, still today (or, perhaps, more than ever before). John Archibald Wheeler (1994: 293) for example, a leading researcher in the development of general relativity and quantum gravity, recently suspected, "that every law of physics, pushed to the extreme, will be found to be statistical and approximate, not mathematically perfect and precise."

However, the statistical or probabilistic re-definition of 'law' escaped attention of linguists of that time. And, generally speaking, one may say it remained unnoticed till today, which explains the aversion of linguists to the concept of law, at the end of the 19th century as well as today... Historically speaking, this aversion has been supported by the spirit of the time, when scholars like Dilthey (1883: 27) established the hermeneutic tradition in the humanities and declared singularities and individualities of socio-historical reality to be the objective of the humanities. It was the time when 'nature itself', as a research object, was opposed to 'nature *ad hominem*', when 'explanation' was increasingly juxtaposed to 'interpretation', and when "nomothetic law sciences" [nomothetische Gesetzeswissenschaften] were distinguished from "idiographic event sciences" [idiographische Ereigniswissenschaften], as Neokantian scholars such as Heinrich Windelband and Wilhelm Rickert put it in the 1890s. Ultimately, this would result in what Snow should term the distinction of *Two Cultures*, in the 1960s – a myth strategically upheld even today. This myth is well prone to perpetuating the overall skepticism as to mathematical methods in the field of the humanities. Mathematics, in this context, tends to be discarded since it allegedly neglects the individuality of the object under study. However, mathematics can never be a substitute for theory, it can only be a tool for theory construction (Bunge 1967: 467).

Ultimately, in science as well as in everyday life, any conclusion as to the question, whether observed or assumed differences, relations, or changes are essential, are merely chance or not, must involve a decision. In everyday life, this decision may remain a matter of individual choice; in science, however, it should obey conventional rules. More often than not, in the realm of the humanities, the empirical test of a given hypothesis has been replaced by the acceptance of the scientific community; this is only possible, of course, because, more often than not, we are concerned with specific hypotheses, as compared to the above Figure 1.1, i.e., with plausible hypotheses.

As soon as we are concerned with empirical tests of a hypothesis, we face the moment where statistics necessarily comes into play: after all, for more than two hundred years, chance has been statistically "tamed" and (re-)defined in terms of probability. Actually, this is the reason why mathematics in general, and particularly statistics as a special field of it, is so essential to science: ultimately, the crucial function of mathematics in science is its role in the expression of scientific models. Observing and collecting measurements, as well as hypothesizing and predicting, typically require mathematical models.

In this context, it is important to note that the formation of a theory is not identical to the simple transformation of intuitive assumptions into the language of formal logic or mathematics; not each attempt to describe (!) particular phenomena by recourse to mathematics or statistics, is building a theory, at least not in the understanding of this term as outlined above. Rather, it is important that there be a model which allows for formulating the statistical hypotheses in terms of probabilities.

At this moment, human sciences in general, and linguistics in particular, tend to bring forth a number of objections, which should be discussed here in brief (cf. Altmann 1985: 5ff.):

a. The most frequent objection is: ≪We are concerned not with quantities, but with qualities.≫ – The simple answer would be that there is a profound epistemological error behind this 'objection', which ultimately is of ontological nature: actually, neither qualities nor quantities are inherent in an object itself; rather they are part of the concepts with which we interpret nature, language, etc.
b. A second well-known objection says: ≪Not everything in nature, language, etc. can be submitted to quantification.≫ – Again, the answer is trivial, since it is not language, nature, etc., which is quantified, but our concepts of them.

In principle, there are therefore no obstacles to formulate statistical hypotheses concerning language in order to arrive at an explanatory model of it; the transformation into statistical meta-language does not depend so much on the object, as on the status of the concrete discipline, or the individual scholar's education (cf. Bunge 1967: 469).

A science of language, understood in the manner outlined above, must therefore be based on statistical hypotheses and theorems, leading to a complete set of laws and/or law-like regularities, ultimately being described and/or explained by a theory. Thus, although linguistics, text scholarship, etc., in the course of their development, have developed specific approaches, measures, and methods, the application of statistical testing procedures must correspond to the following general schema (cf. Altmann 1973: 218ff.):

1. The formulation of a linguistic hypothesis, usually of qualitative kind.
2. The linguistic hypothesis must be translated into the language of statistics; qualitative concepts contained in the hypothesis must be transformed into quantitative ones, so that the statistical models can be applied to them. This may lead to a re-formulation of the hypothesis itself, which must have the form of a statistical hypotheses. Furthermore, a mathematical model must be chosen which allows the probability to be calculated with which the hypothesis may be valid with regard to the data under study.
3. Data have to be collected, prepared, evaluated, and calculated according to the model chosen. (It goes without saying that, in practice, data may stand at the beginning of research – but this should not prevent anyone from going "back" to step one within the course of scientific research.)
4. The result obtained is represented by one or more digits, by a particular function, or the like. Its statistical evaluation leads to an acceptance or refusal of the hypothesis, and to a statement as to the significance of the results.

Ultimately, this decision is not given a priori in the data, but the result of disciplinary conventions.

5. The result must be linguistically interpreted, i.e., re-translated into the linguistic (meta-)language; conclusions must be linguistically drawn, which are based on the confirmed or rejected hypothesis.

Now what does it mean, concretely, if one wants to construct a theory of language in the scientific understanding of this term? According to Altmann (1978: 5), designing a theory of language must start as follows:

> When constructing a theory of language we proceed on the basic assumption that language is a self-regulating system all of whose entities and properties are brought into line with one another in some way or other.

From this perspective, general systems theory and synergetics provide a general framework for a science of language; the statistical formulation of the theoretical model thus can be regarded to represent a meta-linguistic interface to other branches of sciences. As a consequence, language is by no means understood as a natural product in the 19th century understanding of this term; neither is it understood as something extraordinary within culture. Most reasonably, language lends itself to being seen as a specific cultural sign system. Culture, in turn, offers itself to be interpreted in the framework of an evolutionary theory of cognition, or of evolutionary cultural semiotics, respectively. Culture thus is defined as the cognitive and semiotic device for the adaption of human beings to nature. In this sense, culture is a continuation of nature on the one hand, and simultaneously a reflection of nature on the other – consequently, culture stands in an isologic relation to nature, and it can be studied as such.

Therefore culture, understood as the functional correlation of sign systems, must not be seen in ontological opposition to nature: after all, we know at least since Heisenberg's times, that nature cannot be directly observed as a scientific object, but only by way of our culturally biased models and perspectives. Both 'culture' and 'nature' thus turn out to be two specific cultural constructs. One consequence of this view is that the definitions of 'culture' and 'nature' necessarily are subject to historical changes; another consequence is that there can only be a unique theory of 'culture' and 'nature', if one accepts the assumptions above. As Koch (1986: 161) phrases it: " 'Nature' can only be understood via 'Culture'; and 'Culture' can only be comprehended via 'Nature'."

Thus language, as one special case of cultural sign systems, is not – and definitely not *per se*, and not *a priori* – understood as an abstract system of rules or representations. Primarily, language is understood as a sign system serving as a vehicle of cognition and communication. Based on the further assumption that communicative processes are characterized by some kind of economy between the participants, language, regarded as an abstract sign system, is understood as the economic result of communicative processes.

Talking about economy of communication, or of language, any exclusive focus on the production aspect must result in deceptive illusions, since due attention has to be paid to the overall complexity of communicative processes: In any individual speech act, the producer's creativity, his or her principally unlimited freedom to produce whatever s/he wants in whatever form s/he wants, is controlled by the recipient's limited capacities to follow the producer in what s/he is trying to communicate. Any producer being interested in remaining understood (even in the most extreme forms of avantgarde poetry), consequently has to take into consideration the recipient's limitations, and s/he has to make concessions with regard to the recipient.

As a result, a communicative act involves a circular process, providing something like an economic equilibrium between producer's and recipient's interests, which by no means must be a symmetric balance. Rather, we are concerned with a permanent process of mutual adaptation, and of a specific interrelation of (partly contradictory) forces at work, leading to a specific dynamics of antagonistic interest forces in communicative processes. Communicative acts, as well as the sign system serving communication, thus represent something like a dynamic equilibrium.

In principle, this view has been delineated by G.K. Zipf as early as in the 1930s and 40s (cf. Zipf 1949). Today, Zipf is mostly known for his frequency studies, mainly on the word level; however, his ideas have been applied to many other levels of language too, and have been successfully transferred to other disciplines as well.

Most importantly, his ideas as to word length and word frequency have been integrated into a synergetic concept of language, as envisioned by Altmann (1978: 5), and as outlined by Köhler (1985) and Köhler/Altmann (1986). It would be going too far to discuss the relevant ideas in detail here; still, the basic implications of this approach should be presented in order to show that the focus on word length chosen in this book is far from accidental.

Word Length in a Synergetic Context

Word length is, of course, only one linguistic trait of texts, among others. In this sense, word length studies cannot be but a modest *contribution to* an overall *science of language*. However, a focus on the word is not accidental, and the linguistic unit of the word itself is far from trivial.

Rather, word length is an important factor in a synergetic approach to language and text, and it is by no means an isolated linguistic phenomenon within the structure of language. Given one accepts the distinction of linguistic levels, such as (1) phoneme/grapheme, (2) syllable/morpheme, (3) word/lexeme, (4) clause, and (5) sentence, structurally speaking, the word turns out to be hierarchically located in the center of linguistic units: it is formed by lower-level units, and itself is part of the higher-level units. The question here cannot be, of course, in how far each of the units mentioned are equally adequate for linguistic models, in how far their definitions should be modified, or in how far there may be further levels, particularly with regard to specific text types (such as poems, for example, where verses and stanzas may be more suitable units).

At closer inspection (cf. Table 1.1), at least the first three levels are concerned with recurrent units. Consequently, on each of these levels, the re-occurrence of units results in particular frequencies, which may be modelled with recourse to specific frequency distribution models. To give but one example, the famous Zipf-Mandelbrot distribution has become a generally accepted model for word frequencies. Models for letter and phoneme frequencies have recently been discussed in detail. It turns out that the Zipf-Mandelbrot distribution is no adequate model, on this linguistic level (cf. Grzybek/Kelih/Altmann 2004). Yet, grapheme and phoneme frequencies seem to display a similar ranking behavior, which, in both cases depends on the relevant inventory sizes and the resulting frequencies with which the relevant units are realized in a given text (Grzybek/Kelih/Altmann 2005).

Moreover, the units of all levels are characterized by length; and again, the length of the units on one level is directly interrelated with those of the neighboring levels, and, probably, indirectly with those of all others. This is where Menzerath's law comes into play (cf. Altmann 1980, Altmann/Schwibbe 1989), and Arens's law as a special case of it (cf. Altmann 1983).

Finally, systematic dependencies cannot only be observed on the level of length; rather, each of the length categories displays regularities in its own right. Thus, particular frequency length distributions may be modelled on all levels distinguished.

Table 1.1, illustrating the basic interrelations, may be, cum grano salis, regarded to represent something like the synergetics of linguistics in a nutshell.

Table 1.1: Word Length in a Synergetic Circuit

	SENTENCE	Length	Frequency
		↕	
	CLAUSE	Length	Frequency
↱		↰ ↕	
Frequency	WORD / LEXEME	Length	Frequency
↕ ↱		↰ ↕	
Frequency	SYLLABLE / MORPHEME	Length	Frequency
↕ ↱		↰ ↕	
Frequency	PHONEME / GRAPHEME	Length	Frequency

Much progress has been made in recent years, regarding all the issues mentioned above; and many questions have been answered. Yet, many a problem still begs a solution; in fact, even many a question remains to be asked, at least in a systematic way. Thus, the descriptive apparatus has been excellently developed by structuralist linguistics; yet, structuralism has never made the decisive next step, and has never asked the crucial question as to explanatory models. Also, the methodological apparatus for hypothesis testing has been elaborated, along with the formation of a great amount of valuable hypotheses.

Still, much work remains to be done. From one perspective, this work may be regarded as some kind of "refinement" of existing insight, as some kind of detail analysis of boundary conditions, etc. From another perspective, this work will throw us back to the very basics of empirical study. Last but not least, the quality of scientific research depends on the quality of the questions asked, and any modification of the question, or of the basic definitions, will lead to different results.

As long as we do not know, for example, what a word is, i.e., how to define a word, we must test the consequences of different definitions: do we obtain identical, or similar, or different results, when defining a word as a graphemic, an orthographic, a phonetic, phonological, a morphological, a syntactic, a psychological, or other kind of unit? And how, or in how far, do the results change – and if so, do they systematically change? – depending on the decision, in which units a word is measured: in the number of letters, or graphemes, or of sounds, phones, phonemes, of morphs, morphemes, of syllables, or other units? These questions have never been systematically studied, and it is a problem sui generis, to ask for regularities (such as frequency distributions) on each of the levels mentioned. But ultimately, these questions concern only the first degree of uncertainty, involving the qualitative decision as to the measuring units: given, we clearly distinguish these factors, and study them systematically, the next questions concern the quality of our data material: will the results be the same, and how, or in how far, will they (systematically?) change, depending on the decision as to whether we submit individual texts, text segments, text mixtures, whole corpora, or dictionary material to our analyses? At this point, the important distinction of types and tokens comes into play, and again the question must be, how, or in how far, the results depend upon a decision as to this point.

Thus far, only language-intrinsic factors have been named, which possibly influence word length; and this enumeration is not even complete; other factors as the phoneme inventory size, the position in the sentence, the existence of suprasegmentals, etc., may come into play, as well. And, finally, word length does of course not only depend on language-intrinsic factors, according to the synergetic schema represented in Table 1.1. There is also abundant evidence that external factors may strongly influence word length, and word length frequency

Zipf, George K.
1949 *Human behavior and the principle of least effort. An introduction to human ecology.* Cambridge, Mass.

2

HISTORY AND METHODOLOGY OF WORD LENGTH STUDIES

The State of the Art

Peter Grzybek

1. Historical roots

The study of word length has an almost 150-year long history: it was on August 18, 1851, when Augustus de Morgan, the well-known English mathematician and logician (1806–1871), in a letter to a friend of his, brought forth the idea of studying word length as an indicator of individual style, and as a possible factor in determining authorship. Specifically, de Morgan concentrated on the number of letters per word and suspected that the average length of words in different Epistles by St. Paul might shed some light on the question of authorship; generalizing his ideas, he assumed that the average word lengths in two texts, written by one and the same author, though on different subjects, should be more similar to each other than in two texts written by two different individuals on one and the same subject (cf. Lord 1958).

Some decades later, Thomas Corwin Mendenhall (1841–1924), an American physicist and metereologist, provided the first empirical evidence in favor of de Morgan's assumptions. In two subsequent studies, Mendenhall (1887, 1901) elaborated on de Morgan's ideas, suggesting that in addition to analyses "based simply on mean word-length" (1887: 239), one should attempt to graphically exhibit the peculiarities of style in composition: in order to arrive at such graphics, Mendenhall counted the frequency with which words of a given length occur in 1000-word samples from different authors, among them Francis Bacon, Charles Dickens, William M. Thackerey, and John Stuart Mill. Mendenhall's (1887: 241) ultimate aim was the description of the "normal curve of the writer", as he called it:

> [...] it is proposed to analyze a composition by forming what may be called a 'word spectrum' or 'characteristic curve', which shall be a graphic representation of the arrangement of words according to their length and to the relative frequency of their occurrence.

P. Gryzbek (ed.), Contributing in the Science of Text and Language, 15-90.

Figure 2.1, taken from Mendenhall (1887: 237), illustrates, by way of an example, Mendenhall's achievements, showing the result of two 1000-word samples from Dickens' *Oliver Twist*: quite convincingly, the two curves converge to an astonishing degree.

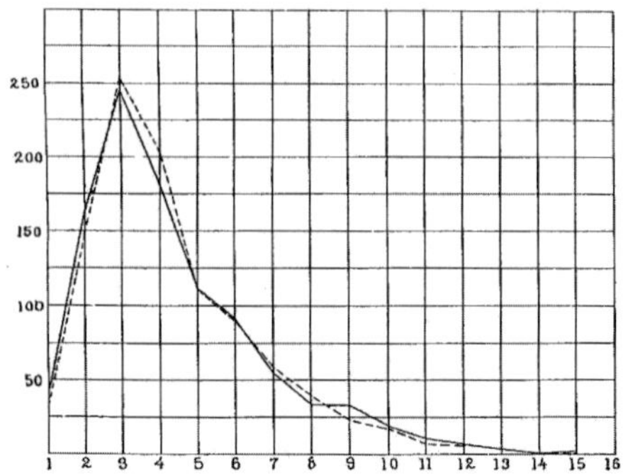

Figure 2.1: Word Length Frequencies in Dickens' *Oliver Twist* (Mendenhall 1887)

Mendenhall (1887: 244) clearly saw the possibility of further applications of his approach:

> It is hardly necessary to say that the method is not necessarily confined to the analysis of a composition by means of its mean word-length: it may equally well be applied to the study of syllables, of words in sentences, and in various other ways.

Still, Mendenhall concentrated on solely on word length, as he did in his follow-up study of 1901, when he continued his earlier line of research, extending it also to include selected passages from French, German, Italian, Latin, and Spanish texts.

As compared to the mere study of mean length, Mendenhall's work meant an enormous step forward in the study of word length, since we know that a given mean may be achieved on the basis of quite different frequency distributions. In fact, what Mendenhall basically did, was what would nowadays rather be called a frequency analysis, or frequency distribution analysis. It should be mentioned, therefore, that the mathematics of the comparison of frequency distributions was very little understood in Mendenhall's time. He personally was mainly attracted to the frequency distribution technique by its resemblance to spectroscopic analysis.

Figure 2.2, taken from Mendenhall (1901: 104) illustrates the curves from two passages by Bacon and Shakespeare. Quite characteristically, Mendenhall's conclusion was a suggestion to the reader: "The reader is at liberty to draw any conclusions he pleases from this diagram."

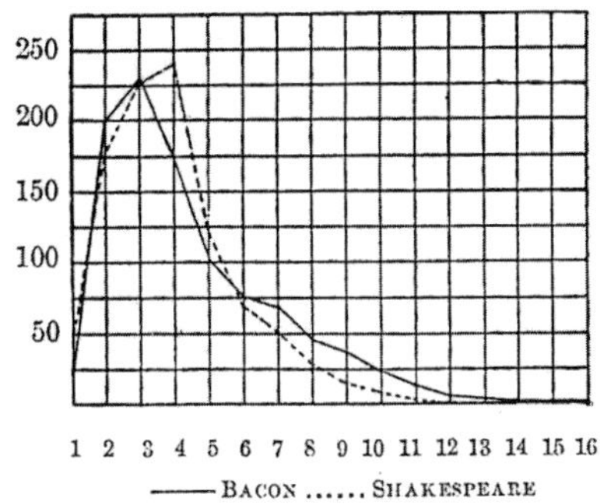

Figure 2.2: Word Length Frequencies in Bacon's and Shakespeare's Texts (Mendenhall 1901)

On the one hand, one may attribute this statement to the author's 'scientific caution', as Williams (1967: 89) put it, discussing Mendenhall's work. On the other hand, the desire for calculation of error or significance becomes obvious, techniques not yet well developed in Mendenhall's time.

Finally, there is another methodological flaw in Mendenhall's work, which has been pointed out by Williams (1976). Particularly as to the question of authorship, Williams (1976: 208) emphasized that before discussing the possible significance of the Shakespeare–Bacon and the Shakespeare–Marlowe controversies, it is important to ask whether any differences, other than authorship, were involved in the calculations. In fact, Williams correctly noted that the texts written by Shakespeare and Marlowe (which Mendenhall found to be very similar) were primarily written in blank verse, while all Bacon's works were in prose (and were clearly different). By way of additionally analyzing works by Sir Philip Sidney (1554–1586), a poet of the Elizabethan Age, Williams (1976: 211) arrived at an important conclusion:

> There is no doubt, as far as the criterion of word-length distribution is concerned, that Sidney's prose more closely resembles prose of Bacon than it does his own verse, and that Sidney's verse more closely resembles the verse plays of Shakespeare than it does his own prose. On the other hand, the pattern of difference between Shakespeare's verse and Bacon's prose is almost exactly comparable with the difference between Sidney's prose and his own verse.

Williams, too, did not submit his observations to statistical testing; yet, he made one point very clear: word length need not, or not only, or perhaps not even primarily, be characteristic of an individual author's style; rather word length, and word length frequencies, may be dependent on a number of other factors, genre being one of them (cf. Grzybek et al. 2005, Kelih et al. 2005).

Coming back to Mendenhall, his approach should thus, from a contemporary point of view, be submitted to cautious criticism in various aspects:

(a) *Word length is defined by the number of letters per word.*– Still today, many contemporary approaches (mainly in the domain of computer sciences), measure word length in the number of letters per word, not paying due attention to the arbitrariness of writing systems. Thus, the least one would expect would be to count the number of sounds, or phonemes, per word; as a matter of fact, it would seem much more reasonable to measure word length in more immediate constituents of the word, such as syllables, or morphemes. Yet, even today, there are no reliable systematic studies on the influence of the measuring unit chosen, nor on possible interrelations between them (and if they exist, they are likely to be extremely language-specific).

(b) *The frequency distribution of word length is studied on the basis of arbitrarily chosen samples of 1000 words.*– This procedure, too, is often applied, still today. More often than not, the reason for this procedure is based on the statistical assumption that, from a well-defined sample, one can, with an equally well-defined degree of probability, make reliable inferences about some totality, usually termed population. Yet, as has been repeatedly shown, studies along this line do not pay attention to a text's homogeneity (and consequently, to data homogeneity). Now, for some linguistic questions, samples of 1000 words may be homogeneous – for example, this seems to be the case with letter frequencies (cf. Grzybek/Kelih/Altmann 2004). For other questions, particularly those concerning word length, this does not seem to be the case – here, any selection of text segments, as well as any combination of different texts, turns out to be a "quasi text" destroying the internal rules of textual self-regulation. The very same, of course, has to be said about corpus analyses, since a corpus, from this point of view, is nothing but a quasi text.

(c) *Analyses and interpretations are made on a merely graphical basis.*– As has been said above, the most important drawback of this method is the lack of objectivity: no procedure is provided to compare two frequency distributions, be it the comparison of two empirical distributions, or the comparison of an empirical distribution to a theoretical one.

(d) *Similarities (homogeneities) and differences (heterogeneities) are unidimensionally interpreted.*– In the case of intralingual studies, word length frequency distributions are interpreted in terms of authorship, and in the case of interlingual comparisons in terms of language-specific factors, only; the possible influence of further influencing factors thus is not taken into consideration.

However, much of this criticism must then be directed towards contemporary research, too. Therefore, Mendenhall should be credited for having established an empirical basis for word length research, and for having initiated a line of research which continues to be relevant still today. Particularly the last point mentioned above, leads to the next period in the history of word length studies. As can be seen, no attempt was made by Mendenhall to find a formal (mathematical) model, which might be able to describe (or rather, theoretically model) the frequency distribution. As a consequence, no objective comparison between empirical and theoretical distributions has been possible.

In this respect, the work of a number of researchers whose work has only recently and, in fact, only partially been appreciated adequately, is of utmost importance. These scholars have proposed particular frequency distribution models, on the one hand, and they have developed methods to test the goodness of the results obtained. Initially, most scholars have (implicitly or explicitly) shared the assumption that there might be one overall model which is able to represent a general theory of word length; more recently, ideas have been developed assuming that there might rather be some kind of general organizational principle, on the basis of which various specific models may be derived.

The present treatment concentrates on the rise and development of such models. It goes without saying that without empirical data, such a discussion would be as useless as the development of theoretical models. Consequently, the following presentation, in addition to discussing relevant theoretical models, will also try to present the results of empirical research. Studies of merely empirical orientation, without any attempt to arrive at some generalization, will not be mentioned, however – this deliberate concentration on theory may be an important explanation as to why some quite important studies of empirical orientation will be absent from the following discussion.

The first models were discussed as early as in the late 1940s. Research then concentrated on two models: the Poisson distribution, and the geometric distribution, on the other. Later, from the mid-1950s onwards, in particular the Poisson distribution was submitted to a number of modifications and generalizations, and this shall be discussed in detail below. The first model to be discussed at some length, here, is the geometric distribution which was suggested to be an adequate model by Elderton in 1949.

2. The Geometric Distribution (Elderton 1949)

In his article "A Few Statistics on the Length of English Words" (1949), English statistician Sir William P. Elderton (1877–1962), who had published a book on *Frequency-Curves and Correlation* some decades before (London 1906), studied the frequency of word lengths in passages from English writers, among them Gray, Macaulay, Shakespeare, and others.

As opposed to Mendenhall, Elderton measured word length in the number of syllables, not letters, per word. Furthermore, in addition to merely counting the frequencies of the individual word length classes, and representing them in graphical form, Elderton undertook an attempt to find a statistical model for theoretically describing the distributions under investigation. His assumption was that the frequency distributions might follow the geometric distribution.

It seems reasonable to take a closer look at this suggestion, since, historically speaking, this was the first attempt ever made to arrive at a mathematical description of a word length frequency distribution. Where are zero-syllable words, i.e., if class $x = 0$ is not empty ($P_0 \neq 0$), the geometric distribution takes the following form (2.1):

$$P_x = p \cdot q^x \qquad x = 0, 1, 2, \ldots \qquad 0 < q < 1 \qquad p = 1 - q \tag{2.1}$$

If class $x = 0$ is empty, however (i.e., if $P_0 = 0$), and the first class are one-syllable words (i.e., $P_1 \neq 0$) – then the geometric distribution looks as follows (2.2):

$$P_x = p \cdot q^{x-1} \qquad x = 1, 2, 3, \ldots \tag{2.2}$$

Thus, generally speaking, for r-displaced distributions we may say:

$$P_x = p \cdot q^{x-r} \qquad x = r, r+1, r+2, \ldots \tag{2.3}$$

Data given by Elderton (1949: 438) on the basis of letters by Gray, may serve as material to demonstrate the author's approach. Table 2.1 contains for each word length (x_i) the absolute frequencies (f_i), as given by Elderton, as well as the corresponding relative frequencies (p_i).[1]

There are various possibilities for estimating the parameter p of the geometric distribution when fitting the theoretical model to the empirical data. Elderton chose one of the standard options (at least of his times), which is based on the mean of the distribution:

$$\bar{x} = \frac{1}{N} \sum_{i=1}^{n} x_i \cdot f_i = \frac{7063}{5237} = 1.3487$$

Since, by way of the maximum likelihood method (or the log-likelihood method, respectively), it can be shown that, for $P_1 \neq 0$ $(x = 1, 2, 3, \ldots)$, p is the reciprocal of the mean, i.e. $p = 1/\bar{x}$; therefore, the calculation is as follows:

$$\hat{p} = 1/\bar{x} = 1/1.3487 = 0.7415$$

and

$$\hat{q} = 1 - p = 1 - 0.7415 = 0.2585.$$

[1] In his tables, Elderton added the data for these frequencies in per mille, and on this basis he then calculated the theoretical frequencies by fitting the geometric distribution to them. For reasons of exactness, only the raw data will be used in the following presentation and discussion of Elderton's data.

Table 2.1: Word Length Frequencies for English Letters by Th.Gray (Elderton 1949)

Number of syllables	Frequency of x-syllable words	
(x_i)	(f_i)	(p_i)
1	3987	0.7613
2	831	0.1587
3	281	0.0537
4	121	0.0231
5	15	0.0029
6	2	0.0004

In Elderton's English data, which are represented in Table 2.1, there are no zero-syllable words ($P_0 = 0$); we are thus concerned with a 1-displaced distribution. Therefore, formula (2.2) is to be applied. We thus obtain:

$$P_1 = P(X = 1) = 0.7415 \cdot 0.2585^{1-1} = 0.7415$$
$$P_2 = P(X = 2) = 0.7415 \cdot 0.2585^{2-1} = 0.1917 \text{ etc.}$$

Based on these probabilities, the theoretical frequencies can easily be calculated:

$$NP_1 = 5237 \cdot 0.7415 = 3883.08$$
$$NP_2 = 5237 \cdot 0.1917 = 1003.89 \text{ etc.}$$

The theoretical data, obtained by fitting the geometric distribution[2] to the empirical data from Table 2.1, are represented in Table 2.2 (cf. p. 22).

According to Elderton (1949: 442), the results obtained show that "the distributions [...] are not sufficiently near to geometrical progressions to be so described". Figure 2.3 (cf. p. 22) presents a comparison between the empirical data and the theoretical results, obtained by fitting the geometrical distribution to them (given in percentages). An inspection of this figure shows that Elderton's intuitive impression that the geometrical distribution is no adequate model to be fitted to the empirical data in a convincing manner, cannot clearly be corroborated.

[2] As compared to the calculations above, the theoretical frequencies slightly differ, due to rounding effects; additionally, for reasons not known, the results provided by Elderton (1949: 442) himself slightly differ from the results presented here, obtained by the method described by him.

Table 2.2: Fitting the Geometric Distribution to English Word Length Frequencies (Elderton 1949)

x_i	NP_i	P_i
1	3883.08	0.7415
2	1003.89	0.1917
3	259.54	0.0496
4	67.10	0.0128
5	17.35	0.0033
6	4.48	0.0009

As was rather usual in his time, Elderton did not run any statistical procedure to confirm his intuitive impression, i.e., to test the goodness of fit. Later, it would become a standard procedure to at least calculate a Pearson χ^2-goodness-of-fit value in order to test the adequacy of the theoretical model. Given this later development, it seems reasonable to re-analyze the result for Elderton's data in this respect.

Pearson's χ^2 is calculated by way of formula (2.4):

$$\chi^2 = \sum_{i=1}^{k} \frac{(f_i - NP_i)^2}{E_i} \tag{2.4}$$

In formula (2.4), k is number of classes, f_i is the observed frequency of a given class, and NP_i is the absolute theoretical frequency. For the data represented above, with $k = 6$ classes, we thus obtain $\chi^2 = 79.33$. The statistical significance of this χ^2 value depends on the degrees of freedom ($d.f.$), which

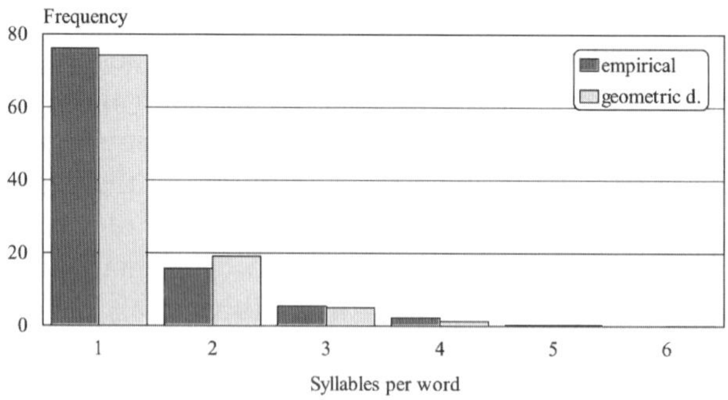

Figure 2.3: Empirical and Theoretical Word Length Frequencies (Elderton 1949)

in turn, are calculated with regard to the number of classes (k) minus 1, and the number of parameters (a) involved in the theoretical estimation: $d.f. = k-a-1$. Thus, with $d.f. = 6 - 2 = 4$ the χ^2 value obtained for Elderton's data can be interpreted in terms of a very poor fit indeed, since $p(\chi^2) < 0.001$.

However, it is a well-known fact that the value of χ^2 grows in a linear fashion with an increase of the sample size. Therefore, the larger a sample, the more likely the deviations tend to be statistically significant. Since linguistic samples tend to be rather larger, various suggestions have been brought forth as to a standardization of χ^2 scores. Thus, in contemporary linguistics, the discrepancy coefficient (C), which is easily calculated as $C = \chi^2/N$, has met general acceptance. The discrepancy coefficient, has the additional advantage that it is not dependent on degrees of freedom: in related studies, one speaks of a good fit for $C < 0.02$, and of a very good fit for $C < 0.01$.

In case of Elderton's data, we thus obtain a discrepancy coefficient of $C = 79.33/5237 = 0.015$; ultimately, this can be regarded to be an acceptable fit. Historically speaking, one should very much appreciate Elderton's early attempt to find an overall model for word length frequencies. What is problematic about his approach is not so much that his attempt was only partly successful for some English texts; rather, it is the fact that the geometrical distribution is adequate to describe monotonously decreasing distributions only. And although Elderton's data are exactly of this kind, word length frequencies from many other languages usually do not tend to display this specific shape.

Nevertheless, the geometric distribution has always attracted researchers' attention. Some decades later, Merkytė (1972), for example, discussed the geometric distribution with regard to its possible relevance for word length frequencies. Analyzing randomly chosen lexical material from a Lithuanian dictionary, he found differences as to the distribution of root words and words with affixes. As a first result, Merkytė (1972: 131) argued in favor of the notion "that the distribution of syllables in the roots is described by a geometric law", as a simple special case of the negative binomial distribution (for $k = 1$).

As an empirical test shows, the geometric distribution indeed turns out to be a good model. Since the data for the root words are given completely, the results given by Merkytė (1972: 128) are presented in Table 2.3 (p. 24).

As opposed to the root words, Merkytė found empirical evidence in agreement with the assumption that words with affixes follow a binomial distribution, i.e.

$$P_x = \binom{n}{x} p^x q^{n-x} \quad x = 0, 1, \ldots n; \quad 0 < p < 1, q = 1 - p \qquad (2.5)$$

Unfortunately, no data are given for the words with affixes; rather, the author confines himself to theoretical ruminations on why the binomial distribution might be an adequate model. As a result, Merkytė (1972: 131) arrives at the

Table 2.3: Fitting the Geometric Distribution to Word Length Frequencies of Lithuanian Root Words (Merkytė 1972)

x_i	f_i	NP_i
1	525	518
2	116	135
3	48	34
4	9	9
5	2	2

hypothesis that the distribution of words is likely to be characterized as a "composition of geometrical and binomial laws".

In order to test his hypothesis, he gives, by way of an example, the relative frequencies of a list of dictionary words taken from a Lithuanian-French dictionary, represented in Table 2.4. Since the absolute sample size ($N = 25036$) is given as well, the absolute frequencies can easily be reconstructed as in Table 2.4.

Merkytė's combination of these two distributions results in the convolution of both for $x = 1, \ldots n$, and the geometric alone for $x = n+1, n+2, \ldots$; with a slight correction of Merkytė's presentation, it can be written as represented in formula (2.6):

$$P_x = \begin{cases} \sum\limits_{i=0}^{x-1} \binom{n}{i} \alpha^i \beta^{n-i} p q^{x-i-1} & \text{for } x \leq n \\ \left(1 - \sum\limits_{j=1}^{n} P_j\right) p q^{x-n-1} & \text{for } x > n \end{cases} \tag{2.6}$$

Here, q is estimated as $\hat{q} = 1/\bar{x}_2$, where $\bar{x}_2$ is the mean word length of the sample's second part, i.e. its tail ($x > n$), and $\hat{p} = 1 - \hat{q}$. Parameter β, in turn, is estimated as $\hat{\beta} = (\bar{x} - \bar{x}_2)/n$, with $\hat{\alpha} = 1 - \hat{\beta}$.

The whole sample is thus arbitrarily divided into two portions, assuming that at a particular point of the data, there is a rupture in the material. With regard to the data presented in Table 2.4, Merkytė suggests $n = 3$ to be the crucial point. The approach as a whole thus implies that word length frequency would not be explained as an organic process, regulated by one overall mechanism, but as being organized by two different, overlapping mechanisms.

In fact, this is a major theoretical problem: Given one accepts the suggested separation of different word types – i.e., words with and without affixes – as a relevant explanation, the combination of both word types (i.e., the complete

Table 2.4: Theoretical Word Length Frequencies for Lithuanian Words: Merkytė-geometric, Binomial and Conway-Maxwell-Poisson Distributions

x_i	f_i	(Merkytė)	(Binomial) NP_i	(CMP)
1	3609	3734.09	3966.55	3346.98
2	9398	9147.28	8836.30	9544.32
3	7969	8144.84	7873.87	7965.80
4	3183	3232.87	3508.13	3240.21
5	752	651.59	781.51	791.50
6	125	125.31	69.64	147.19
	C	0.0012	0.0058	0.0012

material) does not, however, necessarily need to follow a composition of both individual distributions. Yet, the fitting of the Merkytė geometric distribution leads to convincing results: although the χ^2 value of $\chi^2 = 31.05$ is not really good ($p < 0.001$ for $d.f. = 3$), the corresponding discrepancy coefficient $C = 0.0012$ proves the fit to be excellent.[3] The results are represented in the first two columns of Table 2.4.

As a re-analysis of Merkytė's data shows, the geometric distribution cannot, of course, be a good model due to the lack of monotonous decrease in the data. However, the standard binomial distribution can be fitted to the data with quite some success: although the χ^2 value of $\chi^2 = 144,34$ is far from being satisfactory, resulting in $p < 0.001$ (with $d.f. = 3$), the corresponding discrepancy coefficient $C = 0.0058$ turns out be extremely good and proves the binomial distribution to be a possible model as well. The fact that the Merkytė geometric distribution turns out to be a better model as compared to the ordinary binomial distribution, is no wonder since after all, with its three parameters (α, p, n), the Merkytė geometric distribution has one parameter more than the latter.

Yet, this raises the question whether a unique, common model might not be able to model the Lithuanian data from Table 2.4. In fact, as the re-analysis shows, there is such a model which may very well be fitted to the data; we are concerned, here, with the Conway-Maxwell-Poisson (cf. Wimmer/Altmann 1999: 103), a standard model for word length frequencies, which, in its 1-

[3] In fact, the re-analysis led to slightly different results; most likely, this is due to the fact that the data reconstruction on the basis of the relative frequencies implies minor deviations from the original raw data.

displaced form, has the following shape:

$$P_x = \frac{a^{x-1}}{(x-1)!^b T_1}, \qquad x = 1, 2, 3, \ldots, \qquad T_1 = \sum_{j=1}^{\infty} \frac{a^j}{(j!)^b} \tag{2.7}$$

Since this model will be discussed in detail below, and embedded in a broader theoretical framework (cf. p. 77), we will confine ourselves here to a demonstration of its good fitting results, represented in Table 2.4. As can be seen, the fitting results are almost identical as compared to Merkytės specific convolution of the geometric and binomial distributions, although the Conway-Maxwell-Poisson distribution has only two, not three parameters. What is more important, however, is the fact that, in the case of the Conway-Maxwell-Poisson distribution, no separate treatment of two more or less arbitrarily divided parts of the whole sample is necessary, so that in this case, the generation of word length follows one common mechanism.

With this in mind, it seems worthwhile to turn back to the historical background of the 1940s, and to discuss the work of Čebanov (1947), who, independent of and almost simultaneously with Elderton, discussed an alternative model of word length frequency distributions, suggesting the 1-displaced Poisson distribution to be of relevance.

3. The 1-Displaced Poisson Distribution (Čebanov 1947)

Sergej Grigor'evič Čebanov (1897–1966) was a Russian military doctor from Sankt Petersburg.[4] His linguistic interests, to our knowledge, mainly concentrated on the process of language development. He considered "the distribution of words according to the number of syllables" to be "one of the fundamental statistical characteristics of language structures", which, according to him, exhibits "considerable stability throughout a single text, or in several closely related texts, and even within a given language group" (Čebanov 1947: 99).

As Čebanov reports, he investigated as many as 127 different languages and vulgar dialects of the Indo-European family, over a period of 20 years. In his above-mentioned article – as far as we know, no other work of his on this topic has ever been published – Čebanov presented selected data from these studies, e.g., from High German, Iranian, Sanskrit, Old Irish, Old French, Russian, Greek, etc.

Searching a general model for the distribution of word length frequencies, Čebanov's starting expectation was a specific relation between the mean word length $\bar{x}$ of the text under consideration, and the relative frequencies p_i of the individual word length classes. In the next step, given the mean of the

[4] For a short biographical sketch of Čebanov see Best/Čebanov (2001)

distribution, Čebanov assumed the 1-displaced Poisson distribution to be an adequate model for his data. The Poisson distribution can be described as

$$P_x = \frac{e^{-a} \cdot a^x}{x!} \qquad x = 0, 1, 2, \dots \tag{2.8}$$

Since the support of (2.8) is $x = 0, 1, 2, \dots$ with $a \geq 0$, and since there are no zero-syllable words in Čebanov's data, we are concerned with the 1-displaced Poisson distribution, which consequently takes the following shape:

$$P_x = \frac{e^{-a} \cdot a^{x-1}}{(x-1)!} \qquad x = 1, 2, 3, \dots \tag{2.9}$$

Čebanov (1947: 101) presented the data of twelve texts from different languages (or dialects). By way of an example, his approach will be demonstrated here, with reference to three texts. Two of these texts were studied in detail by Čebanov (1947: 102) himself: the High German text *Parzival*, and the Low Frankish text *Heliand*; the third text chosen here, by way of example, is a passage from Lev N. Tolstoj's *Vojna i mir* [War and Peace]. These data shall be additionally analyzed here because they are a good example for showing that word length frequencies do not necessarily imply a monotonously decreasing profile (cf. class $x = 2$) – it will be remembered that this was a major problem for the geometric distribution which failed be an adequate overall model (see above). The absolute frequencies (f_i), as presented by Čebanov (1947: 101), as well as the corresponding relative frequencies (p_i), are represented in Table 2.5 for all three texts.

Table 2.5: Relative Word Length Frequencies of Three Different Texts (Čebanov 1947)

Number of	*Parzival*		*Heliand*		*Vojna i mir*	
syllables (x_i)	f_i	p_i	f_i	p_i	f_i	p_i
1	1823	0.6280	1572	0.4693	466	0.2826
2	849	0.2925	1229	0.3669	541	0.3281
3	194	0.0668	452	0.1349	391	0.2371
4	37	0.0127	83	0.0248	172	0.1043
5			14	0.0042	64	0.0388
6					15	0.0091
$\sum$	2903		3350		1698	

As can be seen from Figure 2.4, all three distributions clearly seem to differ from each other in their shape; particularly the *Vojna i mir* passage, displaying a peak at two-syllable words, differs from the two others.

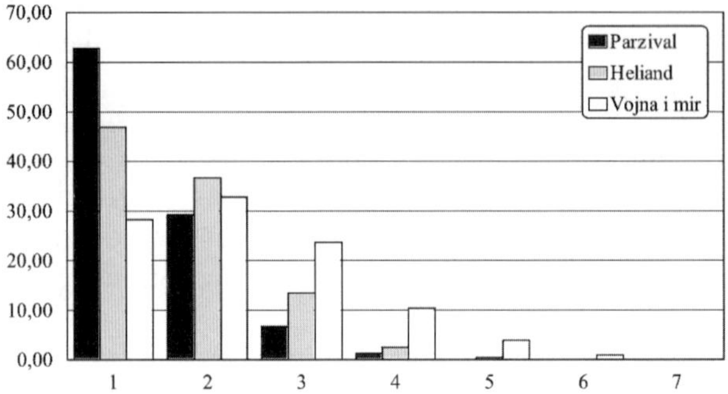

Figure 2.4: Empirical Word Length Frequencies of Three Texts (Čebanov 1947)

How then, did the Poisson distribution in its 1-displaced form fit? Let us demonstrate this with reference to the data from *Parzival* in Table 2.5. Since the mean in this text is $\bar{x} = 1.4643$, with $\hat{a} = \bar{x} - 1$ and referring to formula (2.9) for the 1-displaced Poisson distribution, we thus obtain

$$P_x = \frac{e^{-(1.4643-1)} \cdot (1.4643 - 1)^{x-1}}{(x-1)!} \,. \tag{2.10}$$

Thus, for $x = 1$ and $x = 2$, we obtain

$$P_1 = \frac{e^{-0.4643} \cdot 0.4643^0}{0!} = \frac{2.7183^{-0.4643} \cdot 1}{1} = 0.6285$$

$$P_2 = \frac{e^{-0.4643} \cdot 0.4643^1}{1!} = 2.7183^{-0.4643} \cdot 0.4643 = 0.2918$$

Correspondingly, for $x = 1$ and $x = 2$, we receive the following theoretical frequencies:

$$NP_1 = 2903 \cdot 0.6285 = 1824.54$$

$$NP_2 = 2903 \cdot 0.2918 = 847.10$$

Table 2.6 contains the results of fitting the 1-displaced Poisson distribution to the empirical data of the three texts, or text passages, also represented in Table 2.5 above.[5]

Whereas Elderton, in his analyses, did not run any statistical procedures to statistically test the adequacy of the proposed model, Čebanov did so. Well

[5] As compared to the calculations above, the theoretical frequencies slightly differ, due to rounding effects. For reasons not known, the results also differ as compared to the data provided by Čebanov (1947: 102), obtained by the method described above.

Table 2.6: Fitting the 1-Displaced Poisson Distribution to Word Length Frequencies (Čebanov 1947)

Number of	*Parzival*		*Heliand*		*Vojna i mir*	
syllables (x_i)	f_i	NP_i	f_i	NP_i	f_i	NP_i
1	1823	1824.67	1572	1618.01	466	442.29
2	849	847.28	1229	1177.53	541	582.04
3	194	196.72	452	428.48	391	382.97
4	37	30.45	83	103.94	172	167.99
5			14	18.91	64	55.27
6					15	14.55
$\sum$	2903		3350		1698	

aware of A.A. Markov's (1924) *caveat*, that "complete coincidence of figures cannot be expected in investigations of this kind, where theory is associated with experiment", Čebanov (1947: 101) calculated χ^2 goodness-of-fit values. As a result, Čebanov (ibd.) arrived at the conclusion that the χ^2 values "show good agreement in some cases and considerable departure in others." Let us follow his argumentation step by step, based on the three texts mentioned above.

For *Parzival*, with $k = 4$ classes, we obtain $\chi^2 = 1.45$. This χ^2 value can be interpreted in terms of a very good fit, since $p(\chi^2) = 0.48$ $(d.f. = 2)$.[6] Whereas the 1-displaced Poisson distribution thus turns out to be a good model for *Parzival*, Čebanov interprets the results for *Heliand* not to be: here, the value is $\chi^2 = 10.35$, which, indeed, is a significantly worse, though still acceptable result ($p = 0.016$ for $d.f. = 3$).[7]

Interestingly enough, the 1-displaced Poisson distribution would also turn out to be a good model for the passage from Tolstoj's *Vojna i mir* (not analyzed in detail by Čebanov himself), with a value of $\chi^2 = 5.82$ ($p = 0.213$ for $d.f. = 4$).

On the whole, Čebanov (1947: 101) arrives at the conclusion that the theoretical results "show good agreement in some cases and considerable departure in others." This partly pessimistic estimation has to be corrected however. In fact, Čebanov's (1947: 102) interpretation clearly contradicts the intuitive impression one gets from an optical inspection of Figure 2.5: as can be seen, $P_i(a)$, represented for $i = 1, 2, 3$, indeed seems to be "determined all but completely"

[6] Čebanov (1947: 102) himself reports a value of $\chi^2 = 0.43$ which he interprets to be a good result.

[7] Čebanov (1947: 102) reports a value of $\chi^2 = 13.32$ and, not indicating any degrees of freedom, interprets this result to be a clear deviation from expectation.

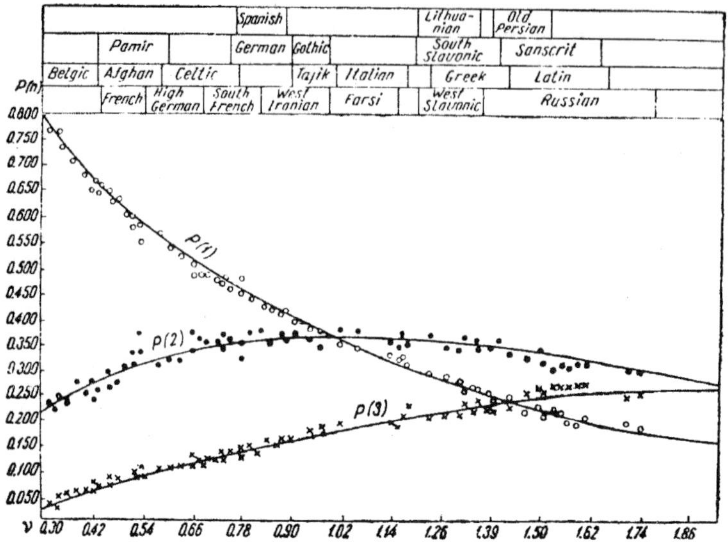

Arrangement of selected data in Poisson's system $P(n)_a$

Figure 2.5: The 1-Displaced Poisson Distribution as a Word Length Frequency Distribution Model (Čebanov 1947)

by the mean of the text under consideration (ibd., 101). In Figure 2.5, Poisson's $P_i(a)$ can be seen on the horizontal, the relative frequencies for p_i on the vertical axis).

The good fit of the 1-displaced Poisson distribution may also be proven by way of a re-analysis of Čebanov's data, calculating the discrepancy values C (see above). Given that in case of all three texts mentioned and analyzed above, we are concerned with relatively large samples ($N = 2903$ for *Parzival*, $N = 1649$ for *Heliand*, and $N = 1698$ for the *Vojna i mir* passage). In fact, the result is $C < 0.01$ in all three cases.[8] In other words: what we have here are excellent fits, in all three cases, which can be clearly seen in the graphical illustration of Figure 2.6 (p. 31).

Unfortunately, Čebanov's work was consigned to oblivion for a long time. If at all, reference to his work was mainly made by some Soviet scholars, who, terming the 1-displaced Poisson distribution "Čebanov-Fucks distribution", would later place him on a par with German physician Wilhelm Fucks. As is well known, Fucks and his followers would also, and independently of

[8] As a corresponding re-analysis of the twelve data sets given by Čebanov (1947: 101) shows, C values are $C < 0.02$ in all cases, and they are even $C < 0.01$ in two thirds of the cases.

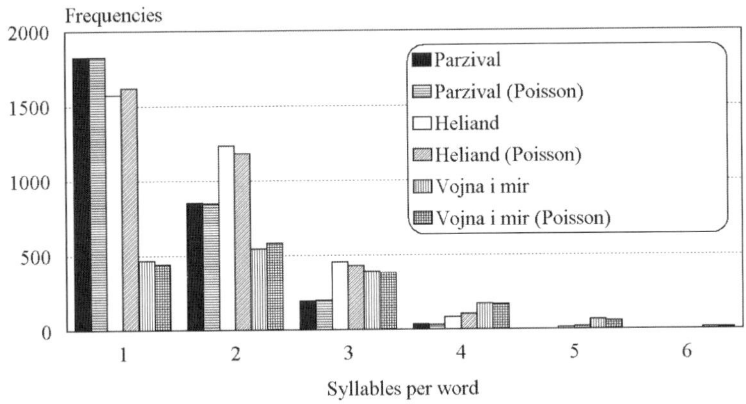

Figure 2.6: Fitting the 1-Displaced Poisson Distribution to Three Text Segments (Čebanov 1947)

Čebanov's work, favor the 1-displaced Poisson distribution to be an important model, in the late 1950s. Before presenting Fucks' work in detail, it is necessary to discuss another approach, which also has its roots in the 1940s.

4. The Lognormal Distribution

A different approach to theoretically model word length distributions was pursued mainly in the late 1950s and early 1960s by scholars such as Gustav Herdan (1958, 1966), René Moreau (1963), and others.

As opposed to the approaches thus far discussed, these authors did not try to find a discrete distribution model; rather, they worked with continuous models, mainly the so-called lognormal model.

Herdan was not the first to promote this idea with regard to language. Before him, Williams (1939, 1956) had applied it to the study of sentence length frequencies, arguing in favor of the notion that the frequency with which sentences of a particular length occur, are lognormally distributed. This assumption was brought forth, based on the observation that sentence length or word length frequencies do not seem to follow a normal distribution; hence, the idea of lognormality was promoted. Later, the idea of word length frequencies being lognormally distributed was only rarely picked up, such as for example by Russian scholar Piotrovskij and colleagues (Piotrovskij et al. 1977: 202ff.; cf. 1985: 278ff.).

Generally speaking, the theoretical background of this assumption can be characterized as follows: the frequency distribution of linguistic units (as of other units occurring in nature and culture) often tends to display a right-sided asymmetry, i.e., the corresponding frequency distribution displays a positive skewness. One of the theoretical reasons for this can be seen in the fact that the variable in question cannot go beyond (or remain below) a particular limit; since it is thus characterized by a one-sided limitation in variation, the distribution cannot be adequately approximated by the normal distribution.

Particularly when a distribution is limited by the value 0 to the left side, one suspects to obtain fairly normally distributed variables by logarithmic transformations: as a result, the interval between 0 and 1 is transformed into $-\infty$ to 0. In other words: the left part of the distribution is stretched, and at the same time, the right part is compressed.

The crucial idea of lognormality thus implies that a given random variable X follows a lognormal distribution if the random variable $Y = \log(X)$ is normally distributed.

Given the probability density function for the normal distribution as in (2.11),

$$y = f(x) = \frac{1}{\sigma \cdot \sqrt{2\pi}} \cdot e^{-\frac{1}{2}\left(\frac{x-\mu}{\sigma}\right)^2}, \qquad -\infty < x < \infty \tag{2.11}$$

one thus obtains the probability density function for the lognormal distribution in equation (2.12):

$$y = f(x) = \frac{1}{\sigma \cdot x \cdot \sqrt{2\pi}} \cdot e^{-\frac{1}{2}\left(\frac{\ln x-\mu}{\sigma}\right)^2}, \qquad 0 < x < \infty \tag{2.12}$$

Herdan based his first analyses of word length studies on data by Dewey (1923) and French et al. (1930). These two studies contain data on word length frequencies, the former 78,633 words of written English, the latter 76,054 words of spoken English. Thus, Herdan had the opportunity to do comparative analyses of word length frequencies measured in letters and phonemes. In order to test his hypothesis as to the lognormality of the frequency distribution, Herdan (1966: 224) confined himself to graphical techniques only. The most widely applied method in his time was the use of probability grids, with a logarithmically divided abscissa (x-axis) and the cumulative frequencies on the ordinate (y-axis). If the resulting graph showed a more or less straight line, one regarded a lognormal distribution to be proven.

As can be seen from Figure 2.7, the result seems to be quite convincing, both for letters and phonemes. In his later monograph on *The Advanced Theory of Language as Choice and Chance*, Herdan (1966: 201ff.) similarly analyzed French data samples, taken from analyses by Moreau (1963). The latter had analyzed several French samples, among them the three picked up by Herdan in Figure 2.7:

1. 3,204 vocabulary entries from George Gougenheim's *Dictionnaire fondamental de la langue française*,
2. 76,918 entries from Émile Littré's *Dictionnaire de la langue française*

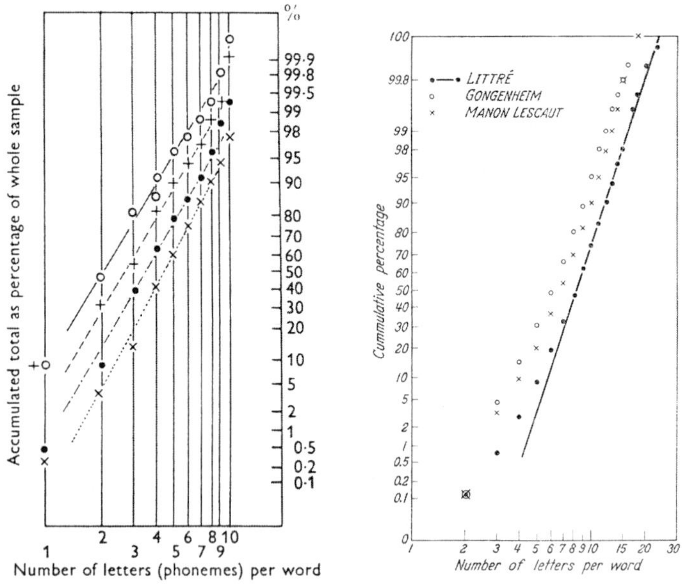

(a) Herdan (1958: 224) (b) Herdan (1966: 203)

Figure 2.7: Word Length Frequencies on a Lognormal Probability Grid (Herdan 1958/66)

3. 6,151 vocubulary items from the *Histoire de Chevalier des Grieux et de Manon Lescaut* by the Abbé Prévost.

The corresponding graph is reproduced in Figure 2.7. Again, for Herdan (1966: 203), the inspection of the graph "shows quite a satisfactory linearity [...], which admits the conclusion of lognormality of the distribution."

In this context, Herdan discusses Moreau's (1961, 1963) introduction of a third parameter (V_0) into the lognormal model, ultimately causing a displacement of the distribution; as can be seen, $\theta \cdot \log k$ is a mere re-parametrization of σ – cf. (2.12).

$$f(x) = \frac{1}{(\theta \log k) \cdot (x + V_0) \cdot \sqrt{2\pi}} \cdot e^{-\frac{1}{2}\left(\frac{\log(x+V_0) - \log k}{\theta \log k}\right)^2} \tag{2.13}$$

Herdan considered this extension not to be necessary. In his book, he offered theoretical arguments for the lognormal distribution to be an adequate model (Herdan 1966: 204). These arguments are in line with the general characteristics of the lognormal distribution, in which the random variables are considered to influence each other in a multiplying manner, whereas the normal distribution

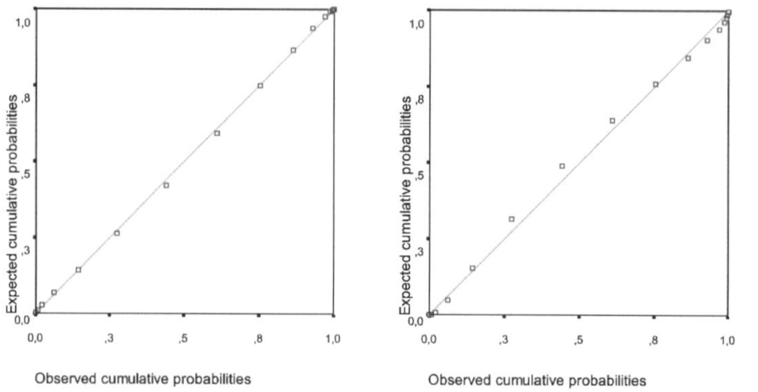

(a) Normal distribution (b) Lognormal distribution

Figure 2.8: *P-P* Plots for Fitting the Normal and Lognormal Distributions to Word Length Frequencies in Abbé Prévost's *Manon Lescaut*

is characterized by the additive interplay of the variables (the variables thus being considered to be independent of one another).

However, Herdan did not do any comparative analyses as to the efficiency of the normal or the lognormal distribution, neither graphically nor statistically. Therefore, both procedures shall be presented here, by way of a re-analysis of the original data.

As far as graphical procedures are concerned, probability grids have been replaced by so-called *P-P* plots, today, which also show the cumulative proportions of a given variable and should result in a linear rise in case of normal distribution. By way of an example, Figure 2.8 represents the *P-P* plots for *Manon Lescaut*, tested for normal and lognormal distribution.

It can clearly be seen that there are quite some deviations for the lognormal distribution (cf. Figure2.8(b)). What is even more important, however, is the fact that the deviations are clearly less expressed for the normal distribution (cf. Figure2.8(a)). Although this can, in fact, be shown for all three data samples mentioned above, we will concentrate on a statistical analysis of these observations.

Table 2.7 contains the relevant Kolmogorov-Smirnov values (KS) and the corresponding p-values with the given degrees of freedom ($d.f.$) for all three samples, both for the normal and the logarithmized values. Additionally, values for skewness (γ_1) and kurtosis (γ_2) are given, so that the effect of the logarithmic manipulation of the data can easily be seen.

Table 2.7: Statistical Comparison of Normal and Lognormal Distributions for Three French Texts (Herdan 1966)

		KS	df	p	γ_1	γ_2
Manon Lescaut	normal distr.	0.105	6151	< 0.0001	0.30	0.22
	lognormal d.	0.135			−0.89	1.83
Littré	normal distr.	0.108	76917	< 0.0001	0.53	0.49
	lognormal d.	0.103			−0.47	0.68
Gougenheim	normal distr.	0.121	3204	< 0.0001	0.80	2.06
	lognormal d.	0.126			−0.55	1.12

As can clearly be seen, the deviations both from the normal and the lognormal distributions are highly significant in all cases. Furthermore, differences between normal and lognormal are minimal; in case of *Manon Lescaut*, the lognormal distribution is even worse than the normal distribution.

The same holds true, by the way, for the above-mentioned data presented by Piotrovskij et al. (1985: 283). The authors analyzed a German technical text of 1,000 words and found, as they claimed, "a clear concordance between the empirical distribution and the lognormal distribution of the random variable". As a justification of their claim they referred to a graphical representation of empirical and theoretical values, only; however, they additionally maintained that the assumed concordance may easily and strongly be proven by way of Kolmogorov's criterium (ibd., 281).

As a re-analysis of the data shows, this claim may not be upheld, however (cf. table 2.8). As in the case of Herdan's analyses, the effect of the logarithmic transformation can easily be deduced from the values for γ_1 and γ_2 (i.e., for skewness and kurtosis). Also, the deviation from the normal distribution is highly significant ($p < 0.001$). However, as can be seen the deviation from the lognormal distribution is highly significant as well, and, strictly speaking, even greater compared to the normal distribution.

Table 2.8: Statistical Comparison of Normal and Lognormal Distribution for German data (Piotrovskij 1985)

	KS	df	p	γ_1	γ_2
normal distr.	0.12	1000	0.0001	0.81	0.20
lognormal d.	0.08			−0.25	−0.52

In summary, one can thus say that neither the normal distribution nor the lognormal distribution model turns out to be adequate in praxis. With regard to this negative finding, one may add the result of a further re-analysis, saying that in case of all three data samples discussed by Herdan, the binomial distribution can very well be fitted to the empirical data, with $0.006 \leq C \leq 0.009$. No such fit is possible in the case of Piotrovskij's data, however, which may be due to the fact that the space was considered to be part of a word.

Incidently, Michel (1982) arrived at the very same conclusion, in an extensive study on Old and New Bulgarian, as well as Old and new Greek material. He tested the adequacy of the lognormal distribution for the word length frequencies of the above-mentioned material on two different premises, basing his calculation of word length both on the number of letters per word, and on the number of syllables per word. As a result, Michel (1982: 198) arrived at the conclusion "that the fitting fails completely".[9]

One can thus say that there is overwhelming negative empirical evidence which proves that the lognormal distribution is no adequate model for word length frequencies of various languages. Additionally, and this is even more important in the given context, one must state that there are also major theoretical problems which arise in the context of the (log-)normal distribution as a possible model for word length frequencies:

a. the approximation of continuous models to discrete data;

b. the doubtful dependence of the variables, due to the multiplying effect of variables within the lognormal model;

c. the manipulation of the initial data by way of logarithmic transformations.

With this in mind, let us return to discrete models. The next historical step in the history of word length studies were the important theoretical and empirical analyses by Wilhelm Fucks, a German physician, whose theoretical models turned out to be of utmost importance in the 1950s and 1960s.

5. The Fucks Generalized Poisson Distribution

5.1 The Background

As mentioned previously, the 1-displaced Poisson distribution had been suggested by S.G. Čebanov in the late 1940s. Interestingly enough, some years later the very same model – i.e., the 1-displaced Poisson distribution – was also favored by German physicist Wilhelm Fucks (1955a,b, 1956b). Completely independent of Čebanov, without knowing the latter's work, and based on completely different theoretical assumptions, Fucks arrived at similar conclusions to

[9] Michel also tested the adequacy of the 1-displaced Poisson distribution (see below, p. 46).

those of Čebanov some years before. However, Fucks' work was much more influential than was Čebanov's, and it was Fucks rather than Čebanov, who would later be credited for having established the 1-displaced Poisson distribution as a standard model for word length frequency distributions.

When Fucks described the 1-displaced Poisson distribution and applied it to his linguistic data, he considered it to be "a mathematical law, thus far not known in mathematical statistics" (Fucks 1957: 34). In fact, he initially derived it from a merely mathematical perspective (Fucks 1955c); in his application of it to the study of language(s) and language style(s), he then considered it to be the "general law of word-formation" (1955a: 88, 1957: 34), or, more exactly, as the "mathematical law of the process of word-formation from syllables for all those languages, which form their words from syllables" (Fucks 1955b: 209).

In fact, Fucks' suggestion was the most important model discussed from the 1950s until the late 1970s; having the 1-displaced Poisson distribution in mind, one used to refer to it as "the Fucks model". Only in Russia, one should later speak of the "Čebanov-Fucks distribution" (e.g., Piotrovskij et al. 1977: 190ff.; cf. Piotrowski et al. 1985: 256ff.), thus adequately honoring the pioneering work of Čebanov, too.

There was one major difference between Čebanov's and Fucks' approaches, however: this difference has to be seen in the fact that Fucks' approach was based on a more general theoretical model, the 1-displaced Poisson distribution being only one of its special cases (see below). Furthermore, Fucks, in a number of studies, developed many important ideas on the general functioning not only of language, but of other human sign systems, too. This general perspective as to the "mathematical analysis of language, music, or other results of human cultural activity" (Fucks 1960: 452), which is best expressed in Fucks' (1968) monograph *Nach allen Regeln der Kunst*, cannot be dealt with in detail, here, where our focus is on the history of word length studies.

5.2 The General Approach

Ultimately, Fucks' general model can be considered to be an extension of the Poisson distribution; specifically, we are concerned with a particularly weighted Poisson distribution. These weights are termed $\varepsilon_k - \varepsilon_{k+1}$, k indicating the number of components to be analyzed.

In its most general form, this weighting generalization results in the following formula (2.14):

$$p_i = P(X = i) = e^{-\lambda} \sum_{k=0}^{\infty} (\varepsilon_k - \varepsilon_{k+1}) \cdot \frac{\lambda^{i-k}}{(i-k)!} \tag{2.14}$$

Here, the random variable X denotes the number of syllables per word, i.e. $X = i, i = 0, 1, 2, 3, \ldots, I$. The probability that a given word has i syllables, is $p_i = P(X = i)$, with $\sum_{i=0}^{I} p_i = 0$, $\lambda = \mu - \varepsilon'$, $\varepsilon' = \sum_{k=1}^{\infty} \varepsilon_k$ and $\mu = E(X)$. The parameters of the distribution $\{\varepsilon_k\}$ are called the ε-spectrum. For (2.14), there are a number of conditions postulated by Fucks which must be fulfilled:

(a) From the necessity that $\varepsilon_k - \varepsilon_{k+1} \geq 0$ it follows that $\varepsilon_{k+1} \leq \varepsilon_k$;

(b) Since the sum of all weights equals 1, we have
$1 = \sum_{k=0}^{\infty} (\varepsilon_k - \varepsilon_{k+1}) = \sum_{k=0}^{\infty} \varepsilon_k - \sum_{k=0}^{\infty} \varepsilon_{k+1} = \varepsilon_0$; it follows that $\varepsilon_0 = 1$.

Finally, from (a) and (b) it follows

(c) $1 = \varepsilon_0 \geq \varepsilon_1 \geq \varepsilon_2 \geq \varepsilon_3 \geq \ldots \geq \varepsilon_k \geq \varepsilon_{k+1} \cdots$

As can be seen from equation (2.14), the so-called "generalized Fucks distribution" includes both the standard Poisson distribution (2.8) and the 1-displaced Poisson distribution (2.9) as two of its special cases. Assuming that $\varepsilon_0 = 1$, and $\varepsilon_1 = \varepsilon_2 = \ldots = \varepsilon_k = 0$ – one obtains the standard Poisson distribution (2.8):

$$p_i = e^{-\lambda} \cdot \frac{\lambda^i}{i!} \qquad i = 0, 1, 2, \ldots$$

Likewise, for $\varepsilon_0 = \varepsilon_1 = 1$, and $\varepsilon_2 = \varepsilon_3 = \ldots = \varepsilon_k = 0$, one obtains the 1-displaced Poisson distribution (2.9) (cf. p. 27):

$$p_i = e^{-\lambda} \cdot \frac{\lambda^{i-1}}{(i-1)!}, \quad i = 1, 2, \ldots$$

As was already mentioned above, the only model which met general acceptance was the 1-displaced Poisson distribution. More often than not, Fucks himself applied the 1-displaced Poisson distribution without referring to his general model, and this may be one more reason why it has often (though rather incorrectly) been assumed to be "the Fucks distribution". In other words: In spite of the overwhelming number of analyses presented by Fucks in the 1950s and 1960s, and irrespective of the broad acceptance of the 1-displaced Poisson distribution as an important model for word length studies, Fucks' generalization as described above can only be found in very few of his works (e.g., Fucks 1956a,b).

It is no wonder, then, that the generalized model has practically not been discussed. Interestingly enough, however, several scholars of East European background became familiar with Fucks' concept, and they not only discussed it at some length, but also applied it to specific data. It seems most reasonable to assume that this rather strange circumstance is due to the Russian translation of Fucks' 1956b paper (cf. Fucks 1957).

Before turning to the East European reception of Fucks' model, resulting not only in its application, but also in some modification of it, let us first discuss some of the results obtained by Fucks in his own application of the 1-displaced Poisson distribution to linguistic data.

5.3 The 1-Displaced Poisson Distribution as a Special Case of Fucks' Generalization of the Poisson Distribution

In his inspiring works, Fucks applied the 1-displaced Poisson distribution on different levels of linguistic and textual analysis: on the one hand, he analyzed single texts, but he also studied word length frequency distribution in text corpora, both from one and the same language and across languages. Thus, his application of the 1-displaced Poisson distribution included studies on (1) the individual style of single authors, as well as on (2) texts from different authors either (2.1) of one and the same language or (2.2) of different languages.

As an example of the study of individual texts, Figure 2.9(a) from Fucks (1956b: 208) may serve. It shows the results of Fucks' analysis of Goethe's *Wilhelm Meister*: on the horizontal x-axis, the number of syllables per word (termed i by Fucks) are indicated, on the vertical y-axis the relative frequency of each word length class (p_i) can be seen. As can be seen from the dotted line in Figure 2.9(a), the fitting of the 1-displaced Poisson distribution seems to result in extremely good theoretical values.

As to a comparison of two German authors, Rilke and Goethe, on the one hand, and two Latin authors, Sallust and Caesar, on the other, Figure 2.9(b) may serve. It gives rise to the impression that word length frequency may be characteristic of a specific author's style, rather than of specific texts. Again, the fitting of the 1-displaced Poisson distribution seems to be convincing.

There can be no doubt about the value of Fucks' studies, and still today, they contain many inspiring ideas which deserve to be further pursued. Yet, in re-analyzing his works, there remains at least one major problem: Fucks gives many characteristics of the specific distributions, starting from mean values and standard deviations up to the central moments, entropy etc. Yet, there are hardly ever any raw data given in his texts, a fact which makes it impossible to check the results at which he arrived. Thus, one is forced to believe in the goodness of his fittings on the basis of his graphical impressions, only; and this drawback is further enhanced by the fact that there are no procedures which are applied to test the goodness of his fitting the 1-displaced Poisson distribution. Ultimately, therefore, Fucks' works cannot but serve as a starting point for new studies which would have to replicate his results.

There is only one instance where Fucks presents at least the *relative*, though not the absolute frequencies of particular distributions in detail. This is when he presents the results of a comparison of texts from nine different languages – eight

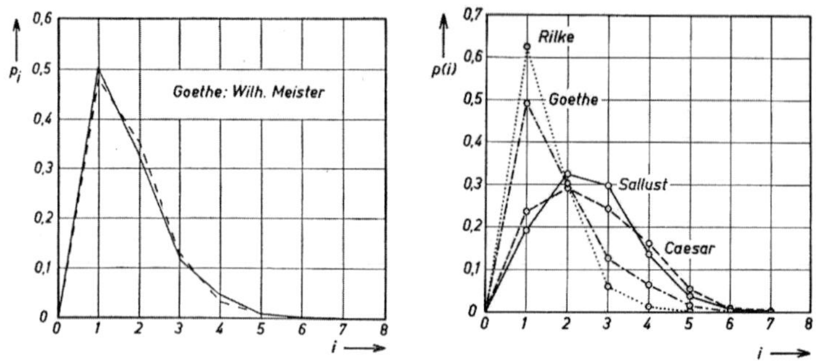

(a) Goethe's *Wilhelm Meister* (b) German and Latin authors

Figure 2.9: Fitting the 1-Displaced Poisson Distribution to German and Latin Text Segments (Fucks 1956)

natural languages, and one artificial (cf. Fucks 1955a: 85ff.). The results for each language are based on what Fucks (1955a: 84) considered to be "representative cross-sections of written documents" of the given languages.

The relative frequencies are reproduced in Table 2.9 which, in addition to the relative frequency of each word length class (measured in syllables per word), also contains the mean ($\bar{x}$), as well as the entropy (H) for each language, the latter being calculated by way of formula (2.15):

$$H = -\sum_{i=1}^{n} p_i \ln p_i \tag{2.15}$$

Unfortunately, quite a number of errors can be found in Fuck' original table, both as to the calculated values of $\bar{x}$ and H; therefore, the data in Table 2.9 represent the corrected results which one obtains on the basis of the relative frequencies given by Fucks and formula (2.15). We will come back to these data throughout the following discussion, using them as exemplifying material. Being well aware of the fact that for each of the languages we are concerned with mixed data, we can ignore this fact, and see the data as a representation of a maximally broad spectrum of different empirical distributions which may be subjected to empirical testing.

Figure 2.10 illustrates the frequency distributions, based on the relative frequencies of the word length classes for each language. The figure is taken from Fucks (1955a: 85), since the errors in the calculation concern only $\bar{x}$ and H and are not relevant here. According to Fucks' interpretation, all shapes fall into one and the same profile, except for Arabic; as a reason for this, Fucks assumed that the number of texts analyzed in this language might not have been sufficient.

Table 2.9: Relative Frequencies, Mean Word Length, and Entropy for Different Languages (Fucks 1955)

	English	**German**	**Esperanto**	**Arabic**	**Greek**
1	0.7152	0.5560	0.4040	0.2270	0.3760
2	0.1940	0.3080	0.3610	0.4970	0.3210
3	0.0680	0.0938	0.1770	0.2239	0.1680
4	0.0160	0.0335	0.0476	0.0506	0.0889
5	0.0056	0.0071	0.0082	0.0017	0.0346
6	0.0012	0.0014	0.0011	–	0.0083
7	–	0.0002	–	–	0.0007
8	–	0.0001	–	–	–
$\bar{x}$	1.4064	1.6333	1.8971	2.1106	2.1053
H	0.3665	0.4655	0.5352	0.5129	0.6118

	Japanese	**Russian**	**Latin**	**Turkish**
1	0.3620	0.3390	0.2420	0.1880
2	0.3440	0.3030	0.3210	0.3784
3	0.1780	0.2140	0.2870	0.2704
4	0.0868	0.0975	0.1168	0.1208
5	0.0232	0.0358	0.0282	0.0360
6	0.0124	0.0101	0.0055	0.0056
7	0.0040	0.0015	0.0007	0.0004
8	0.0004	0.0003	0.0002	0.0004
9	0.0004	–	–	–
$\bar{x}$	2.1325	2.2268	2.3894	2.4588
H	0.6172	0.6355	0.6311	0.6279

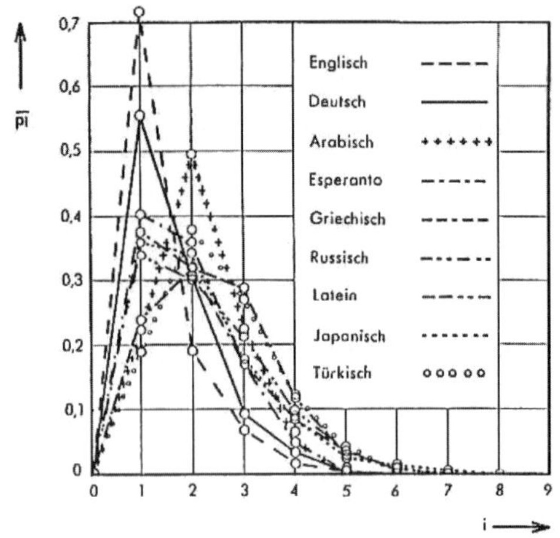

Figure 2.10: Relative Frequencies of Word Lengths in Eight Natural and One Artificial Languages (Fucks 1955)

As was mentioned above, Fucks did not, as was not unusual at his time, calculate any tests as to the significance of the goodness of his fits. It seems that Fucks (1955a: 101) was very well aware of the problems using the χ^2-goodness-of-fit test for this purpose, since he explicitly emphasized that, "for particular mathematical reasons", his data are "not particularly adequate" for the application of the χ^2test.

The problem behind Fucks' assumption might be the fact that the χ^2 value increases in a linear way with an increase of sample size; therefore, results are more likely to display significant differences for larger samples, which is almost always the case in linguistic studies. As was mentioned above (cf. p. 23), the problem is nowadays avoided by calculating the discrepancy coefficient $C = \chi^2/N$, which is not dependent on the degrees of freedom. We may thus easily, by way of a re-analysis, calculate C for the data given by Fucks, in order to statistically test the goodness-of-fit of the 1-displaced Poisson distribution; in order to do so, we simply have to create "artificial" samples of ca. 10,000 each, by multiplying the relative frequencies with 10,000.

Remembering that fitting is considered to be good in case of $0.01 < C < 0.02$ and very good in case of $C < 0.01$, one has to admit that fitting the 1-displaced Poisson distribution to Fucks' data from different languages is not really convincing (see Table 2.10): strictly speaking, it turns out to be adequate only for an artificial language, Esperanto, and must be discarded as an overall valid model.

It is difficult to say whether the observed failure is due to the fact that the data for each of the languages originated from text mixtures (and not from

Table 2.10: Discrepancy Coefficient C as a Result of Fitting the 1-Displaced Poisson Distribution to Different Languages (Fucks 1955)

	English	**German**	**Esperanto**	**Arabic**	**Greek**
C (1-par.)	0.0903	0.0186	0.0023	0.1071	0.0328
	Japanese	**Russian**	**Latin**	**Turkish**	
C (1-par.)	0.0380	0.0208	0.0181	0.0231	

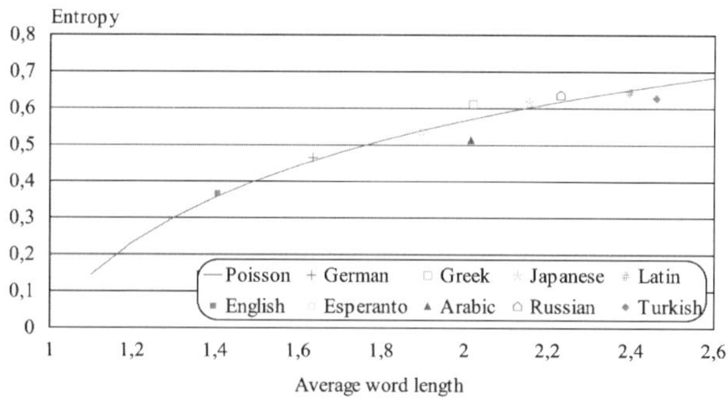

Figure 2.11: Entropy as a Function of Mean Word Length (Fucks 1955a)

individual texts), or if there are other reasons. Still, Fucks and many followers of his pursued the idea of the 1-displaced Poisson distribution as the most adequate model for word length frequencies.

Although Fucks did not calculate any statistics to test the goodness of fit (which in fact many people would not do still today), one must do him justice and point out that he tried to go another way to empirically prove the adequacy of his findings: knowing the values of $\bar{x}$ and H for each language, Fucks graphically illustrated their relationship and interdependency. Figure 2.11 (p. 43) shows the results, with $\bar{x}$ on the horizontal x-axis, and H on the vertical y-axis; the data are based on the corrected values from Table 2.9.

Additionally, Fucks calculated the entropy of the theoretical distribution, estimating $\hat{a}$ as $\bar{x}$; these values can easily be obtained by formula (2.8) (cf. p. 27), and they are reproduced below in Table 2.11. Thus, one arrives at the curve in Figure 2.11, representing the Poisson distribution (cf. Fucks 1955a: 85).

As can be seen with Fucks (1955a: 88, 1960: 458f.), the theoretical distribution "represents the values found in natural texts very well". In other words:

Table 2.11: Empirical and Theoretical Entropy for Nine Word Length Frequency Distributions (Fucks)

$\bar{x}$	$H[y]$	$\hat{H}[\hat{y}]$
1.4064	0.3665	0.3590
1.6333	0.4655	0.4563
1.8971	0.5352	0.5392
2.1032	0.5129	0.5913
2.1106	0.6118	0.5917
2.1325	0.6172	0.6030
2.2268	0.6355	0.6184
2.3894	0.6311	0.6498
2.4588	0.6279	0.6614

evaluating his results, Fucks once again confined himself to merely visual impressions, as he did in the case of the frequency probability distribution. And again, it would have been easy to run such a statistical test, calculating the coefficient of determination (R^2) in order to test the adequacy of the theoretical curve obtained.

Let us shortly discuss this procedure: in a nonlinear regression model, R^2 represents that part of the variance of the variable y, which can be explained by variable x. There are quite a number of more or less divergent formulae to calculate R^2 (cf. Grotjahn 1982), which result in partly significant differences. Usually, the following formula (2.16) is taken:

$$R^2 = 1 - \frac{\sum_{i=1}^{n} (y_i - \widehat{y}_i)^2}{\sum_{i=1}^{n} (y_i - \bar{y})^2} \tag{2.16}$$

With $0 \leq R^2 \leq 1$, one can say that the greater R^2, the better the theoretical fit. In order to calculate R^2, we thus consider $\bar{x}$ to be the independent variable x, and H to be the dependent variable y. Thus, for each empirical x_i, we need both the empirical values (y_i) and the theoretical values ($\widehat{y}_i$) which can be obtained by formula (2.8), and which are represented in Table 2.11. Based on these results, we can now easily calculate R^2, with $\bar{y} = \overline{H[y]}$ (cf. Table 2.11), as

$$R^2 = 1 - \frac{0.0097}{0.0704} = 0.8768 \tag{2.17}$$

As can be seen, the fit can be regarded to be relatively good.[10] This result is not particularly influenced by the fit for Arabic, which, according to Fucks, deviates from the other languages. In fact, the value for R^2 hardly changes if one, following Fucks' argumentation, eliminates the data for Arabic: under this condition, the determination coefficient would result in $R^2 = 0.8763$.

Still, there remains a major theoretical problem with the specific method chosen by Fucks in trying to prove the adequacy of the 1-displaced Poisson distribution: this problem is related to the method itself, i.e., in establishing a relation between $\bar{x}$ and H. Taking a second look at formula (2.15), one can easily see that the entropy of a frequency distribution is ultimately based on p_i, only; p_i, however, in case of the Poisson distribution, is based on parameter a in formula (2.8), which is nothing but the mean $\bar{x}$ of the distribution! In other words, due to the fact that the Poisson distribution is mainly shaped by the mean of the distribution, Fucks arrives at a tautological statement, relating the mean $\bar{x}$ of the Poisson distribution to its entropy H.

To summarize, one has thus to draw an important conclusion: Due to the fact that Fucks did not apply any suitable statistics to test the goodness of fit for the 1-displaced Poisson distribution, he could not come to the point of explicitly stating that this model may be adequate in some cases, but is not acceptable as a general standard model. Still, Fucks' suggestions had an enormous influence on the study of word length frequencies, particularly in the 1960's. Most of these subsequent studies concentrated on the 1-displaced Poisson distribution, as suggested by Fucks.

In fact, work on the Poisson distribution is by no means a matter of the past. Rather, subsequent to Fucks' (and of course Čebanov's) pioneering work on the Poisson distribution, there have been frequent studies discussing and trying to fit the 1-displaced Poisson distribution to linguistic data, with and without reference to the previous achievements.

No reference to Fucks (or Čebanov) is made, for example, by Rothschild (1986) in his study on English dictionary material. Rothschild's initial discussion of previous approaches to word length frequencies, both continuous and discrete, was particularly stimulated by his disapproval of Bagnold's (1983) assumption that word length distributions are not Gaussian, but skew (hyperbolic or double exponential) distributions. Discussing and testing various distribution models, Rothschild did not find any one of the models he tested to be adequate. This holds true for the (1-displaced) Poisson distribution, as well, which, according to Rothschild (1986: 317), "fails on a formal χ^2-test". Nevertheless, he considered it to be "the most promising candidate" (ibd., 321) – quite obviously, *faute de mieux...*

---

[10] Calculating the determination coefficient with the data given by Fucks himself results in R^2=0.8569.

r being the displacement parameter. The coefficient δ can, of course, be calculated not only for theoretical frequencies, but also for empirical frequencies, then having the notation

$$d = \frac{m_2}{\bar{x} - r} \tag{2.22}$$

Given both the empirical value of d and the value of δ, one can easily test the goodness of fitting the Poisson distribution to empirical data, by calculating the deviation of d (based on the empirical data) from δ (as the theoretical value to be expected). Now, since, for the 1-displaced Poisson distribution, the variance $Var(X) = \sigma^2 = \mu - 1$, we have

$$\delta = \frac{\mu - 1}{\mu - 1} = 1.$$

The logical consequence arising from the fact that for the Poisson distribution, $\delta = 1$, is that the latter can be an adequate model only as long as $d \approx 1$ in an empirical sample. Now, based on these considerations, Stadlober (2003) explored the theoretical dispersion quotient δ for the Fucks 2-parameter distribution (2.19), discussed above. Since here, $Var(X) = \mu - 1 - \varepsilon_2^2$, it turns out that $\delta \leq 1$; this means that this 2-parameter model is likely to be inadequate as a theoretical model for empirical samples with $d > 1$.

As in the case of the 1-displaced Poisson distribution, one has thus to acknowledge that the Fucks 2-parameter (1-displaced Dacey-Poisson) distribution is an adequate theoretical model only for a specific type of empirical distributions. This leads to the question whether the Fucks 3-parameter distribution is more adequate as an overall model.

5.5 The 3-Parameter Fucks-Distribution as a Special Case of Fucks' Generalization of the Poisson Distribution

In the above sections, the 1-displaced Poisson distribution and the 1-displaced Dacey-Poisson distribution were derived as two special cases of the Fucks Generalized Poisson distribution as described in (2.14). In the first case, the ε-spectrum had the form $\varepsilon_0 = \varepsilon_1 = 1, \varepsilon_k = 0$ for $k \geq 2$, and in the second case $\varepsilon_0 = \varepsilon_1 = 1,\ \varepsilon_2 = \alpha, \varepsilon_k = 0$ for $k \geq 3$.

Now, in the case of the 3-parameter model, ε_2 and ε_3 have to be estimated, the whole ε-spectrum having the form: $\varepsilon_0 = \varepsilon_1 = 1, \varepsilon_2 = \alpha, \varepsilon_3 = \beta, \varepsilon_k = 0$ for $k \geq 4$, resulting in the following model:

$$p_i = e^{-(\mu-1-\alpha-\beta)} \cdot \sum_{k=1}^{3} (\varepsilon_k - \varepsilon_{i+1}) \frac{(\mu - 1 - \alpha - \beta)^{i-k}}{(i-k)!} \tag{2.23}$$

Replacing $\lambda = mu - \alpha - \beta$, the probability mass function has the following form

$$p_1 = e^{-\lambda} \cdot (1-\alpha)$$

$$p_2 = e^{-\lambda} \cdot [(1-\alpha) \cdot \lambda + (\alpha - \beta)]$$

$$p_i = e^{-\lambda} \left[(1-\alpha) \frac{\lambda^{i-1}}{(i-1)!} + (\alpha-\beta) \frac{\lambda^{i-2}}{(i-2)!} + \beta \frac{\lambda^{i-3}}{(i-3)!} \right], \quad i \geq 3$$

As to the estimation of $\varepsilon_2 = \alpha$ and $\varepsilon_3 = \beta$, Fucks (1956a: 13) suggested calculating them by reference to the second and third central moments (μ_2 and μ_3). It would lead too far, here, to go into details, as far as their derivation is concerned. Still, the resulting 2×2-system of equations shall be quoted:

(a) $\mu_2 = \mu_1 - 1 - (\alpha+\beta)^2 + 2\beta$
(b) $\mu_3 = \mu_3 = \mu_1 + 2(1+\alpha+\beta)^3 - 3(1+\alpha+\beta)^2 - 6(\alpha+\beta)(\alpha+2\beta) + 6\beta$

As can be seen, the solution of this equation system – which can be mathematically simplified (cf. Antić/Grzybek/Stadlober 2005a) – involves a cubic equation. Consequently, three solutions are obtained, not all of which must necessarily be real solutions. For each real solution the values for $\varepsilon_2 = \alpha$ and $\varepsilon_3 = \beta$ have to be estimated (which is easily done by computer programs today, as opposed to in Fucks' time).[11]

Before further going into details of this estimation, let us remember that there are two important conditions as to the two parameters:

(a) $\varepsilon_2 = \alpha \leq 1$ and $\varepsilon_3 = \beta \leq 1$,

(b) $\varepsilon_2 = \alpha \geq \beta = \varepsilon_3$.

With this in mind, let us once again analyze the data of Table 2.9, this time fitting Fucks' 3-parameter model. The results obtained can be seen in Table 2.13; results not meeting the two conditions mentioned above, are marked as $\varnothing$.

It can clearly be seen that in some cases, quite reasonably, the results for the 3-parameter model are better, as compared to those of the two models discussed above. One can also see that the 3-parameter model may be an appropriate model for empirical distributions in which $d > 1$ (which was the decisive problem for the two models described above): thus, in the Russian sample, for example, where $d = 1.1591$, the discrepancy coefficient is $C = 0.0005$. However, as the results for German and Japanese data (with $d = 1.1751$ and $d = 1.2319$, respectively) show, D does not seem to play the crucial role in case of the 3-parameter model.

[11] In addition to a detailed mathematical reconstruction of Fucks' ≪Theory of Word Formation≫, Antić/Grzybek/Stadlober (2005b) have tested the efficiency of Fucks' model in empirical research.

Table 2.13: Discrepancy Coefficient C as a Result of Fitting the Fucks 3-Parameter Poisson Distribution to Different Languages (Fucks 1955)

	English	German	Esperanto	Arabic	Greek
C	∅	∅	0.00004	0.0021	∅
$\hat{\varepsilon}_2$	—	—	0.3933	0.5463	—
$\hat{\varepsilon}_3$	—	—	0.0995	-0.1402	—
d	1.3890	1.1751	0.9511	0.5964	1.2179
	Japanese	**Russian**	**Latin**	**Turkish**	
C	∅	0.0005	0.0003	0.0023	
$\hat{\varepsilon}_2$	—	0.2083	0.5728	0.6164	
$\hat{\varepsilon}_3$	—	0.1686	0.2416	0.1452	
d	1.2319	1.1591	0.8704	0.8015	

In fact, as Antić/Grzybek/Stadlober (2005a) show, the conditions for the Fucks 3-parameter model to be appropriate are slightly different. The details need not be discussed here; it may suffice to say that it is ultimately the difference $M = \bar{x} - m_2$, i.e. the difference between the mean of the empirical distribution ($\bar{x}$) and its variance (m_2). One thus obtains the following two conditions:

1. The sum $a = \hat{\varepsilon}_2 + \hat{\varepsilon}_3 = \hat{\alpha} + \hat{\beta}$ must be in a particular interval:

$$a_i \in \left[\frac{1-\sqrt{4M-3}}{2}, \frac{1+\sqrt{4M-3}}{2}\right] \qquad i = 1, 2, 3$$

   Thus, there are two interval limits a_1 and a_2:

$$a_{i1} = \frac{1-\sqrt{4M-3}}{2} \qquad \text{and} \qquad a_{i2} = \frac{1+\sqrt{4M-3}}{2}$$

2. In order to be $a \in \mathbb{R}$, the root $4M - 3$ must be positive, i.e. $4M - 3 \geq 0$; therefore, $M = \bar{x} - m_2 \geq 0.75$.

From the results represented in Table 2.14 (p. 51) it can clearly be seen why, in four of the nine cases, the results are not as desired: there are a number of violations, which are responsible for the failure of Fucks' 3-parameter model. These violations can be of two kinds:

a. As soon as $M < 0.75$, the definition of the interval limits of a_1 and a_2 involves a negative root – this is the case with the Japanese data, for example;

Table 2.14: Violations of the conditions for Fucks' 3-parameter model

	English	**German**	**Esperanto**	**Arabic**	**Greek**
C	∅	∅	< 0.01	< 0.01	∅
$\hat{\varepsilon}_2$	—	—	0.3933	0.5463	—
$\hat{\varepsilon}_3$	—	—	0.0995	-0.1402	—
$a = \hat{\varepsilon}_2 + \hat{\varepsilon}_3$	-0.0882	-0.1037	0.4929	0.4061	0.2799
a_{i1}	0.1968	0.1270	-0.0421	-0.3338	0.4108
a_{i2}	0.8032	0.8730	1.0421	1.3338	0.5892
$a_{i1} < a < a_{i2}$	–	–	✓	✓	–
$\bar{x}$	1.4064	1.6333	1.8971	2.1032	2.1106
m_2	0.5645	0.7442	0.8532	0.6579	1.3526
$M = \bar{x} - m_2$	0.8420	0.8891	1.0438	1.4453	0.7580
$M \geq 0.75$	✓	✓	✓	✓	✓
	Japanese	**Russian**	**Latin**	**Turkish**	
C	∅	< 0.01	< 0.01	< 0.01	
$\hat{\varepsilon}_2$	—	0.2083	0.5728	0.6164	
$\hat{\varepsilon}_3$	—	0.1686	0.2416	0.1452	
$a = \hat{\varepsilon}_2 + \hat{\varepsilon}_3$	-0.1798	0.3769	0.8144	0.7616	
a_{i1}	$\mathbb{C}$	0.2659	-0.1558	-0.2346	
a_{i1}	$\mathbb{C}$	0.7341	1.1558	1.2346	
$a_{i1} < a < a_{i2}$	–	✓	✓	✓	
$\bar{x}$	2.1325	2.2268	2.3894	2.4588	
m_2	1.3952	1.4220	1.2093	1.1692	
$M = \bar{x} - m_2$	0.7374	0.8048	1.1800	1.2896	
$M \geq 0.75$	–	✓	✓	✓	

b. Even if the first condition is met with $M \geq 0.75$, fitting the Fucks 3-parameter model may fail, if the condition $a_{i1} < a < a_{i2}$ is not fulfilled – this can be seen in the case of the English, German, and Greek data.

Fucks' 3-parameter model thus is adequate only for particular types of empirical distributions, and it can not serve as an overall model for language, not even for syllabic languages, as Fucks himself claimed. However, some of the problems met might be related to the specific way of estimating the parameters suggested by him, and this might be the reason why other authors following him tried to find alternative ways.

5.6 The Georgian Line: Cercvadze, Čikoidze, Cilosani, Gačečiladze

Quite early, three Georgian scholars, G.N. Cercvadze, G.B. Čikoidze, and T.G. Gačečiladze (1959), applied Fucks' ideas to Georgian linguistic material, mainly to phoneme frequencies and word length frequencies. Their study, which was translated into German as early as 1962, and which was later extended by Gačečiladze/Cilosani (1971), was originally inspired by the Russian translation of Fucks' English-language article ≪Mathematical Theory of Word Formation≫. Fucks' article, originally a contribution to the 1956 London Conference on *Information Theory*, had been published in England in 1956, and it was translated into Russian only one year later, in 1957. As opposed to most of his German papers, Fucks had discussed his generalization at some length in this English synopsis of his work, and this is likely to be the reason why his approach received much more attention among Russian-speaking scholars.

In fact, Cercvadze, Čikoidze, and Gačečiladze (1959) based their analyses on Fucks' generalization; the only thing different from Fucks' approach is their estimation of the two parameters ε_2 and ε_3 of Fucks 3-parameter model: as opposed to Fucks, they estimated ε_2 and ε_3 not with recourse to the central moments, but to the initial moments of the empirical distribution. The empirical central moment of the order r

$$m_r = \frac{1}{(N-1)} \sum_x (x - \bar{x})^r f_x$$

is an estimate of the r-th theoretical moment defined as

$$\mu_r = \sum_x (x - \mu)^r P_x$$

As estimate for the theoretical initial moment of the order r

$$\mu'_r = \sum_x x^r P_x$$

serves the empirical r-th initial moment given as:

$$m'_r = \frac{1}{N}\sum_x x^r f_x$$

Since it can be shown that central moments and initial moments can be transformed into each other, the results can be expected to be identical; still, the procedure of estimating is different.

We need not go into details, here, as far as the derivation of the Fucks distribution and its generating function is concerned (cf. Antić/Grzybek/Stadlober 2005a). Rather, it may suffice to name its first three initial moments, which are necessary for the equation system to be established, which, in turn, is needed for the estimation of ε_2 and ε_3. Thus, with

$$\sum_{k=1}^{\infty} \varepsilon_k = \varepsilon' \tag{2.24}$$

we have the first three initial moments of Fucks' distribution:

$$\begin{aligned}
\mu'_1 &= \mu \\
\mu'_2 &= \mu^2 + \mu - \varepsilon'^2 - 2\varepsilon' + 2\sum_{k=1}^{\infty} k\varepsilon_k \\
\mu'_3 &= \mu^3 + 3\mu^2 + \mu + 2\varepsilon'^3 + 3\varepsilon'^2 - \varepsilon' - 3\mu\varepsilon'^2 - 6\mu\varepsilon' + \\
&\quad + \sum_{k=0}^{\infty} k^3 (\varepsilon_k - \varepsilon_{k+1}) + 6(\mu - \varepsilon')\sum_{k=1}^{\infty} k\varepsilon_k
\end{aligned} \tag{2.25}$$

Now, replacing ε_2 with α, and ε_3 with β, we obtain the following system of equations:

$$\begin{aligned}
&\text{(a) } \mu'_2 = \mu^2 + \mu - (1+\alpha+\beta)^2 - 2(1+\alpha+\beta) + 2(1+2\alpha+3\beta) \\
&\text{(b) } \mu'_3 = \mu^3 + 3\mu^2 + \mu + 2(1+\alpha+\beta)^3 + 3(1-\mu)(1+\alpha+\beta)^2 + 6\alpha + \\
&\qquad +18\beta - 6\mu(1+\alpha+\beta) + 6(\mu - 1 - \alpha - \beta)(1+2\alpha+3\beta)\,.
\end{aligned}$$

After the solution for α and β, we thus have the following probabilities:

$$\begin{aligned}
p_1 &= e^{-\lambda} \cdot (1-\alpha) \\
p_2 &= e^{-\lambda} \cdot [(1-\alpha)\cdot\lambda + (\alpha-\beta)] \\
p_i &= e^{-\lambda}\left[(1-\alpha)\frac{\lambda^{i-1}}{(i-1)!} + (\alpha-\beta)\frac{\lambda^{i-2}}{(i-2)!} + \beta\frac{\lambda^{i-3}}{(i-3)!}\right], \quad i \geq 3
\end{aligned}$$

with $\lambda = \mu - 1 - \alpha - \beta$

As was said above, the results are identical as compared to those obtained by recourse to the central moments. Unfortunately, there are several mistakes in the authors' own formula; therefore, there is no sense in reproducing their results on their Georgian sample, here.[12]

Almost twenty years later, Russian scholars Piotrovskij, Bektaev, and Piotrovskja (1977: 193; cf. 1985: 261), would again refer to Fucks' generalized model. These authors quite rightly termed the above-mentioned 1-displaced Poisson distribution (2.9) the "Čebanov-Fucks distribution" (cf. p. 27). In addition to this, they mentioned the so-called "generalized Gačečiladze-Fucks distribution", which deserves some more attention here.

As was seen above, the 1959 paper by Cercvadze, Čikoidze, and Gačečiladze was based on Fuck's generalization of the Poisson distribution. Obviously, these authors indeed once again generalized the Fucks model, which is not inherent in the 1959 paper mentioned, but represented in an extension of it by Gačečiladze/Cilosani (1971). This extension contains an additional factor φ_{nu}, which is dependent on three parameters:

(a) the mean of the sample ($\bar{i}$),

(b) the relevant class i,

(c) the sum of all ε_ν, $A = \sum_{\nu=1}^{\infty} \varepsilon_\nu$ (termed ε' by Fucks).

As a result, the individual weights of the generalized Fucks distribution, defined as $(\varepsilon_k - \varepsilon_{k+1})$, are multiplied by the function φ_ν. Unfortunately, Gačečiladze/Cilosoni (1971: 114) do not explain the process by which φ_{nu} may be theoretically derived; they only present the final formula (2.26):

$$P_i = e^{-\left(\bar{i}-A\right)} \sum_{\nu=0}^{\infty} (\varepsilon_\nu - \varepsilon_{\nu+1}) \frac{(\lambda - A)^{i-\nu}}{(i-\nu)!} \varphi_\nu \left(A, \bar{i}, i\right) \tag{2.26}$$

Here, $\bar{i}$ is the mean of the sample, and $(\varepsilon_k - \varepsilon_{k+1})$ are the weighting factors. Unfortunately, Piotrovskij et al. (1977: 195), who term formula (2.26) the "Fucks-Gačečiladze distribution", also give no derivation for ϕ_ν. Assuming that φ_ν takes account of the contextual environment, they only refer to Fucks' 1955 *Mathematische Analyse von Sprachelementen, Sprachstil und Sprachen.* However, neither Fucks' generalization nor φ are mentioned in this work. Thus, as to the theoretical derivation of φ_ν, there are only sparse references

[12] In fact, in spite of, or rather due to their obvious calculation errors, the authors arrived at a solution for ε_2 and ε_3, which yields a good theoretical result; these values cannot be derived from the correct formula, however, and therefore must be considered to be a casual and accidental ad hoc solution.

by Gačečiladze/Cilosani (1971: 114) who mentioned some of their Georgian publications, which are scarcely available.

Still, it can easily be seen that for $\phi_\nu \to 1$, one obtains the generalized Fucks distribution, which has also been discussed by some Polish authors.

5.7 Estimating the Fucks Distribution With First-Class Frequency (Bartkowiakowa/Gleichgewicht 1964/65)

Two Polish authors, Anna Bartkowiakowa and Bolesław Gleichgewicht (1964, 1965), also suggested an alternative way to estimate the two parameters ε_2 and ε_3 of Fucks' 3-parameter distribution. Based on the standard Poisson distribution, as represented in (2.27),

$$g_k = \frac{\lambda^k}{k!}e^{-\lambda} \qquad k = 0, 1, 2, \ldots \tag{2.27}$$

and referring to Fucks' (2.14) generalization of it, the authors reformulated the latter as seen in (2.28):

$$\begin{aligned} p_i &= \sum_{k=0}^{\infty} (\varepsilon_k - \varepsilon_{k+1}) e^{-\lambda} \frac{\lambda^{i-k}}{(i-k)!} \\ &= \sum_{k=0}^{\infty} (\varepsilon_k - \varepsilon_{k+1}) \cdot g_{i-k} \end{aligned} \tag{2.28}$$

Determining $\varepsilon_0 = \varepsilon_1 = 1$, and $\varepsilon_k = 0$ for $k > 3$, the two parameters $\varepsilon_2 \neq 0$ and $\varepsilon_3 \neq 0$ remain to be estimated on the basis of the empirical distribution. Based on these assumptions, the following special cases are obtained for (2.28):

$$\begin{aligned} p_1 &= (1 - \varepsilon_2) \cdot g_0 \\ p_2 &= (1 - \varepsilon_2) \cdot g_1 + (\varepsilon_2 - \varepsilon_3) \cdot g_0 \\ p_i &= (1 - \varepsilon_2) \cdot g_{i-1} + (\varepsilon_2 - \varepsilon_3) \cdot g_{i-2} + \varepsilon_3 \cdot g_{i-3} \text{ for } i \geq 3 \end{aligned}$$

with $\lambda = \mu - (1 + \varepsilon_2 + \varepsilon_3)$

As to the estimation of ε_2 and ε_3, the authors did not set up an equation system on the basis of the second and third central moments (μ_2 and μ_3), as did Fucks, thus arriving at a cubic equation; rather, they first defined the portion of one-syllable words (p_1), and then modelled the whole distribution on that proportion. Thus, by way of a logarithmic transformation of $p_1 = (1 - \varepsilon_2) \cdot g_0$

in formula (2.28), one obtains the following sequence of transformations:

$$\ln \frac{p_1}{(1-\varepsilon_2)} = \ln g_0$$
$$\ln \frac{p_1}{(1-\varepsilon_2)} = -\lambda$$
$$\ln \frac{p_1}{(1-\varepsilon_2)} = -\left[\mu - (1+\varepsilon_2+\varepsilon_3)\right]$$

Referring to the empirical distribution, a first equation for an equation system to be solved (see below) is thus gained from the first probability (p_1) of the empirical distribution:

$$\ln \frac{\hat{p}_1}{(1-\hat{\varepsilon}_2)} = -\left[\bar{x} - (1+\hat{\varepsilon}_2+\hat{\varepsilon}_3)\right] \tag{2.29}$$

The second equation for that system is then gained from the variance of the empirical distribution. Thus, one gets

$$\mu_2 = \mu - (1+\varepsilon_2+\varepsilon_3)^2 + 2\cdot(\varepsilon_2 + 2\cdot\varepsilon_3)$$

resulting in the second equation for the equation system to be established:

$$m_2 = \bar{x} - (1+\hat{\varepsilon}_2+\hat{\varepsilon}_3)^2 + 2\cdot(\hat{\varepsilon}_2 + 2\hat{\varepsilon}_3) \tag{2.30}$$

With the two equations (2.29) and (2.30), we thus have the following system of equations, adequate to arrive at a solution for ε_2 and ε_3:

$$\text{(a)}\ \ln \frac{\hat{p}_1}{(1-\hat{\varepsilon}_2)} = -\left[\bar{x} - (1+\hat{\varepsilon}_2+\hat{\varepsilon}_3)\right]$$
$$\text{(b)}\ m_2 - \bar{x} = -(1+\hat{\varepsilon}_2+\hat{\varepsilon}_3)^2 + 2\,(\hat{\varepsilon}_2 + 2\hat{\varepsilon}_3)$$

Bartkowiakowa/Gleichgewicht (1964) not only theoretically presented this procedure to estimate ε_2 and ε_3; they also offered the results of empirical studies, which were meant to be a test of their model. These analyses comprised nine Polish literary texts, or segments of them, and the results of these analyses indeed proved their approach to be successful.

Table 2.15 contains the results: as can be seen, the discrepancy coefficient is $C < 0.01$ in all cases; furthermore, in six of the nine samples, the result is indeed better as compared to Fucks' original estimation.

For the sake of comparison, Table 2.15 also contains the results for the (1-displaced) Poisson and the (1-displaced) Dacey-Poisson distributions, which were calculated in a re-analysis of the raw data provided by the Polish authors. A closer look at these data shows that the Polish text samples are relatively homogeneous: for all texts, the dispersion quotient is in the interval $0.88 \leq d \leq 1.04$, and $0.95 \leq M \leq 1.09$.

Table 2.15: Fitting the Fucks 3-Parameter Model to Polish Data, with Parameter Estimation Based on First-Class Frequency

	1	**2**	**3**	**4**	**5**
$\bar{x}$	1.81	1.82	1.96	1.93	2.07
m_2	0.76	0.73	0.87	0.94	1.07
d	0.93	0.88	0.91	1.00	0.99
M	1.05	1.09	1.09	0.99	1.00
C (Poisson)	0.00420	0.00540	0.00370	0.00170	0.00520
C (Dacey-Poisson)	0.00250	0.00060	0.00200	∅	0.00531
C (m_2, m_3)	0.00240	0.00017	0.00226	0.00125	0.00085
C $(\hat{p}_1, m_2)$	0.00197	0.00043	0.00260	0.00194	0.00032

	6	**7**	**8**	**9**
$\bar{x}$	2.12	2.05	2.18	2.16
m_2	1.10	0.98	1.21	1.21
d	0.98	0.94	1.03	1.04
M	1.02	1.07	0.97	0.95
C (Poisson)	0.00810	0.00220	0.01360	0.00940
C (Dacey-Poisson)	0.00862	0.00145	∅	∅
C (m_2, m_3)	0.00084	0.00120	0.00344	0.00383
C $(\hat{p}_1, m_2)$	0.00030	0.00077	0.00216	0.00271

This raises the question in how far the procedure suggested by Bartkowiakowa/Gleichgewicht (1964) is able to improve the results for the nine different languages analyzed by Fucks himself (cf. Table 2.9, p. 41). Table **??** represents the corresponding results.

In summary, one may thus say that the procedure to estimate the two parameters ε_2 and ε_3, as suggested by Bartkowiakowa/Gleichgewicht (1964), may indeed, for particular samples, result in better fittings. However, they cannot overcome the overall limitations of Fucks' 3-parameter model, which have been discussed above.

Table 2.16: Fucks' 3-parameter Model, with Parameter Estimation

	Esperanto	Arabic	Russian	Latin	Turkish
m_2, m_3					
$\hat{\varepsilon}_2$	0.3933	0.5463	0.2083	0.5728	0.6164
$\hat{\varepsilon}_3$	0.0995	-0.1402	0.1686	0.2416	0.1452
C	0.00004	0.0021	0.0005	0.0003	0.0023
$\hat{p}_1, m_2$					
$\hat{\varepsilon}_2$	0.3893	0.7148	0.2098	0.5744	0.6034
$\hat{\varepsilon}_3$	0.0957	0.1599	0.1695	0.2490	0.1090
C	0.00001	0.0042	0.0005	0.0003	0.0018

6. The Doubly Modified Poisson Distribution (Vranić/Matković 1965)

A different approach to modify the standard Poisson distribution has been suggested by Vranić/Matković (1965a,b). The authors analyzed Croatian data from two corpora, each consisting of several literary works and a number of newspaper articles. The data of one of the two samples are represented in Table 2.17

Table 2.17: Word Length Frequencies for Croato-Serbian Text Segments (Vranić/Matković 1965)

i	f_i	p_i
1	13738	0.3420
2	12000	0.2988
3	8776	0.2185
4	4234	0.1054
5	1103	0.0275
6	253	0.0063
7	47	0.0012
8	13	0.0003
9	3	0.0001

In Table 2.17, f_i denotes the absolute and p_i the relative frequencies of i-syllable words.

Referring to the work of Fucks, and testing if their data follow a 1-displaced Poisson distribution, as suggested by Fucks, Vranić/Matković (1965b: 187) observed a clear "discrepancy from the Poisson distribution in monosyllabic and disyllabic words", at the same time seeing "indications of conformity in the distribution of three-syllable, four-syllable, and polysyllabic words." The corresponding data are represented in Figure 2.12.

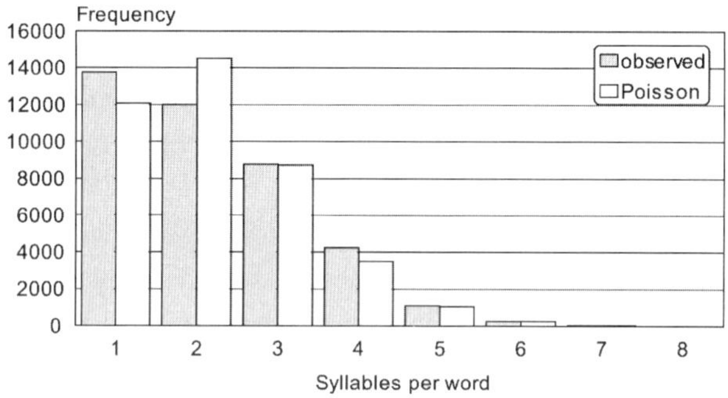

Figure 2.12: Fitting the 1-Displaced Poisson Distribution to Croato-Serbian Text Segments (Vranić/Matković 1965a,b)

We need not concentrate here on questions of the particular data structure. Rather, it is of methodological interest to see how the authors dealt with the data. Guided by the conclusion (supported by the graphical representation of Figure 2.12), the authors tested if the words of length $i \geq 3$, taken as a separate sample, follow the Poisson distribution. Calculating the corresponding χ^2 values, they reduced the whole sample of the remaining 14429 items to an artificial sample of 1000 items, retaining the proportions of the original data set. The reason for this reduction is likely to be the linear rise of χ^2 values with increasing sample size (see above, p. 23). As a result, the authors conclude "that three- and polysyllabic words in Croato-Serbian roughly follow the Poisson distribution" (ibd., 189).

In fact, a re-analysis shows that for fitting the Poisson distribution to the original sample ($N = 40167$), one obtains a rather bad discrepancy coefficient of $C = 0.0206$, whereas for that portion of words with length $i \geq 3$ one obtains $C = 0.0085$. Though convincing at first sight, the question remains why the goodness of the Poisson distribution has not been tested for that portion of words with length $i \geq 2$; curiously enough, the result is even better with $C = 0.0047$. Yet, obviously (mis-)led by the optical impression, Vranić/Matković (1965b: 194) concentrate on a modification of the first two classes, suggesting a procedure which basically implies a double modified Poisson distribution. Referring to the approaches discussed by Fucks and Bartkowiakowa/Gleichgewicht (see above), Vranić/Matković suggest the introduction of particular weights, which, according to their proposal, are obtained by way of the following method.

Taking the relative frequency of $p_1 = 0.342$, one obtains $\lambda = 1.079$ as that parameter of the standard (i.e., unweighted) Poisson distribution, from which $v_1 = 0.340$ results as the theoretical relative frequency:

$$v_i = \frac{\lambda^{i-1} e^{-\lambda}}{(i-1)!} \qquad i = 1, 2, \ldots \tag{2.31}$$

Furthermore, for $\lambda = 1.079$, one obtains $v_2 = 0.367$, and the corresponding values for the remaining frequencies $(v_3 \ldots v_n)$. Given the observation that the empirical values follow a Poisson distribution for $i \geq 3$, the authors consider it to be necessary and sufficient to represent monosyllabic and disyllabic words through superposition by way of introducing two weighting parameters a_1 and a_2 modifying the theoretical frequencies of v_1 and v_2, as obtained from (2.31), thus arriving at the weighted theoretical frequencies p'_1 and p'_2 by assuming:

$$p'_1 = a_1 \cdot v_1 \qquad\qquad p'_2 = a_1 \cdot v_2 + a_2 \cdot v_1$$

Given the condition that $p'_1 + p'_2 = p_1 + p_2 = 0.3420 + 0.2988 = 0.6408$, one has to seek the minimum for formula (2.32):

$$\begin{aligned} F(a_1, a_2) = (p'_1 - a_1 \cdot v_1)^2 + (p'_2 - a_1 \cdot v_2 - a_2 \cdot v_1) - \\ - 2\beta \cdot (v_1 + v_2 - 0.6408) \end{aligned} \tag{2.32}$$

Solving the resulting set of equations, one thus obtains the two weights $a_1 = 1.006$ and $a_2 = -0.2066$; consequently,

$$\begin{aligned} p'_1 &= 1.006 \cdot v_1 = 1.006 \cdot 0.340 = 0.342 \\ p'_2 &= 1.006 \cdot v_2 + a_2 \cdot v_1 = 1.006 \cdot 0.367 - 0.2066 \cdot 0.340 = 0.2988 \end{aligned}$$

We thus obtain the weighted theoretical values NP_i of the doubly modified Poisson distribution, represented in Table 2.18.

As a re-analysis shows, the results must be regarded to be excellent, statistically confirmed by a discrepancy coefficient value of $C = 0.0030$ ($\chi^2_{df=5} = 122.18$). Still, there remain at least two major theoretical problems:

1. No interpretation is given as to why the weighting modification is necessary: is this a matter of the specific data structure, is this specific for Croatian language products?
2. Is it reasonable to stick to the Poisson distribution, though in a modified version of it, as a theoretical model, if almost two thirds of the data sample ($f_1 + f_2 \approx 64\%$) do not seem to follow it?
3. As was mentioned above, the whole sample follows a Poisson distribution not only for $i \geq 3$, but already for $i \geq 2$: Consequently, in this case, only the first class would have to be modified, if it all.

Table 2.18: Fitting the Doubly Modified Poisson Distribution to Croato-Serbian Text Segments (Vranić/Matković 1965a,b)

i	f_i	NP_i
1	13738	13738.00
2	12000	12000.00
3	8776	8599.81
4	4234	4450.40
5	1103	1151.54
6	253	198.64
7	47	25.70
8	13	2.66
9	3	0.23

7. The Negative Binomial Distribution (Grotjahn 1982)

An important step in the discussion of possibly adequate distribution models for word length frequencies was Grotjahn's (1982) contribution. As can be seen above, apart from Elderton's early attempt to favor the geometric distribution, the whole discussion had focused for almost three decades on the Poisson distribution; various attempts had been undertaken to modify the Poisson distribution, due to the fact that the linguistic data under study could not be theoretically modelled by recourse to it. As the re-analyses presented in the preceding chapters have shown, neither the standard Poisson distribution nor any of its straight forward modifications can be considered to be an adequate model. Still, all the attempts discussed above, from the late 1950s until the 1980s, in one way or another, stuck to the conviction that the Poisson distribution is the one relevant model which "only" has to be modified, depending on the specific structure of linguistic data.

Grotjahn, in his attempt, opened the way for new perspectives: he not only showed that the Poisson model per se might not be an adequate model; furthermore, he initiated a discussion concentrating on the question whether one overall model could be sufficient when dealing with word length frequencies of different origin.

Taking into consideration that the 1-displaced Poisson model, basically suggested by Fucks and often, though mistakenly, called the "Fucks distribution", was still considered to be the standard model, it seems to be necessary to put some of Grotjahn's introductory remarks into the right light.

As most scholars at that time would do – and, in fact, as most scholars would do still today –, Grotjahn (1982: 46ff.), at the beginning of his ruminations, referred to the so-called "Fucks distribution". According to him, "the Fucks distribution has to be regarded a special case of a displaced Poisson distribution" (ibd., 46). As was shown above, this statement is correct only if one considers the 1-displaced Poisson distribution to be the "Fucks distribution"; in fact, however, as was shown above, the 1-displaced Fucks distribution is not more and not less than a special case of the generalized Fucks-Poisson distribution.

With this in mind, Grotjahn's own suggestions appear in a somewhat more adequate light. Given a random variable Y, representing the number of syllables per word (which may have the values $k = a, a+1, \ldots$, with $a \in \mathbb{N}_0$), we have formula (2.33) for the displaced Poisson distribution, resulting in the standard Poisson distribution for $a = 0$:

$$P(Y = k) = \frac{e^{-\lambda}\lambda^{k-a}}{(k-a)!}, \qquad k = a, a+1, \ldots \qquad a \in \mathbb{N}^0 \tag{2.33}$$

As a starting point, Grotjahn analyzed seven letters by Goethe, written in 1782, and tested in how far the (1-displaced) Poisson distribution would prove to be an adequate model. As to the statistical testing of the findings, Grotjahn (1982: 52) suggested calculating not only χ^2 values, or their transformation into z values, but also the deviation of the empirical dispersion index (d) from its theoretical expectation (δ). As was pointed out above (cf. p. 48), the Poisson distribution can be an adequate model only in case $d \approx 1$.

However, of the concrete data analyzed by Grotjahn, only some satisfied this condition; others clearly did not, the value of d ranging from $1.01 \leq d \leq 1.32$ for the seven Goethe letters under study. Given this observation, Grotjahn arrived at two important conclusions: the first consequence is that "the displaced Poisson distribution hardly can be regarded to be an adequate model for the word length frequency distribution in German" (ibd., 55). And his second conclusion is even more important, generally stating that the Poisson model "cannot be a general law for the formation of words from syllables" (ibd., 47).

In a way, this conclusion paved the way for a new line of research. After decades of concentration on the Poisson distribution, Grotjahn was able to prove that this model alone cannot be adequate for a general theory of word length distribution. On the basis of this insight, Grotjahn further elaborated his ruminations. Replacing the Poisson parameter λ in (2.33) by $\theta - a$, and obtaining (2.34)

$$P(Y = k) = \frac{e^{-(\theta-a)}(\theta-a)^{k-a}}{(k-a)!}, \qquad k = a, a+1, \ldots \qquad a \in \mathbb{N}_0, \tag{2.34}$$

Grotjahn's (1982: 55) reason for this modification was as follows: a crucial implication of the Poisson distribution is the independence of individual occurrences. Although every single word thus may well follow a Poisson distribution, this assumption does not necessarily imply the premise that the probability is one and the same for all words; rather, it depends on factors such as (linguistic) context, theme, etc. In other words, Grotjahn further assumed that parameter θ itself is likely to be a random variable.

Now, given one follows this (reasonable) assumption, the next question is which theoretical model might be relevant for θ. Grotjahn (1982: 56ff.) tentatively assumed the gamma distribution to be adequate. Thus, the so-called negative binomial distribution (2.35) (also known as 'composed Poisson' or 'multiple Poisson' distribution) in its a-displaced form is obtained, as a result of this super-imposition of two distributions:

$$f(x; k; p) = \binom{k + x - a - 1}{x - a} p^k q^{x-a}, \qquad x = a, a+1, \ldots \qquad a \in \mathbb{N}_0 \tag{2.35}$$

As can be seen, for $k = 1$ and $a = 1$, one obtains the 1-displaced geometric distribution (2.2), earlier discussed by Elderton (1949) as a possible model (see above, p. 20).

$$f(x) = p \cdot q^{x-1}, \qquad x = 1, 2, \ldots \tag{2.36}$$

In fact, the negative binomial distribution had been discussed before by Brainerd (1971, 1975: 240ff.). Analyzing samples from various literary works written in English, Brainerd first tested the 1-displaced Poisson distribution and found that it "yields a poor fit in general for the works considered" (Brainerd 1975: 241). The 1-displaced Poisson distribution turned out to be an acceptable model only in the case of short passages, whereas in general, his data indicated "that a reasonable case can be made for the hypothesis that the frequencies of syllables per word follow the negative binomial distribution" (ibd., 248). In some cases, however (in fact those with $k \to 1$), also the geometric distribution (2.2) suggested by Elderton (1949) turned out to be adequate.

The negative binomial distribution does not only converge to the geometric distribution, however; under particular circumstances, it converges to the Poisson distribution: namely, if $k \to \infty, q \to 0, k \cdot q \to a$ (cf. Wimmer/Altmann (1999: 454). Therefore, as Grotjahn (1982: 71f.) rightly stated, the negative binomial distribution, too, is apt to model frequency distributions with $d \approx 1$.

With his approach, Grotjahn thus additionally succeeded in integrating earlier research, both on the geometric and the Poisson distributions, which had failed to be adequate as an overall valid model. In this context, it is of particular interest, therefore, that the negative binomial distribution is a theoretically adequate model also for data with $d > 1$. Given the theoretical values for σ^2 and μ

$$\sigma^2 = \frac{k \cdot q^2}{p^2} + \frac{k \cdot p}{p}$$
$$\mu = \frac{k \cdot q}{p}$$

it can easily be shown that for the negative binomial distribution,

$$\delta = 1 + \frac{1-p}{p} > 1 \tag{2.37}$$

As Grotjahn (1982: 61) concludes, the negative binomial distribution therefore should be taken into account for empirical distributions with $d > 1$. A comparison of German corpus data from Meier's (1967) *Deutsche Sprachstatistik* clearly proves Grotjahn's argument to be reasonable. The data are reproduced in Table 2.19, which contains the theoretical values both for the Poisson and the negative binomial distributions. In addition to the χ^2 values, given by Grotjahn, Table 2.19 also contains the values of the discrepancy coefficient C discussed above (cf. p. 23), which are calculated anew, here.

Table 2.19: Fitting the Negative Binomial and Poisson Distributions to German Data from Meier's corpus (Grotjahn 1982)

x	f_x	neg. binom. d. NP_x	Poisson d. NP_x
1	25940	25827.1	22357.1
2	14113	14174.9	17994.8
3	5567	6144.5	7241.8
4	2973	2427.2	1942.9
5	1057	912.1	391.0
6	264	332.2	62.9
7	74	118.5	8.4
8	10	41.6	1.0
≥ 9	2	21.9	0.1
$N = 50000$		$\chi^2 = 273.72$	$\chi^2 = 4752.17$
		$C = 0.005$	$C = 0.095$

As can be seen, the negative binomial distribution yields significantly better results as compared to the Poisson model. The results are graphically represented in Figure 2.13.

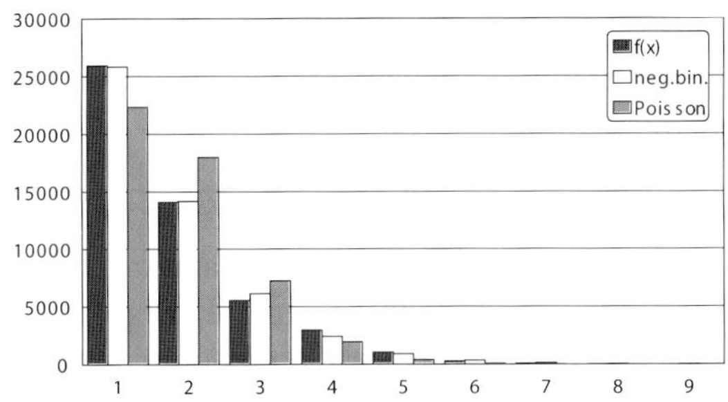

Figure 2.13: Observed and Expected Word Length Frequencies for Meier's German Corpus (Grotjahn 1982)

Concluding, it seems important to emphasize that Grotjahn's (1982: 74) overall advice was that the negative binomial distribution should be taken into account as *one* possible model for word length frequencies, not as *the* only general model. Still, it is tempting to see in how far the negative binomial distribution is able to model the data of nine languages, given by Fucks (cf. Table 2.9, p. 41). Table 2.20 represents the corresponding results, including the estimated values for the parameters k and p.

Table 2.20: Fitting the Negative Binomial Distribution to Fucks' Data From Nine Languages

	English	**German**	**Esperanto**	**Arabic**	**Greek**
$\hat{k}$	1.04	3.62	597.59	9.89	5.09
$\hat{p}$	0.72	0.85	0.99	0.90	0.82
C	0.0026	0.0019	0.0026	0.1503	0.0078

	Japanese	**Russian**	**Latin**	**Turkish**
$\hat{k}$	4.79	7.71	12.47	13.11
$\hat{p}$	0.81	0.86	0.90	0.90
C	0.0036	0.0078	0.0330	0.0440

From Table 2.20, two things can be nicely seen:

1. first, for Esperanto – the only 'language' with a really convincing fitting result of the Poisson distribution (cf. Table 2.10, p. 43) – both parameters behave as predicted: $k \to \infty$, and $q = (1 - p) \to 0$.

the second moment of the distribution on random factors". Kromer therefore suggested not to use this procedure, and to prefer the method of χ^2 minimization.

In the case of this method, we are concerned with a merely numerical solution, fitting λ_1 by minimizing the χ^2 value. Instead of presenting the results of Kromer's fittings, it might be tempting to re-analyze once again Fucks' data (cf. Table 2.9). These data have been repeatedly analyzed above, among others with regard to the negative binomial distribution (cf. Table 2.20, p. 65). Since the negative binomial distribution had proven not to be an adequate model for Latin, Arabic, and Turkish, it is interesting to see the results one obtains with Kromer's model.

Table 2.21 presents the corresponding results. In addition to the values for $\hat{\lambda}_1$ and $\hat{\lambda}_2$, obtained according to the two methods described above, Table 2.21 also contains the results one obtains for the 1-displaced Poisson-uniform distribution, using iterative methods incorporating relevant special software (ALTMANN-Fitter, version 2.1, 2000).

It can clearly be seen that for the 1-displaced Poisson-uniform distribution (with $b > a \geq 0$), there are solutions for all data sets, although for four of the nine languages, the results cannot be called satisfying ($C > 0.02$): these four languages are English, Arabic, Latin, and Turkish. As compared to this, the results for Kromer's modification are better in all cases. Additionally, they prove to be interesting in a different aspect, depending on the manner of estimating λ_1 (and, consequently, of λ_2). Using the method of moments, it turns out that in four of the nine cases (Esperanto, Arabic, Latin, and Turkish), no acceptable solutions are obtained. However, for these four cases, too, acceptable results are obtained with the χ^2 minimization method. Interestingly the values for λ_1 and λ_2, obtained with this method, are almost identical, differing only after the fifth or higher decimal (thus, $\lambda_1 \approx \lambda_2 \approx \lambda_0$).

Now, what is the reason for no satisfying results being obtained, according to the method of moments? Let us once again try to explain this referring to the dispersion quotient δ discussed above (cf. p. 47). As can be seen above, $\delta = Var(X)/[E(X)-1]$. Now, given that, for Kromer's version of the Poisson-uniform distribution in its 1-displaced form, we have the theoretical first and second moments:

$$\mu_1 = \frac{(\lambda_1 - 1) + (\lambda_2 - 1)}{2} + 1 = \frac{\lambda_1 + \lambda_2}{2}$$

$$\mu_2 = \frac{[(\lambda_1 - 1) - (\lambda_2 - 1)]^2}{12} + \frac{(\lambda_1 - 1) + (\lambda_2 - 1)}{2}$$

$$= \frac{(\lambda_1 - \lambda_2)^2}{12} + \frac{\lambda_1 + \lambda_2 - 2}{2}$$

Table 2.21: Fitting the 1-Displaced Poisson-Uniform Distribution to Fucks' Data From Nine Languages

	English	**German**	**Esperanto**	**Arabic**	**Greek**
$b > a \geq 0$					
$\hat{a}$	0.0497	0.1497	0.4675	0.6101	0.3197
$\hat{b}$	0.8148	1.1235	1.3432	1.6686	1.9199
C	0.0288	0.0029	0.0068	0.1409	0.0065
$\bar{x}, m_2'$					
$\hat{\lambda}_1$	0.7178	1.0567	∅	∅	1.2587
$\hat{\lambda}_2$	2.0950	2.2100	∅	∅	2.9625
C	0.0028	0.0027	–	–	0.0047
χ^2-min.					
$\hat{\lambda}_1$	0.7528	1.0904	1.8971	2.1032	1.1556
$\hat{\lambda}_2$	2.0600	2.1763	1.8971	2.1032	3.0656
C	0.0021	0.0024	0.0023	0.1071	0.0023
$d > 1$	✓	✓	–	–	✓

	Japanese	**Russian**	**Latin**	**Turkish**
$b > a \geq 0$				
$\hat{a}$	0.3457	0.3720	0.8373	0.8635
$\hat{b}$	1.9401	2,0900	1.9942	2.0859
C	0.0054	0.0054	0.0282	0.0391
$\bar{x}, m_2'$				
$\hat{\lambda}_1$	1.2451	1.4619	∅	∅
$\hat{\lambda}_2$	3.0199	2.9918	∅	∅
C	0.0053	0.0060	–	–
χ^2-min.				
$\hat{\lambda}_1$	1.3122	1.3088	2.3894	2.4588
$\hat{\lambda}_2$	2.9528	3.1449	2.3894	2.4588
C	0.0037	0.0037	0.0166	0.0207
$d > 1$	✓	✓	–	–

As to the theoretical dispersion quotient δ, we thus obtain the following equation:

$$\delta = \frac{Var(X)}{E(X)-1} = \frac{\dfrac{(\lambda_1-\lambda_2)^2}{12} + \dfrac{\lambda_1+\lambda_2-2}{2}}{\dfrac{\lambda_1+\lambda_2}{2} - 1}$$

$$= \frac{\dfrac{(\lambda_1-\lambda_2)^2 + 6\lambda_1 + 6\lambda_2 - 12}{12}}{\dfrac{\lambda_1+\lambda_2-2}{2}} = \frac{(\lambda_1-\lambda_2)^2 + 6(\lambda_1+\lambda_2-2)}{6(\lambda_1+\lambda_2-2)}$$

$$= \frac{(\lambda_1-\lambda_2)^2}{6\,(\lambda_1+\lambda_2-2)} + 1$$

Because $(\lambda_1 - \lambda_2)^2$ is positive, and because $\lambda_1 > 1$ and $\lambda_2 > 1$ by definition, $(\lambda_1 + \lambda_2 - 2)$ must be positive, as well; therefore, the quotient

$$Q_\delta = \frac{(\lambda_1-\lambda_2)^2}{6\,(\lambda_1+\lambda_2-2)} > 0 \tag{2.41}$$

must be positive as well. Consequently, for the 1-displaced Poisson-uniform distribution to be fitted with the method of moments, a necessary condition is that the dispersion quotient is $d > 1$. Empirically, this is proven by the results represented in Table 2.21: here, for those cases with $d \leq 1$, fitting Kromer's modification of the Poisson-uniform distribution with the method of moments fails.

Additionally, this circumstance explains why in these cases, we have almost identical values for λ_1 and λ_2 (i.e., $\lambda_1 \approx \lambda_2$): As can be shown, the dispersion quotient of the 1-displaced Poisson-uniform distribution is $\delta = 1$, only in the case that the quotient $Q_\delta = 0$ – cf. equation (2.41), as to this point. This however, is the case only if $\lambda_1 = \lambda_2$. Actually, this explains Kromer's assumption that for $\lambda_1 = \lambda_2$, the 1-displaced Poisson-uniform "degenerates" to the 1-displaced Poisson distribution, where, by definition, $\delta = 1$.[13]

According to Kromer (2001a: 96, 2001b: 74), the model proposed by him "degenerates" into the Poisson (Čebanov-Fucks) distribution with $\lambda_1 = \lambda_0$ (and correspondingly $\lambda_2 = \lambda_0$). In principle, this assumption is correct; strictly speaking, however, it would be more correct to say that for $\lambda_1 \cong \lambda_2$, the 1-displaced Poisson-uniform distribution can be approximated by the Poisson distribution. For the sake of clarity, the approximation of the 1-displaced

[13] From this perspective, it is no wonder that the C values obtained for the Poisson-uniform distribution by way of the χ^2 minimization method are almost the same, or even identical to those obtained for the Poisson distribution (cf. Table 2.10, p. 43).

Poisson-uniform distribution suggested by Kromer (personal communication) shall be demonstrated here; it is relevant for those cases when parameter a converges with parameter b in equation (2.39). In these cases, when $b = a + \varepsilon$ with $\varepsilon \to 0$, we first replace b with $a + \varepsilon$ in equation (2.39), thus obtaining formula (2.39'):

$$P_x = \frac{1}{\varepsilon}\left(e^{-a}\sum_{j=0}^{x}\frac{a^j}{j!} - e^{-a-\varepsilon}\sum_{j=0}^{x}\frac{(a+\varepsilon)^j}{j!}\right) \qquad (2.39')$$

In the next step, the binomial expression $(a+\varepsilon)^j$ from equation (2.39') is replaced with its first two terms, i.e.,

$$(a+\varepsilon)^j = \left(a\left(1+\frac{\varepsilon}{a}\right)\right)^j = a^j\left(1+\frac{\varepsilon}{a}\right)^j = a^j\left(1+\frac{\varepsilon}{a}\cdot j + \ldots\right) \approx$$
$$\approx a^j\left(1+\varepsilon\cdot j\cdot a^{-1}\right) = a^j\left(1+\frac{\varepsilon\cdot j}{a}\right) = a^j + a^{j-1}\varepsilon\cdot j,$$

thus obtaining (2.39")

$$P_x = \frac{1}{\varepsilon}\left\{e^{-a}\sum_{j=0}^{x}\frac{a^j}{j!} - e^{-a}\cdot e^{-\varepsilon}\left(\sum_{j=0}^{x}\frac{a^j}{j!} + \sum_{j=0}^{x}\frac{a^{j-1}\varepsilon j}{j!}\right)\right\} \qquad (2.39'')$$

Finally, function $e^{-\varepsilon}$ in equation (2.39") is approximated by the first two terms of the Taylor series of this function, resulting in $1 - \varepsilon$, thus stepwise receiving the ordinary Poisson distribution:

$$P_x = e^{-a}\left(\sum_{j=0}^{x}\frac{a^j}{j!} - \sum_{j=0}^{x}\frac{j\cdot a^{j-1}}{j!}\right) = e^{-a}\frac{a^x}{x!} \qquad (2.39''')$$

Yet, we are concerned here with an approximation of the Poisson-uniform distribution, not with its convergence to the Poisson distribution, since $\lambda_1 = \lambda_2$ would result in zero for the first part of equation (2.39a), and the second part of (2.39a) would make no sense either, also resulting in 0.

Anyway, Kromer's (2001c) further observation – based on the results obtained by the χ^2 minimization – saying that there seems to be a direct dependence of λ_1 on λ_0, is of utmost importance and deserves further attention. In fact, in addition to his assumption that this is the case for homogeneous texts of a given genre only, a re-analysis of Fucks' data (cf. p. 41) as to this question corroborates and extends Kromer's findings; although these data are based on mixed corpora of the languages under study, there is a clear linear dependence of λ_1 on λ_0, for these data as well ($R^2 = 0.91$).

In this respect, another assumption of Kromer's might turn out to be important, here. This assumption is as plausible and as far-reaching, since Kromer postulates two invariant parameters (I and α, in his terminology) to be at work in the generation of word length frequencies. According to Kromer, the first of these two parameters (I) is supposed to be an invariant parameter for the given language, being defined as $I = (\lambda_0 - 1) \cdot (\lambda_1 - \lambda_{1min})$. It is important to note that parameter λ_{1min} should not be confounded here with the result of the χ^2 minimization described above; rather, it is the lower limit of λ_1. On the basis of his analyses, Kromer (2001b,c, 2002) assumes λ_{1min} to be 0.5, approximately. The second parameter α can be derived from the equation $\lambda_1 = \alpha \cdot \lambda_{1min} + (1 - \alpha) \cdot \lambda_0$. Consequently, it is defined as $\alpha = (\lambda_0 - \lambda_1)/(\lambda_0 - \lambda_{1min})$.

According to Kromer, both parameters (I and α) allow for a direct linguistic interpretation. Parameter I, according to him, expresses something like the specifics of a given language (i.e., the degree of a language's syntheticity (Kromer 2001c). As opposed to this, parameter α characterizes the degree of completion of synergetic processes optimizing the code of the given language. According to Kromer (2001c), $\alpha \in (0, 1)$ for real texts, with $\alpha \approx 0.3 - 0.6$ for simple genres (such as letters or children's literature), and $\alpha \approx 0.8$ for more complex genres (such as journalistic or scientific texts).

Unfortunately, most of the above-mentioned papers (Kromer 2001b,c; 2002) have the status of abstracts, rather than of complete papers; as a consequence, only scarce empirical data are presented which might prove the claims brought forth on a broader empirical basis. In summary, one can thus first of all say that Kromer's modification of the Poisson-uniform distribution, as well as the original Poisson-uniform distribution, turns out to be a model which has thus proven its adequacy for linguistic material from various languages. Particularly Kromer's further hope to find language- and text-specific invariants deserves further study. If his assumption should bear closer examination on a broader empirical basis, this might as well explain why we are concerned here with a mixture of two distributions. However, one must ask the question, why it is only the rectangular distribution which comes into play here, as one of two components. In other words: Wouldn't it be more reasonable to look for a model which by way of additional parameters, or by way of parameters taking extreme values (such as $0, 1$, or ∞) allows for transitions between different distribution models, some of them being special cases, or generalizations, of some superordinate model? Strangely enough, it is just the Poisson-uniform distribution, which converges to almost no other distribution, not even to the Poisson distribution, as can be seen above (for details, cf. Wimmer/Altmann 1999: 524).

Ultimately, this observation leads us back to the conclusion drawn at the end of the last chapter, when the necessity to discuss the problems of word length studies from a methodological point of view was mentioned. This discussion was initiated by Grotjahn and Altmann as early as in 1993, and it seems important to call to mind the most important arguments brought forth some ten years ago.

9. Theoretical and Methodological Reflections: Grotjahn/Altmann (1993)

This is not to say that no attention has been paid to the individual points raised by Grotjahn and Altmann. Yet, only recently systematic studies have been undertaken to solve just the methodological problems by way of empirical studies. It would lead too far, and in fact be redundant, to repeat the authors' central arguments here. Nevertheless, most of the ideas discussed – Grotjahn and Altmann combined them in six groups of practical and theoretical problems – are of unchanged importance for contemporary word length studies, which makes it reasonable to summarize at least the most important points, and comment on them from a contemporary point of view.

a. *The problem of the unit of measurement.*– As to this question, it turns out to be of importance what Ferdinand de Saussure stated about a century ago, namely, that there are no positive facts in language. In other words: There can be no a priori decision as to what a word is, or in what units word length can be measured. Meanwhile, in contemporary theories of science, linguistics is no exception to the rule: there is hardly any science which would not acknowledge, to one degree or another, that it has to define its object, first, and that constructive processes are at work in doing so. The relevant thing here is that measuring is (made) possible, as an important thing in the construction of theory. As Grotjahn/Altmann (1993: 142) state with regard to word length, there are three basic types of measurement which can be distinguished: graphic (e.g. letters), phonetic (sounds, phonemes, syllables, etc.), and semantic (morphemes). And, as a consequence, it is obvious "that the choice of the unit of measurement strongly effects the model of word length to be constructed" (ibd., 143).

   What has not yet been studied is whether there are particular dependencies between the results obtained on the basis of different measurement units; it goes without saying that, if they exist, they are highly likely to be language-specific.

   Also, it should be noted that this problem does not only concern the unit of measurement, but also the object under study: the word. It is not even the problem of compound words, abbreviation and acronyms, or numbers and digits, which comes into play here, or the distinction between word forms and lexemes (lemmas) – rather it is the decision whether a word is to be defined on a graphemic, orthographic-graphemic, or phonological level.

f. *The problem of explanation.*– As Grotjahn/Altmann (1993: 150f.) correctly state, striving for explanation is the primary and ultimate aim of science. Consequently, in order to obtain an explanation of the nature of word length, one must discover the mechanism generating it, hereby taking into account the necessary boundary conditions. Thus far, we cannot directly concentrate on the study of particular boundary conditions, since we do not know enough about the general system mechanism at work. Consequently, contemporary research involves three different kinds of orientation: first, we have many bottom-up oriented, partly in the form of ad-hoc solutions for particular problems, partly in the form of inductive research; second, we have top-down oriented, deductive research, aiming at the formulation of general laws and models; and finally, we have much exploratory work, which may be called abductive by nature, since it is characterized by constant hypothesis testing, possibly resulting in a modification of higher-level hypotheses.
As to a possible way of achieving these goals, Grotjahn/Altmann (1993: 147) have suggested to pursue the "synergetic" approach of modelling. In this framework, it is not necessary to know the probabilities of all individual frequency classes; rather, it is sufficient to know the (relative) difference between two neighboring classes, e.g.

$$D = \frac{P_x - P_{x-1}}{P_{x-1}} \text{ , or } D = P_x - P_{x-1}$$

and set up theories about D. Ultimately, this line of research has in fact provided the most important research impulses in the 1990s, which shall be discussed in detail below.

10. From the Synergetic Approach To A Unified Theory of Linguistic Laws (Altmann/Grotjahn/Köhler/Wimmer)

In their 1994 contribution "Towards a theory of word length distribution", Wimmer et al. regarded word length as a "part of several control cycles which maintain the self-organization in language" (ibd., 101). Generally assuming that the distribution of word length in the lexicon and in texts follows a law, the authors further claim that the "empirical distributions actually observed can be represented as specifications of this law according to the boundary and subsidiary conditions which they are subject to in spite of the all-pervasive creativity of speakers/writers" (ibd., 101).

In their search for relevant regularities in the organization of word length, Wimmer et al. (1994: 101) then assume that the various word length classes do not evolve independently of each other, thus obtaining the following basic mechanism:

$$P_x = g(x)P_{x-1} \tag{2.42}$$

With regard to previous results from synergetic linguistics, particular research on the so-called "Menzerath law", modelling the regulation of the size of (sub)systems by the size of the corresponding supersystems, Wimmer et al. state that in elementary cases the function $g(x)$ in (2.42) has the form

$$g(x) = ax^{-b} \tag{2.43}$$

Based on these assumptions, Wimmer et al. (1994: 101ff.) distinguish three levels, if one wants, as to the synergetic modelling of word length distribution: (a) elementary form, (b) modification, and (c) complication.

(a) The most elementary, basic organization of a word length distribution would follow the difference equation

$$P_{x+1} = \frac{a}{(x+1)^b} P_x, \quad x = 0, 1, 2, \dots \quad a, b > 0 \tag{2.44}$$

Depending on whether there are 0-syllable words or not (i.e., $P_0 = 0$ or $P_0 \neq 0$), one obtains one of the two following formulas (2.45) or (2.45a), which are identical except for translation, i.e. either:

$$P_x = \frac{a^x}{(x!)^b} P_0, \quad x = 0, 1, 2, \dots \quad a, b > 0 \tag{2.45}$$

or, in 1-displaced form:

$$P_x = \frac{a^{x-1}}{(x-1)!^b} P_1, \quad x = 1, 2, 3, \dots \quad a, b > 0 \tag{2.45a}$$

This finally results in the so-called Conway-Maxwell-Poisson distribution (cf. Wimmer et al. 1994: 102; Wimmer/Altmann 1999: 103), i.e.:

$$P_x = \frac{a^x}{(x!)^b T_0}, \quad x = 0, 1, 2, \dots, \quad a \geq 0, b > 0, \quad T_0 = \sum_{j=0}^{\infty} \frac{a^j}{(j!)^b} \tag{2.46}$$

with T_0 as norming constant. This model was already discussed above, in its 1-displaced form (2.7), when discussing the Merkytė geometric distribution (cf. p. 26). It has also been found to be an adequate model for word length frequencies from a Slovenian frequency dictionary (Grzybek 2001).

(b) As to the second level of modelling ("first order extensions"), Wimmer et al. (1994: 102) suggested to set parameter $b = 1$ in equation (2.43) and to modify the proportionality function. After corresponding re-parametrizations, these modifications result in well-known distribution models. In 1994, Wimmer et al. wrote that $g(x)$-functions like the following had been found:

$$\text{Hyper-Poisson:} \quad g(x) = \frac{a}{(c+x)}$$

$$\text{Hyper-Pascal:} \quad g(x) = \frac{(a+bx)}{(c+dx)}$$

$$\text{negative binomial:} \quad g(x) = \frac{(a+bx)}{cx}$$

This system of modifications was further elaborated by Wimmer/Altmann in 1996, and shall be presented in detail, below (cf. p. 81ff.).

(c) The third level of modelling is more complex: as Wimmer et al. (1994: 102f.) say, in these more complex models "it is not appropriate to take into account only the neighboring class $(x-1)$. The set of word length classes is organized as a whole, i.e. the class of length x is proportional to all other classes of smaller length $j(j = 1, 2, \ldots, x)$." This can be written as

$$P_x = \sum_{j=1}^{x} h(j) P_{x-j}$$

Inserting the original proportionality function $g(x)$ thus yields (2.47), rendering (2.42) a special case of this more complex form:

$$P_x = g(x) \sum_{j=1}^{x} h(j) P_{x-j} \tag{2.47}$$

If one again chooses $g(x) = a \cdot x^{-b}$ with $b = 1$, as in the case of the first order extensions (b), this results in $g(x) = a/x$; if one furthermore defines $h(j) = j \prod_j$ – where $\prod_j$ itself is a probability function of a variable J –, then the probability P_x fulfills the necessary conditions $P_x \geq 0$ and $\sum_x P_x = 1$.

Now, different distributions may be inserted for $\prod_j$. Thus, inserting the Borel distribution (cf. Wimmer/Altmann 1999: 50f.)

$$P_x = \frac{e^{-ax} \cdot x^{x-1} \cdot x^{x-2}}{(x-1)!}, \qquad x = 1, 2, 3, \ldots \quad 0 \leq a < 1 \tag{2.48}$$

for $\prod_j$ in $h(j) = j \prod_j$, yields

$$P_x = \frac{a}{x} \sum_{j=1}^{x} \frac{e^{-bj} (bj)^{j-1}}{(j-1)!} P_{x-j} \tag{2.49}$$

The solution of this is a specific generalized Poisson distribution (GPD), usually called Consul-Jain-Poisson distribution (cf. Wimmer/Altmann 1999: 93ff.):

$$P_0 = e^{-a}\,,$$
$$P_x = \frac{a\,(a+bx)^{x-1}\,e^{-(a+bx)}}{x!}\,, \quad x = 1, 2, 3, \ldots \tag{2.50}$$

It can easily be seen that for $b = 0$, the standard Poisson is a special case of the GPD. The parameters a and b of the GPD are independent of each other; there are a number of theoretical restrictions for them, which need not be discussed here in detail (cf. Antić/Grzybek/Stadlober 2005a,b). Irrespective of these restrictions, already Wimmer et al. (1994: 103) stated that the application of the GPD has turned out to be especially promising, and, by way of an example, they referred to the results of fitting the generalized Poisson distribution to the data of a Turkish poem. These observations are supported by recent studies in which Stadlober (2003) analyzed this distribution in detail and tested its adequacy for linguistic data. Comparing the GPD with Fucks' generalization of the Poisson distribution (and its special cases), Stadlober demonstrated that the GPD is extremely flexible, and therefore able to model heterogeneous linguistic data. The flexibility is due to specific properties of the mean and the variance of the GPD, which, in its one-displaced form, are:

$$\mu = E(X) = \frac{a+1-b}{1-b} \quad \text{and}$$
$$\sigma^2 = Var(X) = \frac{a}{(1-b)^3}$$

Given these characteristics, we may easily compute δ, as was done in the case of the generalized Fucks distribution and its special cases (see above):

$$\delta = \frac{Var(X)}{E(X)-1} = \frac{1}{(1-b)^2} \geq \frac{1}{4}$$

Thus, whereas the Poisson distribution turned out to be an adequate model for empirical distributions with $d \approx 1$, the 2-parameter Dacey-Poisson distribution with $d < 1$, and the 3-parameter Fucks distribution with $d \geq 0.75$, the GPD proves to be an alternative model for empirical distributions with $D \geq 0.25$ (cf. Stadlober 2004). It is interesting to see, therefore, in how far the GPD is able to model Fucks' data from nine languages, represented in Table 2.9, repeatedly analyzed above; the results taken from Stadlober (2003) are given in Table 2.22.

As can be seen, the results are good or even excellent in all cases; in fact, as opposed to all other distributions discussed above, the Consul-Jain GPD is able to model all data samples given by Fucks. It can also be seen from Table 2.22

Table 2.22: Fitting the Generalized Poisson Distribution (*GPD*) to Fucks' Data From Nine Languages

	English	**German**	**Esperanto**	**Arabic**	**Greek**
$\hat{a}$	0.3448	0.5842	0.9198	1.4285	1.0063
$\hat{b}$	0.1515	0.0775	−0.0254	−0.2949	0.0939
C	0.0030	0.0019	0.0014	0.0121	0.0072

	Japanese	**Russian**	**Latin**	**Turkish**
$\hat{a}$	1.0204	1.1395	1.4892	1.6295
$\hat{b}$	0.0990	0.0712	0.0719	−0.1170
C	0.0037	0.0078	0.0092	0.0053

that the empirical findings confirm the theoretical assumption that there is no dependence between the parameters a and b – this makes it rather unlikely that it might be possible to arrive at a direct interpretation of the results. In this respect, i.e. as to an interpretation of the results, an even more important question remains to be answered, already raised by Wimmer et al. (1994: 103), namely what might be a linguistic justification for the use of the Borel distribution.

As to this problem, it seems however important to state that this is not a problem specifically related to the GPD; rather, any mixture of distributions will cause the very same problems. From this perspective, the crucial question as to possible interpretation remains open for Fucks' generalization too, however, as well as for any other distribution implying weights, as long as no reason can be given for the amount of the specific weights of the elements in the ε-spectrum.

In this respect, it is important that other distributions which imply no mixtures can also be derived from (2.47). Thus, as Wimmer/Altmann (1996: 126ff.) have shown in detail, the probability generating function of X in (2.47) is

$$G(t) = e^{a[H(t)-1]}, \tag{2.51}$$

which leads to the so-called generalized Poisson distributions; the specific solution merely depends on the choice of $H(t)$. Now, if one sets, for example, $H(t) = t$, which is the probability generating function of the deterministic distribution ($P_x = 1,\ P_c \in R$), one obtains the Poisson distribution. And if one sets $a = -k \cdot \ln p$ and $H(t) = \ln(1-qt)/\ln(1-q)$, which is the probability generating function of the logarithmic distribution, then one obtains the negative binomial distribution applied by Grotjahn. However, both distributions can also

it is confined to the first four terms of formula (2.54), with $k_1 = k_2 = \ldots = 1, c_i = 1, a_{i1} = a_i, b_{i1} = b_i, i = 1, 2, \ldots$. Many distributions can be derived from (2.54), which have frequently been used in linguistics studies, and which are thus united under one common roof:

$$P_x = \left(1 + a_0 + \frac{a_1}{x - b_1} + \frac{a_2}{x - b_2}\right) P_{x-1} \tag{2.56}$$

Let us, in order to arrive at an end of the history and methodology of word length studies, discuss the relevant distributions discussed before, on the background of these theoretical assumptions.

Thus, for example, with $-1 < a_0 < 0$, $a_i = 0$ for $i = 1, 2, \ldots$, one obtains from (2.56)

$$P_x = (1 + a_0) P_{x-1} \tag{2.57}$$

resulting in the geometric distribution (with $1 + a_0 = q, 0 < q < 1, p = 1 - q$) in the form

$$P_x = p \cdot q^x \qquad x = 0, 1, 2, \ldots \tag{2.58}$$

Or, for $-1 < a_0 < 0$, $-a_1 < 1 + a_0$ and $a_2 = b_1 = b_2 = 0$, one obtains from (2.56)

$$P_{x+1} = \frac{1 + a_0 + a_1 + (1 + a_0)x}{x + 1} P_x \tag{2.59}$$

With $k = (1 + a_0 + a_1)/(1 + a_0), p = -a_0$, and $q = 1 - p$ this leads to the negative binomial distribution:

$$P_x = \binom{k + x - 1}{x} p^k q^x \qquad x = 0, 1, 2, \ldots \tag{2.60}$$

Finally, inserting $a_2 = 0$ in (2.56), one obtains

$$P_x = \frac{(1 + a_0)(x - b_1) + a_1}{x - b_1} P_{x-1} \tag{2.61}$$

from which the hyper-Poisson distribution (2.52) can be derived, with $a_0 = -1, b_1 = 1 - b, a_1 = a \geq 0$, and $b > 0$.

It can thus be said that the general theoretical assumptions implied in the synergetic approach has experienced strong empirical support. One may object that this is only one of possible alternative models, only one theory among others. However, thus far, we do not have any other, which is as theoretically sound, and as empirically supported, as the one presented.

It seems to be a historical absurdity, therefore, that the methodological discussion on word length studies, which was initiated by Grotjahn/Altmann (1993) about a decade ago, has often not been sufficiently taken account of in the relevant research: more often than not, research has concentrated on word length models for particular languages, not taking notice of the fact that boundary and subsidiary conditions of individual text productions may be so strong that no overall model is adequate, not even within a given language. On the other hand, hardly any systematic studies have been undertaken to empirically study possible influencing factors, neither as to the data basis in general (i.e., text, text segments, mixtures, etc.), nor as to specific questions such as authorship, text type, etc.

Ultimately, the question, what may influence word length frequencies, may be a bottomless pit – after all, any text production is an historically unique event, the boundary conditions of which may never be reproduced, at least not completely. Still, the question remains open if particular factors may be detected, the relevance of which for the distribution of word length frequencies may be proven.

This point definitely goes beyond a historical survey of word length studies; rather, it directs our attention to research desires, as a result of the methodological discussion above. As can be seen, the situation has remained unchanged: in this respect, it will always be a matter of orientation, or of object definition, if one attempts to find "local" solutions (on the basis of a clearly defined data basis), or general solutions, attempting a general explanation of language or text processing.

References

Altmann, Gabriel; Hammer, Rolf
1989 *Diskrete Wahrscheinlichkeitsverteilungen I.* Bochum.

Antić, Gordana; Grzybek, Peter; Stadlober, Ernst
2005a "Mathematical Aspects and Modifications of Fucks' Generalized Poisson Distribution." In: Köhler, R.; Altmann, G.; Piotrovskij, R.G. (eds.), *Handbook of Quantitative Linguistics.* [In print]

Antić, Gordana; Grzybek, Peter; Stadlober, Ernst
2005b "50 Years of Fucks' ≫Theory of Word Formation≪: The Fucks Generalized Poisson Distribution in Theory and Praxis." In: *Journal of Quantitative Linguistics.* [In print]

Bagnold, R.A.
1983 "The nature and correlation of random distributions", in: *Proceedings of the Royal Society of London, ser. A, 388*; 273–291.

Bartkowiakowa, Anna; Gleichgewicht, Bolesław
1962 "O długości sylabicznej wyrazów w tekstach autorów polskich", in: *Zastosowania matematyki, 6*; 309–319. [= On the syllable length of words in texts by Polish authors]

Bartkowiakowa, Anna; Gleichgewicht, Bolesław
1964 "Zastosowanie dwuparametrowych rozkładów Fucksa do opisu długości sylabicznej wyrazów w różnych utworach prozaicznych autorów polskich", in: *Zastosowania matematyki, 7*; 345–352. [= Application of two-parameter Fucks distributions to the description of syllable length of words in various prose texts by Polish authors]

Bartkowiakowa, Anna; Gleichgewicht, Bolesław
1965 "O rozkładach długości sylabicznej wyrazów w różnych tekstach." In: Mayenowa, M.R. (ed.), *Poetyka i matematyka.* Warszwawa. (164–173). [= On the distribution of syllable length of words in various texts.]

Best, Karl-Heinz
1997 "Zur Wortlängenhäufigkeit in deutschsprachigen Pressetexten." In: Best, K.-H. (ed.), *Glottometrika 16: The Distribution of Word and Sentence Length.* Trier. (1–15).

Best, Karl-Heinz; Čebanov, Sergej G.
2001 "Biographische Notiz: Sergej Grigor'evič Čebanov (1897–1966)." In: Best (ed.) (2001); 281–283.

Best, Karl-Heinz
2001 "Kommentierte Bibliographie zum Göttinger Projekt." In: Best, K.-H. (ed.) (2001); 284–310.

Best, Karl-Heinz (ed.)
2001 *Häufigkeitsverteilungen in Texten.* Göttingen.

Brainerd, Barron
1971 "On the distribution of syllables per word", in: *Mathematical Linguistics [Keiryo Kokugogaku], 57*; 1–18.

Brainerd, Barron
1975 *Weighing evidence in language and literature: A statistical approach.* Toronto.

Cercvadze, G.N./Čikoidze, G.B./Gačečiladze, T.G.
1959 Primenenie matematičeskoj teorii slovoobrazovanija k gruzinskomu jazyku. In: *Soobščenija akademii nauk Gruzinskoj SSR, t. 22/6*, 705–710.

Cercvadze, G.N./Čikoidze, G.B./Gačečiladze, T.G.
1962 see: Zerzwadse et al. (1962)

Čebanov s. Chebanow

Chebanow, S.G.
1947 "On Conformity of Language Structures within the Indo-European Familiy to Poisson's Law", in: *Comptes Rendus (Doklady) de l'Adadémie des Sciences de l'URS, vol. 55, no. 2*; 99–102.

Dewey, G.
1923 *Relative Frequencies of English Speech Sounds.* Cambridge; Mass.

Elderton, William P.
1949 "A Few Statistics on the Length of English Words", in: *Journal of the Royal Statistical Society, series A (general), vol. 112*; 436–445.

French, N.R.; Carter, C.W.; Koenig, W.
1930 "Words and Sounds of Telephone Communications", in: *Bell System Technical Journal, 9*; 290–325.

Fucks, Wilhelm
1955a *Mathematische Analyse von Sprachelementen, Sprachstil und Sprachen.* Köln/Opladen. [= Arbeitsgemeinschaft für Forschung des Landes Nordrhein-Westfalen; 34a]

Fucks, Wilhelm
1955b "Theorie der Wortbildung", in: *Mathematisch-Physikalische Semesterberichte zur Pflege des Zusammenhangs von Schule und Universität, 4*; 195–212.

Fucks, Wilhelm
1955c "Eine statistische Verteilung mit Vorbelegung. Anwendung auf mathematische Sprachanalyse", in: *Die Naturwissenschaften, 42_1*; 10.

Fucks, Wilhelm
1956a "Die mathematischen Gesetze der Bildung von Sprachelementen aus ihren Bestandteilen", in: *Nachrichtentechnische Fachberichte, 3 [= Beiheft zu Nachrichtentechnische Fachzeitschrift]*; 7–21.

Fucks, Wilhelm
1956b "Mathematische Analyse von Werken der Sprache und der Musik", in: *Physikalische Blätter, 16*; 452–459 & 545.

Fucks, Wilhelm
1956c "Statistische Verteilungen mit gebundenen Anteilen', in: *Zeitschrift für Physik, 145*; 520–533.

Fucks, Wilhelm
1956d "Mathematical theory of word formation." In: Cherry, Colin (ed.), *Information theory.* London, 1955. (154–170).

Fucks, Wilhelm
1957 "Gibt es allgemeine Gesetze in Sprache und Musik?", in: *Umschau, 57_2*; 33–37.

Fucks, Wilhelm
1960 "Mathematische Analyse von Werken der Sprache und der Musik", in: *Physikalische Blätter, 16*; 452–459.

Fucks, Wilhelm; Lauter, Josef
1968 "Mathematische Analyse des literarischen Stils." In: Kreuzer, H.; Gunzenhäuser, R. (eds.), *Mathematik und Dichtung.* München, ^{4}1971.

Fucks, Wilhelm
1968 *Nach allen Regeln der Kunst. Diagnosen über Literatur, Musik, bildende Kunst – die Werke, ihre Autoren und Schöpfer.* Stuttgart.

Gačečiladze, T.G./Cilosani, T.P.
1971 Ob odnom metode izučenija statističeskoj struktury teksta. In: *Statistika reči i avtomatičeskij analiz teksta.* Leningrad, Nauka: 113–133.

Grotjahn, Rüdiger
1982 "Ein statistisches Modell für die Verteilung der Wortlänge", in: *Zeitschrift für Sprachwissenschaft, 1*; 44–75.

Grotjahn, Rüdiger; Altmann, Gabriel
1993 "Modelling the Distribution of Word Length: Some Methodological Problems." In: Köhler, R.; Rieger, B. (eds.), *Contributions to Quantitative Linguistics.* Dordrecht, NL. (141–153).

Grzybek, Peter
2001 "Pogostnostna analiza besed iz elektronskega korpusa slovenskih besedel", in: *Slavistična Revija, 48(2) 2000 [2001]*; 141–157.

Grzybek, Peter (ed.)
2004 *Studies on the Generalized Fucks Model of Word Length.* [In prep.]

Grzybek, Peter; Kelih, Emmerich; Altmann, Gabriel
2004 Graphemhäufigkeiten (Am Beispiel des Russischen) Teil II: Theoretische Modelle. In: *Anzeiger für Slavische Philologie*, (32); 25–54.

Grzybek, Peter; Kelih, Emmerich
2005 "Texttypologie in/aus empirischer Perspektive." In: Bernard, J.; Fikfak, J.; Grzybek, P. (eds.), *Text und Realität – Text and Reality.* Ljubljana etc. [In print]

Grzybek, Peter; Stadlober, Ernst
2003 "Zur Prosa Karel Čapeks – Einige quantitative Bemerkungen." In: Kempgen, S.; Schweier, U.; Berger, T. (eds.), *Rusistika • Slavistika • Lingvistika.* München. (474–488).

Grzybek, Peter; Stadlober, Ernst; Antić, Gordana; Kelih, Emmerich
2005 "Quantitative Text Typology: The Impact of Word Length." In: Weihs, C. (ed.), *Classification – The Ubiquitous Challenge.* Heidelberg/Berlin. [In print]

Herdan, Gustav
1958 "The relation between the dictionary distribution and the occurrence distribution of word length and its importance for the study of quantitative linguistics", in: *Biometrika, 45*; 222–228.

Herdan, Gustav
1966 *The Advanced Theory of Language as Choice and Chance.* Berlin etc.

Kelih, Emmerich; Antić, Gordana; Grzybek, Peter; Stadlober, Ernst
2005 "Classification of Author and/or Genre? The Impact of Word Length." In: Weihs, C. (ed.), *Classification – The Ubiquitous Challenge.* Heidelberg/Berlin. [In print]

Kromer, Victor V.
2001a "Word length model based on the one-displaced Poisson-uniform distribution", in: *Glottometrics, 1*; 87–96.

Kromer, Victor V.
2001b "Dvuchparametričeskaja model' dliny slova 'jazyk –žanr' . [= A Two-Parameter Model of Word Length: ≪Language – Genre≫.]" In: *Electronic archive* Computer Science, March 8, 2001 [http://arxiv.org/abs/cs.CL/0103007.

Kromer, Victor V.
2001c "Matematičeskaja model' dliny slova na osnove raspredelenija Čebanova-Fuksa s ravnomernym raspredeleniem parametra. [= A Mathematical Model of Word Length on the Basis of the Čebanov-Fucks Distribution with Uniform Distribution of the Parameter.]" In: *Informatika i problemy telekommunikacij: meždunarodnaja naučno-tekhničeskaja konferencija SibGUTI, 26-27 aprelja 2001 g. Materialy konferencii.* Novosibirsk. (74–75). [http://kromer.newmail.ru/kvv_c_18.pdf]

Kromer, Victor V.
2002 "Ob odnoj vozmožnosti obobščenija matematičeskoj modeli dliny slova. [= On A Possible Generalization of the Word Length Model.]" In: *Informatika i problemy telekommunikacij: meždunarodnaja naučno-tekhničeskaja konferencija SibGUTI, 25-26 aprelja 2002 g. Materialy konferencii.* Novosibirsk. (139–140). [http://kromer.newmail.ru/kvv_c_23.pdf]

Lord, R.D.
1958 "Studies in the history of probability and statistics. VIII: De Morgan and the statistical study of literary style", in: *Biometrika, 45*; 282.

Markov, Andrej A.
1924 *Isčislenie verojatnostej.* Moskva.

Mendenhall, Thomas C.
1887 "The characteristic curves of composition", in: *Science, supplement, vol. 214, pt. 9*; 237–249.

Mendenhall, Thomas C.
1901 "A mechanical solution of a literary problem", in: *Popular Science Monthly, vol. 60, pt. 7*; 97–105.

Merkytė, R.Ju.
1972 "Zakon, opisyvajuščij raspredelenie slogov v slovach slovarej", in: *Lietuvos matematikos rinkinys, 12/4*; 125–131.

Michel, Gunther
1982 "Zur Häufigkeitsverteilung der Wortlänge im Bulgarischen und im Griechischen." In: *1300 Jahre Bulgarien. Studien zum 1. Internationalen Bulgaristikkongress Sofia 1981.* Neuried. (143–208).

Moreau, René
1961 "Linguistique quantitative. Sur la distribution des unités lexicales dans le français écrit", in: *Comptes rendus hebdomaires des séances de l'académie des sciences, 253*; 2626–2628.

Moreau, René
1963 "Sur la distribution des formes verbales dans le français écrit", in: *Études de linguistique appliquée, 2*; 65–88.

Piotrovskij, Rajmond G.; Bektaev, Kaldybaj B.; Piotrovskaja, Anna A.
1977 *Matematičeskaja lingvistika.* Moskva. [German translation: Piotrowski, R.G.; Bektaev, K.B.; Piotrowskaja, A.A.: *Mathematische Linguistik.* Bochum, 1985]

Rothschild, Lord
1986 "The Distribution of English Dictionary Word Lengths", in: *Journal of Statistical Planning and Inference, 14*; 311–322.

Stadlober, Ernst
2003 "Poissonmodelle und Wortlängenhäufigkeiten." [Ms.]

Vranić, V.
1965a "Statističko istraživanje hrvatskosrpskog jezika", in: *Statistička revija, 15(2-3)*; 174–185.

Vranić, V.; Matković, V.
1965b "Mathematic Theory of the Syllabic Structure of Croato-Serbian", in: *Rad JAZU (odjel za matematičke, fizičke i tehničke nauke; 10) (331)*; 181–199.

Williams, Carrington B.
1939 "A note on the statistical analysis of sentence-length as a criterion of literary style", in: *Biometrika, 31*; 356–361.

Williams, Carrington B.
1956 "Studies in the history of probability and statistics. IV: A note on an early statistical study of literary style", in: *Biometrika, 43*; 248–256.

Williams, Carrington B.
1967 "Writers, readers and arithmetic", in: *New Scientist, 13*; 88–91.

Williams, Carrington B.
1976 "Mendenhall's studies of word-length distribution in the works of Shakespeare and Bacon", in: *Biometrika, 62*; 207–212.

Wimmer, Gejza; Altmann, Gabriel
1996 "The Theory of Word Length: Some Results and Generalizations." In: Schmidt, P. (ed.), *Glottometrika 15: Issues in General Linguistic Theory and the Theory of Word Length.* Trier. (112–133).

Wimmer, Gejza; Altmann, Gabriel
1999 *Thesaurus of univariate discrete probability distributions.* Essen.

Wimmer, Gejza; Altmann, Gabriel
2005 "Unified derivation of some linguistic laws." In: Köhler, R.; Altmann, G.; Piotrovskij, R.G. (eds.), *Handbook of Quantitative Linguistics.* [In print]

Wimmer, Gejza; Köhler, Reinhard; Grotjahn, Rüdiger; Altmann, Gabriel
1994 "Towards a Theory of Word Length Distribution", in: *Journal of Quantitative Linguistics, 1/1*; 98–106.

Wimmer, Gejza; Witkovský, Viktor; Altmann, Gabriel
1999 "Modification of Probability Distributions Applied to Word Length Research", in: *Journal of Quantitative Linguistics, 6/3*; 257–268.

Zerzwadse, G./Tschikoidse, G./Gatschetschiladse, Th.
1962 Die Anwendung der mathematischen Theorie der Wortbildung auf die georgische Sprache. In: *Grundlagenstudien aus Kybernetik und Geisteswissenschaft* 4, 110–118.

Ziegler, Arne
1996 "Word Length Distribution in Brazilian-Portuguese Texts", in: *Journal of Quantitative Linguistics,* 3_1; 73–79.

Ziegler, Arne
1996 "Word Length in Portuguese Texts", in: *Journal of Quantitative Linguistics,* 5_{1-2}; 115–120.

3

INFORMATION CONTENT OF WORDS IN TEXTS

Simone Andersen, Gabriel Altmann

1. Introduction

In a previous study, Andersen (2002a) postulated that information of words in texts has to be examined from two aspects yielding two distinct measures called "speaker's information content" (SIC) and "hearer's information content" (HIC) which may differ in amount, i.e. $SIC \neq HIC$, and cannot always be mechanically evaluated from the frequencies of words in the text. The idea is derived from the Fitts–Garner controversy in mathematical psychology (cf. Fitts et al. 1956; Garner 1962, 1970; Garner, Hake 1951; Coombs, Dawes, Tversky 1970; Evans 1967; Attneave 1959, 1968). Obviously, the problem is quite old but has not penetrated into linguistics as yet.

A word in a text can be thought of as a realization of a number of different alternative possibilities, see Fig. 3.1, in which for each word in the sequence the probability distribution of its alternatives is shown.

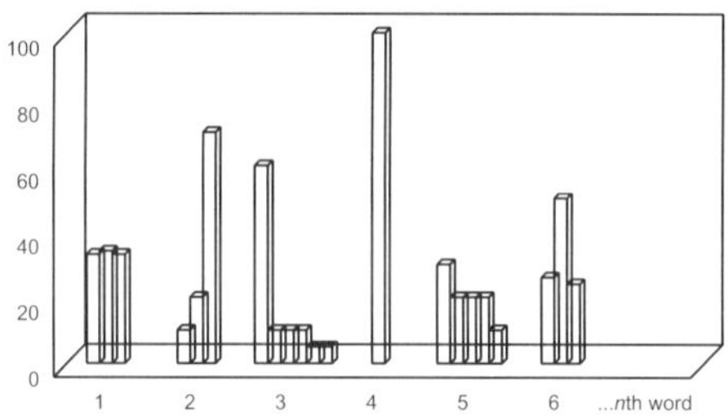

Figure 3.1: Probability Distributions of Word Alternatives in a Sequence

The number of alternatives is varying for different words, and the probabilities for the alternatives are distributed in varying ways (in detail: Andersen 2002b). They can even be understood in different ways, e.g. they can be used when counting the number of cases in which an alternative can be found as an admitted substitute for the word or the number of cases of a given alternative in a corpus (without considering its ability as substitute). For greater simplicity, only the number of alternatives is taken into account, regardless of their dif-

P. Gryzbek (ed.), Contributing in the Science of Text and Language, 91-115.

fering probability distributions, treating them as being equal. So the classical concept of "uncertainty" can be used here, according to Hartley (1928), where "information" is interpreted in terms of freedom of choice or decision content and where the alternatives are supposed to be equal.

For every word in the text the degree of uncertainty can be determined by entering for $p = 1/s$ into the information content formula

$$h(x_i) = -\text{ld } p(x_i)$$

yielding the uncertainty U or $h(x_i)$ as

$$h(x_i) = \text{ld } s$$

which is a function of the number of alternatives s.

The p that is replaced by $1/s$ here, is not the p denoting the relative frequency in the total text. Neither is it the conditional probability resulting from hearer's/reader's guessings depending on the preceding words. It is the p related to the possible occurrence a specific word has at a specific place: here defined as either zero or $1/s$, where s is not the total sum of words in the entire text, but the set of words conceivable at the specific place. So speaker's p and hearer's p need not to be equal.

As Attneave (1959, 1968) already remarked, the amount of information content and redundancy in metric figures depends on whether they are calculated from construction or from reception perspective; correspondingly, the probability of a word occuring at a specific place in a text also depends on whether it is evaluated from the hearer's or from the speaker's perspective.

The conditions for determining *HIC* (hearer's information content or: h from hearer's perspective) for a specific word are the possibilities of inferencing it in case of missing ("surprise potential", Berlyne 1960; cf. also Andersen 1985; Piotrowski, Lesohin, Lukjanenkov 1990). On the other hand, determining SIC (speaker's information content or: h from speaker's perspective) depends on the decision content of the special place in the text: the freedom of choice. The constraints for the speaker's uncertainty h are in his intentions of transmission, not in the predictability of the message. What is neglected when correlating the lengths and the frequencies of words in real texts is the fact that for the text producer there is not at all free choice of all existing words at every moment.

An example for $SIC \neq HIC$: In the sentence "Tomorrow he will be in Cologne" the word 'Cologne' is being deleted, replaced by a blank. Trying to fill in the blank is a model for determining the uncertainty of the missing word. From the hearer's perspective, trying to anticipate what could be intended to be said, the word 'Cologne' stands in a "hearer's distribution" with a nearly infinite number of alternatives – presumed, there is no prior pragmatic knowledge – its information (HIC) is extremely high. However, when p is defined from the speaker's distributions, other values result. Provided he wants to transmit the message that a certain person will be in Cologne tomorrow, then there is no alternative for 'Cologne', so $s = 1$ and $SIC = 0$.

According to Andersen's (2002) conjecture, SIC is a variable which is simultaneously correlated with frequency (F) and length (L) of words in text. It must be noted that SIC or HIC are associated not only with words but also with whole phrases or clauses, so that they represent rather polystratic structures and sequences. The present approach is the first approximation at the word level.

2. Preparation

In order to illustrate the variables which will be treated later on, let us first define some quantities. The cardinality of the set X will be symbolized as $|X|$.

P the set of positions in a text, whatever the counting unit. The elements of this set are natural numbers $k \in N$

$|P|$ the length of the text

W the set of all different types (or word forms) in the text

$|W|$ the number of different types (word forms) in the text

w_i type i, $i = 1, 2, \dots, |W|$ (element of set W)

J_i the number of tokens of the type i

T the set of all *tokens* in the text, i.e. the set of realizations of the types. The elements of this set are tokens t_{ij_k}, i.e. t_{ij_k} is the jth realization of the ith type at position k ($i. = 1, 2, \dots, |W|, j = 1, 2, \dots, Ji, k = 1, 2, \dots, |P|$). If the type and its token are known, the indices i and j can be left out. $|T| = |P|$

A_{ij} the set of latent entities which can be substituted for the token j of type i at position k without changing the sense of the sentence. The elements of this set, a_{ij}, are not necessarily synonyms but in the given context they are admissible alternatives of the given token. That is $A_{ij} = \{a_{ij_1}, a_{ij_2}, a_{iJ_i}\}$. The index k can be omitted

$|A_{ij}|$ the number of elements in the set A_{ij}, i.e. the number of latent elements of token j of type i

a_i $\sum_{j=1}^{J_i} |A_{ij}|$, i.e. the number of all latent entities of type i

M_{ij} the set consisting of a token and the specific set of alternatives at a specific position, i.e. $M_{ij} = t_{ij} \cup A_{ij}$. This entity can be called **tokeme**. By defining M_{ij}, we are able to distinguish between tokens of the same type but with different alternatives and different number a_i – so they are different tokemes. If two tokens of a type i differ in kind and number of alternatives, they are two different tokemes

$|M_{ij}|$ size of the tokeme $= |A_{ij}| + 1$

$s_i = a_i + J_i$, i.e. the number of all latent entities of type i + the number of tokens of i, i.e.

$$s_i = \sum_{j=1}^{J_i} |M_{ij}|$$

$$\bar{s}_i = \frac{1}{J_i}(a_i + J_i) = \frac{1}{J_i}\sum_{j=1}^{J_i} |M_{ij}| \tag{3.1}$$

i.e., the number of all latent entities of type $i+$ the number of tokens of i. This is the mean of the size of all tokemes of type i

$$SIC_i = \text{ld }(\bar{s}_i), i = 1, 2, \ldots, |W| \tag{3.2}$$

i.e., speaker's information content is the dual logarithm of the mean tokeme size. Thus, as a matter of fact, SIC is a new variable which should be embedded in Köhler's control cycles of synergetic linguistics.

Example

Using Table 9 (cf. appendix, p. 108ff.) representing the analysis of the text taken from a German newspaper (*Hamburger Morgenpost*, 24.04.2002) we can illustrate these concepts. The text is reproduced word for word in the second column of Table 9 (p. 108ff.).

There are $|P| = 128$ positions in the text.

The set $W = \{$ein, Taschenbuch, ist, das, $\ldots\}$

$|W| = 102$ i.e. there are 102 different types (word forms) in the text, realized by $|T| = 128$ tokens in the text: $|P| = |T|$

The type 'die' is realized by five tokens in the text ($J_{die} = 5$): At positions 31, 120, 126 it is used in a tokeme of size $|M_{die,31}| = |M_{die,120}| = |M_{die,126}| = 1$ (only word 'die' is possible in this context, $a_{die} = 0$); at positions 64 and 81 it is used in a tokeme of size $|M_{die,64}| = |M_{die,81}| = 2$ ('die' and also 'diese' are possible alternatives in this context, $a_{die} = 1$ every time); so the type 'die' is used here three times with $|M| = 1$ and two times with $|M| = 2$, or with $\bar{s}_{die} = (1+1+1+2+2)/5 = 7/5 = 1.4$ alternatives per mean in this text.

The SIC for the type 'die' results as $SIC_{die} = \text{ld }(\bar{s}_{die}) = \text{ld }(1.4) = 0.48$.

Thus, the mean decision content or uncertainty for the word 'die' in this text is 0.48, which is not very much; in contrast, the word/type 'Taschenbuch' is used in one tokeme with size $|M| = 16$ and $SIC = 4$ (it is used here once: 1 token, position 2, so the $SIC(\bar{s})$ is also 4), so this type has a far greater decision content – or speaker's information content – in this text. The type 'die' here is much nearer to the "forced choice" situation than 'Taschenbuch', for which there is much more freedom.

The uncertainty cannot be infinite: there is no infinite number of alternative words for any token, and for psychological reasons we can determine about 30 alternatives with $SIC \approx 5$ as an upper limit: speakers will hardly handle more than 50 or 100 alternative words; if we take into respect Miller's magical number 7 ± 2 as a kind of short term memory capacity, we even could determine a realistic upper limit of $SIC \approx 3$ resulting from ≈ 8 alternatives), the uncertainty lies in an interval which is specific for every text. In the given text it lies within $< 0.4 >$.

3. Latent Length (LL)

We define further $L_k = L(word)$ the length of a word in text. The length is measured in terms of the number of syllables of the word. Thus, e.g. the length of "Taschenbuch" is $L(Taschenbuch) = L_2 = 3$.

$$LL_k = \frac{1}{|M_k|} \sum_{m=1}^{|M_k|} L(M_{km}); \tag{3.3}$$

i.e., the mean length of all possible alternatives at this specific position k including the realized token j. We can define it for types too: then it is the mean of all LLs of all tokens of this type in the text. LL is usually a positive real number.

We consider for every token in the text its length L as a random variable which is realized out of the distribution of possible alternatives at the specific position (for many of the tokens the local variance is $\sigma^2 = 0$). The deviation of L from LL can be considered as "error" in terms of classical test theory. The errors compensate each other in the long run, so the distribution of L equals that of LL. The distribution of LL is the "real" distribution of lengths in texts. It can be ascertained for any text. We can set up the hypothesis that

Hypothesis 1
The longer the token, the longer the tokeme at the given position.

This hypothesis can be tested in different ways.

1. As an empirical consequence of hypothesis (1) it can be expected that the distribution of L and LL is approximately equal. A token of length L has alternatives which are on average the same length, i.e. $L \approx LL$ yielding the most elementary linear regression. Since LL is a positive real number (it is an average) we divide the range of lengths in the text in continuous intervals and ascertain the number of cases (the frequency) in the particular intervals. This can easily be made using the third and the sixth column of Table 9 (p. 108ff.). The result is presented in Table 3.1.
   It can easily be shown that the frequencies differ non-significantly. For example, the chi-square test for homogeneity – after pooling the three highest classes – yields $\chi^2_4 = 4.93, P = 0.29$, signalizing non-significant difference.

Table 3.1: The Frequencies of Token Lengths (L) and Tokeme Lengths (Latent Lengths) (LL) From Table 9

Length interval x	$f(L_x)$	$f(LL_x)$
≤ 1.5	59	61
$(1.5, 2.5>$	42	36
$(2.5, 3.5>$	15	22
$(3.5, 4.5>$	5	7
$(4.5, 5.5>$	6	1
$(5.5, 6.5>$	0	0
> 6.51	1	1

2. Since the distributions are equal, they must abide by the same theoretical distribution. Using the well corroborated theory of word length (cf. Wimmer et al. 1994; Wimmer/Altmann 1996) we choose one of the simplest distributions resulting from the theory, namely the 1-displaced geometric distribution

$$P_x = pq^{x-1}, \qquad x = 1, 2, \ldots \tag{3.4}$$

and assume that the parameter p will be equal for both distributions. As a matter of fact, for the distribution of LL we take the middles of the intervals as variable. It would, perhaps, be more correct to use for both data the continuous equivalent of the geometric distribution, namely the exponential distribution – however, again not quite correct. Thus we adhere to discreteness without loss of validity. The result of fitting the geometric distribution to the data from Table 3.1 are shown in Table 3.2.

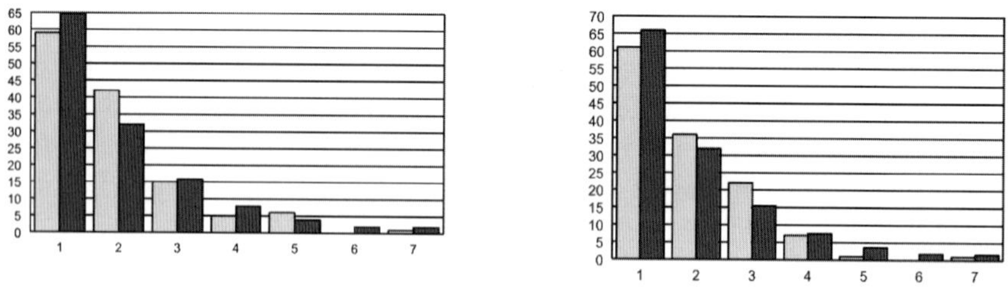

Figure 3.2: Fitting the Geometric Distribution to Token Length / Tokeme Length (Latent Length)

Table 3.2: Fitting the Geometric Distribution to the Data From Table 3.1

Length x	$f(L_x)$	$NP(L_x)$	$f(LL_x)$	$NP(LL_x)$
1	59	64.60	61	65.93
2	42	32	36	31.97
3	15	15.85	22	15.50
4	5	7.85	7	7.52
5	6	3.89	1	3.65
6	0	1.93	0	1.77
7	1	1.89	1	1.66
$p = 0.5047, \chi^2_5 = 8.18; P = 0.15$			$p = 0.5151, \chi^2_5 = 7.59, P = 0.18$	

Any other test would yield the same result, namely the equality of length distributions of tokens and tokemes.

4. Length Range in Tokemes

In each tokeme the lengths of words (local latent lengths) are distributed themselves in a special way. It is not fertile to study them individually since the majority of them is deterministic (i.e. one-point) or two-point distribution, e.g. zero-one. It is more prolific to consider the ranges of latent lengths for the whole text. For this phenomenon we set up the hypothesis

Hypothesis 2
The range of latent lengths within the tokemes is geometric-Poisson.

Since the latent length distribution (LL_x) is geometric and each LL_x is almost identical on average with that of L_x (the alternatives tend to keep the length of the token), the range of the latent lengths in the tokeme is very restricted. The deviations seem to be distributed at random, i.e. without any trend. If we take the range of latent lengths

$$Rg_x = LL_x(a_{ij_{\max}}) - LL_x(a_{ij_{\min}}) \tag{3.5}$$

i.e., the length of the longest elements of the tokeme minus that of the shortest one (excluding the case of $\emptyset$ = "saying nothing"), as a measure of this deviation, then we must simply note that for each separate token length they follow the Poisson distribution with parameter $a < 1$

$$P_x = \frac{a^x e^{-a}}{x!}, \qquad x = 0, 1, 2, \ldots \tag{3.6}$$

Since LL_x follows the geometric distribution – for the sake of simplicity we consider the not-displaced form of (3.4) which is a question of convention – and the ranges within a length class are Poissonian, the distribution of ranges of latent lengths in the text must consequently be geometric-Poisson. In order to obtain this result we replace t in the probability generating function of the geometric distribution

$$G(t) = p(1 - qt)^{-1} \tag{3.7}$$

by that of the Poisson distribution

$$H(t) = e^{a(t-1)} \tag{3.8}$$

resulting in

$$G(t) = p[1 - qe^{a(t-1)}]^{-1} \tag{3.9}$$

From (3.9) we obtain the probability mass function as

$$P_x = \frac{1}{x!}\left[\frac{d^x G(t)}{dt^x}\right]_{t=0} \tag{3.10}$$

yielding in our case

$$P_x = \sum_{j=0}^{\infty} \frac{e^{-aj}(aj)^x pq^j}{x!}, \qquad x = 0, 1, 2, \ldots \tag{3.11}$$

The fitting of (3.11) to the empirical distribution of latent length ranges yields results presented in Table 3.3 and Fig. 3.3. Evidently, the fitting is very good and corroborates in addition hypothesis 1, too.

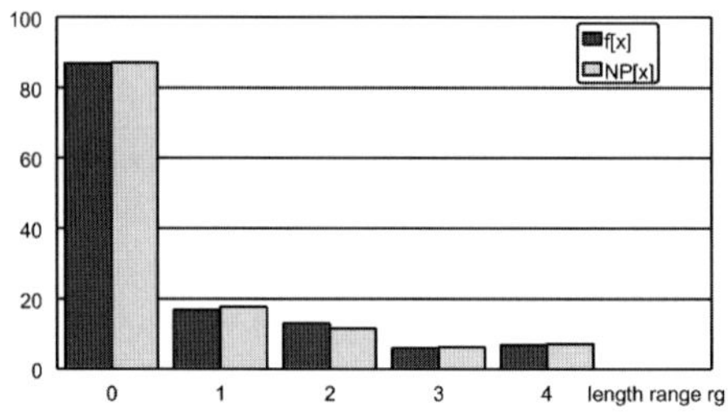

Figure 3.3: Fitting (3.11) to the Length Range of Tokeme Elements

The interpretation of this is that there is a very small chance for the length L of a word to differ from its latent length LL. Thus latent length is a kind of latent mechanism controlling the token length at the given position. Latent length is not directly measurable, it is an invisible result of the complex flow of information. Nevertheless, it can be made visible – as we tried to do above – or it can be approximately deduced on the basis of token lengths.

Table 3.3: Fitting the Geometric-Poisson Distribution (3.11) to the Length Ranges of Tokeme Elements

Length range of tokeme elements x	Frequency f(x)	NP_x (3.11)
0	87	81.16
1	17	17.68
2	13	11.57
3	6	6.37
4	7	7.22
	$a = 0.9029, p = 0.4525,$ $\chi_2^2 = 0.23, P = 0.89$	

5. Stable Latent Length

Consider the deviations of the individual token lengths from those of the respective tokeme lengths as shown in Table 9 (p. 108ff.), symbolized by

$$d_x = L_x - LL_x. \tag{3.12}$$

One can see that the deviations are small and very regular up and down – as far as the text is sufficiently long. This encourages us to set up the hypothesis that

Hypothesis 3
There is no tendency to choose the smallest possible alternative at the given position in text.

The hypothesis can easily be tested. Let the mean deviation be defined as

$$\bar{d} = \frac{1}{|P|}\sum_{x=1}^{|P|} d_x\,; \tag{3.13}$$

then for our data we obtain $0, 15/128 = 0.0018$. Let $E(\bar{d}) = 0$. Since the variance of the deviations is $\sigma_d^2 = 0, 26$ and there are 128 positions, we obtain

$$z = \frac{|\bar{d} - E(\bar{d})|}{\frac{\sigma}{\sqrt{|P|}}} = \frac{|0.0018|}{\frac{0.51}{\sqrt{128}}} = 0.04 \tag{3.14}$$

which is not significant.

6. SIC of the Text

Above, we defined SIC of a type as the dual logarithm of the mean size of all tokeme sizes of the given type, as shown in formula (3.2). Now, the speaker's information content for the whole text can again be characterized by an index by means of which texts can be compared. Two possibilities can be proposed.

(i) Since $SIC_i = \text{ld }(\bar{s}_i), i = 1, 2, \ldots, |W|$, we can construct an index:

$$\overline{SIC}_1 = \frac{1}{|W|}\sum_{i=1}^{|W|} \text{ld }(\bar{s}_i) \tag{3.15}$$

where one must first compute the SICs for individual types i, a procedure that is the more tedious the longer the text.

(ii) Another procedure is to take simply the local sizes of tokemes and define

$$\overline{SIC}_2 = \frac{1}{|T|}\sum_{k=1}^{|T|} \text{ld } |M_k|. \tag{3.16}$$

The difference between (3.15) and (3.16) consists merely in weighting: (3.16) is a weighted measure considering each local alternation separately, while (3.15) takes a mean of means into account. We shall use here (3.16).

For the given text it can be computed directly using the fifth column of Table 9 (p. 108ff.) where one finds the tokeme sizes. Here we obtain

$$\overline{SIC}_2 = (1/128)[\text{ld } 1 + \text{ld } 16 + \text{ld } 3 + \ldots + \text{ld } 1 + \text{ld } 1 + \text{ld } 3]$$

or, if we collect the frequencies

$$\begin{aligned}\overline{SIC}_2 &= (1/128)[70\text{ld } 1 + 21\text{ld } 2 + 6\text{ld } 3 + 9\text{ld } 4 + 15\text{ld } 8 + 7\text{ld } 16]\\ &= (1/128)[0 + 21 + 9.5097 + 18 + 45 + 28] = 0.9493\end{aligned}$$

$\overline{SIC}$ is a content – informational characteristic of the text seen from the speaker's perspective. We suppose that it is the smaller the more formal the text. Thus for scientific or juridical texts $\overline{SIC}_2 \to 0$ because the number of alternatives is very restricted, while for poetic texts it will be much higher. We can build about it a confidence interval. We easily compute the variance

$$\sigma^2_{\overline{SIC}} = \frac{\sigma^2_{\text{ld }|M|}}{|T|} = 0.0124$$

Using our result as a first estimation for journalistic texts we obtain a 95% confidence interval as

$$|\overline{SIC}_2| < 0.9493 \pm 1.96\sqrt{0.0124} = 0.9493 \pm 0.2183$$

The variance of (3.16) can approximatively be computed directly from tokeme sizes $|M_k|$, i.e. without first taking their logarithms. Using Taylor expansion we obtain

$$\sigma_{\overline{SIC}^2} = \frac{(\log_2 e)^2 \sigma^2_{|M|}}{|T||\bar{M}|^2} \tag{3.17}$$

7. The Sequences of SICs

Consider again the fifth column of Table 9 (p. 108ff.). Here the tokeme sizes build a sequence of

(a) 1, 16, 3, 2, 1, 8, 2, 1,...

Taking the dual logarithms we obtain a new sequence

(b) 0, 4, 1.585, 1, 0, 3, 1, 0,...

The zeroes in this sequence signalize content rigidity restricting speaker's selection possibilities, numbers greater than 0 signalize greater or smaller stylistic freedom. In order to control the information flow and at the same time to allow *licentia poetica*, zeros and non-zeroes must display some pattern which is characteristic of different text types. In the first approximation we leave the zeroes as they are and symbolize all other numbers (> 0) as 1. Thus we obtain the two state sequence

(c) 0, 1, 1, 1, 0, 1, 1, 0,...

which can be analyzed in different ways. We begin with the examination of runs of 0 and 1 and set up the hypothesis that

Hypothesis 4
The building of text blocks with zero uncertainty (0) and those with selection possibilities (1) is random

i.e., there is no tendency either to enlarge or to reduce passages with the same (dichotomized) information content. In practice it means that the runs of zeroes and ones are distributed at random.

For testing the hypothesis on great samples one usually applies the normal distribution and computes the quantity

$$z = \frac{n(r-1) - n_0 n_1}{\left[\dfrac{2n_0 n_1(2n_0 n_1 - n)}{n-1}\right]^{1/2}} \tag{3.18}$$

Pos.	Text word	Length L_k	Alternatives A_{ijk}	Tokeme size $\|M_k\|$	LL_k	Range rg	d
19.	wurde:	2	-	1	2.00	0.00	0.00
20.	Fünf	1	-	1	1.00	0.00	0.00
21.	Meter	2	-	1	2.00	0.00	0.00
22.	dick	1	breit, tief	3	1.00	0.00	0.00
23.	ist	1	war	2	1.00	0.00	0.00
24.	der	1	dieser	2	1.50	1.00	-0.50
25.	Monster-	2	Mammut-, Riesen-, Mörder-, Mega-, Super-, Wahnsinns-, ∅	8	1.75		0.25
26.	Wälzer	2	Schmöker, Schinken, Roman	4	2.00	0.00	0.00
27.	und	1	-	1	1.00	0.00	0.00
28.	wiegt	1	-	1	1.00	0.00	0.00
29.	250	5	-	1	5.00	0.00	0.00
30.	Kilo.	2	Kilogramm	2	2.50	1.00	-0.50
31.	Die	1	-	1	1.00	0.00	0.00
32.	Stiftung	2	-	1	2.00	0.00	0.00
33.	Lesen	2	-	1	2.00	0.00	0.00
34.	hatte	2	-	1	2.00	0.00	0.00
35.	zum	1	-	1	1.00	0.00	0.00
36.	“Welttag	2	-	1	2.00	0.00	0.00
37.	des	1	-	1	1.00	0.00	0.00
38.	Buches”	2	-	1	2.00	0.00	0.00
39.	Schüler	2	Kinder, Schulkinder, Leseratten	4	2.75	2.00	-0.75
40.	in	1	aus	2	1.00	0.00	0.00
41.	ganz	1	∅	2	0.50	0.00	0.50
42.	Deutschland	2	-	1	2.00	0.00	0.00
43.	aufgerufen	4	aufgefordert, gebeten, angeregt	4	3.50	1.00	0.50

Pos.	Text word	Length L_k	Alternatives A_{ijk}	Tokeme size $\|M_k\|$	LL_k	Range rg	d
44.	einen	2	-	1	2.00	0.00	0.00
45.	spannenden	3	∅, aufregenden, spannungsreichen, tollen, interessanten, fesselnden, packenden	8	3.00	3.00	0.00
46.	Kinder-	2	-	1	2.00	0.00	0.00
47.	Krimi	2	Kriminalroman, Thriller	3	3.00	3.00	-1.00
48.	zu	1	-	1	1.00	0.00	0.00
49.	schreiben	2	dichten, erfinden, verfassen, erstellen, erzählen, texten, erdenken	8	2.63	1.00	-0.63
50.	Kinderbuchautor	5	Autor, Schriftsteller, Kinderbuchschriftsteller	4	4.00	4.00	1.00
51.	Andreas	3	-	1	3.00	0.00	0.00
52.	Steinhöfel	3	-	1	3.00	0.00	0.00
53.	dachte	2	-	1	2.00	0.00	0.00
54.	sich	1	∅, lediglich	3	1.33	2.00	-0.33
55.	den	1	einen	2	1.50	1.00	-0.50
56.	Anfang	2	Beginn, Start	3	1.67	1.00	0.33
57.	aus	1	-	1	1.00	0.00	0.00
58.	und	1	-	1	1.00	0.00	0.00
59.	18000	4	-	1	4.00	0.00	0.00
60.	Jungen	2	-	1	2.00	0.00	0.00
61.	und	1	sowie	2	1.50	1.00	-0.50
62.	Mädchen	2	-	1	2.00	0.00	0.0
63.	"strickten"	2	bastelten, schrieben, dichteten, führten, erdachten, texteten, brachten, dachten, erfanden, sponnen, häkelten, ergänzten, erarbeiteten, webten, erzählten	16	2.69	3.00	-0.69
64	die	1	diese	2	1.50	1.00	-0.50

Pos.	Text word	Length L_k	Alternatives A_{ijk}	Tokeme size $\|M_k\|$	LL_k	Range rg	d
65.	Geschichte	3	Story, Erzählung, Handlung	4	2.50	1.00	0.50
66.	rund	1	∅	2	0.50	0.00	0.50
67.	um	1	-	1	1.00	0.00	0.00
68.	eine	2	-	1	2.00	0.00	0.00
69.	geheimnisvolle	5	mysteriöse, seltsame, merkwürdige, eigenartige, unheimliche, rätselhafte, zwielichtige	8	4.25	2.00	0.75
70.	Weltuhr	2	Uhr	2	1.50	1.00	0.50
71.	und	1	-	1	1.00	0.00	0.00
72.	einen	2	-	1	2.00	0.00	0.00
73.	bösen	2	fiesen, verbrecherischen, finsteren, schlimmen, gemeinen, gefährlichen, üblen, schurkigen, hinterhältigen, miesen, arglistigen, tückischen, bedrohlichen, durchtriebenen, ∅	16	3.00	3.00	-1.00
74.	Gauner	2	Gangster, Verbrecher, Schurken, Kriminellen, Dunkelmann, Bösewicht, Spitzbuben	8	2.75	2.00	-0.75
75.	zu	1	-	1	1.00	0.00	0.00
76.	Ende	2	-	1	2.00	0.00	0.00
77.	47000	7	-	1	7.00	0.00	0.00
78.	Seiten	2	-	1	2.00	0.00	0.00
79	kamen	2	-	1	2.00	0.00	0.00
80.	zusammen	3	-	1	3.00	0.00	0.00
81.	die	1	diese	2	1.50	1.00	-0.50
82.	Aktion	3	Leistung, Tat, Sache	4	2.00	2.00	1.00
83.	soll	1	wird	2	1.00	0.00	0.00
84.	ins	1	-	1	1.00	0.00	0.00
85.	Guinness	2	-	1	2.00	0.00	0.00

Pos.	Text word	Length L_k	Alternatives A_{ijk}	Tokeme size $\lvert M_k \rvert$	LL_k	Range rg	d
86.	Buch	1	-	1	1.00	0.00	0.00
87.	der	1	-	1	1.00	0.00	0.00
88.	Rekorde	3	-	1	3.00	0.00	0.00
89.	aufgenommen	4	eingetragen, übernommen, geschrieben	4	3.75	1.00	0.25
90.	werden	2	-	1	2.00	0.00	0.00
91.	Zur	1	-	1	1.00	0.00	0.00
92.	Präsentation	5	Vorführung, Vorstellung, Ausstellung, Enthüllung, Darbietung, Musterung, Begutachtung	8	3.38	2.00	1.63
93.	des	1	dieses	2	1.50	1.00	-0.50
94.	Gemeinschafts-werkes	5	Werkes, Buches, Krimis, Riesenbuchs, Wälzers, Mammutwerks, Projekts	8	2.88	3.00	2.13
95.	kamen	2	reisten, fuhren, eilten, zogen, pilgerten, drängten, sausten	8	2.13	1.00	-0.13
96.	viele	2	Dutzende, einige, etliche, zahlreiche, zahllose, scharenweise, Unmengen	8	3.00	2.00	-1.00
97.	der	1	-	1	1.00	0.00	0.00
98.	Nachwuchs-autoren	5	Schüler, Kinder, Autoren, Schreiber, Krimiautoren, Nachwuchs-schreiber, Starschreiber, Kinderautoren, Teilnehmer, Beteiligten, Schulkinder, Kriminalautoren, Krimischreiber, Schreiberlinge, Jungschrift-steller	16	3.69	4.00	1.31
99.	nach	1	-	1	1.00	0.00	0.00
100.	Altona	3	Hamburg	2	2.50	1.00	0.50
101.	Und	1	-	1	1.00	0.00	0.00
102.	weil	1	da	2	1.00	0.00	0.00

Pos.	Text word	Length L_k	Alternatives A_{ijk}	Tokeme size $\|M_k\|$	LL_k	Range rg	d
103.	es	1	-	1	1.00	0.00	0.00
104.	in	1	-	1	1.00	0.00	0.00
105.	dem	1	diesem	2	1.50	1.00	-0.50
106.	Buch	1	Werk, Krimi, Wälzer, Roman, Schmöker, Plot, Kriminalroman	8	2.00	4.00	-1.00
107.	um	1	-	1	1.00	0.00	0.00
108.	zwei	1	∅	1	0.50	0.00	0.50
109.	junge	2	∅, jugendliche, kleine, eifrige, begabte, echte, richtige	8	2.38	2.00	-0.38
110.	Spürnasen	3	Detektive, Schnüffler, Ermittler, Spurensucher, Privatdetektive, Auskundschafter, Späher, Beobachter, Lauscher, Beschatter, Aufpasser, Schlauberger, Schlauköpfe, Derricks	16	3.19	4.00	-0.19
111.	geht	1	-	1	1.00	0.00	0.00
112.	spielten	2	stellten, empfanden, sangen, tanzten, mimten, machten, agierten	8	2.25	1.00	-0.25
113.	Stella-	2	∅	2	1.00	0.00	1.00
114.	Musical	3	∅	2	1.50	0.00	1.50
115.	Stars	1	Schauspieler, Sänger, Akteure, Mitglieder, Leute, Darsteller, Künstler	8	2.38	2.00	-1.38
116.	in	1	-	1	1.00	0.00	0.00
117.	der	1	-	1	1.00	0.00	0.00
118.	Bahnhofshalle	4	Halle, Vorhalle, Wandelhalle	4	3.25	2.00	0.75
119.	für	1	-	1	1.00	0.00	0.00
120.	die	1	-	1	1.00	0.00	0.00

Pos.	Text word	Length L_k	Alternatives A_{ijk}	Tokeme size $\|M_k\|$	LL_k	Range rg	d
121.	Kinder	2	Schüler, Autoren, Schreiber, Krimiautoren, Nachwuchsautoren, Nachwuchsschreiber, Starschreiber, Kinderautoren, Teilnehmer, Beteiligten, Schulkinder, Kriminalautoren, Krimischreiber, Schreiberlinge, Jungschriftsteller	16	3.69	4.00	-1.69
122.	Szenen	2	Bilder, Teile, Partien	4	2.00	0.00	0.00
123.	aus	1	-	1	1.00	0.00	0.00
124.	Emil	2	-	1	2.00	0.00	0.00
125.	und	1	-	1	1.00	0.00	0.00
126.	die	1	-	1	1.00	0.00	0.00
127.	Detektive	4	-	1	4.00	0.00	0.00
128.	nach	1	vor, $\emptyset$	3	0.67	0.00	0.33

4

ZERO-SYLLABLE WORDS IN DETERMINING WORD LENGTH*

Gordana Antić, Emmerich Kelih, Peter Grzybek

1. Introduction

This paper concentrates on the question of zero-syllable words (i.e. words without vowels) in Slavic languages. By way of an example, special emphasis will be laid on Slovenian, subsequent to general introductory remarks on the quantitative study of word length, which focus on the basic definition of 'word' and 'syllable' as linguistic units.

The problem of zero-syllable words has become evident in a number of studies on word length in Slavic languages, dealing with the theoretical modelling of frequency distributions of x-syllable words (as for example Best/Zinenko 1998, 1999, 2001; Girzig 1997; Grzybek 2000; Nemcová/Altmann 1994; Uhlířová 1996, 1997, 1999, 2001). As an essential result of these studies it turned out that, due to the specific structure of syllable and word in Slavic languages (a) several probability distribution models have to be taken into account, and this depends (b) on the fact if zero-syllable words are considered as a separate word class in its own right or not.

Apart from the question how specific explanatory factors may be submitted to linguistic interpretations with regard to the parameters given by the relevant model(s), we are faced with the even more basic question, to what extent the specific definition of the underlying linguistic units (as, in the given case, the definition of 'syllable' as the measure unit), causes the necessity to introduce different models.

Instead of looking for an adequate model for the frequency distribution of x-syllable words, as is done in works theoretically modelling word length in a synergetic framework, as developed by Grotjahn/Altmann (1993), Wimmer et al. (1994), Wimmer/Altmann (1996), Altmann et al. (1997), Wimmer/Altmann (in this volume), we rather suggest to first follow a different line in this study:

* This study was conducted in the context of the Graz Project "Word Length (Frequencies) in Slavic Language Texts", financially supported by the Austrian Fund for Scientific Research (FWF, P-15485).

P. Gryzbek (ed.), Contributing in the Science of Text and Language, 117-156.

our interest will be to find out, which empirical effects result from the choice (or definition) of the observed units 'word' or 'syllable'. Predominantly putting a particular accent on zero-syllable words, we examine if and how the major statistical measures are influenced by the theoretical definition of the above-mentioned units. We do not, of course, generally neglect the question if and how the choice of an adequate frequency model is modified depending on these pre-conditions – it is simply not pursued in this paper which has a different accent.

Basing our analysis on 152 Slovenian texts, we are mainly concerned with the following two questions:

(a) How can word length reasonably be defined for automatical analyses, and

(b) what influence has the determination of the measure unit (i.e. the syllable) on the given problem?

Thus, subsequent to the discussion of (a), it will be necessary to test how the decision to consider zero-syllable words as a specific word length class in its own right influences the major statistical measures.

Any answer to the problem outlined should lead to the solution of specific problems: among others, it should be possible to see to what extent the proportion of x-syllable words can be interpreted as a discriminating factor in text typology – to give but one example. Also, it is our hope that by analyzing the influence the definition of 'word' and 'syllable' (as the two basic linguistic units) have, and further testing the consequences of considering zero-syllable words as a separate word class in its own right, we can contribute to current word length-research at least of Slavic languages (and other languages with similar problems).

In a way, the scope of this study may be understood to be more far-reaching, however, insofar as it focuses relevant pre-conditions which are of general methodological importance.

In order to arrive at answers to at least some of these questions, it seems reasonable to test the operationality of different definitions of the units 'word' and 'syllable'. For these ends, we will empirically test, on a basis of 152 Slovenian texts, which effects can be observed in dependence of diverging definitions of these units.

2. Word Definition

Without a doubt, a consistent definition of the basic linguistic units is of utmost importance for the study of word length. It seems that, in an everyday understanding of the relevant terms, one easily has a notion of what the term 'word' implies. Yet, as has already been said in the introduction, there is no generally accepted definition of this term, not even in linguistics; thus the 'word' has to be operationally defined according to the objective of the research in question.

Irrespective of the theoretical problems of defining the word, there can be no doubt that the latter is one of the main formal textual and perceptive units in linguistics, which has to be determined in one way or another.
Knowing that there is no uniquely accepted, general definition, which we can accept as a standardized definition and use for our purposes, it seems reasonable to discuss relevant available definitions. As a result, we should then choose one intersubjectively acceptable definition, adequate for dealing with the concrete questions we are pursuing.

With the framework of quantitative linguistics and computer linguistics, one can distinguish, among others, the following alternatives:

(a) The 'word' is defined as a so-called "rhythm group", a definition related to the realm of phonetics, which is, among others, postulated in the work by Lehfeldt (1999: 34ff.) and Lehfeldt/Altmann (2002: 38). This conception, which is methodologically based on Mel'čuk's (1997) theoretical works, strictly distinguishes between 'slovoforma' [словоформа] and 'lexema' [лексема]: whereas 'slovoforma' is the individual occurrence of the linguistic sign (частный случай языкового знака), the 'lexema' is a multitude of word forms [slovoforms] or word fusions, which are different from each other only by inflectional forms.

    In our context, only the concept of 'slovoforma' is of relevance; in further specifying it, one can see that it is defined by a number of further qualities, first and foremost by suprasegmental marks, i.e. by the presence of an accent (*accentogene word forms* vs. *clitics*). Based on this phonematic criterium, phonotactical, morphophonological and morphological ("word end signals") criteria will have to be pursued additionally.

(b) In a number of works by Rottmann (1997, 1999), the word is, without further specification, defined as a semantic unit. Taking into consideration syntactic qualities, and differentiating autosemantic vs. synsemantic words, a more or less autonomous role is attributed to prepositions as a class in their own right.

(c) The definition of the word according to orthographic criteria can be found throughout the literature, and it is also used in quantitative linguistics. According to this definition, "words are units of speech which appear as sequences of written letters between spaces" (cf. Bühler et al. 1972, Bünting/Bergenholtz 1995). Such a definition has been fundamentally criticized by many linguists, as, for example, by Wurzel (2000: 30): "With this criterium, we arrive at a concept of word, which is not morphological, but orthographic and thus, from the perspective of theoretical grammar, irrelevant: it reflects the morphological aspects of a word only insufficiently and incoherently." – Similar arguments are brought forth by Mel'čuk (1997: 198 ff.), who objects that the orthographical criterium can have no linguistic meaning because (i) some languages have never been alphabetized, (ii) the space (and other punctuation marks) does not have a word-separating function in all languages, and (iii) the space must not be generally considered to be a reliable and consistent means of separating words.

Subsequent to this discussion of three different theoretical definitions, we will try to work with one of these definitions, of which we demand that it is acceptable on an intersubjective level. The decisive criterium in this next step will be a sufficient degree of formalization, allowing for an automatic text processing and analysis.

2.1 Towards the choice of definition

Given the contradictory situation of arguments outlined above, it is self-evident that the present article cannot offer a solution to the discussion outlined above. Rather, what can be realized, is an attempt to show which consequences arise if one makes a decision in favor of one of the described options. Since this, too, cannot be done in detail for all of the above-mentioned alternatives, within the framework of this article, there remains only one reasonable way to go: We will tentatively make a decision for one of the options, and then, in a number of comparative studies, empirically test which consequences result from this decision as compared to the theoretical alternatives.

By way of pragmatic solution, we will therefore tentatively adopt the graphematic-orthographic word definition; accordingly, a 'word' is understood as a "perceptible unit of written text", which can be recognized according to the spaces or some additional special marks" (Bünting/Bergenholtz 1995: 39).

In accepting this procedure, it seems reasonable, however, to side with Jachnow's (1974: 66) warning that a word – irrespective of its universal character – should be described as a language-specific phenomenon. This will be briefly analyzed in the following work and only in the Slovenian language, but under special circumstances, and with specific modifications.

In the previous discussion, we already pointed out the weaknesses of this definition; therefore, we will now have to explain that we regard it to be reasonable to take just the graphematic-orthographic definition as a starting point. Basically, there are three arguments in favor of this decision:

(a) First, there seems to be general agreement that the orthographic-graphematic criterium is the less complex definition of the word, the 'least common denominator' of definitions, in a way. This is the reason why this definition can be and is used in an almost identical manner by many researchers, though with a number of "local modifications" (cf. Best/Zinenko 1980: 10). It can therefore be expected that the results allow for some intersubjective comparability, at least to a particular degree.

(b) Second, since the definition of the units involves complex problems of quantifying linguistic data, this question can be solved only by way of the assumption that any quantification is some kind of a process which needs to be operationally defined. Thus, any kind of clear-cut definition guarantees that the claim of possible reproduction of the experiment can be fulfilled, which guarantees the control over the precision and reliability of the applied measures (see Altmann/Lehfeldt 1980).

(c) Third, it must be emphasized that when studying the length of particular linguistic units, we are not so much concerned with the phonetic, morphological and syntactic structure of langauge, or of a given language, but with the question of regularities, which underly language(s) and text(s).

The word thus being defined according to purely formal criteria – i.e., as a unit delimited by spaces and, eventually, additional special marks – finds well its place and approval in pragmatically and empirically oriented linguistics. With a number of additional modifications, this concept can easily be integrated in the following model:

TEXT ———— WORD FORM ———— WORD (LEXEME)

MORPHE ———————— MORPHEME

(Schaeder/Willée 1989: 189)

This scheme makes it clear that the determination of word forms is an important first step in the analysis of (electronically coded) texts. This, in turn, can serve as a guarantee that an analysis on all other levels of language (i.e., word, lexeme, morpheme) remains open for further research.

In summary, we will thus understand by 'word' that kind of 'word form' which, in corpus linguistics and computer linguistics, uses to be termed 'token' (or 'running word'), i.e., that particular unit which can be obtained by the formal segmentation of concrete texts (Schaeder/Willée 1989: 191).

The definition chosen above is, of course, of relevance for the automatic processing and quantitative analysis of text(s). In detail, a number of concrete textual modifications result from the above-mentioned definition.[1]

(a) **Acronyms** – being realized as a sequence of capitals from the words' initial letters, or as letters separated by punctuation marks – have to be transformed into a textual form corresponding to their unabbreviated pronunciation. Therefore, vowelless acronyms often have to be supplemented by an additional 'vowel' to guarantee the underlying syllabic structure, as, e.g.:

[1] The "Principles of Word Length Counting" applied in the Graz Project (see fn. 1) can be found under: http://www-gewi.uni-graz.at/quanta

SMS	Slovenska mladinska stranka	→	EsEmEs
SDS	Socialdemokratska stranka Slovenije	→	EsDeEs
NK	Nogometni klub	→	EnKa
JLA	Jugoslovanska ljudska armada	→	JeLeA

In all these cases, the acronyms are counted as words with two or three syllables respectively.

(b) **Abbreviations** are completely transformed, in correspondence with the orthographical norm, and in congruence with the relevant grammatical and syntactical rules.

c.k.	→	cesarsko-kraljevi
sv.	→	sveti, svetega
g.	→	gospod

(c) **Numerals** (numeralia, cardinalia, ordinalia, distributiva) in the form of Arabic or Latin figures (year, date, etc.) will be processed homogeneously: figures will be written in their complete, graphemic realization:

Example: *Bilo je leta 1907 → Bilo je leta tisoč devetsto sedem.* In this case, '1907' will be counted as three words consisting of seven syllables.

(d) **Foreign language passages** will be eliminated in case of longer passages. In case of single elements, they are processed according to their syllabic structure. For example, the name "Wiener Neustadt", occurring in a Slovenian text, will be "transliterated" as *Viner Nejstadt*, in order to guarantee the underlying syllabic structure. Particularly with regard to foreign language elements and passages, attention must be paid to syllabic and non-syllabic elements which, for the two languages under consideration, differ in function: cf. the letter "Y" in *lorry → lori* vs. *New York → Nju Jork.*

(e) **Hyphenated words**, including hyphenated adjective and noun composites such as "Benezi-Najstati", etc., will be counted as two words.

It should be noted here that irrespective of these secondary manipulations the original text structure remains fully recognizable to a researcher; in other words, the text remains open for further examinations (e.g., on the phonemic, syllabic, or morphemic level).

2.2 On the Definition of 'Syllable' as the Unit of Measurement

In quantitative analyses of word length in texts, a word usually is measured by the number of syllables (cf. Altmann et al. 1997: 2), since the syllable is considered as a direct constituent of the word.

The syllable can be regarded as a central syntagmatic-paradigmatic, phonotactic and phonetic-rhythmic unit of the word, which is characterized by increased sonority, and which is the carrier of all suprasegmental qualities of a language (cf. Unuk 2001: 3). In order to automatically measure word length it is therefore not primarily necessary to define the syllable boundaries; rather, it is sufficient to determine all those units (phonemes) which are characterized by an increased sonority and thus have syllabic function.

Analyzing the Slovenian phoneme inventory in this respect, the following vowels and sonants can potentially have syllabic function:

(i) vowels [/a/, /ɛ/, /e/, /i/, /ɔ/, /o/. /u/, /ə/]

(ii) sonants [/v/, /j/, /r/, /l/, /m/, /n/] (cf. Unuk 2001: 29)

The phonemes listed under (i) are graphemically realized as [a, e, i, o, u]; they all, including the half-vowel /ə/ – which is not represented by a separate grapheme, but realized as [e] (Toporišič 2000: 72) – have syllabic function.

The sonants /m/, /n/, /l/, /j/ – except for some special cases in codified Slovenian (cf. Toporišič 2000: 87) – can not occur in syllabic position, and are thus not regarded to be syllabic in the automatic counting of syllables.

The sonant /r/ can be regarded to be syllabic only within a word, between two consonants: ['smrt', 'grlo', 'prt'].

As to the phoneme /v/, there has been a long discussion in (Slovenian) linguistics, predominantly concerning its orthographic realization and phonematic valence. On the one hand (see Toporišič 2000: 74), it has been classified as a sonant with three different consonantal variants, namely as

1) /u̯/ in siv, sivka – a non-syllabic bilabial sound, a short /u/ from a quantitative perspective
2) /w/ in vzeti, vreti – a voiced bilabial fricative, and
3) /ʍ/ in vsak, vsebina – a voiceless bilabial fricative.

On the other hand, empirical sonographic studies show that there are no bilabial fricatives in Slovenian standard language (cf. Srebot-Rejec 1981). Instead, it is an unaccentuated /u/ which occurs in this position and which, in the initial position, is shortened so significantly that it occurs in a non-syllabic position.

We can thus conclude that a consistent picture of the syllabic valence of /v/ cannot be derived either from normative Slovenian grammar or from any other sources.[2]

Once again, it appears that it is necessary to define an operational, clearly defined inventory, as far as the measurement of word length is concerned. Of course,

[2] For further discussions on this topic see: Tivadar (1999), Srebot Rejec (2000), *Slovenski pravopis* (2001); cf. also Lekomceva (1968), where the sonants /r/, /l/, /w/, /j/, /v/ are both as vowels and as consonants, depending on the position they take.

this question is also relevant regarding the Slovenian inventory of zero-syllable words, as e.g., the non-vocalic valence of the sonant /v/ as a preposition: partly – in particular when slowly spoken (see Toporišić 2000: 86) – /v/ is pronounced as a short /u/ in non-vocalic surrounding, whereas the preposition "v", when preceding vowels, can be phonetically realized as either /u̯/, /w/, or /u/.

In spite of these ambiguities, it is necessary to exactly define the syllabic units of the phoneme as well as of the grapheme inventory, if an automatic analysis of word length is desired. Since the valence of the phoneme /v/ cannot be clearly defined, we will, in the following analyses, proceed as follows: both the vowels listed above under (i) and the sonant /r/, in combination with the half vowel /ə/ (in the positions mentioned), will be regarded to be syllabic, and consequently will be treated as the basic measuring unit.

3. On the Question of Zero-Syllabic Words

The question whether there is a class of zero-syllabic words in its own right, is of utmost importance for any quantitative study on word length. With regard to this question, two different approaches can be found in the research on the frequency of x-syllabic words.

On the one hand, in correspondence with the orthographic-graphematic paradigm, zero-syllabic words have been analyzed as a separate category in the following works:

Slowak	Nemcová/Altmann (1994)
Czech	Uhlířová (1996, 1997, 1999)
Russian	Girzig (1997)
Slovenian	Grzybek (2000)
Bulgarian	Uhlířová (2001)

On the other hand, there are studies in which scholars have not treated zero-syllabic as a category in its own right: Best/Zinenko (1998: 10), for example, who analyzed Russian texts, argued in favor of the notion that zero-syllabic words can be regarded to be words in the usual understanding of this term, but that they are not words in a phonetic and phonological sense. Instead of discussing the partly contradictory results in detail, here (see Best/Zinenko 1999, 2001), we shall rather describe and analyze the Slovenian inventory of zero-syllable words: subsequent to a description of the historical development of this word class, we will shift our attention to a statistical-descriptive analysis. In this context, it will be important to see if consideration or neglect of this special word class results in statistical differences, and how much information consideration of them offers for quantitative studies.

Inventory of Slovenian zero-syllable Words. In addition to interjections[3] not containing a syllable, there are two words in Slovenian, which are to be considered as zero-syllable words (provided, one regards the preposition 'v' to be consonantal, according to its graphematic-orthographical realization). Both words may be realized in two graphematic variants, depending on their specific position:

- ◇ the preposition *k*, or *h*;
- ◇ the preposition *s*, or *z*.

As can be seen, we are concerned with two zero-syllable prepositions and with corresponding orthographical-graphematic variants for their phonetic realizations. In Slovenian, as in other Slavic languages as well, these words, which originally had one syllable, were shortened to zero-syllable words after the loss of /ъ/ in weak positions. Whereas in Old Church Slavonic only the preposition /kъ/ is documented, in Slovenian, according to Bajec (1959), only the form without vowels, /k/, occurs. According to contemporary Slovenian orthography, the preposition "k" tends to be modified as follows: preceding the consonants 'g' or 'k', the preposition 'k' is transformed to "h".

The situation is similar in the case of the prepositions *s*, or *z* respectively: (*s* precedes the graphemes "p, f, t, s, c, č, š"), which are documented as one-syllable "sъ" in Old Church Slavonic as well as in the *Brižinski spomeniki* (Bajec 1959: 106ff.). As opposed to this, these prepositions are treated as zero-syllable words in modern Slovenian; they thus exemplify the following general trend: original one-syllable words have been transformed into zero-syllable words. Obviously, there are economic reasons for this reduction tendency. From a phonematic point of view, one might add the argument that these prepositions do not display any suprasegmental properties, i.e., they are not stressed, and therefore are proclitically attached to the subsequent word (cf. Toporišić 2000: 112). Following this (diachronic) line of thinking might lead one to assume that zero-syllable words should (or need) not be considered as a specific class in linguo-statistic studies.

Incidently, the depicted trend (i.e., that zero-syllable prepositions are proclitically attached to the subsequent word) can also be observed in the case of some adverbs: according to Bajec (1959: 88), expressions such as *kmalu, kvečjemu, hkrati* can be regarded as frozen prepositional fusions. Adverbs with the preposition "s/z" can be dealt with accordingly: *zdavnaj, zdrda, zlahko, skupa, zgoraj,* etc. Yet, due to modern Slovenian vowel reduction, it is not always clear whether these fusions originate from the preposition "s/z" or from "iz".

---

[3] A list of interjections without syllable can be found in Toporišić (2000: 450 ff.); here, one can also find a suggestion how to deal with this inventory.

Once again it turns out that diverging concepts and definitions run parallel to each other. Yet, as was said above, it is not our aim to provide a theoretical solution to this open question. Nor do we have to make a decision, here, whether zero-syllable words should or should not be treated as a specific class, i.e., whether they should or should not, in accordance with the phonetic-phonological argument, be defined as independent words. Rather, we will leave this question open and shift our attention to the empirical part of our study, testing what importance such a decision might have for particular statistical models.

4. Descriptive Statistics

The statistical analyses are based on 152 Slovenian texts, which are considered to represent the text corpus of the present study. The whole number of texts is divided into the following groups[4]: literary prose, poetry, journalism. The detailed reference for the prose and poetic texts are given in Tables 4.8 and 4.9 (pp. 144ff.); the sources of the journalistic texts are given in Table 4.1.

Table 4.1: Sources of Journalistic Prose Texts

Text #	Source	Text sort	Year
104-120	www.delo.si	Essays, News	2001
121-129	www.mladina.si	Reports	2001
130-139	www.delo.si	News	2001
140-152	www.dnevnik.si	News	2001

Homogeneous texts (or parts of texts) were chosen as analytical units, i.e., complete poetic and journalistic texts. Furthermore, based on Orlov's (1982: 6) suggestions, chapters of longer prose text (such as novels) are treated as separate analytical units.

Based on these considerations, and taking into account that the text data basis is heterogeneous both with regard to content and text types, statistical measures, such as mean, standard deviation, skewness, kurtosis, etc., can be calculated on different analytical levels, illustrated in Figure 4.1 (p. 128).

Level I

The whole corpus is analyzed under two conditions, once considering zero-syllable words to be a separate class in their own right, and once not doing so. One can thus, for example, calculate relevant statistical measures or analyze the distribution of word length within one of the two corpora. Alternatively,

[4] For our purposes, we do note really need a theoretical text typology, as would usually be the case

one can compare both corpora with each other; one can thus, for example, measure the correlation between the average word length of corpus with zero-syllable words ($\overline{W}_{C(0)}$) and average word length of corpus without zero-syllable words ($\overline{W}_C$).

Level II
Corresponding groups of texts in each of the two corpora can be compared to each other: one can, for example, compare the poetic texts, taken as a group, in the corpus with zero-syllable words, with the corresponding text group in corpus without zero-syllable words.

Level III
Individual texts are compared to each other. Here, one has to distinguish different possibilities: the two texts under consideration may be from one and the same text group, or from different text groups; additionally, they may be part of the corpus with zero-syllable words or the corpus without zero-syllable words.

Level IV
An individual text is studied without comparison to any other text.

By way of an introductory example, let us analyze a literary prose text, chapter 6 of Ivan Cankar's *Hlapec Jernej in njegova pravica*. The text is analyzed twice: In the first analysis, zero-syllable words are treated as a separate class, whereas in the second analysis, zero-syllable words are "ignored". Table 4.2 represents characteristic statistical measures (mean word length, standard deviation, skewness, kurtosis) for the analyses under both conditions: with (0) and without (∅) considering zero-syllable words as a separate category.

Table 4.2: Characteristic Statistical Measures of Chapter 6 of Ivan Cankar's (*Hlapec Jernej in njegova pravica* (With/Without Zero-Syllable Words))

	TL in words	Mean word length	Standard deviation	Skewness	Kurtosis
0	890	1.8101	0.9915	0.9555	0.2182
∅	882	1.8265	0.9808	1.0029	0.2170

It is self-evident that text length (TL) varies according to the decision as to this point; furthermore, it can clearly be seen that the values differ in the second or the third decimal place. A larger positive skewness implies a right skewed distribution. In the next step, we analyze which percentage of the whole text corpus is represented by x-syllable words. The results of the same analysis,

Figure 4.1: Different Levels of Statistical Analysis

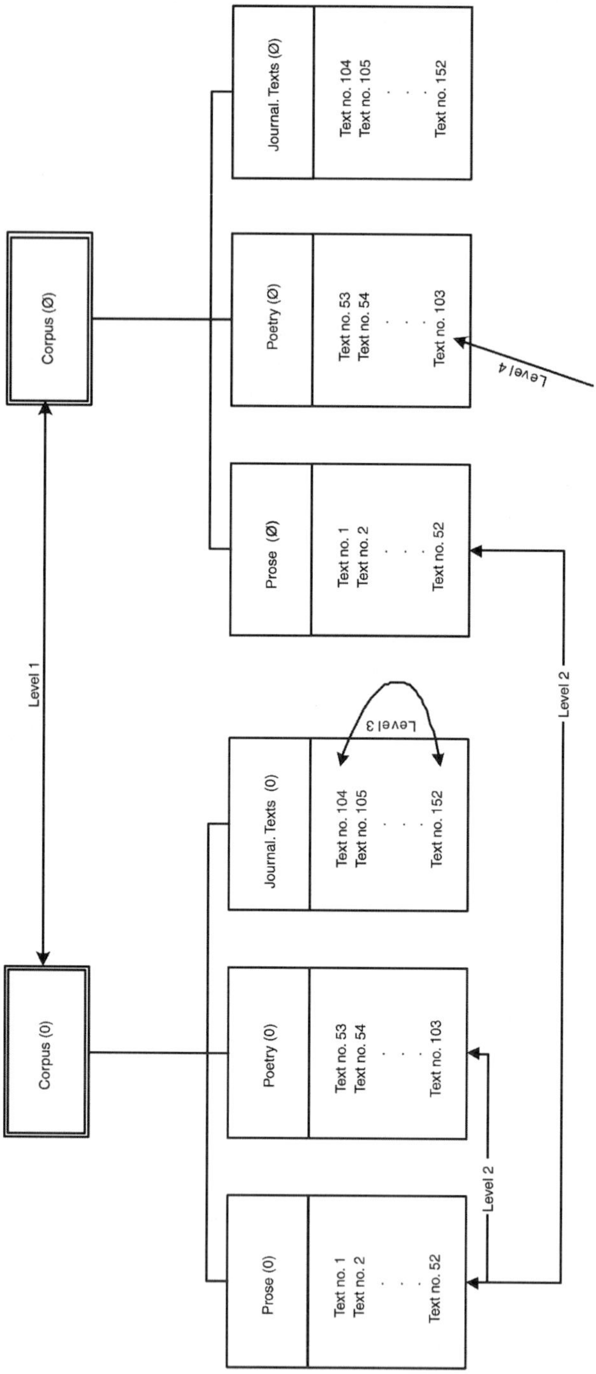

but separate for each of the three text types, are represented in Figure 4.2; the corresponding data can be found below Figure 4.2.

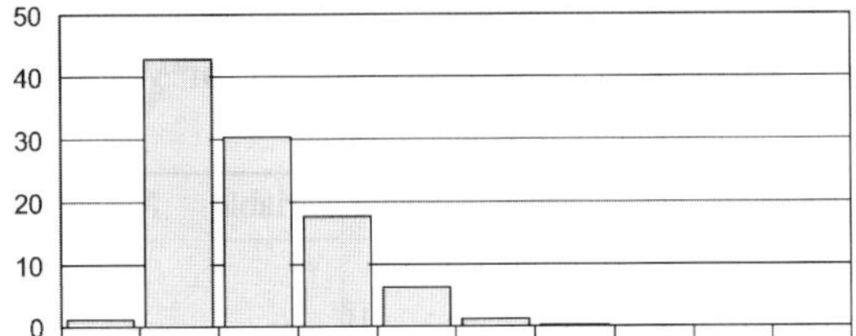

	0	1	2	3	4	5	6	7	8	9
text corpus	1,19	42,87	30,37	17,71	6,38	1,23	0,19	0,05	0,006	0,0007
L	1,17	44,26	31,21	16,91	5,55	0,79	0,1	0,01	0	0
P	0,71	46,38	36,26	14,73	1,79	0,13	0	0	0	0
J	1,42	35,16	24,45	22,47	11,82	3,67	0,72	0,25	0,034	0,004

Figure 4.2: Percentage of x-syllable Words: Corpus vs. Three Text Types

Figure 4.2 convincingly shows that the percentage of zero-syllable words is very small, both as compared to the whole text corpus, and to isolated samples of the three text types mentioned above. It should be noted that many poetic texts do not contain any 0-syllable words at all. Of the 51 poetic texts, only 26 contain such words.

5. Analysis of Mean Word Length in Texts

The statistical analysis is carried out twice, once considering the class of zero-syllable words as a separate category, and once considering them to be proclitics. Our aim is to answer the question, whether the influence of the zero-syllable words on the mean word length is significant. In the next step concentrating on the mean word length value of all 152 texts (Level I), two vector variables are introduced, each of them with 152 components: $\overline{W}_{C(0)}$ and $\overline{W}_C$.

The i-th component of the vector variable $\overline{W}_{C(0)}$ defines the mean word length of the i-th text including zero-syllable words. In analogy to this, the i-th component of the vector variable $\overline{W}_C$ gives the mean word length of the i-th text excluding zero-syllable words (see Table 4.10, column 5 and 6; p. 147). In order to obtain a more precise structure of the word length mean values, the analyses will be run both over all 152 texts of the whole corpus (Level I), and over the given number of texts belonging to one of the following three text types, only (Level II):

(i) literary prose (L),

(ii) poetry (P),

(iii) journalistic prose (J).

Alternatively, if the data do not originate from a normal distribution, Kendall's or Spearman's correlation coefficient can be used. As to our data, a strong dependence (at the 0.01 significance level, 2-sided) for all pairs of variables can be observed (see Table 4.4).

Table 4.4: Kendall and Spearman Correlations Between Mean Word Lengths in Texts With and Without Zero-syllable Words

	$\overline{W}_{C(0)}$ & $\overline{W}_C$	$\overline{W}_{L(0)}$ & $\overline{W}_L$	$\overline{W}_{P(0)}$ & $\overline{W}_P$	$\overline{W}_{J(0)}$ & $\overline{W}_J$
Kendall	0.964	0.927	0.940	0.937
Spearman	0.997	0.986	0.991	0.992

5.2 Test of Normal Distribution

In the next step, we have to examine whether the variables are normally distributed, since this is a necessary condition for further investigations. Let us therefore take a look at the histograms of each of the eight new variables. The first pair of histograms (cf. Figure 4.4) represents the distribution of mean word length for the whole text corpus, with and without zero-syllable words (Level I).

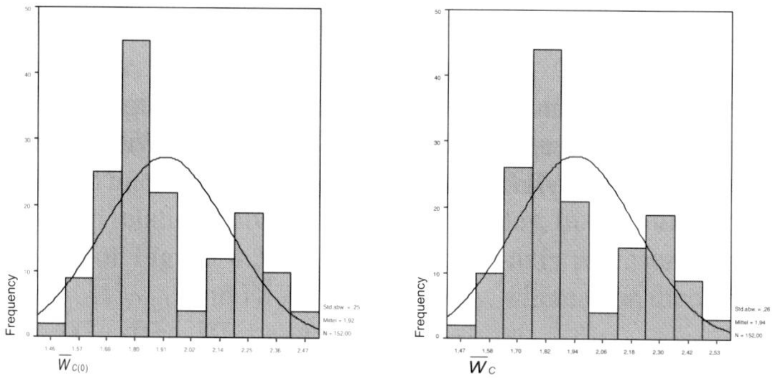

(a) Corpus With Zero-Syllable Words (b) Corpus Without Zero-Syllable Words

Figure 4.4: Distribution of Mean Word Length

The subsequent three pairs of histograms (Figures 4.5(a)–4.5(f)) represent the corresponding distributions for each of the three text types: L, P, and J (Level II).

Whereas the first pair of histograms (Figure 4.4) gives reason to assume that the mean word lengths of the whole text corpus (with and without zero-syllable) are not normally distributed, the other three pairs of histograms (Figure 4.5) seem to indicate a normal distribution. Still, we have to test these assumptions. Usually, either the Kolmogorov-Smirnov test or the Shapiro-Wilk test are applied in order to test if the data follow the normal distribution. However, the Kolmogorov-Smirnov test is rather conservative (and thus loses power), if the mean and/or variance (parameters of the normal distribution) are not specified beforehand; therefore, it tends not to reject the null hypothesis.

Since, in our case, the parameters of the distribution must be estimated from the sample data, we use the Shapiro-Wilk test, instead. This test is specifically designed to detect deviations from normality, without requiring that the mean or variance of the hypothesized normal distribution are specified in advance. We thus test the null hypothesis (H_0) against the alternative hypothesis (H_1):

H_0 : *The mean word length of texts with (without) zero-syllable words is normally distributed*

H_1 : *The mean word length of texts with (without) zero-syllable words is not normally distributed*

The Shapiro-Wilk test statistic (W) is calculated as follows:

$$W = \frac{\left(\sum_{i=1}^{n} a_i \cdot x_{(i)}\right)^2}{\sum_{i=1}^{n} (x_i - \overline{x})^2}$$

where $\bar{x} = \frac{1}{n} \sum_{i=1}^{n} x_i$ is the sample mean of the data.

$x_{(i)}$ are the ordered sample values, and a_i (for $i = 1, 2, \ldots, n$) are a set of "weights" whose values depend on the sample size n only. For $n \leq 50$, exact tables are available for a_i (Royston 1982); for $50 < n \leq 2000$, the coefficients can be determined by way of an approximation to the normal distribution. To determine whether the null hypothesis of normality has to be rejected, the probability associated with the test statistic (i.e., the p-value), has to be examined. If this value is less than the chosen level of significance (such as 0.05 for 95%), then the null hypothesis is rejected, and we can conclude that the data do not originate from a normal distribution.

Table 4.5 (p. 135) shows the results of the Shapiro-Wilk test (as obtained by SPSS). The obtained p-values support our assumptions, i.e., the mean word length of the text types 'literary prose', 'poetry', and 'journalistic prose' (Level II) are normally distributed, though the mean word lengths (with and without zero-syllable words) in the whole text corpus (Level I) are not normally distributed.

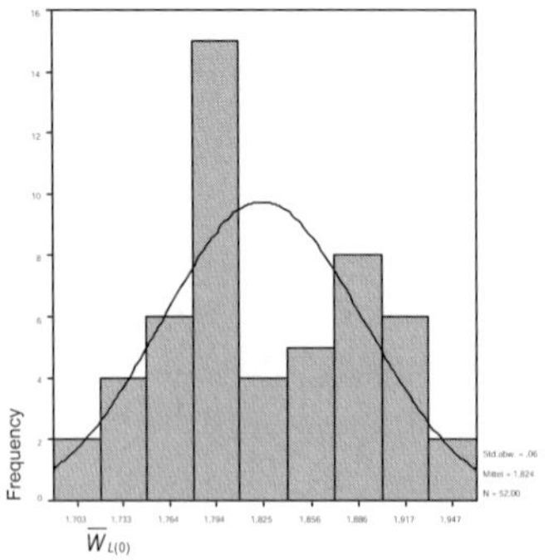

(a) L With Zero-Syllable Words

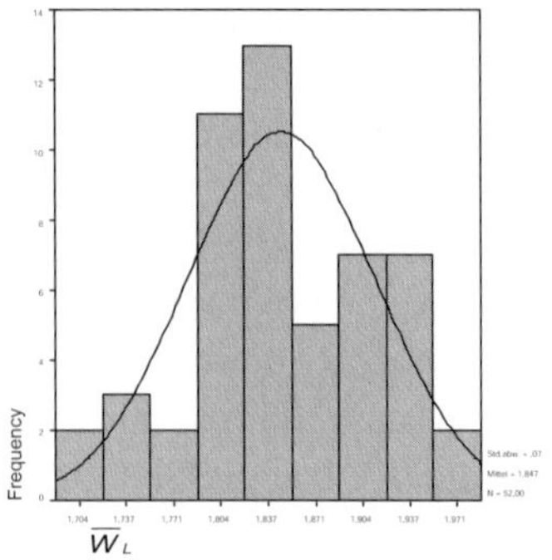

(b) L Without Zero-Syllable Words

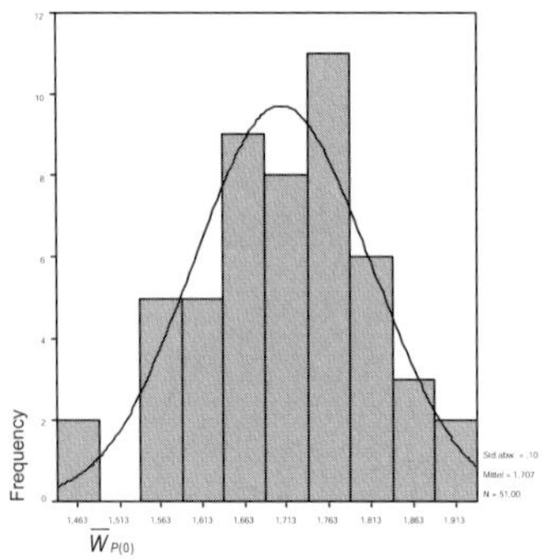

(c) P With Zero-Syllable Words

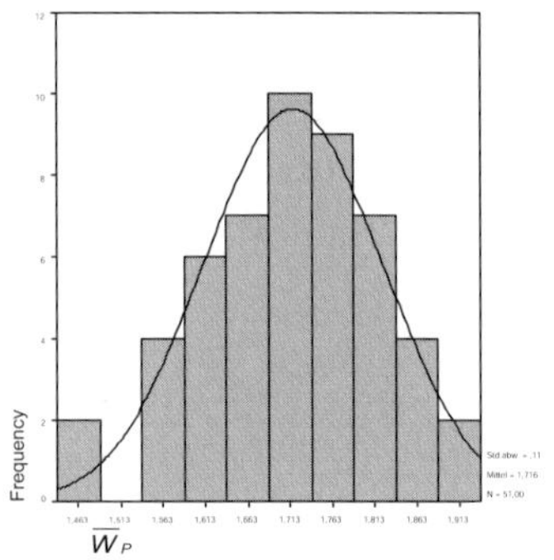

(d) P Without Zero-Syllable Words

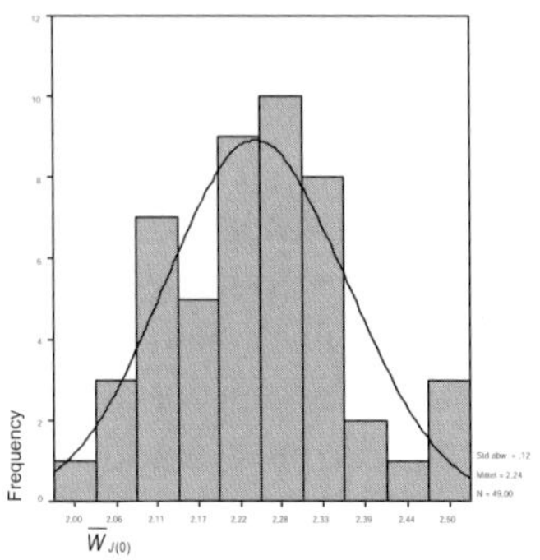

(e) J With Zero-Syllable Words

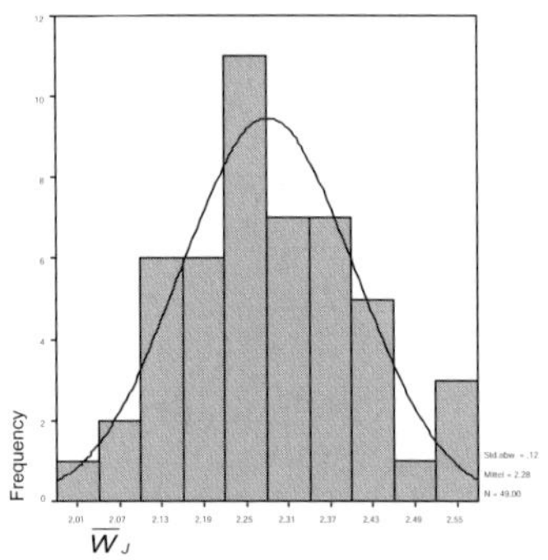

(f) J Without Zero-Syllable Words

Figure 4.5: Distribution of Mean Word Length For Literary Prose (L), Poetry (P), and Journalistic Prose (J), With and Without Zero-Syllable Words

Table 4.5: Results of the Shapiro-Wilk Test For the Three Text Types

Text type	**variable**	p **value**
Literary prose		
with zero-syllable words	$\overline{W}_{L(0)}$	0.140
without zero-syllable words	$\overline{W}_{L}$	0.267
Poetry		
with zero-syllable words	$\overline{W}_{P(0)}$	0.864
without zero-syllable words	$\overline{W}_{P}$	0.620
Journalistic prose		
with zero-syllable words	$\overline{W}_{J(0)}$	0.859
without zero-syllable words	$\overline{W}_{J}$	0.640
Corpus		
with zero-syllable words	$\overline{W}_{C(0)}$	$3.213 \cdot 10^{-7}$
without zero-syllable words	$\overline{W}_{C}$	$5.020 \cdot 10^{-7}$

Given this finding, we will now concentrate on the six normally distributed variables. In the following analyses, we shall focus on the second analytical level, i.e., between-group comparisons within a given corpus.

5.3 Analysis of Paired Observations

In this section, we will investigate whether the mean values of these new variables differ significantly from each other, within each of the three text types. In order to test this, we can apply the t-test for paired samples. This test compares the means of two variables; it computes the difference between the two variables for each case, and tests if the average difference is significantly different from zero. Since we have already shown that the necessary conditions for the application of t-test are satisfied (normal distribution and correlation of variables), we can proceed with the test; therefore, we form the differences between corresponding pairs of variables:

$$d_L = \overline{W}_L - \overline{W}_{L(0)} \quad d_P = \overline{W}_P - \overline{W}_{P(0)} \quad d_J = \overline{W}_J - \overline{W}_{J(0)}$$

For each text type, we consider one selected example (text #1, #53, and #104, respectively); these three texts are characterized by the values represented in Table 4.6 (for all texts see appendix, p. 147ff., Table 4.10).

Table 4.6: Differences (d) Between Mean Word Length of Two Variables

	mean word length of texts without zero-syllable	with zero-syllable	Difference (d)
Text # 1	1.8409	1.8073	0.0336
Text # 53	1.8000	1.7895	0.0105
Text #104	2.2745	2.2431	0.0314

Instead of a t-test for paired samples, we now have a one-sample t-test for the new variables d_L, d_P, d_J. This means that we test the following hypothesis:

H_0 : *There is no significant difference between the theoretical means (i.e., expected values) of the two variables:* $E(d_i) = 0 \;\left(E(\overline{W}_i) = E(\overline{W}_{i(0)})\right), i = L, P, J$

H_1 : *There is a significant difference between the theoretical means of the two variables:* $E(d_i) \neq 0$

We thus test for each text type, whether the mean value of the difference equals zero or not. In other words, we test if the mean values of the variables 'mean word length with zero-syllables' and 'mean word length without zero-syllables' differ. Before applying the t-test, we have to test if the variables d_L, d_P, d_J are also normally distributed. As they are linear combinations of normally distributed variables, there is sound reason to assume that this is the case. The Shapiro-Wilk test yields the p-values given in Table 4.7.

Table 4.7: Results of the Shapiro-Wilk Tests For Differences (d) For the Three Text Types

	Differences	p value
Literary prose	d_L	0,084
Poetry	d_P	$3,776 \cdot 10^{-7}$
Journalistic prose	d_J	0,059

According to the Shapiro-Wilk test, we may conclude that the variables d_L and d_J are normally distributed at the 5% level of significance, whereas the variable d_P does not seem to be normally distributed. Once more checking our data, we can see that 25 of the poetic texts (almost 50% of this text type) contain no zero-syllable words at all; it is obvious that this is the reason why the mean word lengths of those 25 texts are exactly the same for both conditions, and why the corresponding differences are equal to zero. The histogram of the variable d_P shows the same result (cf. Figure 4.6).

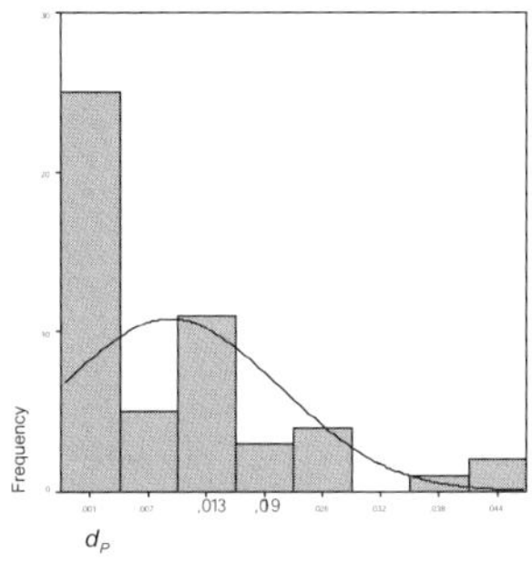

Figure 4.6: Histogram of d_P

We may thus conclude that the variable d_P is not normally distributed because of this exceptional situation in our data set. In spite of the result of the Shapiro-Wilk test, we therefore apply a one sample t-test assuming that d_P is normally distributed.

The t-test statistic is given as:

$$t = \frac{\bar{d_i}}{s_{d_i}/\sqrt{n}} \quad \text{for } i = L, P, J.$$

The t-test yields p-values close to zero for all three text types; therefore, we reject the null hypothesis, and conclude that the mean values of the mean word lengths with and without zero-syllable words differ significantly. All six variables ($\overline{W}_{i(0)}$ and $\overline{W}_i, i = L, P, J$) are thus normally distributed with different expected values. Two distribution functions (for variables which denote mean word length of texts with and without zero-syllable words) have the same shape, but they are shifted, since their expected values differ.

The following Figures 4.7(a)– 4.7(c) show the density functions of the pairs of variables for the three text types L, P, J, where the black line always represents the variable "mean word length with zero-syllables", and the dot line represents the variable "mean word length without zero-syllables" in each text type.

It should be noted that this conclusion can not be generalized. As long as the variables d_L, d_P, d_J are normally distributed, our statement is true. Yet, normality has to be tested in advance and we can not generally assume normally distributed variables.

In the next step we show the box plots and error bars of the variables d_L, d_P, d_J. A box plot is a graphical display which shows a measure of location (the median-center of the data), a measure of dispersion (the interquartile range, i.e. $iqr = q_{0.75} - q_{0.25}$), and possible outliers; it also gives an indication of the

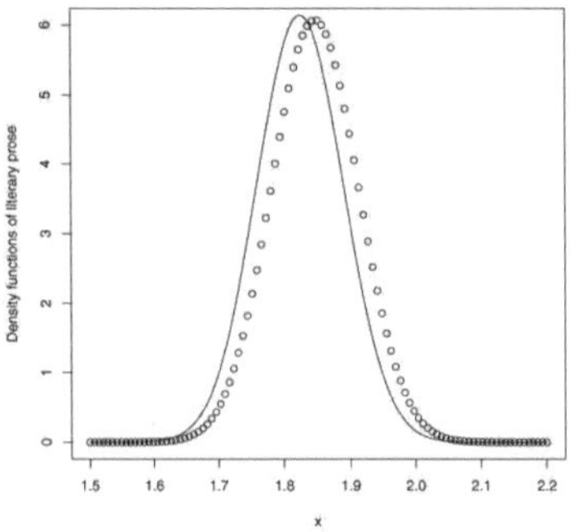

(a) Literary Prose

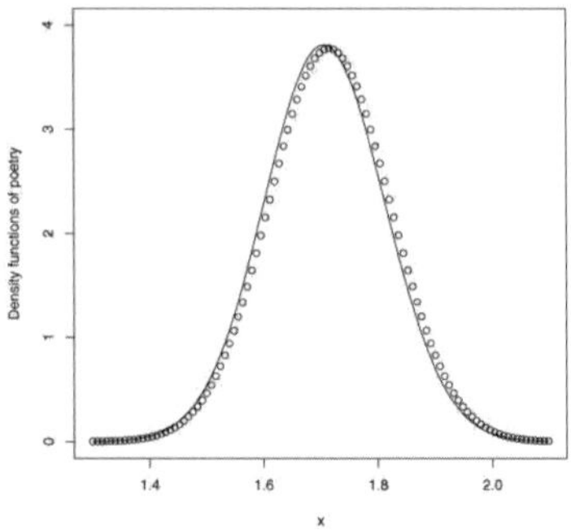

(b) Poetry

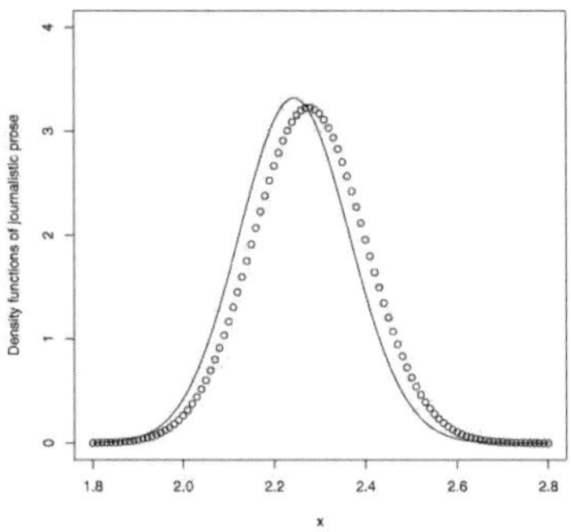

(c) Journalistic Prose

Figure 4.7: Density of Mean Word Length of the Pairs of Vari-ables (With/Without Zero-Syllable Words) for the Three Text Types

symmetry or skewness of the distribution. Horizontal lines are drawn both at the median – the 50th percentile ($q_{0.50}$) –, and at the upper and lower quartiles – the 25th percentile ($q_{0.25}$), and the 75th percentile ($q_{0.75}$), respectively. The horizontal lines are joined by vertical lines to produce the box. A vertical line is drawn up from the upper quartile to the most extreme data point (i.e. from the lower quartile to the minimum value); this distance is $= 1.5 \cdot iqr$. The most extreme data point thus is $min(x(n), q_{0.75} + 1.5 \cdot iqr)$. Short horizontal lines are added in order to mark the ends of these vertical lines. Each data point beyond the ends of the vertical lines is called an outlier and is marked by an asterisk ('*').

Figure 4.8 shows the box plot series of the variables d_L, d_P, and d_J for the three text types L, P and J. The difference in the mean values of the three samples is obvious; also it can clearly be seen that all three samples produce symmetric distributions, variable d_J displaying the largest variability.

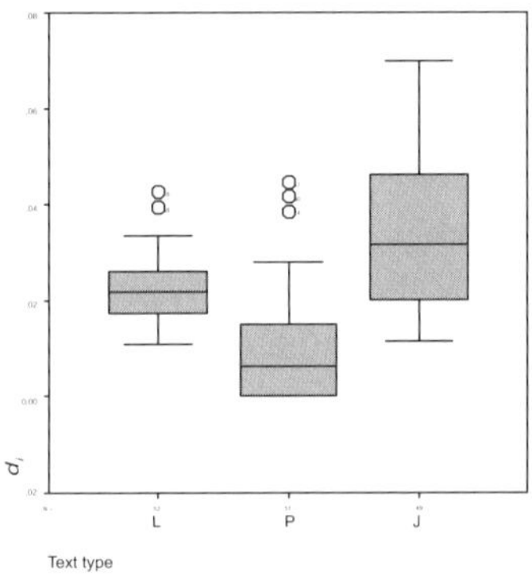

Figure 4.8: Boxplot Series of the Variables d_L, d_P, and d_J

The Error bars in Figure 4.9 provide the mean values, as well as the 95% confidence intervals of the mean of the variables d_L, d_P and d_J. As can be seen, the confidence intervals do not overlap; we can therefore conclude that the percentage of zero-syllable words possibly may allow for a distinction between different text types.

6. Conclusions

In order to conclude, let us summarize the most important findings of the present study:

(a) In a first step, the theoretical essentials of the linguistic units 'word' and 'syllable' are discussed, in order to arrive at an operational definition adequate for automatic text analyses. Based on this discussion, (involving phonological, semantic, and orthographic approaches to define the word),

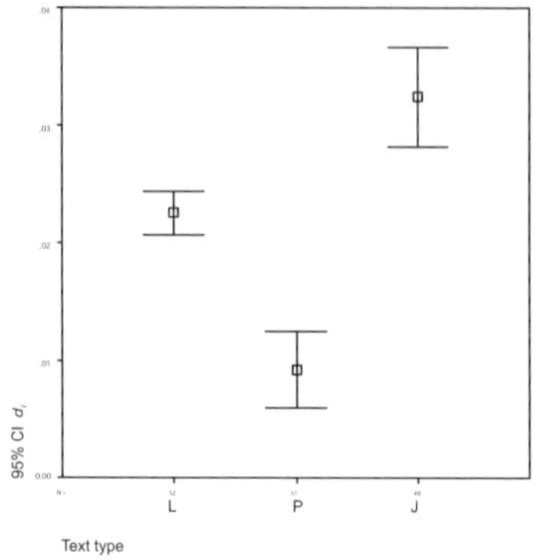

Figure 4.9: Error Bars of the Variables d_L, d_P, and d_J

an orthographic-graphematic concept of word [slovoforma] is used, for the present study, representing the least common denominator of all definitions.

(b) Subsequent to the operational definition of the linguistic unit 'word', described in (a), an adequate choice of the analytical unit in which word length is measured, has to be made. For our purposes, the 'syllable' is regarded as the direct constituent of the word. It turns out that the number of syllables per word (i.e., word length) can be automatically calculated, at least as far Slovenian texts are concerned, which represent the text material of the present study.

(c) The decisions made with regard to the theoretical problems described in (a) and (b), lead to the problem of zero-syllable words; the latter are a result of the above-mentioned definition of the word as an orthographic-graphematic defined unit: we are concerned here with words which have no vowel as a constituting element (to be precise, the prepositions k/h and s/z). This class of words may either be considered to be a separate word-length class in its own right, or as clitics. Without making an a priori decision as to this question, the mean word length of 152 Slovenian texts is analyzed in the present study, under these two conditions, in order to test the statistical effect of the theoretical decision.

(d) As is initially shown, there are a whole variety of possible analytical options (cf. Figure 4.1, page 128), depending on the perspective from which the 152 texts are being analyzed. In the present study, the material is analyzed from two perspectives, only: mean word length is calculated both in the whole text corpus (Level I), and in three different groups of text types, representing Level II: literary, journalistic, poetic. These empirical analyses are run under two conditions, either including the zero-syllable words as a separate word length class in its own right, or not doing so.

Based on these definitions and conditions, the major results of the present study may be summarized as follows:

(1) As a first result, the proportion of zero-syllable words turned out to be relatively small (i.e., less than 2%).

(2) Generally speaking, mean values differ only slightly, at first sight, under both conditions. Furthermore, it can be shown that the mean word length in texts under both conditions are highly correlated with each other; the positive linear trend, which is statistically tested in the form of a correlation analysis and graphically represented in Figure 4.3, (p. 131).

(3) In order to test if the expected values significantly differ or not, under both conditions, data have to be checked for their normal distribution. As a result, it turns out that mean word length is normally distributed in the three text groups analyzed (Level II), but, interestingly enough, not in the whole corpus (Level II). Based on this finding, further analyses concentrate on Level II, only. Therefore, t-tests are run, in order to compare the mean lengths between the three groups of texts on the basis of the differences between the mean lengths under both conditions. As a result, the expected values of mean word length significantly differ between all three groups.

(4) As can be clearly seen from Figure 4.7 (p. 138), representing the probability density function of mean word length (with and without zero-syllable words as a separate category) there is reason to assume that the choice of a particular word definition results in a systematic displacement of word lengths.

To summarize, we thus obtain a further hint at the well-organized structure of word length in texts.

References

Altmann, G.
1988 "Verteilungen der Satzlänge." In: Schulz, K.-P. (Hrsg.): *Glottometrika, 9.* [= Quantitative Linguistics, Vol. 35]. (147–171).

Altmann, G.; Best, K.H.; Wimmer, G.
1997 "Wortlänge in romanischen Sprachen." In: Gather, A.; Werner, H. (Hrsg.): *Semiotische Prozesse und natürliche Sprache. Festschrift für Udo L. Figge zum 60. Geburtstag.* Stuttgart. (1–13).

Altmann, G.; Lehfeldt, W.
1980 *Einführung in die Quantitative Phonologie.* [= Quantitative Linguistics, Vol. 7].

Bajec, A.
1959 *Besedotovorje slovenskega jezika, IV. Predlogi in predpone.* Ljubljana. [= SAZU, Razred za filološke in literarne vede, Dela 14.]

Best, K.H.; Zinenko, S.
1998 "Wortlängenverteilung in Briefen A.T. Twardowskis," in: *Göttinger Beiträge zur Sprachwissenschaft, 1*; 7–19.

Best, K.-H.; Zinenko, S.
1999 "Wortlängen in Gedichten des ukrainischen Autors Ivan Franko." In: J. Genzor; S. Ondrejovič (eds.): *Pange lingua. Zborník na počest' Viktora Krupu.* Bratislava. (201–213).

Best, K.-H.; Zinenko, S.
2001 "Wortlängen in Gedichten A.T. Twardowskis." In: L. Uhlířová; G. Wimmer; G. Altmann; R. Köhler (eds.), *Text as a Linguistic Paradigm: Levels, Constituents, Constructs. Festschrift in honour of Luděk Hřebíček.* Trier. (21–28).

Bühler, H.; Fritz, G., Herlitz, W.
^{3}1972 *Linguistik I. Lehr- und Übungsbuch zur Einführung in die Sprachwissenschaft.* Tübingen.

Bünting, K.D.; Bergenholtz, H.
^{3}1995 *Einführung in die Syntax.* Stuttgart.

Girzig, P.
1997 "Untersuchungen zur Häufigkeit von Wortlängen in russischen Texten." In: Best, K.H. (ed.): *The Distribution of Word and Sentence Length.* [= Glottometrika 16.] (152–162).

Grotjahn, R.; Altmann, G.
1993 "Modelling the Distribution of Word Length: Some Methodological Problems." In: Köhler, R.; Rieger, B. (eds.): *Contributions to Quantitative Linguistics: Proceedings of the First International Conference on Quantitative Linguistics, QUALICO, Trier; 1991.* Dordrecht. (141–153).

Grzybek, P.
2000 "Pogostnostna analiza besed iz elektronskega korpusa slovenskih besedil", in: *Slavistična revija, 48*$_{2}$; 141–157.

Jachnow, H.
1974 "Versuch einer Klassifikation der wortabgrenzenden Mittel in gesprochenen russischen Texten", in: *Die Welt der Slaven, 19*; 64–79.

Lehfeldt, W.
1999 "Akzent." In: H. Jachnow (ed.), *Handbuch der sprachwissenschaftlichen Russistik und ihrer Grenzdisziplinen.* Wiesbaden. (34–48).

Lehfeldt, W.; Altmann, G.
2002 "Der altrussische Jerwandel", in: *Glottometrics, 2*; 34–44.

Lekomceva, M.I.
1968 *Tipologija struktur sloga v slavjanskich jazykach.* Moskva.

Mel' čuk, I.A.
1999 *Kurs obščej morfologii. Tom 1. Vvedenie. Čast' pervaja. Slovo.* Wien. [= Wiener Slawistischer Almanach, Sonderband 38/1).

Nemcová, E., Altmann, G.
1994 "Zur Wortlänge in slowakischen Texten". In: Zeitschrift für Empirische Textforschung, 1994 (1); 40–44.

Rottmann, Otto A.
1997 "Word–Length Counting in Old Church Slavonic." In: Altmann, G.; Mikk, J.; Saukkonen, P.; Wimmer. G. (eds.), *Festschrift in honour of Juhan Tuldava.* [= Special issue of: *Journal of Quantitative Linguistics, 4,* $_{1-3}$; 252–256.

Rottmann, Otto A.
1999 "Word and Syllable Lengths in East Slavonic", in: *Journal of Quantitative Linguistics,* 6_3; 235–238.

Royston, P.
1982 "An Extension of Shapiro and Wilk's *W* Test for Normality to Large Samples", in: *Applied Statistics, 31*; 115–124.

Schaeder, B.; Willée, G.
1989 "Computergestützte Verfahren morphologischer Beschreibung." In: Bátori, I.S.; Lenders, W.; Putschke,W. (eds.), *Computerlinguistik. An International Handbook on Computer Oriented Language Research and Applications.* Berlin/New York. (188–203).

Srebot-Rejec, T.
1981 "On the Allophones of /v/ in Standard Slovene", in: *Scando-Slavica, 27*; 233–241.

Srebot-Rejec, T.
2000 "Še o fonemu /v/ in njegovih alofonih", in: *Slavistična revija,* 48_1; 41–54.

2001 *Slovenski pravopis.* Ljubljana.

Tivadar, H.
1999 "Fonem /v/ v slovenskem govorjenem knjižnem jeziku", in: *Slavistična revija,* 47_3; 341–361.

Toporišič, J.
2000 *Slovenska slovnica.* Maribor.

Uhlířová, L.
1996 "How long are words in Czech?" In: Schmidt, P. (ed.), *Issues in General Linguistic Theory and The Theory of Word Length.* [= Glottometrika 15]. (134–146).

Uhlířová, L.
1997 "Word length Distribution in Czech: On the Generality of Linguistic Laws and Individuality of Texts." In: Best, K.-H. (ed.), *The Distribution of Word and Sentence Length.* [= Glottometrika 16.] (163–174).

Uhlířová, L.
1999 "Word Length Modelling: Intertextuality as a Relevant Factor?", in: *Journal of Quantitative Linguistics, 6*; 252–256.

Uhlířová, L.
2001 "On Word length, clause length and sentence length in Bulgarian", In: Uhlířová, L.; Wimmer, G.; Altmann, G.; Köhler, R. (eds.), *Text as a Linguistic Paradigm: Levels, Constituents, Constructs. Festschrift in honour of Luděk Hřebíček.* Trier. (266–282).

Unuk, D.
2001 *Zlog v slovenskem jeziku. Doktorska disertacija.* Maribor.

Wimmer, G.; Köhler, R.; Grotjahn, R.; Altmann, G.
1994 "Towards a Theory of Word Length Distribution", in: *Journal of Quantitative Linguistics, 1*; 98–106.

Wimmer, G.; Altmann, G.
1996 "The Theory of Word Length: Some Results and Generalizations." In: Schmidt, P. (ed.), *Issues in General Linguistic Theory and The Theory of Word Length.* [= Glottometrika 15.] Trier. (112–133).

Wimmer, G.; Altmann, G.
2005 "Towards a Unified derivation of Some Linguistic Laws." [In this volume]

Wurzel, W.U.
2000 "Was ist ein Wort?" In: Thieroff, R. et al. (eds.), *Deutsche Grammatik in Theorie und Praxis.* Tübingen. (29–42).

Appendix

Table 4.8: Sources of the Literary Prose Texts

Text #	Author	Title	ch.	Year
1-18	Cankar, Ivan	Hlapec Jernej in njegova pravica	1-18	1907
19-27		Hiša Marije pomočnice	1-9	1904
28		Mimo življenja	1	1920
29		O prešcah	1	1920
30		Brez doma	1	1903
31-33		Greh	1-3	1903
34		V temi	1-3	1903
35-40		Tinica	1-6	1903
41	Kočevar, Matija	Izgubljene stvari	1	2001
42		Ko je vsega konec	1	2001
43		Ko se vrnem v postelju	1	2001
44		Moja vloga	1	2001
45		Nevidni svet	1	2001
46		Noč	1	2001
47	Kočevar, Ferdo	Papežev poslanec	1	1892
48		Stiriperesna deteljica	1	1892
49		Sužnost	1	1892
50		Vbežnik vjetnik	1	1892
51		Volitev načelnika	1	1892
52		Grof in menih	1	1892

Table 4.9: Source of the Poetic Texts

Text #	Author	Title	Year
53	Gregorčič, Simon	Čas	1888
54		Človeka nikar!	1877
55		Cvete, cvete pomlad	1901
56		Daritev	1882
57		Domovini	1880
58		Izgubljeni raj	1882
59		Izgubljeni cvet	1882
60		Kako srčno sva se ljubila	1901
61		Kesanje	1882
62		Klubuj usodi	1908
63		Kropiti te ne smem	1902
64		Kupa življenja	1872
65		Moj crni plašč	1879
66		Mojo srčno kri škropite	1864
67		Na bregu	1908
68		Na potujčeni zemlji	1880
69		Na sveti večer	1882
70		Naša zvezda	1882
71		Njega ni!	1879
72		O nevihti	1878
73		Oj zbogom, ti planinski svet!	1879
74		Oljki	1882
75		Pogled v nedolžno oko	1882
76		Pozabljenim	1881
77		Pri zibelki	1882
78		Primula	1882
79		Sam	1872
80		Samostanski vratar	1882
81		Siroti	1882
82		Srce sirota	1882
83		Sveta odkletev	1882
84		Ti veselo poj!	1879
85		Tri lipe	1878
86		Ujetega ptica tožba	1878
87		V mraku	1870
88		Veseli pastir	1871

Table 4.9 (cont.)

Text #	Author	Title	Year
89	Gregorčič, Simon	Vojak na poti	1879
90		Zaostali ptič	1876
91		Zimski dan	1879
92		Življenje ni praznik	1878
93	Vodnik, Valentin	Zadovoljni kranjec (Zadovolne Kraync)	1806
94		Vršač	1806
95		Dramilo (Krajnc tvoja dežela je zdrava)	1795
96		Kos in brezen (Kos inu Sušic)	1798
97		Sraka in mlade (sraka inu mlade)	1790
98		Petelinčka (Pravlica)	1795
99		Ilirja oživljena	1811
100		Moj spominik	1810
101	Stritar, Josip	Konju	1888
102		Koprive	1888
103		Mladini	1868

Table 4.10: Characteristic Statistical Measures of the Texts

Text #	TL in words 0	TL in words $\emptyset$	TL in syllables	$\overline{W}_i$	$\overline{W}_{i(0)}$	Difference d
1	591	602	1088	1.8409	1.8073	0.0336
2	969	977	1665	1.7183	1.7042	0.0141
3	1029	1038	1807	1.7561	1.7408	0.0153
4	790	796	1403	1.7759	1.7626	0.0133
5	803	809	1395	1.7372	1.7244	0.0128
6	882	890	1611	1.8265	1.8101	0.0164
7	957	973	1743	1.8213	1.7914	0.0299
8	1447	1473	2608	1.8023	1.7705	0.0318
9	922	939	1679	1.8210	1.7881	0.0329
10	1121	1134	1956	1.7449	1.7249	0.0200
11	925	937	1675	1.8108	1.7876	0.0232
12	1191	1203	2177	1.8279	1.8096	0.0183
13	1558	1583	2828	1.8151	1.7865	0.0286
14	942	956	1691	1.7951	1.7688	0.0263
15	1376	1388	2502	1.8183	1.8026	0.0157
16	1188	1203	2138	1.7997	1.7772	0.0225
17	1186	1203	2127	1.7934	1.7681	0.0253
18	296	303	546	1.8446	1.8020	0.0426
19	2793	2836	5437	1.9467	1.9171	0.0296
20	2733	2775	5400	1.9759	1.9459	0.0300
21	3240	3271	6107	1.8849	1.8670	0.0179
22	3548	3588	6418	1.8089	1.7887	0.0202
23	4485	4547	8442	1.8823	1.8566	0.0257
24	3698	3761	6760	1.8280	1.7974	0.0306
25	3054	3090	5922	1.9391	1.9165	0.0226
26	3172	3220	5806	1.8304	1.8031	0.0273
27	2592	2616	4899	1.8900	1.8727	0.0173
28	1425	1448	2765	1.9404	1.9095	0.0309
29	4411	4452	7993	1.8121	1.7954	0.0167
30	970	978	1786	1.8412	1.8262	0.0150
31	2906	2944	5239	1.8028	1.7796	0.0232
32	2874	2902	4897	1.7039	1.6875	0.0164
33	2872	2890	4981	1.7343	1.7235	0.0108
34	3416	3458	6260	1.8326	1.8103	0.0223
35	1104	1115	2089	1.8922	1.8735	0.0187

Table 4.10 (cont.)

Text #	TL in words 0	$\emptyset$	TL in syllables	$\overline{W}_i$	$\overline{W}_{i(0)}$	Difference d
36	910	922	1665	1.8297	1.8059	0.0238
37	1086	1101	1987	1.8297	1.8047	0.0250
38	716	732	1290	1.8017	1.7623	0.0394
39	971	984	1841	1.8960	1.8709	0.0251
40	686	694	1288	1.8776	1.8559	0.0217
41	2337	2361	4380	1.8742	1.8551	0.0191
42	1563	1578	2982	1.9079	1.8897	0.0182
43	1493	1513	2748	1.8406	1.8163	0.0243
44	1458	1473	2852	1.9561	1.9362	0.0199
45	1999	2023	3763	1.8824	1.8601	0.0223
46	916	926	1750	1.9105	1.8898	0.0207
47	2388	2406	4601	1.9267	1.9123	0.0144
48	4899	4944	9346	1.9077	1.8904	0.0173
49	4120	4157	8009	1.9439	1.9266	0.0173
50	7380	7477	14188	1.9225	1.8976	0.0249
51	5018	5075	9707	1.9344	1.9127	0.0217
52	5528	5588	10524	1.9038	1.8833	0.0205
53	170	171	306	1.8000	1.7895	0.0105
54	228	228	393	1.7237	1.7237	0.0000
55	101	101	165	1.6337	1.6337	0.0000
56	81	81	151	1.8642	1.8642	0.0000
57	150	154	257	1.7133	1.6688	0.0445
58	48	48	92	1.9167	1.9167	0.0000
59	69	69	110	1.5942	1.5942	0.0000
60	121	124	208	1.7190	1.6774	0.0416
61	186	188	345	1.8548	1.8351	0.0197
62	37	37	54	1.4595	1.4595	0.0000
63	81	81	125	1.5432	1.5432	0.0000
64	62	62	110	1.7742	1.7742	0.0000
65	164	166	258	1.5732	1.5542	0.0190
66	69	69	121	1.7536	1.7536	0.0000
67	68	68	124	1.8235	1.8235	0.0000
68	193	193	307	1.5907	1.5907	0.0000
69	121	123	209	1.7273	1.6992	0.0281
70	70	71	121	1.7286	1.7042	0.0244

Table 4.10 (cont.)

Text #	TL in words 0	$\emptyset$	TL in syllables	$\overline{W}_i$	$\overline{W}_{i(0)}$	Difference d
71	109	110	183	1.6789	1.6636	0.0153
72	225	226	385	1.7111	1.7035	0.0076
73	167	167	259	1.5509	1.5509	0.0000
74	640	654	1151	1.7984	1.7599	0.0385
75	141	142	222	1.5745	1.5634	0.0111
76	131	131	216	1.6489	1.6489	0.0000
77	119	120	209	1.7563	1.7417	0.0146
78	129	129	209	1.6202	1.6202	0.0000
79	59	59	105	1.7797	1.7797	0.0000
80	246	247	445	1.8089	1.8016	0.0073
81	95	96	158	1.6632	1.6458	0.0174
82	70	70	120	1.7143	1.7143	0.0000
83	196	198	314	1.6020	1.5859	0.0161
84	181	181	266	1.4696	1.4696	0.0000
85	333	336	586	1.7598	1.7440	0.0158
86	248	252	414	1.6694	1.6429	0.0265
87	94	94	162	1.7234	1.7234	0.0000
88	134	135	240	1.7910	1.7778	0.0132
89	50	50	83	1.6600	1.6600	0.0000
90	137	138	242	1.7664	1.7536	0.0128
91	256	257	417	1.6289	1.6226	0.0063
92	176	177	311	1.7670	1.7571	0.0099
93	154	156	282	1.8312	1.8077	0.0235
94	165	166	308	1.8667	1.8554	0.0113
95	60	60	108	1.8000	1.8000	0.0000
96	126	127	211	1.6746	1.6614	0.0132
97	72	72	120	1.6667	1.6667	0.0000
98	23	23	44	1.9130	1.9130	0.0000
99	265	267	492	1.8566	1.8427	0.0139
100	87	87	155	1.7816	1.7816	0.0000
101	158	158	272	1.7215	1.7215	0.0000
102	411	413	725	1.7640	1.7554	0.0086
103	306	306	522	1.7059	1.7059	0.0000
104	714	724	1624	2.2745	2.2431	0.0314
105	510	519	1195	2,3431	2,3025	0,0406

Table 4.10 (cont.)

Text #	TL in words 0	TL in words ∅	TL in syllables	$\overline{W}_i$	$\overline{W}_{i(0)}$	Difference d
106	1932	1966	4344	2.2484	2.2096	0.0388
107	775	781	1659	2.1406	2.1242	0.0164
108	386	390	886	2.2953	2.2718	0.0235
109	314	319	658	2.0955	2.0627	0.0328
110	490	495	1144	2.3347	2.3111	0.0236
111	441	450	1118	2.5351	2.4844	0.0507
112	584	593	1251	2.1421	2.1096	0.0325
113	1560	1582	3533	2.2647	2.2332	0.0315
114	785	800	1772	2.2573	2.2150	0.0423
115	341	343	799	2.3431	2.3294	0.0137
116	681	687	1468	2.1557	2.1368	0.0189
117	573	590	1391	2.4276	2.3576	0.0700
118	312	319	750	2.4038	2.3511	0.0527
119	936	942	2008	2.1453	2.1316	0.0137
120	976	981	2217	2.2715	2.2599	0.0116
121	141	143	283	2.0071	1.9790	0.0281
122	460	463	1004	2.1826	2.1685	0.0141
123	291	295	688	2.3643	2.3322	0.0321
124	438	441	945	2.1575	2.1429	0.0146
125	254	256	582	2.2913	2.2734	0.0179
126	777	793	1853	2.3848	2.3367	0.0481
127	826	837	1878	2.2736	2.2437	0.0299
128	219	224	458	2.0913	2.0446	0.0467
129	202	203	474	2.3465	2.3350	0.0115
130	422	433	939	2.2251	2.1686	0.0565
131	394	402	843	2.1396	2.0970	0.0426
132	606	612	1357	2.2393	2.2173	0.0220
133	406	412	887	2.1847	2.1529	0.0318
134	397	406	825	2.0781	2.0320	0.0461
135	682	698	1646	2.4135	2.3582	0.0553
136	439	448	1009	2.2984	2.2522	0.0462
137	430	439	1007	2.3419	2.2938	0.0481
138	191	194	429	2.2461	2.2113	0.0348
139	200	170	484	2.4556	2.4412	0.0144
140	215	219	546	2.5395	2.4932	0.0463

Table 4.10 (cont.)

Text #	TL in words 0	TL in words $\emptyset$	TL in syllables	$\overline{W}_i$	$\overline{W}_{i(0)}$	Difference d
141	334	337	766	2.2934	2.2730	0.0204
142	138	139	302	2.1884	2.1727	0.0157
143	236	239	510	2.1610	2.1339	0.0271
144	214	218	461	2.1542	2.1147	0.0395
145	325	330	793	2.4400	2.4030	0.0370
146	827	836	1847	2.2334	2.2093	0.0241
147	114	117	269	2.3596	2.2991	0.0605
148	299	302	687	2.2977	2.2748	0.0229
149	200	201	484	2.4200	2.4080	0.0120
150	201	203	448	2.2289	2.2069	0.0220
151	162	164	372	2.2963	2.2683	0.0280
152	159	162	403	2.5346	2.4877	0.0469

Table 4.11: Proportion of x-syllable Words

			Syllables per word							
Text #	0	1	2	3	4	5	6	7	8	9
1	11	266	194	93	35	3				
2	8	478	325	130	33	3				
3	9	507	315	164	37	6				
4	6	376	250	131	32	1				
5	6	381	280	119	19	3	1			
6	8	434	237	151	50	10				
7	16	441	306	157	46	7				
8	26	672	449	270	52	4				
9	17	423	288	169	37	5				
10	13	560	336	181	39	5				
11	12	441	269	165	49	1				
12	12	566	339	213	71	2				
13	25	726	477	283	61	11				
14	14	466	265	156	48	7				
15	12	645	423	230	69	9				
16	15	573	361	185	58	10	1			
17	17	585	340	188	67	6				
18	7	136	94	46	16	4				
19	43	1126	944	500	197	22	3	1		
20	42	1099	872	527	203	29	2	1		
21	31	1397	1057	579	180	23	4			
22	40	1669	1104	581	174	18	2			
23	62	1961	1444	780	252	43	5			
24	63	1675	1223	592	180	25	3			
25	36	1326	895	573	218	37	5			
26	48	1472	1005	497	165	25	8			
27	24	1131	832	439	168	17	5			
28	23	581	477	255	96	15	1			
29	41	1993	1524	658	208	22	6			
30	8	452	313	130	59	14	2			
31	38	1386	886	474	143	15	2			
32	28	1460	918	389	101	6				
33	18	1424	924	406	99	19				
34	42	1540	1131	554	162	26	3			
35	11	474	353	214	51	10	1	1		
36	12	430	272	150	49	9				

Table 4.11 (cont.)

	Syllables per word									
Text #	0	1	2	3	4	5	6	7	8	9
37	15	508	315	210	46	7				
38	16	336	226	118	32	4				
39	13	434	288	177	62	8	2			
40	8	302	216	128	32	7	1			
41	24	1067	695	404	148	20	2	1		
42	15	692	462	289	102	17	1			
43	20	691	446	270	76	9	1			
44	15	643	399	278	115	21	2			
45	24	890	615	360	110	21	3			
46	10	400	271	182	53	10				
47	18	1021	744	433	159	29	2			
48	45	2102	1599	805	340	47	6			
49	37	1724	1282	784	283	45	2			
50	97	3101	2398	1327	473	68	13			
51	57	2117	1589	917	327	56	11	1		
52	60	2381	1770	974	344	50	8	1		
53	1	72	62	34	2					
54	119	66	33	7	3					
55	50	39	11	1						
56	27	38	16							
57	4	75	48	22	5					
58	21	14	9	4						
59	35	27	7							
60	3	58	42	18	3					
61	2	77	63	42	4					
62	26	5	6							
63	42	34	5							
64	26	25	10	1						
65	2	98	44	16	6					
66	29	29	10	1						
67	27	26	15							
68	106	63	21	3						
69	2	59	37	24	1					
70	1	29	33	6	2					

Table 4.11 (cont.)

	Syllables per word									
Text #	0	1	2	3	4	5	6	7	8	9
71	1	45	55	8	1					
72	1	104	84	35	2					
73		99	50	12	6					
74	14	278	226	125	9	2				
75	1	78	47	14	2					
76		65	49	15	2					
77	1	50	48	21						
78		65	49	14	1					
79		25	23	10	1					
80	1	104	91	45	6					
81	1	48	34	11	3					
82		30	33	4	3					
83	2	103	69	23	1					
84		107	63	11						
85	3	151	117	59	6					
86	4	123	89	32	3	1				
87		40	41	12	1					
88	1	57	53	24	2					
89		22	23	5						
90	1	61	49	25	2					
91	1	131	93	28	4					
92	1	81	58	34	3					
93	2	64	55	32	3					
94	1	55	84	19	7					
95		23	27	9	1					
96	1	53	62	10	1					
97		36	25	10	1					
98		10	6	6	1					
99	2	115	85	54	10	1				
100		38	31	17	1					
101		69	67	19	3					
102	2	187	145	70	7	2				
103		144	117	37	7	1				
104	10	267	167	145	96	32	5	2		
105	9	167	127	122	68	20	6			

Table 4.11 (cont.)

	Syllables per word									
Text #	0	1	2	3	4	5	6	7	8	9
106	34	699	484	443	210	75	15	5	1	
107	6	278	236	163	77	15	5	1		
108	4	142	82	99	38	19	6			
109	5	124	76	82	25	6	1			
110	5	170	113	120	54	27	5	1		
111	9	132	94	110	72	23	5	5		
112	9	220	155	134	60	12	2	1		
113	22	564	359	368	209	52	5	3		
114	15	280	201	174	87	38	5			
115	2	121	69	90	45	9	5	1	1	
116	6	259	185	147	58	27	4	1		
117	17	179	139	128	94	26	5	2		
118	7	87	81	95	36	7	5	1		
119	6	362	256	182	99	30	7			
120	5	326	269	216	134	24		7		
121	2	54	47	26	13	1				
122	3	187	108	85	62	10	8			
123	4	103	61	76	29	14	7	1		
124	3	178	112	77	46	23	1	1	0	
125	2	97	60	48	31	13	3	2		
126	16	254	174	191	127	19	9	3		
127	11	295	200	201	80	41	8	1		
128	5	74	80	43	17	3	2			
129	1	65	61	33	30	10	3			
130	11	150	118	86	49	17	1		1	
131	8	164	89	88	37	11	2	2	1	
132	6	227	137	149	62	27	2	2		
133	6	156	104	79	51	14	2			
134	9	170	103	68	43	8	2	3		
135	16	202	174	174	98	26	4	4		
136	9	141	121	105	57	10	2	3		
137	9	148	104	96	54	22	5	1		
138	3	66	50	45	24	4	2			
139	1	54	38	39	25	11	1	1		
140	4	71	38	43	45	18				

Table 4.11 (cont.)

	Syllables per word									
Text #	0	1	2	3	4	5	6	7	8	9
141	3	108	94	84	31	13	1	1	2	
142	1	54	30	32	19	2	1			
143	3	95	52	58	21	7	3			
144	4	86	49	50	22	5	2			
145	5	101	72	90	40	16	4	2		
146	9	307	200	189	90	35	4	2		
147	3	42	23	24	16	9				
148	3	107	73	61	39	19				
149	1	69	36	53	32	7	2			1
150	2	73	49	52	16	9	2			
151	2	52	41	40	27	2				
152	3	46	33	49	20	6	3		2	

5

WITHIN-SENTENCE DISTRIBUTION AND RETENTION OF CONTENT WORDS AND FUNCTION WORDS

August Fenk, Gertraud Fenk-Oczlon

1. Serial Position Effects in the Recall of Sentences

Experiments with free immediate recall of lists of unconnected words usually reveal a saddle-shaped 'serial position curve': high frequency of recall in the items obtaining the first positions ('primacy effect') of the list and those obtaining the last positions ('recency effect'), and, in the words of Murdock Jr., "a horizontal asymptote spanning the primacy and recency effect" (cf. Figure 5.1).

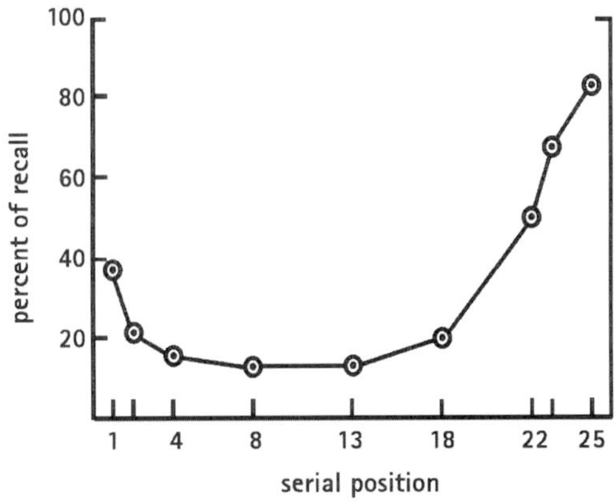

Figure 5.1: A "Typical" Serial Position Curve Resulting From Immediate Free Recall of Unconnected Words (Murdock Jr. 1962: 484, modified)

Murdock Jr. (1962: 488) suggested "that the shape of the curve may well result from proactive and retroactive inhibition effects occurring within the list itself." Assumptions regarding the underlying mechanisms became more differentiated

P. Gryzbek (ed.), Contributing in the Science of Text and Language, 157-170.

in later experiments introducing – in addition to input-order – sense-modality of list presentation as a second independent variable (Murdock & Walker 1969) and evaluating – in addition to frequency of recall – output-order in recall as a second dependent variable (Fenk 1979). Many of the relevant psychological findings seem to be interesting for linguistics as well: the results reported e.g. by Murdock Jr. (1962) suggesting that the recency effect extends over the last 7 plus minus 2 words; the observation of Murdock & Walker (1969) that in auditory presentation the recency effect is higher and more extensive than in visual presentation ('modality effect'); the observation that 'sequential clusters', i.e. word groups with the words recalled in the same order as represented, are in the recency part of auditorily presented word strings significantly larger and significantly more frequent than in the recency part of visually presented word strings – in series of unconnected nouns as well as in real sentences, and despite the tendency to start the recall of auditorily presented word strings with words and word groups from the end of the string (Fenk 1979: 14). Of particular linguistic interest is the question whether the serial position effects shown in the recall of lists of unconnected words show in the recall of real sentences as well. Are the underlying processes also efficient in real sentence processing and in connected discourse?

Indications reported so far (Jarvella 1971; Fenk 1979, 1981; Rummler 2003) are not fully convincing: In Jarvella's study, subjects were presented sentences like "... Having failed to disprove the charges, Taylor was later fired by the president" (p. 410). The fragment starting with "Taylor..." is not only localized in the 'recency part' of the sentence but also represents the main constituent of this sentence, so that one has to suspect a confusion of the effects of these conditions. The marked and plateau-shaped 'recency effect' in the serial position curves (p. 411) might suggest some additive effects on the performance of recall (see Figure 5.2).

Rummler (2003: 96) states that the so-called "subordination effect" (subordinating conjunctions achieve a better verbatim recall than coordinating conjunctions) mainly comes off by better retention of the second clause. This better recall of the second clause might again be a consequence of the restricted "span" of the recency effect and/or of the fact that in the subordinating conjunction the internal redundancy is higher and the informational content (and cognitive load) of the second clause lower than in the coordinating conjunction.

The serial position curve reported by Fenk (1981: 25) shows a marked recency effect (only) in auditory presentation of the sentence. (And, in addition, an 'inverse modality effect', i.e. a superiority of visual presentation in the primacy part.) But these results originate from only two different sentences presented simultaneously in two different sense modalities.

For a more systematic approach, the subjects in an experiment by Auer, Bačik & Fenk (2001) were presented a text by Glasersfeld (1998). Speech was interrupted

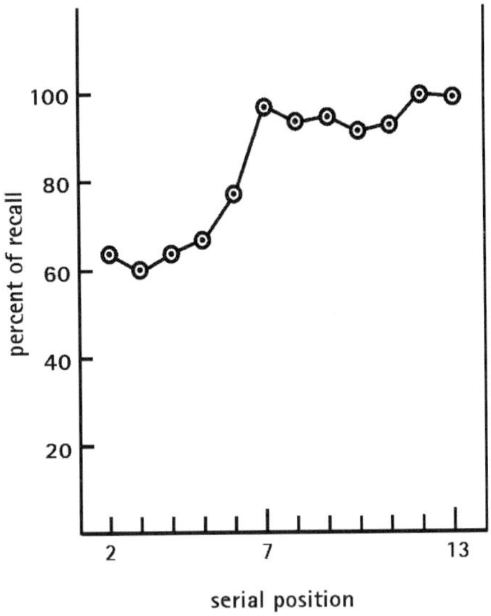

Figure 5.2: One of the Serial Position Curves For Free Recall of Sentences (Jarvella 1971: 414, modified)

after some of the sentences by a certain signal. Subjects were instructed to write down as much as they could remember from the last sentence before the test pause. Since the position of a word is by far not the only factor determining its chance to be recalled, the serial position curves obtained differ not only from the "ideal" curve (Figure 5.1) that approximately shows when different groups of subjects are presented different lists with the single items changing their positions in systematic rotation. They differed also from sentence to sentence, since these individual sentences ($n = 10$) differed in all possible respects – lexemes, syntactic structure, length. Nevertheless the family of curves shows a (rather weak) primacy effect and a marked recency effect. Data from this experiment were re-analyzed in order to investigate further questions.

2. Wordclass-specific Effects on the Serial Position Curve?

2.1 Two hypotheses

The aim of our statistical reanalysis was to test the following assumptions:

Hypothesis 1
In content words the likelihood of recalling is higher than in function words.

Hypothesis 2
In the recency part the difference predicted in assumption I will be smaller than in earlier parts of the serial position curve.

The basic consideration leading to these assumptions was that the fundamental difference between content words and function words (a) should be in some way reflected in sentence processing, especially in our 'semantic memory' (b).

Ad (a):

Within linguistics, content words are often characterized as 'open class words' opposed to function words as 'closed class words'. Rather relevant with respect to our hypotheses is the fact that content words are more significant for the specific topic, just for the particular and concrete 'content' of texts and sentences, while the function of function words is to bring about certain references between more or less exchangeable contents and content words. In brief: The relevant division here is between context-specific content words and rather context-independent function words. Function words are, moreover, rather short, very frequent, and 'multifunctional' in the sense of Zipf (1949).

Ad (b):

A widely accepted model concerning our memory says: After having extracted the meaning of an actual clause, its verbatim form (words and syntax) is rapidly lost from memory, while the meaning is preserved (and affects e.g. our interpretation of the following clauses). This conception is strongly influenced by Sachs (1967). Her findings could be reproduced in later experiments by Luther & Fenk (1984) which showed moreover that this outcome is not grounded in the nature and incapability of our long term memory but is the result of a cognitive strategy which is successful under 'normal' conditions, i.e. in the absence of the instruction and motivation to concentrate on other aspects of sentences.

This principle – rapid loss of the form after the meaning has been extracted – is actually also supported by two findings already mentioned in the present paper:

(i) The tendency to repeat some of the words in the 'input order' especially from the recency part of auditorily presented word strings (Fenk 1979: 14) indicates that verbatim representation is a speciality of immediate acoustic memory.

(ii) The plateau at the end of Jarvella's (1971) serial position curves. Jarvella's comment on his findings:

> "Various verbatim measures of recall support only the immediate sentence and immediately heard clause as retrievable units in memory" (p. 409). "Apparently only these immediate sentences hold a retrievable form in memory; this form also leads to superior recall of their most recent clause. On the other hand, recall of previous sentences indicates that they had received a relatively thorough semantic interpretation. It appears that the propositional meaning of sentences was remembered shortly after they were heard, although, as measured by verbatim recall, the form of sentences was quickly forgotten" (p. 415).

2.2 Method

In order to test our assumptions, each of the test-sentences used in the Auer, Bačik & Fenk experiment was divided into four quarters, rounding off where necessary. The first quarter (I) was defined as the primacy part of the sentence, II and III taken together as the medium part, and the last 25 percent of the words (IV) as the recency part. Then we determined, separately for the three parts (I, II+III, IV) of each sentence, the number of content words – nouns, verbs, adjectives, manner adverbs – and the number of function words such as articles, prepositions, pronouns, conjunctions, negations, particles, auxiliary verbs.

Our operationalization of 'primacy part' (first 25% of words) and 'recency part' (last 25% of words) might, at a first glance, appear as a rather arbitrary and rough method, since a 'quarter' means different things in sentences of differing length: e.g. five words in a 20-word sentence or ten words in a 40-word sentence. But the alternative – to define the primacy part and the recency part in terms of a fixed number of words – would again be arbitrary: How many words should be fixed? And it would restrict the application to rather long sentences: A fixed number of, let us say, six words for the primacy part and six words for the recency part would, in the case of a 12-word sentence, reduce the 'medium part' to zero, and would exclude shorter sentences altogether.

Our operationalization, however, offers a wide range of applications and establishes a firm proportion between, on the one hand, the primacy and recency part, and, on the other hand, the part in between and the sentence as a whole. And it has proved to bring about significant results.

2.3 Results

A problem for the quantification of a primacy and recency effect in our two word classes was the unexpected observation that the proportion of content words to function words showed a considerable variation between the interesting parts of the sentences. Thus, a quantification in absolute terms did not make much sense, and the recall scores had to be related to the number of words presented. Table 5.1 lists the results – number of words occurring, number of words recalled, and the 'relative' recall scores R/O.

Table 5.1: Number of Words Occurring (O) in and Recalled (R) from the First Quarter (I), the Medium Part (II + III), and the Last Quarter (IV) of a Total of 10 Sentences; R/O = Mean Frequency of Recall Per Word Given

	I			II + III			IV		
Wordclasses	O	R	R/O	O	R	R/O	O	R	R/O
Content Words (C)	22	55	2.5000	75	152	2.0267	37	132	3.5676
Function Words (F)	37	68	1.8378	68	98	1.4412	25	75	3.0000
Total ($C + F$)	59	123	2.0847	143	250	1.7483	62	207	3.3387
Difference ($C - F$)			0.6622			0.5855			0.5676
Level of significance (p)			$< 5\%$			$< 5\%$			$< 1\%$

The results of the statistical evaluation (Wilcoxon tests) in words:

- The primacy effect – the gradient we can see in Figure 5.3 between middle part and primacy part – was not significant.
- The recency effect, i.e. the gradient between middle part and recency part, was more marked (Figure 5.3) and was significant in all possible evaluations: in the content words ($p < 1\%$), in the function words ($p < 2\%$), and when both word classes were taken together ($p < 1\%$).
- **Hypothesis 1** was clearly confirmed: Level of relative recall scores was significantly higher in content words than in function words throughout the sentences. (Table 5.1 presents in its lowest line the error probabilities for parts I, II+III, and IV).
- **Hypothesis 2** would predict a convergence between the recall curves for content words and function words at least between the middle part and the recency part (Figure 5.3). Actually there is, as can be seen from the values in Table 5.1, a slight convergence from I to II+III and from II+III to IV. But in both cases this convergence is far from significant.

3. Three More or Less Hypothetical Regularities

The formulation of the first of the following assumptions is motivated by the occasional observation that our test sentences taken from a Glasersfeld text showed a tendency of an increase of content words and a decrease of function words during a sentence. As to this tendency we carried out a little follow-up

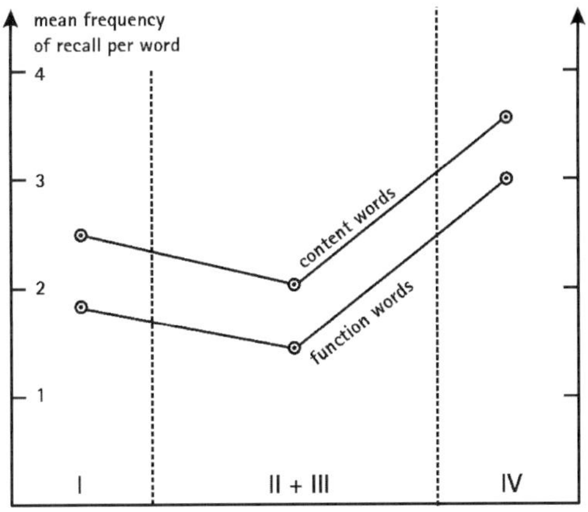

Figure 5.3: Differences Between Content and Function Words in a Serial Position Curve For Free Recall of Sentences of Different Length (I = first quarter, IV = last quarter)

study (3.1). Results strongly indicate that this is a general tendency at least in German texts. And if our tentative explanation (section 4) of this regularity holds, its scope should not be restricted to German texts.

Regularities 3.2 and 3.3 have the status of as yet unexamined lawlike hypotheses.

Regularity 3.2 proceeds from the assumption that the token frequency of function words is higher than the token frequency of content words. If these function words tend to occupy initial positions of sentences, this should contribute to the regularity "the more frequent before the less frequent". This statistical regularity has proven to be the most powerful one in the explanation of word order in frozen conjoined expressions (Fenk-Oczlon 1989), and it seems that its range of validity can be extended on clauses in general. In this present paper we will state this generalized rule mainly as an inferential step to our third regularity (3.3) which perfectly fits with the topic of this volume on "word length".

3.1 Decrease of Function Words and Increase of Content Words Within Sentences

As Table 5.1 shows, function words tend to decrease and content words to increase in the course of a sentence. Figure 5.4 illustrates these tendencies.

Despite the small sample of only ten sentences, the relevant differences proved to be significant in the Wilcoxon test (Table 5.2).

These differences in the distribution of the instances of the two word classes were, as already mentioned in section 2.3, a problem for a simple evaluation of the recall scores. But we suspected that it might indicate an interesting

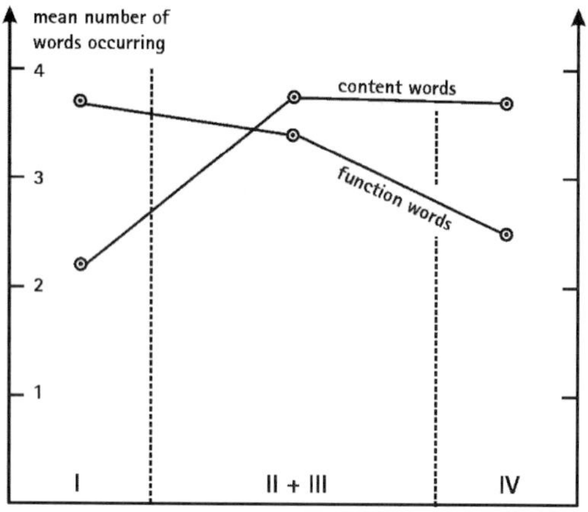

Figure 5.4: Differences Found in the Within-Sentence Distribution of Content and Function Words

phenomenon within the scope of quantitative linguistics – provided, that these tendencies are not a special feature of a certain text of a certain author. A pilot study was conducted in order to find some indications of possible generalizations of this tendency. The sample of authors was increased – nine more German text passages, four of them from scientific books, five from literary books. Taken together with the already analysed text passages from Glasersfeld this is a sample of ten (five scientific, five literary) text passages, and a sample of ten sentences from each of these passages, i.e. a total of $10 \times 10 = 100$ sentences. (Source texts are listed at the end of the paper.)

Table 5.2: Differences Between the Frequency of Function Words and Content Words Occurring in the Primacy Part (I) and in the Recency Part (IV) of 10 Sentences from a Text by Glasersfeld (1998)

difference	quarter I – quarter IV	error probability
function words	12	$p < 1\%$
content words	-15	$p < 1\%$
difference	function w. – content w.	
quarter I	15	$p < 1\%$
quarter IV	-12	$p < 5\%$

The evaluation was carried out by a student who did not know our assumptions. She was instructed not to collect ten successive sentences from each passage into the sample, but – where possible – each third sentence. Sometimes she had to overleap more than two sentences, e.g. when one of the intervening 'sentences' was too short (less than four words) or the heading of a new section. As already suggested by Niehaus (1997: 221), a colon was accepted as the end of the sentence when the following word started with a capital letter. The results: The gradient of the decrease of function words and increase of content words from the first quarter to the last quarter is not as steep as in Glasersfeld, but still significant (Fenk-Oczlon & Fenk 2002). These results suggest that the tendency of function words to decrease and of content words to increase in the course of a sentence is a general tendency at least in German texts. And the provisional results of Müller (in preparation) indicate that this tendency is not restricted to German texts.

3.2 The More Frequent Before the Less Frequent

This regularity was originally stated in order to explain and predict the order of the two main elements forming a frozen conjoined expression such as *knife and fork*, *salt and pepper*, *peak and valley*. From all the rules examined (e.g. "short before long", "the first word has fewer initial consonants than the second"), the rule "the more frequent before the less frequent" showed the highest explanatory power as to the word order in 400 freezes (Fenk-Oczlon 1989). Our regularity 3.1 should establish or enhance such a tendency in sentences as well to the effect that regularity 3.2 is not restricted to freezes.

If the tendency "the more frequent before the less frequent" fits to sentences as well – as a consequence of 3.1 or for whatever reason – then it is plausible to assume a further regularity:

3.3 Increase of Word Length in the Course of a Sentence

A more general regularity of this sort was already postulated in Behaghel (1909): "Das Gesetz der wachsenden Glieder", i.e. "the law of increasing elements, parts, links, constituents...". Behaghel illustrates this law with many examples from classical texts in a variety of languages such as ancient Greek, Latin, Old High German and German. In most of his examples the comparison was between word groups of different size or between single words and word groups: *auf der* ***Türbank*** *und im* ***dunklen Gang*** (p. 110), ***ih*** *inti* ***father min*** (p. 111). In a little experiment by Behaghel the subjects got four sheets of paper with the following words and word groups: *Gold / edles Geschmeide / und / sie besitzt*. They were instructed to form a sentence from these fragments, and the result was always the same: sie besitzt ***Gold*** und ***edles Geschmeide***. (Behaghel 1909: 137). He offers the following interpretation:

> Man wird nicht nur die länger dauernde Arbeit auf den Zeitraum verlegen, wo man den Abschluß leichter hinausschieben kann; man wird auch, wenn man sich Zeit lassen kann, die Arbeit gründlicher tun, mehr ins Einzelne gehen, oder, sprachlich ausgedrückt: man wird nicht nur für den umfangreicheren Ausdruck die spätere Stelle wählen, sondern auch für die spätere Stelle den umfangreicheren Ausdruck sich zubereiten. So bildet sich unbewußt in den Sprachen ein eigenartiges rhythmisches Gefühl, die Neigung, vom kürzeren zum längeren Glied überzugehen; so entwickelt sich das, was ich, um einen ganz knappen Ausdruck zu gewinnen, als das *Gesetz der wachsenden Glieder* bezeichnen möchte. (Behaghel 1909: 138f.)

Our regularity "increase of word length during a sentence" is similar to Behaghel's law but more specific in that it is localized at the single word level. A special case of Behaghel's law, so to speak! At present we cannot offer results of empirical tests of this lawlike assumption. (But see Müller, in preparation.) But we can contribute two new perspectives:

1. An operationalization that allows for a statistical examination of the law: Define words as the relevant 'Glieder' or 'constituents', determine their 'size' in terms of 'number of syllables', and compare the mean size of words in the early and late parts of sentences.
2. An interpretation specifying a concrete factor that might at least contribute to the rhythmic pattern described by Behaghel. This factor is the concentration or accumulation of function words in the first parts of clauses (sentences, subordinate clauses). And since function words are generally extremely frequent and frequent words tend – for economic reasons – to be rather short (Zipf 1929, 1949), the concentration of these rather short units in the first part of clauses results in an increase of the mean word length in the course of a sentence. This hypothesized tendency will of course depend on the respective language type and is expected to be more pronounced in languages with a tendency to agglutinative morphology and a tendency to OV order.

4. Conclusions

A possible explanation for our regularity "decrease of function words and increase of content words": In a running text, almost any clause has to refer to what was said in the clauses before ("old before new", "topic before comment", "theme before rheme"). This reference is – most probably not only in German texts – first of all brought about by function words (e.g. anaphoric pronouns, conjunctions) right at the beginning of the new clause. If this is an appropriate explanation of our regularity 3.1, then it is – indirectly – also relevant for the hypothesized regularities 3.2 "the more frequent before the less frequent" and 3.3 "within-sentence increase of word length". The last steps of the arguments in other words: Function words accumulate at the beginning of clauses; they are very frequent and 'therefore' very short in terms of number of syllables; members of our second word class 'content words' are, on average, composed of a higher number of syllables, and the number of these content words tends to increase during the sentence. This means, first of all: The regularity "the more frequent before the less frequent" found in frozen binomials holds true for sentences as well. As a consequence, one may expect an increase of word length in the course of a sentence. All the regularities outlined above ("the more frequent before the less frequent", "short before long") fit to and contribute to the more general law (Fenk-Oczlon 2001) of an economic and rather 'constant' flow of linguistic information.

5. Appendix: Sources of the Test Sentences

Bachmann, I. (1980 [1971]). Malina. Frankfurt: Suhrkamp Verlag (suhrkamp taschenbuch 641).
▷ pp. 200–202, beginning with section "Malina ist ..."

Frisch, M. (1975). Montauk. Gütersloh: Bertelsmann Reinhard Mohn OHG.
▷ pp. 157–159, beginning with section "Money"

Gigerenzer, G., Swijtink, Z., Porter, Th., Daston, L., Beatty, J., Krüger, L. (1999). Das Reich des Zufalls. Heidelberg/Berlin: Spektrum Akademischer Verlag.
▷ pp. 212–213, beginning with section "5.8 Diskontinuität, eine Grundlage aller Veränderung"

Glasersfeld, E. von (1998). Konstruktivismus statt Erkenntnistheorie. In: W. Dörfler & J. Mitterer (eds.), Ernst von Glasersfeld – Konstruktivismus statt Erkenntnistheorie. Klagenfurt: Drava Verlag.
▷ pp. 11–17

Hesse, H. (1972). Der Steppenwolf. Gütersloh: Bertelsmann Reinhard Mohn OHG
▷ pp. 269–271, beginning with section "Die Fremdenstadt im Süden"

Mann, Th. (5. Aufl. 1997 [1947]). Doktor Faustus. Frankfurt a. M.: Fischer Taschenbuch Verlag.
▷ pp. 47–50, beginning with section "VI"

Musil, R. (1960; A. Frisé, ed.). Der Mann ohne Eigenschaften. Stuttgart: Deutscher Bücherbund.
▷ pp. 445–447, beginning with section "98. Aus einem Staat, der an einem Sprachfehler zugrundegegangen ist"

Niehaus, B. (1997). Untersuchung zur Satzlängenhäufigkeit im Deutschen. In: Best, K.-H. (ed.), The Distribution of Word and Sentence Length. Glottometrika 16, Quantitative Linguistics 58, 213–275. Trier: WVT Wissenschaftlicher Verlag Trier.
▷ pp. 263–264, beginning with section "6. Ausblick"

Spies, M. (1993). Unsicheres Wissen. Heidelberg/Berlin/Oxford: Spektrum Akademischer Verlag.
▷ pp. 20–21, beginning with section "3. Perspektive: Kognitive Modelle der Informationsverarbeitung"

Stegmüller, W. (1957). Das Wahrheitsproblem und die Idee der Semantik. Wien: Springer-Verlag.
▷ pp. 38–40, beginning with section "III. Die Trennung von Objekt- und Metasprache als Weg zur Lösung und die Idee der Semantik als exakter Wissenschaft. Semantische Systeme von elementarer Struktur"

References

Auer, L.; Bačik, I.; Fenk, A.
2001 "Die serielle Positionskurve beim Behalten echter Sätze." Vortrag am 26.10.2001 im Rahmen der 29. Österreichischen Linguistiktagung in Klagenfurt.

Behaghel, O.
1909 "Beziehungen zwischen Umfang und Reihenfolge von Satzgliedern", in: *Indogermanische Forschungen, 25*; 110–142.

Fenk, A.
1979 "Positionseffekte und Reihenfolge der Wiedergabe bei optisch und akustisch gebotenen Wortketten", in: *Archiv für Psychologie / Archives of Psychology, 132(1)*; 1–18.

Fenk, A.
1981 " 'Ein Bild sagt mehr als tausend Worte...?' Lernleistungsunterschiede bei optischer, akustischer und optisch-akustischer Präsentation von Lehrmaterial", in: *AV-Forschung, 23*; 3–50.

Fenk-Oczlon, G.
1989 "Word frequency and word order in freezes", in: *Linguistics, 27*; 517–556.

Fenk-Oczlon, G.
2001 "Familiarity, information flow, and linguistic form." In: Bybee, J.; Hopper, P. (eds.), *Frequency and the emergence of linguistic structure.* Amsterdam / Philadelphia. (431–448).

Fenk-Oczlon, G.; Fenk, A.
2002 "Zipf's Tool Analogy and word order", in: *Glottometrics, 5*; 22–28.

Jarvella, R.J.
1971 "Syntactic processing of connected speech", in: *Journal of Verbal Learning and Verbal Behavior, 10*; 409–416.

Luther, P.; Fenk, A.
1984 "Wird der Wortlaut von Sätzen zwangsläufig schneller vergessen als ihr Inhalt?", in: *Zeitschrift für experimentelle und angewandte Psychologie, 31*; 101–123.

Müller, B.
in prep. *Die statistische Verteilung von Wortklassen und Wortlängen in lateinischen, italienischen und französischen und italienischen Sätzen.* Phil. Diss., University of Klagenfurt.

Murdock, B.B., Jr.
1962 "The serial position effect in free recall", in: *Journal of Experimental Psychology, 64*, 482–488.

Murdock, B.B.; Walker, K.D.
1969 "Modality effects in free recall", in: *Journal of Verbal Learning and Verbal Behavior, 8*; 665–676.

Niehaus, B.
1997 "Untersuchung zur Satzlängenhäufigkeit im Deutschen." In: Best, K.-H. (ed.), *The Distribution of Word and Sentence Length.* Trier. (213–275). [= Glottometrika 16, Quantitative Linguistics; 58]

Rummler, R.
2003 "Das kurzfristige Behalten von Sätzen", in: *Psychologische Rundschau, 54(2)*; 93–102.

Sachs, J.S.
1967 "Recognition memory for syntactic and semantic aspects of connected discourse", in: *Perception & Psychophysics, 2(9)*; 437–442.

Zipf, G.K.
1929 "Relative frequency as a determinant of phonetic change", in: *Harvard Studies in Classical Philology, 40*; 1–95.

Zipf, G.K.
1949 *Human behavior and the principle of least effort. An introduction to human ecology.* Cambridge, Mass. [^{2}1972, New York.]

6

ON TEXT CORPORA, WORD LENGTHS, AND WORD FREQUENCIES IN SLOVENIAN

Primož Jakopin

1. Introduction

From the first beginnings in the mid-1990s, availability of electronic text corpora in Slovenian, all with an Internet user interface, has grown to a level comparable to many European languages with a long history of quantitative linguistic research. There are two established corpora with 100 million running words, an academic one which is freely accessible and a commercial one, prepared by industrial and academic partners. The two are complemented by a sizeable collection of works of fiction, available for reading in a free virtual library and several specialized corpora, compiled for the needs of particular institutions. The majority of Slovenian newspapers are also accessible online, at least in the form of selected articles.

Lists of word forms with frequencies can be downloaded in chunks of 1000 from the *Nova beseda* corpus, and a lemmatization service is also available from the companion page (`http://bos.zrc-sazu.si/dol_lem.html`). Online translation from Slovenian into English for short texts (up to 500 characters) is already at hand (`http://presis.amebis.si/prevajanje`), with English-Slovenian in preparation.

The basic infrastructure for word-length analysis is in place and in the following chapters these topics are discussed in some more detail.

2. Online Text Corpora

There are two online text corpora in the narrow sense of this word, each 100 million running words in size and each equipped with an Internet user interface including a concordancer and some other searching facilities. Other text collections have been built with different uses in mind and they complement the Slovenian corpus scene.

P. Gryzbek (ed.), Contributing in the Science of Text and Language, 171-185.

2.1 Nova beseda

Nova beseda is a text corpus, built and run by the Corpus Laboratory of the Fran Ramovš Institute of Slovenian Language ZRC SAZU. It is available to everyone, together with three monolingual dictionaries developed at the Institute, with word lemmatisation and word-frequency service, at the URL `http://bos.zrc-sazu.si`. The corpus was online in November 1999 with three million running words of fiction from the author's doctoral thesis, on the server of his then home university, Faculty of Arts, University of Ljubljana at the URL `http://www.ff.uni-lj.si/cortes`, under the name CORTES (CORpus of TExts in Slovenian). In April 2000 it was expanded with newspaper texts to 28 million words, and in May 2000 it was moved to the current server (in unforgettable circumstances) and given two more modest names: *Beseda* ('word' in Slovenian) for the fiction subcorpus and *Nova beseda* ('new word') for the complete corpus. Nova beseda was upgraded to 48 million words in September 2000, to 76 million words in October 2002, to 93 million words in April 2003 and to 100 million words of text in Slovenian in July 2003.

The current corpus contents can be classified as: DELO daily newspaper 1998–2003 – 88.5 million words, fiction – 5.6 million words (it includes the complete works of Drago Jančar, Ciril Kosmač and Ivan Cankar), non-fiction (essays, correspondence) – 1.0 million words, scientific and technical publications – 1.6 million words, Monitor computer magazine 1999–2001 – 3.2 million words and Viva healthy living magazine 2002–2003 – 0.5 million words. All texts have undergone an extensive word form check-up and correction process and so the level of noise is kept to a minimum (over 45,000 errors, mostly typing errors, but also other errors which usually appear during the preparation of electronic publications or its transfer from one format or platform to another, have been detected and corrected). The corpus web pages are accessed over 500 times a day and an overview of the referring URLs in the first three months of 2003 are shown in Table 6.1 (Jakopin 2003).

The domain `.net` is mostly used by Slovenian users from home (`siol.net` 12.155, `volja.net` 2.969, `slon.net` 237, `telemach.net` 227, `k2.net` 192, `amis.net`190), domain `.si` by in-house users, academic and office use, (`zrc-sazu.si` 8.642, `arnes.si` 2.411, `uni-lj.si` 873, `uni-mb.si` 631, `select-tech.si` 587, `delo.si` 424, `rtvslo.si` 370, `ijs.si` 183); there is also quite a sizeable amount of use from Italy (`interbusiness.it` 2.365) and Poland (`edu.pl` 1.747).

2.2 FIDA

FIDA is a text corpus (URL `http://www.fida.net`), compiled by four partners; two academic – the Faculty of Arts of the University of Ljubljana (whence the **F** at the beginning of the acronym FIDA, and the Jožef Stefan Institute pro-

Table 6.1: Identifiable Web Domains of the *Nova beseda* Users, January–March 2003

net	16.514	uk	165	dk	18	es	6	ch	2
si	15.058	edu	81	au	17	fr	6	il	2
it	2.435	hr	66	ca	16	mil	6	int	2
pl	1.792	de	56	bg	11	tw	6	mx	2
com	1.388	hu	56	be	9	lu	5	pt	2
yu	453	org	42	jp	9	sk	5	cn	1
cz	276	nl	27	lt	8	tr	5	info	1
at	203	ru	21	se	8	us	3	ro	1

viding the **I** in it) – and two commercial partner: DZS, a publishing house with a long history of lexical publications, including dictionaries (cf. the **D**. DZS was also the coordinator and leading partner. Amebis, the main Slovenian enterprise in the field of language resources, mostly spell-checkers, provides the **A** in FIDA). Publications about FIDA are in Slovenian (e.g. Gorjanc 1999), the corpus contains 100 million running words of mostly newspaper text, it went operational in 1999 and was completed in the first half of 2000; the corpus has remained unchanged since that time. The project, aiming at a reference corpus of modern Slovenian, has been financed by the two commercial partners and so is not freely available. Free use is restricted to 10 concordance lines per search and the number of concurrent free users is also limited; full use requires the signing of a contract which regulates eventual publications based on the use of the FIDA corpus and a yearly fee in the vicinity of 500€ per user.

2.3 Web Index NAJDI.SI

In the past two years NAJDI.SI (`http://www.najdi.si`), owned and operated by Noviforum from Ljubljana, has become the main Slovenian search engine with over 100,000 unique users per day (400,000 searches per day). Words from around 1.5 million web pages are included in its index, the amount of words in Slovenian can be estimated at around 500 million. An automatic procedure based on n-gram frequencies, is used to identify the page language – it is usually successful after two or three lines of text. The distribution of languages represented in March 2002 can be seen in Table 6.2 (Jakopin 2002).

The search engine's word index, as can be expected for such a source, contains a considerable amount of noise, which is reflected in a very large number of different tokens – close to 7,500,000. Nevertheless, it is an excellent source of new words in Slovenian. The search engine does not yet include a lemmatizer; a simple stemmer is used instead and it usually performs remarkably well. To

Table 6.2: NAJDI.SI Languages of Web Pages and Their Number

1.	Slovenian	920.215	12.	Polish	582	23.	Norwegian	82
2.	English	493.894	13.	Danish	580	24.	Bulgarian	20
3.	German	12.730	14.	Finnish	547	25.	Albanian	18
4.	Croatian	4.892	15.	Czech	499	26.	Korean	17
5.	Serbian	2.625	16.	Portuguese	471	27.	Ukrainian	10
6.	Italian	2.530	17.	Japanese	383	28.	Icelandic	4
7.	French	2.063	18.	Latin	305	29.	Arab	3
8.	Russian	1.851	19.	Dutch	248	30.	Macedonian	3
9.	Spanish	1.084	20.	Slovak	181	31.	Chinese	1
10.	Hungarian	848	21.	Swedish	161	32.	Greek	1
11.	Romanian	606	22.	Bosnian	147	33.	Thai	1

query for an individual word form without all its anticipated close relatives, a '+' (plus) character has to be entered in front of the word. The entry *prod* (Engl. *gravel*) delivers a lot of unwanted hits coming from *prodaja* (Engl. *sale*), while the entry +*prod* limits the search to a more sensible outcome.

2.4 Virtual Library BESeDA

BESeDA is a free service of electronic books in Slovenian, accessible through the web page `http://www.omnibus.se/beseda`. It is maintained in Stockholm by Franko Luin, a Slovenian from Triest. Over the past three years the collection of books, mainly fiction, all in well-designed, attractive and legible PDF format (clipboard copy is disabled), has grown to the current 281 titles with over 40,000 pages. It all began with some 20 works from the project *Zbirka slovenskih leposlovnih besedil* by Miran Hladnik, started in 1995, with books in HTML format and available through the web page `http://www.ijs.si/lit/leposl.html`. Besides many classic works from late 19th and early 20th century, mainly scanned in by Mr. Luin, BESeDA now also contains a sizeable proportion of modern literature, donated by the authors.

2.5 Evrokorpus and Evroterm

Evrokorpus (at `http://www.gov.si/evrokorpus`) was compiled from translation memory databases (mainly English and Slovenian), which were generated during the translation of EU legislation into Slovenian at the Translation department of the Government Office for European Affairs. The corpus with its own web interface (developed by Miran Željko) can be searched for free and contains more than 7 million words. Evrokorpus is accompanied by Evroterm, which is not a standard web dictionary with terms in two or more languages, but a terminology database of the translated acquis communautaire. The terminology in the database conforms to the characteristics of the fields of the

EU activities, the purpose of the database and the needs of users, mainly the translators. It contains more than 40,000 entries and in April 2003 alone there were 316,000 queries, which makes Evroterm the second most popular web page on the Slovenian government server (`www.gov.si`).

2.6 Electronic Theses and Dissertations

There have been several initiatives to make available, in full text, the academic theses, produced at the end of graduate, master's and doctoral studies. An example is an extensive collection at the Faculty of Economics at the University of Ljubljana (`http://www.cek.ef.uni-lj.si/dela`, 1107 titles, it does not include doctoral dissertations) with search on meta data and with full text accessible in PDF format. An inter-faculty project with much wider ambitions, involving electronic theses and dissertations, supported by a grant from the Ministry of Information Society, was initiated at the end of 2002 and at the beginning of 2003. It aimed at establishing the required logistical and software infrastructure for inclusion of all new master's and doctoral theses in a common data base with a corpus-like full text search engine and entire texts downloadable in PDF format. There are three participating faculties of the University of Ljubljana: the Faculty of Medicine, the Faculty of Arts and the Faculty of Mathemathics and Physics. Currently 51 theses are online (44 + 1 + 6); for the Faculty of Medicine the URL is `http://pelin.mf.uni-lj.si/ETD-mf`.

The awareness that academic production should be readily accessible is gaining momentum and probably the best path to take would be to open a way for the authors to publish their articles and monographs on the web themselves, without the intervention of a librarian and using the existing Co-operative Online Bibliographic System & Services (COBISS at the URL `http://cobiss.izum.si`). The idea has been suggested by Žiga Turk (Turk 2003) and though it is feared by many it is worth a shot. Democracy can be chaos but it is, however, also the most effective way of doing things.

2.7 Newspapers

There are eight daily newspapers in the Slovenian language, seven published in Slovenia and one in Italy. The more important five have a free online presence – not with complete coverage but with a selection of articles available in full text. *DELO* is the standard daily with wide reader coverage, it is published in Ljubljana and a selection of articles is available at the address `http://www.delo.si/delofax.php`. *Dnevnik* is the second daily from Ljubljana, a selection of the articles is available at `http://www.dnevnik.si`; its machine-translated English version, not what one would want, but nevertheless a start, can be found at `http://www.dnevnik.si/eng`. *Finance*, the Slovenian version of the Wall Street Journal also comes from Ljubljana, has a very neat internet interface and can be checked at `http://www.finance-on.net`. *Večer* is published in Maribor, covers the northeastern part of Slovenia and is available at `http://www.vecer.si`. *Primorski dnevnik* is published in Triest and covers the Slovenian readership in Italy; the newspaper is online at `http://www.primorski.it`.

There are many more weekly (103), biweekly and monthly (587) magazines in Slovenian and every year a larger number is available online, at least with a selection of articles. One of them is *Monitor*, a computer magazine with good coverage of modern technology, at `http://www.monitor.si`.

2.8 Other Initiatives

The idea of a complete text corpus which would contain everything published in Slovenian, has become technically feasible in the past several years (Jakopin 2002). Yearly growth has been estimated to roughly 1.5 billion words (Jakopin 2002: serial publications 1.0 billion, monographs 315 million and Internet pages at 150 million), an amount that could now be processed even on ordinary desktop computers. A copy of every printed publication is collected and stored by the national and university library (NUK), under an instrument of legal deposit. As virtually every publication nowadays is printed from a computer file, i.e. from electronic form, it would only make sense that the NUK would also act as a collector and guardian of those files. An initiative of the NUK for preservation of texts found on the web has come in the past two years (contribution of Alenka Kavčič-Čolić at the Digital library conference – at `http://www.zbds-zveza.si/eng_referati2001.html`) and recently also for storing the electronic layouts of printed material.

Besides all of the above mentioned text corpora or text collections there are also a few other, usually much smaller resources gathered by other centers of research in language technology, such as the web concordance service of the Department of Intelligent Systems at the Jožef Stefan Institute in Ljubljana, available at the URL `http://nl2.ijs.si/index-mono.html`.

3. Words, Word Lengths

More often than not, words are the basic units of linguistic research, and word lengths in particular are a very welcome object in quantitative linguistics (Grzybek 2000, 2002). The definition of a word was of no particular importance in classic works, such as grammars, but in corpus construction, for instance, it can be a real problem. How far to go, what to treat as a basic (word) token of a frequency dictionary? The following definitions of the term word represent some standard definitions and/or relevant references:

- "speech, utterance, verbal expression" – *The Oxford English Dictionary*, 1989, pp. 526–531.

- "six characters including spaces" – standard use by an editor in a publishing house, Rothman, C. 2001: *What is a word* – http://www.sfwa.org/writing/wordcount.htm
- "a single unit of language which has meaning and can be spoken or written" – *Cambridge International Dictionary of English* – http://dictionary.cambridge.org
- "a group of letters or sounds that mean something" – *Cambridge Learner's Dictionary* – http://dictionary.cambridge.org
- "a collection of letters indicating a concept" – Goldstein, D. L. (2001): *Hyperflow, hypertextual dictionary* – http://www.haileris.com/cgi-bin/dict
- "any segment of written or printed discourse ordinarily appearing between spaces or between a space and a punctuation mark, a number of bytes processed as a unit and conveying a quantum of information in communication and computer work" – Merriam-Webster 1997
- Di Sciullo, A.; Williams, E. (1987): *On the definition of word.* Cambridge, Mass.: MIT Press.

Most definitions are close to what one would intuitively expect – a sequence of letters that can be pronounced and has meaning. In corpus construction, large groups of tokens also emerge which do not fulfill the above criterion but which definitely have a meaning and which obviously should not be wasted. Usually these tokens amount to about 1–2% of the entire lot. The author of these lines described them as wordlike terms and as nonwords; they could be classified according to the following schemas (examples and frequencies, where given, are taken from the DELO 1998–2000 subcorpus, 47 million running words).

Wordlike terms from DELO 1998–2000

1. Hyphen-connected terms

Top 10:

le-ta, črno-bel, slovensko-hrvaški, hrvaško-slovenski, obveščevalno-varnosten, kmetijsko-gozdarski, cestno-hitrosten, operativno-komunikacijski, ekonomsko-socialen, hat-trick

10 longest:

plešem-v-sandalcih-in-pisanih-hlačah-in-mam-rada-Križanke-juhu, poveljniško-nadzorno-računalniško-komunikacijsko-obveščevalen, ta-gospa-pa-že-mora-znati-nemško-saj-je-hodila-v-slovensko-gimnazijo, bio-psiho-socialno-kulturno-zgodovinsko-ekonomsko-filozofski, gorenjsko-ljubljansko-dolenjsko-notranjsko-belokranjski, športno-poslovno-loterijsko-medijsko-

oglaševalski, francosko-ameriško-slovensko-judovsko-madžarski, vlada-o-tem-še-ni-razpravljala-bo-pa-v-kratkem, glicidilmetalkrilaten-etilen-dimetakrilaten, mi-si-balkansko-politiko-že-lahko-privoščimo

2. Words with Parentheses

total(itar)ne, T(ušar), uradni(č)ki, (tragi)komične, T(wist), U(rbančič), varne(jše)m, T(rakl), (u)branila, urednik(ca), var(ov)al, (trans)estetsko, učitelja(e), U(roš), V(asja), T(renet), (u)lov, U(šeničnik), (več)vrednosti, T(ul), upa(j)mo, V(alentin), (vele)mestnega, T(urner), (u)porabi, V(alič), velik(a)

3. Incomplete Words

.afukala, .aterna, .izda, j..i, k..c, pizd...ije, prapraprapra....predniki, prapra... vnuk, p...da, r..i, ...ski, slo...nske, sr...nje, s....a, .urba, zaje...vati..

Hyphen-connected terms can be quite long, the longest is 68 characters long, and in the ten longest there are five writer-invented multiword expressions, four adjectives, one noun, and a chemical formula. Words with parentheses are either explained abbreviations of names or two words written as one. Incomplete words would often look very strange if written without dots, and besides terms such as *prapra... vnuk* (Engl. *great-great... grandson*) they are all part of obscene speech.

Nonwords from DELO 1998–2000

1. **numbers**

   1. simple numbers
      5,400 instances (284,000 total frequency): *0, 1, 2, ..., 99, 100, ... 33455432112332233455432112321* – Ode to Joy by Ludwig van Beethoven (as keyed in for Ericsson GF 768 mobile phone)
   2. ordinal numbers
      1,100 instances (284,000 total frequency): *1., 2., 3., ...*
   3. composite numbers 250 instances (cumulative frequency 161.100): *6,5, 6:2, 7:5, 2:4, 50.000, 1,3, 1:0, 2:1, 4:6, 0:3, 1:4, 15.000,* the longest: *2.235.197.406.895.366.368.301.599.999* – about a group from Ipswich, playing whist
   4. number-prefixed adjectives and nouns
      6,000 instances (total frequency 42.000): *-leten (25800), -milijonski (195), -litrski (80), -sekunden (25), -lukenjski (12), -odstoten (8237), -kilometrski (189), -kilovolten (76), -megaherčen (25), -obletnica (12), -letnica (1499), -kraten (169), -kilogramski (75), -milijarden (24), -tisočglavi (11), -krat (1150), -minuten (159), -glavi (71), -palčen (24), -km (11), -članski (692), -oktanski (149), -tonski (62),*

-tedenski (20), -stranski (11), -metrski (528), -milimetrski (122), -l (45), -megavaten (19), -mesten (10), -m (452), -ti (110), -let (43), -gramski (18), -hektarski (10), -letnik (420), -metrovka (104), -centimetrski (41), -nadstropen (17), -kratnik (10), -dneven (373), -mesečen (103), -biten (32), -karaten (14), -mikronski (8), -urni (304), -kubičen (86), -sedežen (28), -vaten (12), -dolarski (8).

5. times and dates 2,010 instances (total frequency 108.500): *1999, 2000, 2000-2006, 15.5.2001*
6. ISBN, ISSN, ISO numbers: *ISBN 892, ISSN 19, ISO* 27 (total frequency 1394)
7. UDC (Universal Decimal Classification) classifiers
   550 instances (total frequency 860): *663.2(035), 666.1/.2 (497.4 Novo mesto) (091), 681.3.06(075.2), 681.816.61(497.4):929 Škrabl A.*
8. car license plate numbers
   1000 instances (total frequency 1030): *NM 94-83J, LJ LAZE*

2. **URLs, file names, dotted names**
   2,183 instances (total frequency 2,661): *offline@online = Festival of modern electronic art, b.ALT.ica Modern gallery (Ljubljana) project, Marcel.li Catalan artist Antunez Roca.*

3. **e-mail addresses**
   121 instances (total frequency 262): *abuse@arnes.si, alojzij.oblak@siol.net, 555555@linux.mobitel.si, anda.klancic@guest.arnes.si, amavko@yahoo.com*

4. **measures and weights**
   130 instances (total frequency 42,863): *m (17885), km (5926), cm (5661), kg (3475), h (2516), Mb (1200), g (774), km/h (716), min (671), l (644).*

Nonwords, especially numbers, represent the bulk of what in corpus does not fit the standard definition for word and if not treated properly they would seriously pollute the word form dictionary; each full URL, for instance, contains at least four strings of letters.

In Table 6.3, the most frequent word forms from three subcorpora of the *Nova beseda* corpus are shown, the complete works of Ciril Kosmač, probably most prominent mid-twentieth century writer (0.4 million running words, not much but delicately composed, he knew all his works by heart), the complete works of Ivan Cankar, the paramount master of Slovenian, from the early twentieth century (2 million words) and DELO, the main Slovenian newspaper 1998–2000 (47 million words).

Table 6.3: Top 20 Word Forms With Frequencies – C. Kosmač, I. Cankar, DELO

	Ciril Kosmač		Ivan Cankar		DELO 1998–2000	
1.	je	25.798	je	123.281	je	1 570.404
2.	in	18.471	in	78.807	v	1 350.680
3.	se	13.330	se	56.101	in	1 171.370
4.	v	7.809	v	38.931	na	759.128
5.	da	5.412	da	34.552	za	656.814
6.	na	5.124	na	25.983	se	604.642
7.	pa	4.625	ne	24.117	da	583.347
8.	so	4.243	so	22.109	so	561.073
9.	ne	3.695	bi	21.678	ki	510.010
10.	bi	3.221	sem	19.675	pa	472.056
11.	z	3.181	ni	14.182	z	344.917
12.	ga	3.039	pa	13.796	tudi	332.187
13.	ki	2.995	kakor	13.528	bi	314.828
14.	po	2.948	ki	12.741	po	287.911
15.	sem	2.812	bil	12.469	s	281.805
16.	ni	2.636	z	12.107	ne	271.777
17.	s	2.441	še	11.754	bo	251.951
18.	še	2.410	mi	11.116	še	241.063
19.	za	2.327	za	10.719	kot	234.457
20.	tako	2.155	bilo	10.010	ni	190.827

As can be expected, no open class word, such as noun, adjective or verb, can be found in any of the above lists, the only exception being *je* (Engl. *is*) in the role of auxiliary verb (*je bil – he was*). There is a remarkable match between the two fiction corpora in the top six places (*je, in, se, v, da* and *na* – Engl. *is, and, pertaining to oneself, in, that* and *on*). In general there are four words from the first list which do not show in the DELO column (five from the second) and only three words (*ga, sem, tako*) from the C. Kosmač column which cannot be found in the DELO list.

How various corpora can really be quite different and how it shows in the top list of nouns can be seen from the Table 6.4. The list of top nouns from the British National Corpus has been taken from the standard source (Leech, Rayson & Wilson 2001) and the frequencies are normalized; they are given per million running words. In the lists of the two fiction subcorpora words from ordinary life, of communication in romantic circumstances, such as eyes, heart, head, hand or cheek are to be found, while in the newspaper subcorpus words related to politics, economy and sports are easily recognized. In the BNC corpus and in the NAJDI.SI web index the origin of top nouns is more difficult to explain. From the table it is also clear that fiction operates with a smaller noun apparatus of higher frequency than is the case in other corpora.

Figure 6.1 presents a distribution of word forms, where every occurrence is accounted for, for three different units: fiction (white), composed of the Beseda subcorpus (3 million words, includes the complete works of Ciril Kosmač) and the complete works of Ivan Cankar (2 million words), DELO 1998–2000 (tiled pattern, 47 million words) and NAJDI.SI (black, from the index of March 2002, 460 million Slovenian words).

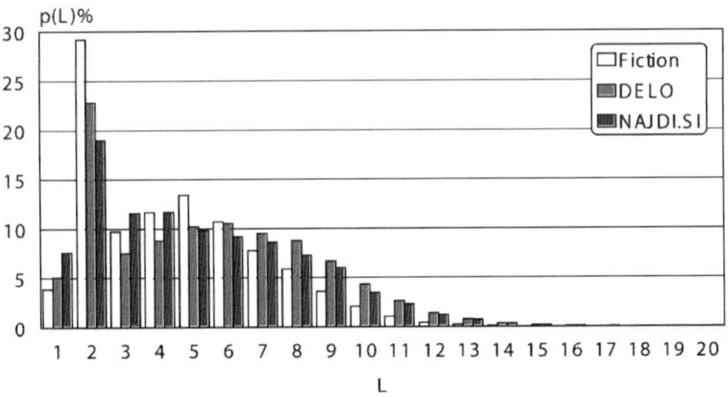

Figure 6.1: All word forms (Length Frequency Distribution): Fiction, DELO, NAJDI.SI

It is clearly evident that fiction has a much more fluent language, the share of function class words, most of them two letters long (also see Table 6.3), is 29% as opposed to 23% for the newspaper language and 19% for texts from

Table 6.4: Top 20 Nouns From Different Corpora

	Ciril Kosmač		Ivan Cankar		DELO 1998–2000		*BNC*		NAJDI.SI	
1.	hand	3, 866	eyes	3, 153	state	1, 906	time	1, 833	article	2, 107
2.	head	2, 415	heart	2, 739	year	1, 824	year	1, 639	page	1, 666
3.	eyes	2, 042	face	2, 675	time	1, 394	people	1, 256	day	1, 526
4.	child	2, 013	hand	2, 620	city, place	1, 309	way	1, 108	year	1, 267
5.	day	1, 836	man	2, 351	president	1, 167	man	1, 003	work	1, 252
6.	house	1, 716	word	1, 646	law	1, 022	day	940	world	1, 073
7.	year	1, 539	life	1, 570	percent	1, 021	thing	776	time	827
8.	door	1, 314	day	1, 435	day	989	child	710	law	799
9.	word	1, 258	head	1, 335	end	973	Mr.	673	group	790
10.	father	1, 191	people	1, 153	people	921	government	670	contribution	776
11.	man	1, 110	way, path	1, 134	tolar	860	work	653	system	773
12.	voice	1, 074	night	1, 123	party (pol.)	796	life	645	city, place	717
13.	heart	1, 039	Mr.	1, 113	million	789	woman	631	connection	690
14.	village	1, 015	time	1, 081	group	774	system	619	data item	680
15.	face	971	cheek	1, 055	minister	744	case	613	school	638
16.	table	961	road	1, 036	enterprise	737	part	612	community	608
17.	leg	941	window	1, 023	government	732	group	607	right	600
18.	life	914	voice	995	case	694	number	606	use	559
19.	people	905	mother	959	question	694	world	600	court	558
20.	water	887	table	938	sport match	669	house	598	change	556

web pages. It is also interesting that the curve tail peaks at 5-letter words for fiction, 6-letter words for DELO and 4-letter words for the web index. The share of long words, 14 letters or more, is negligible.

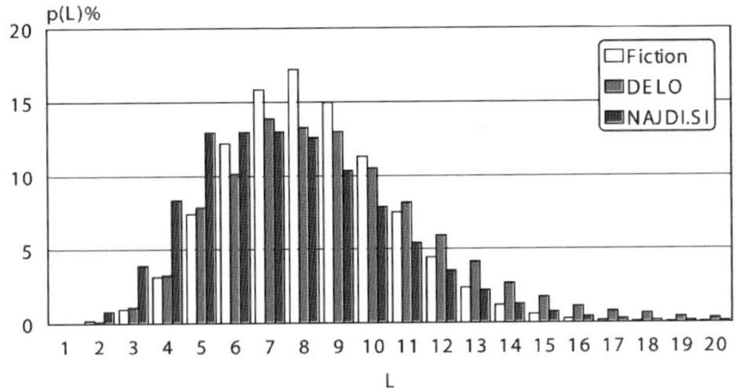

Figure 6.2: Different word forms (Length Frequency Distribution): Fiction, DELO, NAJDI.SI

These trends are further illustrated in Figure 6.2, where word form lengths are shown with every word form accounted for only once. For fiction the distribution curve is fairly regular and peaks at 8-letter words, with 17% share, and tails off quickly to the length of 16. In newspaper texts the shares of 7-letter (peak at 14%), 8-letter and 9-letter words are close enough. This fact may be attributed to the large share of names; the tail diminishes much more slowly to the length of 20. In the web index the peak is very broad, it stretches from 5-letter to 8-letter words, and it remains to be further explored in the future.

In Table 6.5, finally, a brief history of quantitative research, at least in the size of texts analyzed, is shown.

Table 6.5: Size of Statistically Evaluated Slovenian Texts in Time

year	words	publication
1962	4.000	Gyergyék (1962)
1973	6.000	Gyergyék (1973)
1974	60.000	Gyergyék et al. (1974)
1980	100.000	Vasle (1980)
1994	650.000	Kristan et al. (1994)
1995	1.600.000	Jakopin (1995)
1998	3.100.000	Jakopin (2002a)
2002	512.000.000	this paper

Computers did not really exist in Slovenia before Gyergyék initiated the first research (students counted the letters by hand) with publication in April 1962; the first computer, Zuse Z 23, was installed at the Institute for Mathematics, Physics and Mechanics on November 15, 1962. In the early seventies a quantum leap was achieved with the installation of the CYBER mainframe computer (1971) at the Republic Computing Centre (RRC) and everything seemed within reach. The disappointment which followed lasted nearly two decades, until the mid-nineties when desktop (personal) computers grew to a scale suitable for serious quantitative linguistic research. The adequate system needed to provide a detailed analysis of immense text collections such as Slovenian online texts, incorporating a robust part-of-speech tagger and lemmatizer combined with a guesser familiar with an encyclopaedia of names and words in all relevant languages besides Slovenian (from English to C++), still does not exist.

4. Conclusion

In this paper a brief overview of what is currently available in the domain of electronic text corpora has been given. The situation has moved from very little to two 100-million-word corpora in the past five years, and further prospects are open.

The infrastructure which would push word- and word-length studies to the absolute levels we all strive for is slowly emerging. With the combined efforts of all players and with the wide availability of quantitative resources from major European languages, such high goals could be achieved in this generation.

5. References

Gorjanc, Vojko
1999 "Kaj in kako v korpus FIDA?", in: *Razgledi, 13*, 23.6.1999; 7–8.

Grzybek, Peter
2002 *Einflussfaktoren auf die Wortlänge und ihre Häufigkeitsverteilung in Texten slawischer Sprachen. Projekt-Skizze 2002.* (29.10.2003) [http://www-gewi.uni-graz.at/quanta/projects/wol/wol_descr.htm]

Grzybek, Peter
2000 "Pogostnostna analiza besed iz elektronskega korpusa slovenskih besedil", in: *Slavistična revija, 48(2)*; 141–157.

Gyergyék, Ludvik
1962 "Nekateri stavki iz teorije o informacijah in srednja vrednost informacije na črko slovenske abecede", in: *Avtomatika, III/april*; 74–80.

Gyergyék, Ludvik
1973 "Prispevek k statistični obdelavi slovenskega pisanega besedila", in: *Elektrotehniški vestnik, 40/11-12*; 247–252.

Gyergyék, Ludvik et al.
1974 "Prispevek k statistični obdelavi slovenskega jezika", in: *Raziskovalna naloga 122*; Fakulteta za elektrotehniko, Ljubljana.

Jakopin, Primož
2003 "O spletnih virih slovenskega jezika, tretjič", in: *DELO*, 19.5.2003; 14.

Jakopin, Primož
2002 "The feasibility of a complete text corpus." In: *Proceedings of LREC 2002 International Conference, Vol. II.* Las Palmas. (437-440).

Jakopin, Primož
2002a *Entropija v slovenskih leposlovnih besedilih.* Ljubljana.

Jakopin, Primož
2000 "Beseda: a Slovenian text corpus." In: Fraser, M.; Williamson, N.; Deegan, M. (eds.), *Digital Evidence: selected papers from DRH2000, Digital Resources for the Humanities Conference*. University of Sheffield, September 2000. (229–241).

Jakopin, Primož
1995 "Nekaj številk iz Slovarja slovenskega knjižnega jezika", in: *Slavistična revija, 43/3*; 341–375.

Kristan, Blaž et al.
1994 "Entropija slovenskih besedil", in: *Elektrotehniški vestnik, 61/4*; 171–179.

Leech, Geoffrey; Rayson, Paul; Wilson, Andrew
2001 *Word Frequencies in Written and Spoken English: based on the British National Corpus.* London.

Turk, Žiga
2003 "Založniki postajajo ovira", in: *DELO*, 5.5.2003; 12.

Vasle, Tomaž
1980 *Statistična obdelava slovenskega besedila.* Diplomska naloga. Fakulteta za elektrotehniko, Ljubljana.

The effort involved in the task of corpus compilation justifies some additional thought and work in order to guarantee that as much use as possible can be made of the result:

(a) The use of a corpus which has been set up by others is also connected with a lot of thought and work, and this effort should be minimized if possible;

(b) it would be a shame if someone had to redo all the work because of a tiny detail of a given corpus preventing him from using it for his own purpose.

A frequently found problem is the less-than-optimal conservation of original data (in short: annihilation of information). An illustrative example is a corpus compiled by, say, a linguist who has access to data he receives from a newspaper publisher in the form of the daily typeset tapes. These tapes contain all the text including some 'strange' control characters for positioning and layouting the text portions. As a rule, our linguist will remove all these strange and 'useless' control characters from the data stream when forming his corpus. As a consequence, a researcher interested in problems of content analysis, who would need information about position and size of the newspaper articles – exactly the information which was, among others, hidden in the 'strange' character strings – cannot use our linguist's corpus.

From an *a posteriori* point of view of a potential user of the corpus, the above method of preparing a corpus is hardly comprehensible – a lot of work has been done with the result that valuable data have been destroyed. On the other hand, we would have to admit two things:

(1) Our linguist did not have the faintest idea that what he removed could have been of any interest to anyone, and if he did, he would never know whether anyone would ever want to use it.

(2) The simplified version of the corpus is much more transparent and more efficient with respect to his own purposes because corpus inspection becomes easier, and the computer programs for analysing the data do not have to cope with possibly complicated technical details which do not contribute in any way to the solution of the problem under consideration.

However, the more optimized a corpus is with respect to a given task (not only in a purely technical sense) the harder it is to use for purposes other than from the original one.

Clearly, there are much more less extreme technical questions to be considered before setting up a corpus, and a lot of these questions are discussed at length in the literature: Which of the currently popular mark-up languages (such as SGML, HTML, XML,...) should be used (if any), the choice of one of the most prominent morphological tag sets, the pros and cons of document representation systems (PDF), and many others. Moreover, there is a large variety of formats (document structures) in which the texts can be presented: Plain text with marks to separate individual texts, text with annotations (such as part of speech information assigned to the words, syntactic trees in form of labelled brackets or in form of indented lines, files with a line structure where each line contains just one running word together with annotated data, files which contain plain texts accompanied by annotation files, referenced by position or with pointers from the annotations to the linguistic items). There are always good reasons to select among the possibilities, depending on the given circumstances and on the purposes.

Furthermore, every corpus has certain technical characteristics which are, in general, not at the disposal of the persons that compile the corpus: operation systems, file systems, character codes (such as ASCII, EBCDIC, Unicode, to name a few of the contemporarily most common ones), place of storage and access methods (the corpus may consist of one large file or of thousands of files, it may be distributed over several computers in a network or reside on a single CD-ROM. The technical representation may even change dynamically).

What is rarely seen is the fact that virtually every possible feature becomes realized with a number of corpora and, as a consequence, users who want to use, and authors of analytical software meant to work with, more than one specific corpus are confronted with a wide spectrum of structures and technical details – every corpus is a special case. To make things even worse, whenever a design feature or a technical detail of a corpus has to be changed, all the computer programs which are supposed to work on the data have to be changed, too.

Surprisingly, not much attention is paid to these kinds of problems although standard solutions are available. It is the purpose of the present paper to propose such a solution.

2. Abstract Data Types and Abstract Data Structures

Let us consider a much simpler example: the programming task of calculating the sum of two numbers. To perform this task, in the early days of computer technology, a programmer had to know where the corresponding numbers were stored in the computer's storage (in which register or index cell, or the address in the core memory or elsewhere), and *how* it was represented on the given computer (e.g. four bytes for the mantissa and one for the exponent in a certain sequence, where two specific bits represent the signs of mantissa and exponent, others care for error detection etc.; which nibble (half-byte) counts as high and which as low; how many bytes make a machine word; which is the high/low sequence of the bytes in a word; which access methods to bytes and/or machine words are available etc.). Only with this information was it possible to write a program for adding the corresponding numbers. Later, programming languages simplified this task considerably. Operators such as addition (symbolized in most cases by the '+' sign) were introduced, which could be used without knowing any details of the machine representation of the operands. It is a good design principle of a programming language if it *prevents* programmers from knowing how the operands are represented on the given machine and how the algorithm which realizes the operator works. In software engineering, this principle is called *information hiding*, and many good reasons support this principle. The two most important ones are:

1. If you do not have to know the details when formulating your program, because the programming language takes care of these details, then your program will run on every computer hardware and with all existing and future operating and file systems in the world where the programming language you used is available.

2. Information hiding prevents the programmer from making assumptions on specific representations and other technical details, which – if used in an algorithm – would cause errors in a different environment.

A further improvement is the introduction of data types in programming languages, which make sure that a programmer does not compare apples with pears or multiply a number with a character. Each operator is defined with respect to its possible operands (arguments) and with respect to the properties of its result. Modern programming languages enable the programmer to define his own operators in the form of functions or procedures.

Teachers of programming style emphasize that one should use procedures and functions also in order to improve program structure (readability, changeability, and other software quality criteria) and to write code that is re-usable. A procedure that has been written for, say, finding the maximum value in a list of numbers or for sorting a list according to a given criterion can be used not only for the program it has been written for originally, but also for numerous other programs where a similar task occurs – if the corresponding procedure has been designed in a general enough way.

Re-usability is the main concern of *abstract data structures* (ADS) and *abstract data types* (ADT), which go a step further: They enable the programmer to define not only operators on the basis of predefined data types but even to create their own data types together with possible operations. What is special about ADS and ADT is that the implementation details are hidden: They consist of an object together with the corresponding access procedures in the case of an ADS and of a class of objects in the case of an ADT. The latter allows to create more than one data item of the given type during runtime. Let us consider the following example. Many complex data structures are rather common but in the framework of traditional programming techniques, every programmer writes his own code for, say, a matrix, a stack, or a tree each time he needs one (he will copy and modify, of course, as much as possible from previous implementations and will, of course, make some mistakes). For an ADS or ADT, the mechanism of the corresponding data structure is considered separately from the given problem and programmed in a *general* way, i.e. regardless of whether it is a stack for a parser, for a compiler, or for a search program. What counts is that a stack defines a constructor (such as CREATE or NEW), modifiers (such as PUSH or POP), and inspectors (such as TOP or EMPTY) and their effect on the data. The user of the stack need not and should not know how these procedures work or how the data structure is realized (e.g. as unidirectional or bi-directional pointer chain or simply as an array) in the same way as you are not told how a set type or an array is implemented, but just the preconditions and the postconditions of the procedures. Here, the constructor CREATE has no precondition (a new stack can always be created); its postcondition is that EMPTY has the value TRUE. The modifier PUSH(x) has the precondition that the stack exists. Its postcondition is that TOP has the value x.

3. The Corpus as an ADS

It is obvious that the principles from software engineering sketched above can be applied to the problems discussed in the first section. We can compare the situation of a programmer who wants to add two numbers (and does not necessarily want to re-invent binary or BCD addition techniques) to the corpus user who wants to examine in a loop syllable after syllable (and does not really want to find out how to identify and find the next syllable in a given corpus). We should therefore encapsulate all the features and details which are particular and present the corpus contents to the user on a level which is close to his interest (cf. Figure 7.1). This implies that there could be more than one presentation or interface.

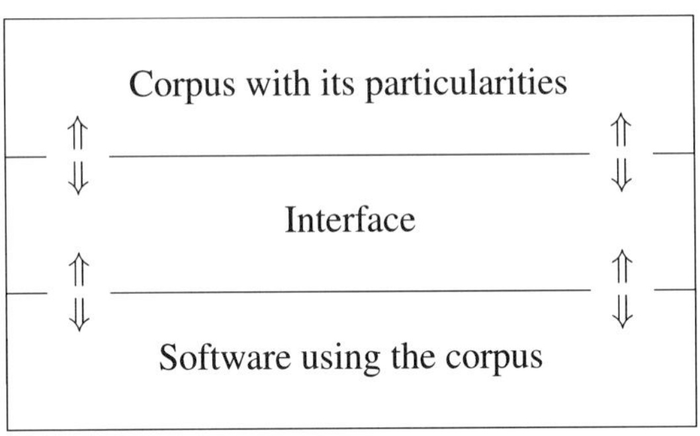

Figure 7.1: Corpus Interface Principle

Thus, the interface should translate commands such as “Give me the next syllable” into procedures which provide the next syllable, where the interface has the knowledge of how to find and identify the next syllable in the given corpus whereas the software using it has not. In general, the interface should offer access procedures which can pass all the items the corpus contains to the using program, i.e. units and categories, together with annotations if available. On the string level, character strings (separated by spaces or interpunction) should be accompanied by information on the separators, on the characters (upper/lower case), font, size, and style (bold, italics, ...), position of the string (relative to sentence, paragraph, text) etc. – everything that is either explicitly annotated in the corpus or can easily be inferred by the interface software. Similarly, on the syllable, morph(eme), word, phrase, sentence etc. levels, all linguistic or typographical (or other) information should be passed as a value of a complex procedure parameter.

The corpus interface should be made bi-directional, i.e. there should also be procedures that allow to write annotations (provided the linguistic application program has the corresponding rights). In this way, the linguistic application program (which could be, e.g. an interactive editor for manual/intellectual annotations as well as an automatic tagger or parser) would not have any information about the way in which the annotations are stored (in analogy to the lack of knowledge when reading from the corpus).

A basic function of the interface is the procedure which tells the linguistic application program which facilities, categories, items, annotations are available in the given corpus version, the alphabet used, special symbols, limitations etc.

Finally, the question remains where the interface gets all that information from. Clearly, the information should not be hard coded in the interface software. The disadvantages are obvious: The interface software would have to be changed and re-compiled for every corpus it is used with, and for every change which is made to a corpus. Moreover, numerous versions of the interface software would result, of which only one would work with the corresponding corpus while others would yield errors or, worse, provide incorrect data.

Therefore, an independent corpus description is needed: a file which contains the information about the corpus, including which files it consists of, where they can be found, and how accessed. The best way to describe the corpus for the interface module is to use a formal language, which should be a LL(1) language. Such languages possess properties which make them particularly easy to parse (cf. Aho et al. 1988; Mössenböck/Rechenberg 1985; Wirth 1986). The description must be set up together with the corpus by the corpus compiler. The overall architecture of the interface technique proposed here is shown in Figure 7.2.

In the appendix (cf. p. 195ff.), an example of a formal description of a corpus can be found – in this case, a dictionary of Maori with data for quantitative analysis.

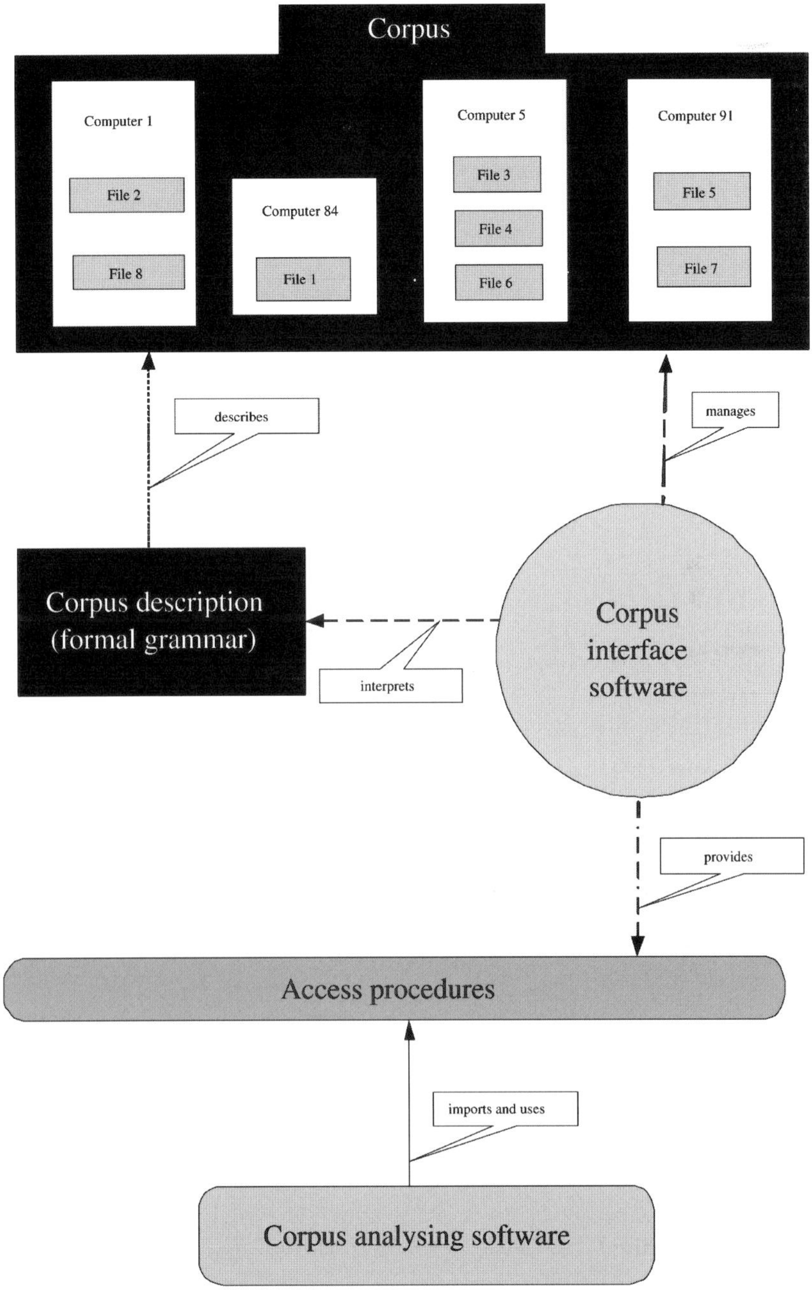

Figure 7.2: The Architecture of a Corpus Interface

References

Aho, Alfred; Sethi, Ravi; Ullman, Jeffrey D.
[2]1988 *Compilers. Principles, Techniques, and Tools.* Reading.

Mössenböck, Hanspeter; Rechenberg, Peter
1985 *Ein Compiler-Generator für Mikrocomputer: Grundlagen, Anwendung, Programmierung in Modula-2.* München.

Wirth, Niklas
[4]1986 *Compilerbau.* Stuttgart.

Appendix

A Maori dictionary description using a formal LL(1) language

```
&Language = "maori"

&Columns
&Separator = ';'

&Column 1
&Name = "Phonological transliteration of the lemma"
&Characters = {'a','e','h','i',chr(231),'k','m','n','o','p','r',
't','u','w','A','E','H','I','K','M','N','O','P','R','T','U','V',
'W','X','#','(',')','-','=','/','.','1','2','3','4','7','9','0'}
&Value range = {"a","e","h","i","k","m","n","o","p","r","t","u",
"w","A","E","H","I","K","M","N","O","P","R","T","U","V","W","X",
"#","(",")","-","=","/",".","1","2","3","4","7","9","0","II","III",
"IV","VI","VII","VIII","IX","(1)","(2)","(3)","(4)","(7)","(9)",
"(0)"}

&Column 2
&Name = "part of speech"
&Character = {'a','c','d','e','g','i','j','l','m','n','o','p','r',
's','t','u','v',','}
&List separator = ','
&Value range = {"a","ad","adv","c","conj","int","l","loc","m","n",
"num","pe","pr","pron","pt","ptg","ptm","ptmod","ptv","rp","st",
"u","v"}

&Column 3
&Name = "Inflectional paradigm"
&Characters = {'0','1','2','3','4','5','6','7','8','9'}
&List separator = ','
&Value range = [0..12]

&Column 4
&Name = "Morphological status"
&Characters = 'c','d','e','f','i','n','o','q','r','s','t','u','z'
&Value range = {"c","cd","cdr","ced","cr","crd","crqint","ct","d",
"dc","dcr","de","dr","drc","drd","dt","f","n","o","r","rc","rcd",
"rd","ru","rz","s","se","sr","t","u","uc","ur"}
```

```
&Column 5
&Name = "Function"
&Characters = 'a','b','c','d','e','f','g','i','l','m','n','o','p',
'q','r','s', 't','u','v','x','-','+','2'
&Value range =
{"an","al","crint+","dem","dempl","demplur","detplur","dur","ex",
"fr","freg","ftu-","fut","fut+","gn","gnfut","gnplur","gu",
"inr+","int","int+","int-","intfr","intfreg","intr","intr+2",
"intchr(374)","n","ndet","neg","nom","nposal","nprep","pers",
"persposs","perssing","plur","plurposs","posalpl","poss",
"possalpl","possalplur","possplural","prep","q","qu","rec",
"recfreg","recint+","red","rep","restr","s","sim","simint-",
"st","tr","ubt+","v","vb","verb","vimp"}

&Column 6
&Name = "Number of meanings"
&Characters = '-','0','1','2','3','4','5','6','7','8','9'
&Value range = [1..23]

&Column 7
&Name = "Style characteristics"
&Characters = {'a','c','d','g','h','i','l','m','n','o','p','r',
's','t','u','w','z','(',')','/'}
&Value range = {"a","c","col","d","d(po)","d(tahu)","d(tu)",
"d/rau/","d/si/","d/tah/","d/tahu/","d/whang/","dngi","doz",
"dpo","drar","dtahu","dtai","dtu","dwha","l","m","mod","p"}

&Column 8
&Name = "Lemma length"
&Characters = {'0','1','2','3','4','5','6','7','8','9'}

&Column 9
&Name = "Syllable number"
&Characters = '0', '1', '2', '3', '4', '5', '6', '7', '8', '9'

&Column 10
&Name = "Mean syllable number"
&Characters = '.','+','e','0','1','2','3','4','5','6','7','8','9'

&Column 11
&Name = "Morpheme number"
&Characters = '0','1','2','3','4','5','6','7','8','9'

&Column 12
&Name = "Mean morpheme number"
&Characters = '.','+','e','0','1','2','3','4','5','6','7','8','9'
```

```
&Files = "D:\dictionaries\maori\"
"maori11k.lex"
"maori11t.lex"
"maori1k.lex"
"maoria1.lex"
"maorif1.lex"
"maorig1.lex"
"maorih1.lex"
"maorii1.lex"
"maorip1.lex"
"maorir1.lex"
```

8

ABOUT WORD LENGTH DISTRIBUTION

Victor V. Kromer

The author of the present paper earlier proposed a mathematical model of word length based on the Čebanov-Fucks distribution with equal distributions of the parameter (Kromer 2001). The Čebanov-Fucks distribution is the known Poisson distribution when the obligatory (first) syllable is not taken into account:

$$p_x = \frac{(\lambda_0 - 1)^{x-1}}{(x-1)!} e^{-(\lambda_0 - 1)} \qquad x = 1, 2, 3, \dots \tag{8.1}$$

The parameter λ_0 of the model is the average word length in the text, which is determined by the formula:

$$\lambda_0 = \frac{1}{N} \sum_{i=1}^{N} x_i = \frac{1}{N} \sum_{x=1}^{\infty} n_x x \ , \tag{8.2}$$

where N is the text size measured by the number of word occurrences, x_i is the word length of the i-th word, measured in syllables, and n_x is the number of words having length x. In Fucks' model the only parameter λ_0 is strictly determined by the text, i.e., the Fucks model does not contain fitting parameters.

It has been suggested, that Fucks' model would be more flexible, if the text would be parted into groups of words with equal mathematical expectation of word length, and word length distribution would be calculated separately for each word group in accordance with formula (8.1) and subsequent adding of separate particular distributions based on their weights. The text might be parted, for example, into groups of words with equal frequency, polysemy, age etc. To construct a model, it is nessary to know the dependence of word length on the chosen group characteristic in the text. The most investigated are the frequency distributions (in the form of the frequency spectrum and rank-frequency distribution) and the dependence of the word length from the frequency or rank. Let us construct a model on the base of these dependencies. The model construction has been detailed in (Kromer 2001).

Let us repeat in brief the main course of considerations. Let us order text words according to the decreasing frequency, giving each word a number i from

P. Gryzbek (ed.), Contributing in the Science of Text and Language, 199-210.

1 to N, where N stands for text size in running words. Supposing that Zipf's law (8.3) holds true

$$F_r = \frac{kN}{r} \, , \tag{8.3}$$

where F_r is frequency of the word with rank r, and k is parameter, the following relation holds:

$$i = \sum_{m=1}^{r} F_m = kN \sum_{m=1}^{r} \frac{1}{m} = kN(\psi(r+1) + C) \approx kN(\ln r + C) \, , \tag{8.4}$$

where m are the numbers of natural order, and $C = 0.5772\ldots$ is Euler's constant. An average word length dependence in function from the rank is known:

$$\bar{x} = d_1 + d_2 \ln r \, , \tag{8.5}$$

where d_1 and d_2 are coefficients. This dependence has been verified empirically more than once. Some authors deduce it from theoretical considerations. Arapov (1998: 123) deduces this formula for written Russian from the following hypothesis:

i) the number of places in the word structure is directly proportional to the cubic root of the word rank;

ii) the probability of filling the place in the word structure with a unit-syllable is related to the number of the place (the number of the place is not related to the spatial orientation in the unity-word).

The mentioned probabilities, arranged in a non-increasing order, are inverse to the numbers of natural order. Substituting the member $\ln r$ in (8.5) by the same member from (8.4), and designating the coefficient of word coverage of the text in word successive appearance in the word frequency list as $Q_i = \frac{i}{N}$, we obtain (after some transformations) that there exists a linear dependence between $\bar{x}$ and Q_i. The parameter λ_0 in (8.1) should be replaced by the variable parameter $\lambda = \lambda_1 + (\lambda_2 - \lambda_1)Q_i$, where Q_i is uniformly distributed on $[0, 1]$, and λ_1 and λ_2 are the mathematical expectations of word length correspondingly at the beginning and the end of the rank frequency list. By integrating the obtained expression in limits of 0 to 1 on dQ_i, and after replacing the variables for the sought for expression for p_x, we obtain

$$p_x = \frac{1}{\lambda_2 - \lambda_1} \left(e^{-(\lambda_1 - 1)} \sum_{t=1}^{x} \frac{(\lambda_1 - 1)^{t-1}}{(t-1)!} - e^{-(\lambda_2 - 1)} \sum_{t=1}^{x} \frac{(\lambda_2 - 1)^{t-1}}{(t-1)!} \right) \tag{8.6}$$

with the support $x = 1, 2, 3, \ldots$.

The obtained expression is the known Poisson uniform or Bhattacharya-Holla distribution (Wimmer/Altmann 1999: 524f.). Since the average word length throughout the text λ_0 is equal to $\lambda_0 = (\lambda_1 + \lambda_2)/2$, the values λ_2 and λ_1 are related by the dependence $\lambda_2 = 2\lambda_0 - \lambda_1$. The value of λ_0 is strictly determined by the text (formula 8.2), and there exists only one fitting parameter (λ_1), fitted in order to obtain better agreement between theoretical and empirical data. The monotonically increasing $\bar{x}(r)$ dependence reflects the synergetic regulation of language. Ideally, the word length dependence from word rank is consistent with a language without redundancy:

$$G_r \approx \log_G r = \frac{1}{\ln G} \ln r$$

where G stands for the number of letters in the alphabet (cited from Leopold 1998: 225); there are no restrictions on letter combinability, all possible letter combinations are realized in the language lexicon. We are thus concerned with a language with equal probabilities of all letters and language optimal organization, which means that the shortest words are the most frequent ones and vice versa.

Let us make the supposition that the synergetic organization of the language is carried out on a certain abstract "language as a whole". The frequency dictionaries, on the base of which theoretical dependencies are constructed and verified, are representative of a concrete sublanguage (language of a particular text corpus, author or text). The optimum relations between word length and word rank are broken on such dictionaries, as word ranks in the dictionaries of the sublanguage and the language as whole do not match, which leads to retaining the value of λ_0 to λ_1-value increasing and λ_2-value decreasing. In the case $\lambda_1 = \lambda_0 = \lambda_2$, the dependence (8.6) degenerates into dependence (8.1). This case corresponds to the assumption (used as the base for dependence (8.1)) that the word has a certain average length in the given language, not depending on its frequency. It seems that a language (sublanguage) with such a degenerate word distribution is synergetically chaotic to a larger extent. However, there exist languages with larger degrees of chaos. Such languages can be described by the dependence (8.6), with parameter values λ_1 and λ_2, equal to $\lambda_1 = \lambda_0 - ig$ and $\lambda_2 = \lambda_0 + ig$, where g is a certain positive real number, and $i = \sqrt{-1}$ is the imaginary unit. With such conjugate complex values of parameters λ_1 and λ_2, the values of p_x are nevertheless real, and the range of the model feasibility extends.

The question arises about lower limit of λ_1-value. If the ideal Mandelbrot's distribution $x(r)$ of the word length in the dependence of word rank is realized, which means stepped distribution with step height of unity and equal steps length (in log scale), the graph of linear dependence of type (8.5), approximating stepped distribution, cuts the middles of horizontal steps, which results in $\lambda_1 = 0.5$. Considering that the text with the minimum value with $\lambda_{1_{min}}$ is totally synergetically regulated, and the text with $\lambda_1 = \lambda_0$ value is totally synergetically disordered, a possibility occurs to introduce the parameter

$$\alpha = \frac{\lambda_0 - \lambda_1}{\lambda_0 - \lambda_{1\,\mathrm{min}}}\,, \tag{8.7}$$

which is the coefficient of completeness of synergetic processes of linguistic code optimization. For real values of parameter λ_1, the values of α are in the range of $0 \leq \alpha \leq 1$, for complex values of λ_1, the values of α are imaginary.

There exists another variant of describing the empirical distribution in the way of composition of two distributions of type (8.6) with $\alpha = 1$ (with corresponding $\lambda_1 = 0.5$) and $\alpha = 0$ (with corresponding $\lambda_2 = \lambda_1$), which means $p_x(\beta) = \beta p_x|\alpha = 1| + (1-\beta)p_x|\alpha = 0|$. The model parameter $\beta \in (-\infty, 1)$. Now find out, in which way the parameters α and β of a mixed text are dependent of the same parameters of constituent texts.

We took data from two newspaper texts in Austrian-German from the paper by Best (1997a). Texts #2 and #4, as the most diverging ones according to the results of parameterization done by Best (1997), are chosen. The results of the parameterization of the original texts and the mixed texts are given in the Table 8.1.

Table 8.1: Parameters of the Original Texts #2, #4, and of the mixed text #2+4

Text	N	λ_0	λ_1	α	α^*	β	β^*
Text 2	770	1.996	1.211	0.515	–	0.223	–
Text 4	621	2.222	0.794	0.829	–	0.668	–
Text 2+4	1391	2.081	0.990	0.690	0.655	0.448	0.422

The defined values of parameter λ_1 for texts #2 and #4 slightly differ from those for the same texts, defined by Kromer (2001: 93). The difference can be assigned to use of a different (modified) χ^2-criterion.

As α^* and β^* are designated weighted (in accordance with the sizes of constituent texts) average parameters of the corresponding parameters, so

$$\alpha^*_{2+4} = \frac{\alpha_2 N_2 + \alpha_4 N_4}{N_2 + N_4}\,,$$

where α_2 and α_4 are values of parameter α for texts correspondingly #2 and #4, and N_2 and N_4 are the sizes of corresponding texts in running words. Comparison of α_{2+4} with α^*_{2+4} and β_{2+4} with β^*_{2+4} reveals that the measured values are greater than the weighted means for both parameters. With the aim of revealing the possible reason for this let us switch from real texts to modelled texts with controlled values of parameters.

Let us model four texts A, B, C and D of equal size N with given values of parameters λ_0 and β (Table 8.2), where n_x stands for number of words in the modelled texts of the given size x (measured in syllables).

Table 8.2: Data on modelled texts A, B, C and D

Text	N	λ_0	β	x								
				1	2	3	4	5	6	7	8	9
				n_x								
A	1000	2.000	0.100	383	349	182	63	17	4	1	0	0
B	1000	2.000	0.900	507	198	164	78	34	13	4	1	0
C	1000	1.500	0.500	660	218	93	22	6	1	0	0	0
D	1000	2.500	0.500	314	253	214	120	58	25	11	4	1

The results of parameterization of all four modelled texts and two mixed texts (A+B) and (C+D) in the context of the investigated model are given in Table 8.3.

Table 8.3: Parameters of modelled texts A, B, C and D and mixed texts (A+B) and (C+D)

Text	N	λ_0	λ_1	α	α^*	β	β^*
A	1000	2.000	1.529	0.314	–	0.100	–
B	1000	2.000	0.562	0.959	–	0.900	–
C	1000	1.500	0.778	0.722	–	0.500	–
D	1000	2.500	1.026	0.737	–	0.500	–
A + B	2000	2.000	0.906	0.729	0.637	0.500	0.500
C + D	2000	2.000	0.688	0.875	0.730	0.740	0.500

The comparison of weighted parameters α^* and β^* with measured parameters α and β for the mixed text (A + B) allows us to come to the conclusion that parameter β unlike parameter α normally has an additive function on texts with the same word length. The same comparison for mixed text (C + D) reveals the violation of parameter β additivity on texts with different average word length in the direction of parameter β increasing.

Considering that parameter λ_0 depends on text topic, the increase of parameter β for the mixed text, composed from model texts with different average word length λ_0 can be explained by increasing thematic variety of mixed texts, which counts in favor of defining β as a parameter, reflecting the degree of synergetic regularity in the text (the mixed text is closer to the "language as a whole", as single texts). Earlier, Polikarpov (personal communication, november 2001); suggested in the course of model discussion that parameter α expresses genre diversity of the text. As parameters α and β are directly related, this suggestion is supported.

Parameter α, calculated using formula (8.7), is an imaginary number with complex values of λ_1 and real value of λ_0. For the same texts β is a real negative number. If α is positive (for real values of λ_0), β is positive too. After analyzing many pairs of values of parameters α and β, a statistical relation between parameters $\alpha \approx \sqrt{\beta}$ is revealed, which is valid both for positive and for negative values of β.

Data on 28 typologically different ancient and modern languages were processed in order to test the model checking and to reveal possible regularities. For some languages, data were processed for texts of different genres (styles). It was revealed that there exists a direct dependence between parameters λ_1 and λ_0 for single-genre texts. The dependence $\lambda_1(\lambda_0)$ for six European languages, and the most consistently represented in the available data genre of letters, is reflected in the graph Figure 8.1 (points 1–16). The corresponding data concerning processed mixed samples are given in the Table 8.4 (p. 205).

The trend line, described by the equation $\lambda_1 = 0.40 + 0.35\lambda_0$, is drawn through the points 1–16 (excluding point 7). The processed material does not include Luther's letters. The Latin phrases occurring in them lead to sharp deviation of the word structure from the general tendency, in particular the λ_1-value is overstated. The determination coefficient is equal to $R^2 = 0.38$. Let us calculate coefficient α for the points of the trend line (we consider $\lambda_{1_{min}}$ to be equal to 0.5).

$$\alpha = \frac{\lambda_0 - \lambda_1}{\lambda_0 - 0.5} = \frac{\lambda_0 - 0.40 - 0.35\lambda_0}{\lambda_0 - 0.5} = 0.65 - \frac{0.075}{\lambda_0 - 0.5}$$

The analysis of the obtained expression permits to conclude that α is constant for the chosen genre of letters, at least for the processed six modern languages. At the same time this simple relation breaks for languages of the synthetic type, not belonging to German or Roman language groups, as well as for other Indo-European languages, where α-values tend to be zero or to become imaginary.

A dependence between the values of the parameters λ_1 and λ_0, as reflected by the formula $I = (\lambda_0 - 1)(\lambda_1 - 0.5)$ – where I is a certain constant, equal to 0.36 – is determined for the German language: here exists an inversely proportional dependence between the values of λ_0 and λ_1, shifted at 1 and 0.5

Table 8.4: Parameters of 26 mixed texts in six languages

Point number	Language	Sample	N	λ_0	λ_1	α	β
1	English	Letters	6480	1.368	0.753	0.709	0.477
2	English	Sidney's letters	4459	1.370	0.845	0.604	0.338
3	English	Austin's letters	5610	1.383	0.824	0.633	0.374
4	German	Dürer's letters	7255	1.467	1.077	0.403	0.152
5	French	Letters	9572	1.484	0.874	0.620	0.363
6	German	Tucholsky's letters	12531	1.605	1.003	0.544	0.260
7	German	Luther's letters	8471	1.618	$1.618-0.211i$	$0.189i$	−0.019
8	Swedish	Ekelöf's letters	6876	1.685	0.968	0.605	0.325
9	German	Lichtenberg's letters	4028	1.687	1.161	0.443	0.183
10	German	Lessing's letters	7215	1.693	1.148	0.456	0.191
11	German	Letters	10031	1.757	0.946	0.645	0.383
12	German	Hoffmann's letters	5014	1.770	0.925	0.665	0.416
13	German	Behaim's letters	5163	1.901	1.100	0.572	0.305
14	Spanish	Mistral's letters	10444	1.901	1.168	0.523	0.252
15	Spanish	Lorca's letters	5503	1.993	1.042	0.637	0.379
16	Italian	Pasolini's letters	5848	2.045	1.003	0.674	0.426
17	German	Low German texts	7121	1.391	0.829	0.630	0.373
18	German	Luther's songs and fables	6016	1.420	1.241	0.195	−0.001
19	German	Middle High German texts	13728	1.448	1.358	0.095	−0.007
20	German	Baroque Poetry	12638	1.454	1.273	0.190	0.031
21	German	Children's textbooks	7286	1.524	1.209	0.307	0.057
22	German	Children's textbooks	8517	1.679	1.052	0.532	0.247
23	German	Old High German Poetry	2159	1.708	$1.708-0.332i$	$0.275i$	−0.115
24	German	Texts	18425	1.914	0.877	0.733	0.513
25	German	Biology	19174	1.995	0.851	0.765	0.556
26	German	Press texts	9583	2.080	0.825	0.795	0.617

correspondingly, i.e. counted off from their lowest possible values. Hence I is an invariant of the German language and does not depend on the text genre. The points of this dependence and the line of hyperbolic trend are also plotted in Figure 8.1.

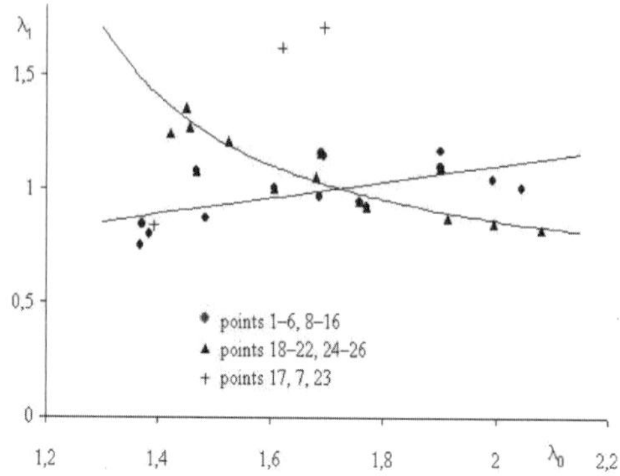

Figure 8.1: The dependencies $\lambda_1(\lambda_0)$ and $I(\lambda_0)$

The trend line is drawn through all points, related to German texts (Table 8.4, p. 205), excluding Luther's letters (point 7), Low German texts (point 17) and Old High German texts (point 23). Points 7 and 23 with complex values of λ_1 do not belong to the graph of Figure 8.1 (one more coordinate axis is needed for adequate mapping). The coefficient of determination is equal to 0.95. For other languages from the six listed, the value of I changes from 0.11 (English language) to 0.53 (Italian language) and reflects the degree of language syntheticity. The invariance of I-value, i.e., its independence of the genre, needs to be verified for those languages on the basis of additional material.

Of special interest is the comparison of α (or β) values for texts of different genres of the same language. A general rule can be observed: the values of those parameters increase when passing from simple genres to sophisticated ones. So, for the genre of Children's textbooks in German $\alpha \approx 0.30 - 0.53$, for the genre of letters $\alpha \approx 0.60$, for scientific and journalistic texts $\alpha \approx 0.80$. At the same time low and zero values of α (sometimes even imaginary ones) are characteristic for ancient texts. Old High German and Middle High German texts are satisfactorily described by Poisson's distribution (Best 1997b), which is a special case of the distribution under consideration at $\alpha = 0$.

The historical dynamics of structural reorganization of modern languages are of special interest. Such reorganization could be represented as the movement of a point in a multi-dimensional space with time and language parameters as coordinates. In the contest of the model under consideration, a coordinate system $\beta\lambda_0$, where parameter β is plotted on the abscissa axis, and parameter λ_0 on the ordinates axis, is very illustrative. The results are given in Table 8.5 and in Figure 8.2.

Table 8.5: Data on the Structural Reorganization of the German Language

Language	Old High German	Middle High German	Modern High German: Early Modern High German	Modern High German: Contemporary Standard German
Point no.	1	2	3	4
λ_0	1.708	1.448	1.450	1.812
λ_1	$1.708 - 0.332i$	1.358	1.183	0.907
α	$0.275i$	0.095	0.281	0.690
β	−0.115	−0.007	0.065	0.446

Old High German is represented by poetry. Middle High German is represented by songs by Walter von der Vogelweide and other authors from the minnesang collection *Deutscher Minnesang*, by texts from the *Codex Karlsruhe*, and from the *Sachsenspiegel*. Early Modern High German is represented by letters and poetic works (songs and fables) by Luther, letters by Dürer, and baroque poetry. Among Modern Standard German texts were selected: 18th-20th century letters, texts from schoolbooks, newspaper texts, texts with natural science topics. Parameter β is characterized by a direct chronological dependence, while parameter λ_0 has a local minimum. The decrease of λ_0 from Old

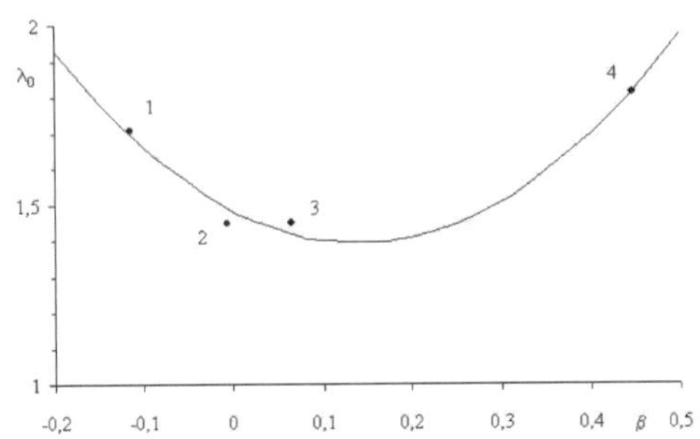

Figure 8.2: The Dependence $\lambda_0(\beta)$, Reflecting the Structural Reorganization of German Language

High German to Middle High German is explained by the development towards relative analyticity of the language, in particular, by the formation of the article as a new category (Arsen'eva et al. 1998: 267). The increase of λ_0 from Early Modern High German on is due to the rise of compounding and the appearance of numerous derived verbs with prefixes and suffixes, and also of derived and complex adjectives (Arsen'eva et al. 1998: 274). The Results of the parameterization of mixed texts on 23 languages are given in Table 8.6 (p. 209).

The quality of adaptation is estimated by the discrepancy coefficient C, which is somehow different from the coefficient, used by the research group of Göttingen Quantitative Linguistics Project (Best 1998). The adaptation of theoretical data to the empirical ones is considered as acceptable if $C \leq 0.02$. Three languages (Icelandic, Mordvinian and Korean), on which the adaptation is unsatisfactory ($0.02 \leq C \leq 0.04$), are marked with a star (*) in Table 8.6 (p. 209). Nevertheless, the data are given owing to their significance.

The fit in accordance with the proposed model in its current state is not sufficient for Arabic, Old Hebrew and Sámi. It is worth mentioning that word structure in Mao Zedong's letters in Chinese could not be described satisfactorily, whereas mixed Chinese texts are described as very satisfactory.

Acknowledgments

The author of the present paper processed data on word length distributions in different languages, given in papers of S. Abbe, A. Ahlers, G. Altmann, S. Ammermann, C. Balschun, S. Barbaro, O. Bartels, H.-H. Bartens, C. Becker, G. Behrmann, M. Bengtson, K.-H. Best, B. Christiansen, S. Dieckmann, H. Dittrich, J. Drechsler, E. Erat, S. Feldt, J. Frischen, P. Girzig, A. Hasse, M. Hein, C. Hollberg, L. Hřebíček, M. Janssen, B. Judt, I. Kaspar, I. Kim, S. Kuhr, S. Kuleisa, F. Laass, P. Medrano, B. Müller, H. G. Riedemann, W. Röttger, O.A. Rottman, A. Schweers, M. Strehlow, L. Uhlířová, M. Weinbrenner, J. Zhu, A. Ziegler, S. Zinenko, T. Zöbelin and M. Zuse, written in the frames of the Göttingen Quantitative Linguistics Project on word length (Best, 1998).

The author is personally grateful to Dr. K.-H. Best for supporting the present investigation.

Table 8.6: Parameters of mixed texts in 23 languages

	Language	Genre	N	λ_0	λ_1	α	β
1	Chinese	Mixed sample	14917	1.187	0.872	0.458	0.185
2	Gaelic	Mixed sample	23333	1.494	1.091	0.405	0.168
3	French	Fiction	1888	1.513	1.016	0.491	0.243
4	Icelandic*	Old Songs & Prose Texts	17818	1.547	$1.547-0.466i$	$0.445i$	−0.264
5	Faeroe	Letters	5044	1.557	1.457	0.094	−0.037
6	French	Press	4276	1.611	0.896	0.644	0.389
7	French	Press	9918	1.650	0.753	0.780	0.581
8	English	Press	15188	1.666	0.739	0.795	0.609
9	English	Biology	5441	1.810	0.616	0.912	0.834
10	Czech	Fiction	40936	1.917	1.680	0.167	0.061
11	Ukrainian	Poems (Franko)	2426	1.940	$1.940-0.318i$	$0.221i$	−0.020
12	Czech	Stories for Children	10919	1.949	$1.949-0.408i$	$0.282i$	−0.063
13	Russian	Poems (Tvardovskij)	2630	1.976	$1.976-0.431i$	$0.292i$	−0.055
14	Polish	Mixed Sample	4956	1.983	$1.983-0.240i$	$0.162i$	−0.035
15	Swedish	Press	4292	1.988	0.732	0.844	0.698
16	East Slavonic	Old Russian Reader	5298	1.995	0.809	0.793	0.592
17	Russian	Poems	3801	2.017	$2.017-0.390i$	$0.257i$	−0.028
18	Portuguese	European P.	8686	2.086	0.974	0.701	0.458
19	Portuguese	Brazilian P.	20263	2.087	1.100	0.622	0.352
20	Japan	Press	2796	2.117	1.080	0.641	0.394
21	Mordvinian*	Mixed sample	9134	2.176	$2.176-0.961i$	$0.573i$	−0.392
22	Estonian	Mixed sample	6998	2.181	$2.181-0.280i$	$0.167i$	−0.100
23	Czech	Press	2870	2.208	1.010	0.116	0.035
24	Italian	Press	8027	2.212	1.377	0.488	0.237
25	Russian	Fiction	6096	2.220	1.994	0.131	0.020
26	Hungarian	Mixed sample	12615	2.236	1.213	0.589	0.330
27	Latin	Letters (Cicero)	6092	2.312	1.636	0.373	0.150
28	Czech	Letters (Answers)	2895	2.371	$2.371-0.634i$	0.339i	−0.084
29	Czech	Letters (Questions)	2546	2.372	$2.372-0.605i$	$0.323i$	−0.047
30	Old Church Slavonic	OCS Holy texts	9118	2.575	1.694	0.424	0.171
31	Turkish	Mixed sample	11655	2.720	$2.720-0.711i$	$0.320i$	−0.085
32	Korean*	Mixed sample	25384	2.894	$2.894-1.138i$	$0.475i$	−0.200
33	Kechua	Poems & Fairy tales	3057	3.420	$3.420-0.781i$	$0.267i$	−0.124

References

Arapov, M.V.
1988 *Kvantitativnaja lingvistika.* Moskva.

Arsen'eva, M.G. et al.
1998 *Vvedenie v germanskuju filologiju: Učebnik dlja filologičeskich fakul'tetov.* Moskva.

Best, K.-H.
1997a "Zur Wortlängenhäufigkeit in deutschsprachigen Pressetexten." In: Best, K.-H. (ed.), The Distribution of Word and Sentence Length. [= Glottometrika 16.] Trier. (1–15).

Best, K.-H.
1997b "Wortlängen in mittelhochdeutschen Texten." In: Best, K.-H. (ed.), The Distribution of Word and Sentence Length. [= Glottometrika 16.] Trier. (40–54).

Best, K.-H.
1998 "Results and perspectives of the Göttingen project on quantitative linguistics", in: *Journal of Quantitative Linguistics, 5*; 155–162.

Kromer, V.V.
2001 "Word length model based on the one-displaced Poisson-uniform distribution", in: *Glottometrics, 1*; 87–96.

Kromer, V.V.
2002 "Ob odnoj vozmožnosti obobšçenija matematičeskoj modeli dliny slova." In: *Informatika i problemy telekommunikacii: Meždunarodnaja naučno-techničeskaja konferencija (SibGUTI, 25–26 aprelja 2002 g.). Materialy konferencii.* Novosibirsk. (139–140).

Leopold, E.
1998 "Frequency spectra within word length classes", in: *Journal of Quantitative Linguistics, 5*; 224–231.

Wimmer, G.; Altmann, G.
1996 "The theory of word length: Some results and generalizations." In: *Glottometrika 15.* (112–133).

Wimmer, G.; Altmann, G.
1999 *Thesaurus of univariate discrete probability distributions.* Essen.

9

THE FALL OF THE JERS IN THE LIGHT OF MENZERATH'S LAW

Resumee

Werner Lehfeldt

It was the aim of the lecture on which this paper is based to model one of the most important sound changes in Slavic on the basis of Menzerath's law in order to establish an explanation for this process. The sound change in question is the fall of the "reduced" vowels ь and ъ – the jers – in "weak" position; cf. in Russian *otьcь* > *otec*, *pъtica* > *ptica*, *sъnъ* > *son*. The fall of the jers had far reaching consequences for the phonological systems of all Slavic languages. In Russian, for instance, the whole vowel and consonantal system was restructured, one result being the development of the correlation of palatalization, so characteristic for the Russian consonantal system. Another consequence of the fall of the jers was the restructuring of syllable structure: Before the sound change there had only been open syllables in Slavic, i.e. syllables ending in a vowel, but as a result of the fall of the jers closed syllables also became possible. There also developed consonantal sequences "forbidden" in the period before the fall of the jers. The fall, i.e. the elimination of a jer automatically led to the reduction of the number of syllables in the word in question. At the same time longer and more complex syllables emerged. So, for instance, the three-syllable word *otьcь* became the two-syllable word *otec*, the second syllable of which now comprises three instead of two phonemes, the three-syllable word *pъtica* resulted in the two- syllable word *ptica*. The onset of the first syllable of this new word comprises three instead of two phonemes, with a sequence of two plosives, formerly "forbidden" in Slavic.

Such observations and speculations led to the hypothesis that it should be possible to model the fall of the jers with the help of Menzerath's law. In its most general form, this law states that the increase of a linguistic construct results in a decrease of its constituents, and vice versa. Gabriel Altmann (1980) gave the law the following mathematical form:

$$y = a \cdot x^{-b} \cdot e^{-cx}$$

P. Gryzbek (ed.), Contributing in the Science of Text and Language, 211-213.

In this formula, y represents constituent size – e.g., mean syllable length, measured as the number of phonemes –, x represents the size of the linguistic construct in question – e.g. the mean number of syllables per word –, whereas a, b and c are parameters.

In the research program reported in the lecture, the following hypothesis had to be tested: As a consequence of the fall of the jers, the mean syllable length of words comprising i $(i = 1, 2, 3, \ldots)$ syllables increased significantly in principal accordance with Menzerath's law. In order to test this hypothesis two text samples were analyzed: The first sample was taken from the earliest surviving dated East Slavic manuscript book, the famous *Ostromir Gospel* of 1056-57, which represents the situation before the fall of the jers. This sample was compared with a corresponding sample taken from the *Gennadius Bible* written in the 15th century and representing the situation after the fall of the jers. For both samples the mean syllable length for words comprising one to six syllables was determined. As expected, curve fitting with the help of Menzerath's law led to an unsatisfactory result for the *Ostromir Gospel* sample, whereas for the *Gennadius Bible* sample a theoretical curve in excellent accordance with Menzerath's law resulted.

In order to put our research on a broader basis and to reexamine the reported result, the following experiment was carried out in a second step: The *Poučenie Vladimira Monomakha*, a text written in the 12th century and thus representing the situation after the fall of the jers was artificially archaized by restituting all eliminated jers and by reversing all sound contractions. As expected, curve fitting on the basis of Menzerath's law gave an extremely unsatisfactory result for this artificial text, whereas curve fitting for the original *Poučenie* led to an excellent result. It can thus be assumed that before the fall of the jers some factor existed which distorted the mechanism of Menzerath's law, a factor which was eliminated by the sound change in question. Examination of a number of texts ranging from the 15th to the 20th century showed that, apparently, Menzerath's law never again lost its effect after the fall of the jers. In the meantime several Serbian and Polish texts were also analyzed. In all these cases curve fitting on the basis of Menzerath's law gave very good results.

We plan to found our research on an ever broadening basis, i.e. to analyze all Slavic languages, taking into account texts from all periods of language history. It is the aim of this research program to test the hypothesis according to which by the fall of the jers, Menzerath's law became effective in the whole Slavic language area. This is meant to further underline the great significance of the sound change in question.

The results reached so far have been published in the following articles: Lehfeldt/Altmann (2002a,b; 2003).

References

Altmann, G.
1980 "Prolegomena to Menzerath's law", in: *Glottometrika 2*; 1–10.

Lehfeldt, W.; Altmann, G.
2002a "Der altrussische Jerwandel", in: *Glottometrics, 2*; 34–44.

Lehfeldt, W.; Altmann, G.
2000b "Padenie reducirovannykh v svete zakona P. Mencerata", in: *Russian Linguistics, 26*; 327–344.

Lehfeldt, W.; Altmann, G.
2003 "The Process of the Fall of the Reduced Vowels in Old Russian in the Light of the Piotrovskii Law", in: *Russian Linguistics, 27*; 141–149.

10

TOWARDS THE FOUNDATIONS OF MENZERATH'S LAW

On the Functional Dependence of Affix Length On their Positional Number Within Words

Anatolij A. Polikarpov

Introductory Remark

Based on the suggestions of the Model of a sign's life cycle, this article offers a foundation of the logics of the word formation process, from which general regularities are derived concerning the length relation of words and of morphemes. Furthermore, a representative sample of Russian language data is analyzed (50787 Russian root words and affixal-derivational words) for a preliminary test of the suggested model. Primary attention is paid to one of the most fundamental regularities in the organization of language – the negative dependence of the length of affixes and the magnitudes of the ordered numbers of their sequence within a word. The conclusion is drawn that this dependence can be formalized in the form of a logarithmic dependence: $y = a \cdot \ln(x+c)+b$, where y is the mean length of affixes in position x in some numbered position in their word forms, a the coefficient of proportionality; b the average length of affixes in the initial (-3rd) position within word forms present in the analyzed dictionary; and c – the coefficient for converting a negative-positive scale into a purely positive one.

Also, an attempt is made to explain the empirically observed oscillation of the values of suffix length, depending on their even or odd position in a word. Finally, observations are made as to the specific characteristics of Menzerathian regularities for morphemes of various quality (root, prefix, suffix) and for all kinds of morphemes combined within the limits of words of different age categories.

P. Gryzbek (ed.), Contributing in the Science of Text and Language, 215-240.

1. The Unexplained State of the "Menzerath's Law" Phenomenon

"Menzerath's Law" is widely accepted to be one of the most fundamental regularities in human language organization. In its initial form (Menzerath 1954) it described the negative correlation between the length of words (measured according to the number of syllables), and the length of syllables (measured according to the numbers of letters or phonemes). Later on this "law" was extended to the description of word length, measured not only in syllables, but also in morphemes, and even extended to the description of collocation and the sentence level and the like. Finally the law has been applied for describing some other phenomena such as semiotic, biologic, astrologic etc. In the most general formulation, Menzerathian regularity has been defined by Altmann and his followers (cf. Altmann/Schwibbe 1989; Hřebíček 1995) as follows: the longer a language "construct" (the whole) the shorter its "constituents" (parts).

Nevertheless, Menzerath's law has not been theoretically substantiated, either in linguistics or in any other relevant science.[1] Moreover, not much empirical research has been carried out on this phenomenon up to the present in the area in which it was discovered, namely linguistics.

What is most striking is that the Menzerathian regularity has not been adequately studied empirically even on the basic semiotic level of the organization of human language, the level of its morphemic units in word boundaries. Up to now only sporadic word/morphemic studies exist on the relation between word length and morpheme length, and these in only three languages – German (Gerlach 1982), Turkish (Hřebíček 1995), and Russian (Polikarpov 2000, 2000a). Meanwhile, it would be natural to expect that regularities of the most basic units of human language should determine to some significant extent regularities for units on any other upper levels of language.

So, in principle, it is not possible to elaborate a relatively complete linguistic theory (including a quantitatively-oriented theory of the length of syntactic and suprasyntactic units) without a deep understanding of the regularities of the formation of the most elementary sign-units of a language, namely words and morphemes. Therefore, there is a vital need first and foremost for a substantiated theory of a possibly ontological mechanism which would lead to "Menzerath's Law", in relation to words and morphemes. Further, in order to test this theory, it is necessary to gather and analyse extensive and systematically characterised data of a multi-aspectual nature on morphemic structures of words in various languages.

---

[1] The most interesting attempts at a theoretical study of the "Law" are presented in the works of Altmann (1980), Altmann/Schwibbe (1989), Köhler (1989), Fenk/Fenk-Oczlon (1993), Hřebíček (1995).

This paper is a step towards building a theory of word/morpheme relationship and a step towards widening the empirical basis for testing a model of word/morpheme length regularities using Russian language data.

2. An Evolutionary Model as a Basis for Revealing the Structure of Word-Formational Regularities

2.1 Directionality of Word-Formational Process as a Derivative of Directionality of Basic Semantic Drift

According to the Model of sign life cycle (Polikarpov 1993, 1998, 2000, 2000a, 2000b, 2001, 2001a; Khmelev/Polikarpov 2000), it is natural to expect that the most probable (statistically dominant) direction for the categorial order within the branches of any nest of derivationally related words will be the movement from more objective words at the beginning of the word-building chain towards their derivatives of gradually more abstract, subjectively oriented and functional quality, i.e. towards words of gradually more grammatical parts of speech. So, there should be a tendency to begin a word-formational tree mainly with nouns, to continue it with adjectives, verbs, adverbs, pronouns, etc., and to end it typically with words of pure syntactic (functional) quality like conjunctions and prepositions. This general direction of the categorial development of words within any nest is predetermined most fundamentally by two basic semantic processes acting together in the same direction in the history of any given word (as well as in the history of morphemic, phrasemic or other linguistic signs):

(1) by the inescapable gradual drift in character of any lexical item's meaning in time (word, morpheme, phraseme), during each speech act, mainly in the direction of its gradually greater abstractness and subjectivity,

(2) by the predominant relative change of new word meanings (also of morphemes, phrasemes etc.) in the direction of their relatively greater abstractness as compared to their maternal meanings.

Such a tendency of a lexical item's meaning to change over time, points to a general tendency towards the semantic abstractness and subjectivity of words, morphemes, phrasemes, etc., with increasing age.

According to the principle of necessity for close correspondence between lexical and categorial semantics of words (Polikarpov 1998), increasingly more abstract lexical units "seek" their correspondingly more abstract categorial (part-of-speech) form to achieve the closer correspondence. This "seeking" and "finding" of a more organic categorial form results in acts of word-formation, in the production of word derivatives of a relatively more abstract categorial nature. A basic way of modifying the character of the categorial form of words, including the character of the lexical content, is what is called the "syntactic derivation" (a term introduced by Kurylowicz). In other words, from a given word, a more grammatical derivative is formed, which transparently demonstrates the exact semantic inheritance, even if only in relation to one of the meanings of a maternal word. For example, in such a correlation of syntactic derivation, there are many relative adjectives which are derived from nouns.

Naturally, acts of word formation involve not only the syntactical type of derivation, but also the lexical type which differs from various kinds of the syntactical type by the noticeable changes in the lexical semantics of a derived word as compared to the basic word. But according to our data, about 40 per cent of new words are formed by way of "syntactic derivation". This means that this type of derivative has a significant impact on the general pattern of change in the categorial semantics of words, for each following step of derivation – in increasing their relative categorial abstractness.

The production of derivatives of more grammatical word categories at each next step of word formation is reached usually by means of adding relatively more abstract, more grammatical suffixes to corresponding word-bases. With time, a formerly derived "new word" becomes "old" and semantically more abstract than it was initially. Therefore it loses semantic-grammatical concord obtained initially, and correspondingly tends to give birth to a new, categorically more abstract derivative than it is now itself. Repeated acts of word formation, though gradually retarded in time and intensity, eventually can lead in some nests to the formation of pure grammatical (functional) words.

2.2 Prefixes vs. Suffixes: Principle Difference in Function

Prefixes added step by step to the left of a root during the word-formational process, on the contrary, are usually relatively more semantically specific, more concrete than those prefixes which were put into the word form before them. This significant difference in semantic quality direction of relative changes between prefixes and suffixes within their growing chains, is explained by the principle difference in function of these two different kinds of affixes. The function of prefixes is not confined to establishing new grammar categories of words (as is the case for suffixes), but to varying aspectually already established categories (with the help of suffixes) by way of "multiplying" categorial meaning of suffixes by different aspectual meanings of prefixes. Thus the relative modification of lexical and categorial meaning of derived words with the help of prefixes, begins in each chain of prefixes from the most general categories to the more specific prefixes, in meaning and function.

2.3 Correlation of Categorial, Age, Frequency and Length Ordering of Morphemes within Word-Forms with their Positional Ordering

More grammatical affixes usually are the result of some longer history in language. Therefore, they should be more aged and more frequent than less grammatical ones. Greater frequency of use of more grammatical affixes determines their corresponding shortening. Growing in two opposite directions (to the right and to the left of a root), chains of affixes correspondingly change their age, grammar, frequency and length features also in two opposite directions.

The above mentioned issue of functional difference between prefixes and suffixes predetermines significant difference (even opposition) in the direction of the positional dependence of semantic quality, frequency and length of suffixes and prefixes in any word form, subject to their distance from the root, to the right or to the left of the root.

The most remarkable consequence of the above mentioned processes is the correlation between categorial-, age-, frequency- and length related characteristics of all type of affixes and their corresponding position in a word.

This correlation can be seen as follows:

(i) suffixal units which are further away from their root should be proportionally more grammatical, more frequent, and, finally, shorter than less distant ones;

(ii) prefixal units which are further away from their root, on the contrary, should be proportionally less grammatical, less frequent, and, finally, longer than less distant ones;

(iii) in the process of the functioning of roots in a language, they tend not only to become more semantically abstract and more frequent and therefore shorter with time, but also tend to be "packed" by "chains" of a growing number of affixes, cumulated during the word-formational process.

So, in general, morpheme length change brought about by the gradual increase of the number of all morphemes in word formation, is determined by three interrelated but different process regularities. Prefixes and suffixes follow two different, even opposite tendencies of the development of their functional and structural characteristics depending on the positional number of their placing in relation to the root. Roots follow yet another specific law of length- and function changes over time, including of course the growing affixal chain to the right and the left of the root.

In sum, our ontological model predicts a negative correlation of suffix length and a positive correlation of prefix length with their growing positional number within their word forms. Correspondingly, we predict a positive correlation between prefix length and their overall quantity, and a negative correlation of suffix length and their overall quantity within word forms. So, dealing with the dependence of average affix length on overall number of affixes (suffixes and prefixes together) we, seemingly, do not obtain a homogeneous dependence. This fact has not yet been mentioned in any Menzerathian study to date, because too often the problem has been dealt with in too abstract a manner, not taking into account the regularities of real mechanisms of the word-formational process.

The specific role and dynamics of roots within lengthening word forms have not yet been examined either. Therefore the positional numbers of prefixes and suffixes are of primary interest in the model being elaborated. The positional numbers are oriented to a root as a center of word-formational process and a zero point in word-formational static structure. Positional features of morphemes constitute a basic system of coordinates which have to be taken into account, especially when examining the correlation between length of morphemes and word structure. The overall number of morphemes in a word (which is usually taken as the main determinant of "Menzerath's Law") is not more than a combined (mixed) parameter. The exact form of this parameter's influence on average morpheme length can only be analytically considered, taking into account the three more fundamental dependencies mentioned previously.

If however the growth of number of prefixes in any word form is correlated with the growth of number of suffixes, and if the degree of corresponding gradual changes for the average length of suffixes and prefixes is correlated, this could present an opportunity to come to a more reasonable conclusion as to a less sophisticated dependence of affix length on the overall number of affixes (and correspondingly on the overall number of morphemes in a word form, which means including the morpheme units and roots in the total). The question of the integration of regularities of length change of roots and affix morphemes, requires separate study which is still ahead. Especially the change of root length with the increasing affix length, follow a certain regularity.

All in all it can be said that the "Menzerath's Law" for word/morphemic relations is a mixed result of three different independent fundamental laws (each affecting prefixal, root, and suffixal length respectively), which should be considered one by one in order to be able to arrive at a conclusion as to their integration in the form of some complex law.

Below we will firstly characterize the sources of the data on which we base our experimental investigation to confirm our prediction of two types of positional dependence of affix length.

Further we will undertake an initial attempt to formally integrate the two types of dependence on the basis of the prognosis of a logarithmic dependence, the correlation between average affix length and positional number of affixes on a uniform position scale of morphemes in an affix-derived word.

3. Source of Data and Analytical Tools

In the submitted paper, data were analysed which concerns morphemic structures of root and affix-derived Russian words (50,747 different words). These data were taken from the *Chronological Morphemic and Word-Formational Dictionary of Russian Language* – a database containing more than 180,000 words, prepared at the Laboratory for General and Computational Lexicology and Lexicography of Moscow State Lomonosov University. The data from this dictionary were previously characterized and analyzed (Polikarpov / Bogdanov / Krjukova 1998; Polikarpov 2000, 2000a). The data were presented and analyzed with the help of Access97 and Excel97 DB shells.

4. A Possible Mathematical Form for the Law of Affix Length Dependence on their Positional Number

4.1 From a Three-Factor-Model to a Two-Factor Model

Our experimental investigation of the material from the above-mentioned *Chronological Dictionary* shows that this three-factor model of morpheme length dependence can be simplified, or reduced to a two-factor one, if we take into account that prefixal and suffixal tendencies of change are really correlated and can be considered as components of the integral construction – as different, but closely correlated results of some unified process. On this basis it is possible to establish a unified distant scale for prefixes and suffixes, where a root "center" is symbolized by a zero ordinal number of its position – suffixes by increasing positive numbers and prefixes by increasing (in absolute value) negative ones. It is possible to see (table 10.1 and figures 10.1, 10.2 below) that this statement is valid, except for the oscillative nature of the positional dynamics of suffixes (discussed below, cf. point 4.4). Yet there is a necessity to examine these dependencies independently, and to explain the close correlation between them by further investigation into the quality nature of word-formational process. In the meantime, we will attempt here to develop a general mathematical form which will show the correlation between affix length dependence and their positional number.

4.2 An attempt at Revealing the General Form for the Positional Dependence of Affix Length

Based on the theoretical positions described above, we have considered different possible mathematical forms of defining the positional effect of affix placement within word forms. We have arrived at the conclusion that this can best be formalized by a logarithmic dependence:

$$y = a \cdot ln(x + c) + b, \qquad (10.1)$$

where

y – the average length of affixes being in some numbered position in their word-forms;

x – the positional number of affixes;

a – the coefficient of proportionality;

b – the average length of affixes in the initial (-3rd) position within word forms present in the analyzed dictionary;

c – the coefficient for converting a negative-positive scale into a purely positive one (c is here maximum ordinal number of prefixes plus one in words of any given dictionary).

4.3 Parameters of the Positional Dependence for Length of Affixes in Russian Words from the "Chronological Dictionary"

The results obtained on the basis of analysis of the above-mentioned "Chronological Dictionary" clearly show the validity of the theoretically derived dependence. Besides, we revealed significant oscillations of the dependence (see point 4.4 below) and stable variations in the positional dependence for affixial word structures of differing age and categorial form as well as significant differences in the parameters of average root length, and of the affixes in words of different grammar and age categories.

The empirical values achieved from the study of the chronological dictionary, for parameters a,b and c in the proposed positional dependence of affix length are presented as follows

$$\begin{aligned} a &= -0.3953 \\ b &= 2.5473 \\ c &= 4 \end{aligned}$$

The equation for the dependence of the average length of Russian affix morphemes on their positional numbers therefore is as follows:

$$y = -0.3953 \cdot ln(x+4) + 2.5473 \qquad (10.2)$$

The parameters of the above equation have been calculated on the basis of the data presented in Table 10.1 (for a detailed presentation of the data see Table 10.4 in the Appendix below (cf. pp. 234ff.). The graphical projection of the results which are presented in Table 10.4 may be seen in Figures 10.1 and 10.2 below.

The primary data, regarding the correlation of length of different type and age words, to the length of morphemes of different quality (roots, prefixes and suffixes), forming the words, are represented in Table 10.4 (see Appendix below), separately for each single position within the word.

Table 10.1: Dependence of Lengths of Morphemes of Different Type on the Ordinal Number of their Positions in a Word

Suffixes in words	**0**	**1**	2	3	4	5	6	7	total
Pos. of morphemes in words	*Average letter length of morphemes*								
-3	2.00	1.83	2.93	2.55	2.50	2.75			2.56
-2	1.89	2.18	2.33	2.20	2.28	2.25	1.73	1.5	2.25
-1	2.22	2.11	2.10	2.05	1.97	1.94	1.98	1.60	2.08
0	4.15	3.70	3.63	3.45	3.37	3.17	2.91	2.70	3.59
1		1.95	1.71	1.66	1.48	1.42	1.23	1.00	1.70
2			1.93	1.87	2.03	2.14	2.27	2.80	1.92
3				1.84	1.80	1.72	2.27	2.50	1.83
4					1.85	1.90	1.54	2.50	1.85
5						1.70	1.77	1.10	1.70
6							1.76	1.90	1.78
7								1.40	1.40
All morphemes	3.47	2.69	2.37	2.18	2.09	2.01	1.96	1.92	2.31
All prefixes	2.19	2.12	2.12	2.06	2.00	1.98	1.94	1.57	2.09
All suffixes		1.70	1.92	1.83	1.85	1.70	1.78	1.40	1.81

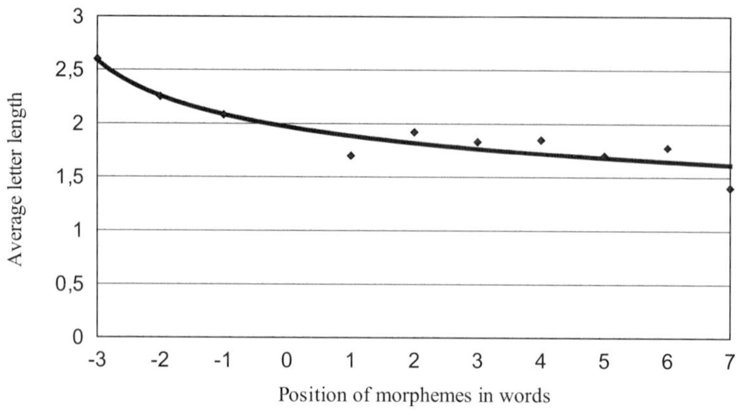

Figure 10.1: Dependence of Average Letter Length of Morphemes of Different Types on Their Positional Features

Length of morphemes is measured by the number of letters in them. According to the specific features of the Russian alphabet there is a very close (almost one-to-one) correspondence between Russian letters and phonemes. So, it is possible to use both kinds of units without any noticeable difference.

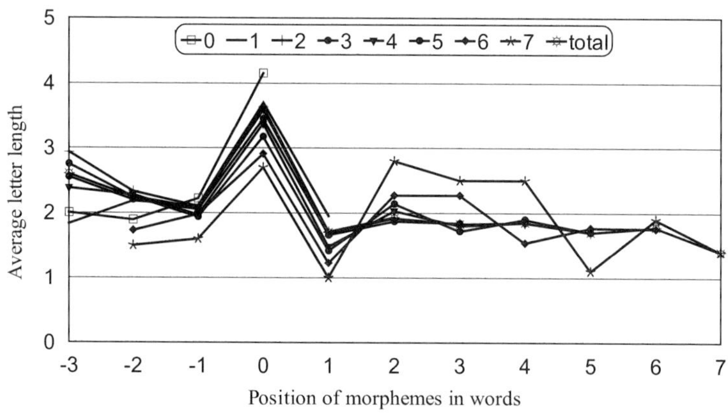

Figure 10.2: Dependence of Average Morpheme Length on the Ordinal Number of Their Position Within a Word (separately for words of different number of suffixes)

4.4 Oscillations in the Dependence of Suffix Length on Their Positional Features

On analyzing the data presented in Table 10.1 and figures 10.1 and 10.2, one can easily notice, in addition to the expected correlation between positional and length features of suffixes, a lesser phenomena of oscillations, local rhythmic deviations of average suffix length from the theoretically drawn general tendency. The phenomena of oscillation of word length features (as well as frequency and other range of other word features) have already been noticed (see, for instance, Köhler 1986). Apparently, however, it was not evaluated fully and was not declared as one of the most remarkable features of the word-formational process in language. A proper evaluation of the oscillation phenomenon can only be made on the basis of the present evolutionary model of the word-formational process described above. We suppose that these oscillations represent small rhythmic deviations from a general tendency of change of affix length according to their position, which could be interpreted as a basic rhythm of the word-formational process.

For modelling this phenomenon it is enough to make two assumptions. The first and main assumption (already explained above) is that there is a proportionally greater probability to produce at each next step of the word-formational process, a relatively more grammatical affix, than at each previous step. The second assumption is that acts of production of more and less categorially abstract affixes should take turns for the whole chain of derivatives in any nest.

Despite the seemingly contradictory nature of these two statements, there is no real inconsistency. The first assumption concerns only the summarized picture of the whole chain of all derivatives on average, without taking into account their closer pair relations. The second assumption, on the contrary, takes into account only relations of contiguous derivatives in successions of Markovian-like pairs. The real interaction between the two tendencies is present in the form of modulations of the general tendency (of diminishing affix length from left to right within a word) by some rhythmic, auto-correlative "plus" and "minus" deviations of real length values from those values which are determined by the main tendency. It should be admitted, however, that, due to the brevity of the prefixal part of the affixal structure of the word, it is still uncertain, whether oscillations also concern prefixes or not.

The backward tendency within derivational pairs (like the derivational movement from an adjective back to a noun) is explained by the necessity to produce those derivatives which could be used for expressing almost the same meanings, but in greater variety of syntactic conditions than was possible for their immediate derivational predecessor. For instance, substantivation of the form of expressing various static and dynamic features of objects (expressed usually by adjectives and verbs) is one means of using the substantivized name of a feature (a feature itself is characterising some set of objects in nature) in the most syntactically open and flexible – object – position. This syntactic position provides some additional opportunities for the specification of the denoted feature (if necessary), by the possible additional use of attributes and predicates, and object determinants (circumstantial).

If we take for granted that in the majority of cases, a word of the initial, zero degree of derivation within a word-formational nest is represented by a noun (usually having physical object reference and not having any affixal "clothes", i.e. being represented by a pure root), this means that the first step of suffixation (at suffixal position # 1, just after a root) would most suitably be taken up by an adjectival or verbal affix with a movement mainly in the direction of a relatively greater categorial abstractness using a relatively shorter suffix. The second step of suffixation can be in either of two directions – (1) towards greater or (2) lower categorial abstractness. But in a substantial number of cases it is realized into the second – categorially more concrete, direction and, correspondingly, with a relative increase of suffix average length. This is because of the strong negative correlation between quality of contiguous derivation steps within any nest, mentioned above. But this substantivizing "revenge" prepares some additional abstractivizing opportunities for those words which have undergone substantivizing at the previous step. So, the third word-formation step – according to the global abstractivizing tendency together with the minor tendency of negative correlation between the direction of quality changes for contiguous derivation steps – should be towards the relatively greater categorial abstractness as compared to that of their word-bases and, and correspondingly in the direction of a relative shortening of the third suffix in comparison to the second one.

This, in turn, gives additional opportunities in the next step for relative substantivization of derivatives of it (as compared to word bases), for relative categorial and semantic specification of suffixes and, correspondingly, to the relative increase in their length. As can be seen, the third step will repeat the relative logic of the first step, the fourth step will repeat the relative logic of the second one, and so on. But each next odd and even step is made from the higher level of abstractness of suffixal semantics than a previous one, leading eventually to the shaping of a global abstractivizing tendency.

All in all, on the basis of the correlation between the two recorded tendencies, one should be able to notice a strong negative correlation between the quality of each next step of derivation and the previous one, whereas a strong positive correlation between each previous and each next odd and even step. So, the general pattern of suffix length dynamics is determined by a process of global shortening of suffix length. The process is modulated by rhythmic ("plus" and "minus") deviations from the general pattern as a result of negative correlation between contiguous steps of derivation. The phenomenon of specific progression of characteristic and nominative derivatives, during the word-formational process, with a global movement towards the increasingly abstract quality of word lexical and categorial semantics is now being experimentally examined and analysed on the basis of data from the "Chronological Dictionary" and prepared for publishing.

5. The Specifics of Menzerathian Regularities Separately for Roots, Prefixes and Suffixes

For a deeper understanding of this process and a more differentiated analysis of morphemes of different quality, we have obtained a series of projections of root-, prefix- and suffix length dependence on length features of words. Here we present the dependence of length features of the above-mentioned kinds of morpheme units on the number of suffixes in words (see Figure 10.3).

An initial consideration shows significant differences in dependence for morphemes of different quality. It is most important to note, firstly, that roots are opposed to affixes on the whole and, secondly, that prefixes on the whole spectrum of word-lengths are, on average, considerably longer than suffixes, which also means that according to their function and length, that they are nearest to the roots after the affix. This is obviously produced by the oscillation in the above examined positional dependence. Thirdly, the general pattern of dependence of length of all morphemes together, on the number of suffixes in the words studied, is most smooth. As we now understand, this is the result of a mixture of the three types of dependence (for prefixes, roots and suffixes) which are represented in Figure 10.3).

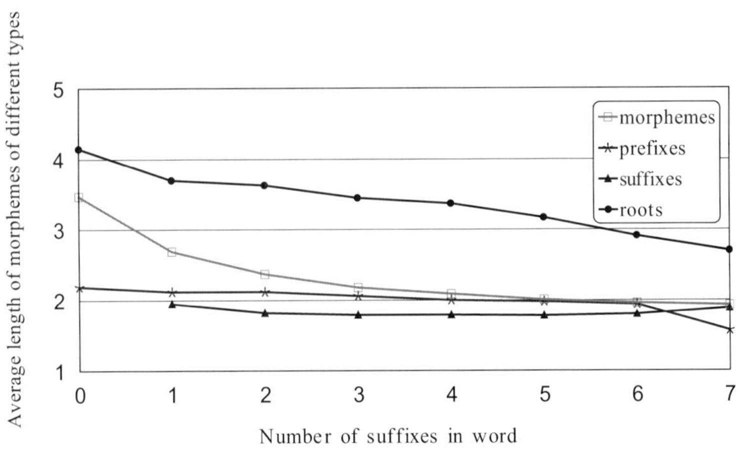

Figure 10.3: Dependence of Average Letter Length of Morphemes of Different Types on the Number of Suffixes in Words

Table 10.2: Dependence of Average Letter Length of Morphemes on the Number of Morphemes

Qmrf	age 1	age2	age 3	age 4	age 5	age 6	age 7	all ages
1	3.28	4.35	4.87	4.96	4.75	4.86	4.34	4.58
2	2.15	2.68	2.92	3.08	3.11	3.18	3.50	3.01
3	1.88	2.25	2.39	2.45	2.58	2.66	2.74	2.53
4		2.02	2.15	2.21	2.29	2.34	2.43	2.27
5		1.84	2.04	2.07	2.17	2.22	2.23	2.17
6		1.58	1.94	1.98	2.08	2.10	2.19	2.10
7			1.87	1.88	2.02	2.08	2.06	2.04
8			1.84	1.88	1.98	2.01	1.97	1.98
9			2.11	2.00	1.83	1.99	2.04	2.01
10				2.10	1.95	2.00		2.00
Total	2.52	2.36	2.19	2.30	2.30	2.33	2.37	2.31

6. Menzerathian Regularity for Morphemes of Words of Different Age

According to our data collected from the *Chronological Dictionary*, there are seven grades of ages – from the 1st, most ancient words of Indo-European (and older) origin, to gradually younger words of the 2nd (Common Slavic) period, 3rd (Old Russian), 4th (15-17th centuries of origin), 5th (18th century), 6th (19th century) up to 7th age period (words of the origin in 20th century).

It can be seen from the data that words of different age follow the same Menzerathian law of correlation with the specification that words of older age but of the same length (i.e., with the same number of morphemes) are built with the use of gradually shorter morphemes (see table 10.2 and 10.3 – cf. figures 10.4 and 10.5).

This can presumably be explained by the fact that, on average, younger, and therefore less semantically abstract and less grammatical words (which can be seen in the relationship of words within each of the age categories, cf. table 10.4) are usually built by relatively younger (and, correspondingly, by less grammatical, less frequent, and, therefore – longer) morphemes than, on average, older words.

One of the reasons for this is that new morphemic material, for example root material, will be required to form new signs (for example through borrowing from other languages), when new concepts emerge in reality. Another reason is that morphemic units entering the language earlier – both root- and suffix units – in time become too empty, less effective in denoting and therefore less

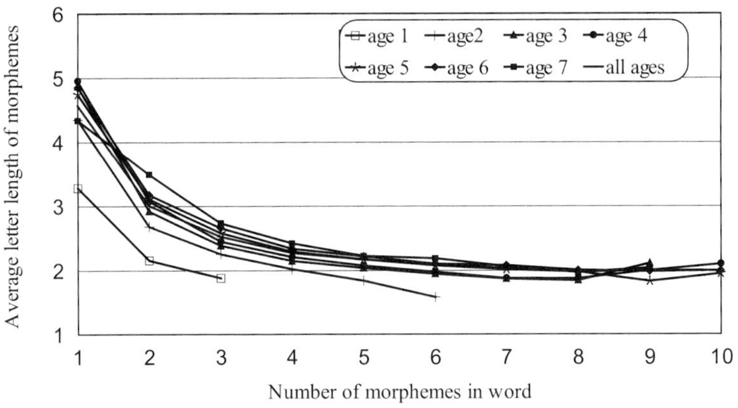

Figure 10.4: Dependence of Average Letter Length of Morphemes of Different Types on the Number of Morphemes in Words of Different Age Periods

used and eventually obsolete, which means that they gradually rid themselves of the word-forming process.

Thus the need arises to find and use relatively new, relatively more specific morphemes to signify the lexical content of new words. This brings about the necessity to discriminate between the influence of the length of words and their age on the average length of affixes. Presumably, length and age of words are correlated, albeit separately-acting factors, in the complex process of affix length formation.

It is necessary to develop a further formal apparatus of modelling positional and Menzerathian-like dependencies, which would include not only positional features of words as well as average number of morphemes, but also age properties, for an independent calculation of the influence of both of these factors.

One more projection of word age ↔ morphemic length relations is presented in Figure 10.5 below. It shows even more clearly the fact of the dependence of the average length of morphemes of any kind on age of words containing those morphemes.

7. Conclusion

In this study, we demonstrated the predicted phenomenon of the correlation between average affix length and their positional number on the unified ordinal scale of affixes within a word, on the basis of the model of life cycle of a sign, as a natural effect of the word-formational process. "Menzerath's Law" from this point of view, turns out to be a regularity which is produced from the fundamental dependence of morpheme units on their positional number in

Table 10.3: Dependence of Average Letter Length of Morphemes on the Number of Morphemes in Words (for words of different age periods)

Age period	Average Letter Length			
	Prefixes	**Suffixes**	**Affixes**	**Roots**
1	1.0000	1.3678	1.3556	3.1279
2	2.0365	1.5926	1.6314	3.5961
3	2.0575	1.6741	1.7721	3.4328
4	2.1935	1.7053	1.8289	3.5042
5	2.0579	1.8358	1.8873	3.5751
6	2.0970	1.8567	1.9113	3.6699
7	2.0868	1.9417	1.9726	3.6809

the word structure, and correspondingly on their function in each position. We predicted and demonstrated a general growth in the degree of semantic and categorial abstractness of suffixes, in increasing distance rightwards of the root, and conversely a decrease in the degree of semantic and categorial abstractness of prefixes, in increasing distance leftwards of the root. The harmonised positional dynamics is expressed by the equation elaborated in this study of a logarithmical dependency of the average length of affixes on their positional number on the unified ordinal scale within the word morphemic structure.

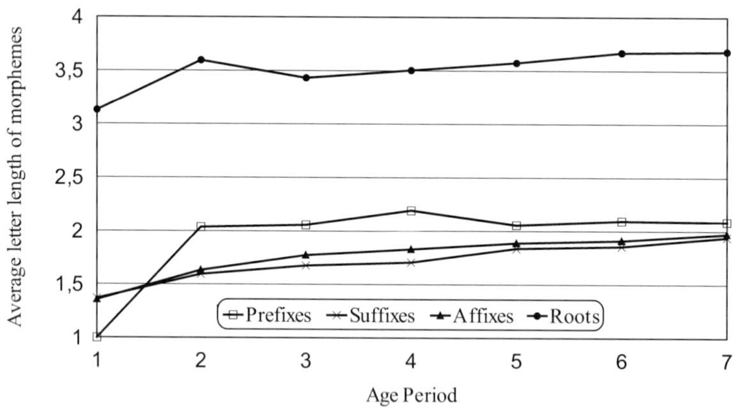

Figure 10.5: Dependence of Average Letter Length of Morphemes on the Number of Morphemes in Words (for words of different age periods)

For a deeper understanding of the observed features it is necessary to also take into account age features of words and morphemes.

The phenomenon of oscillation of suffix length within a word is of primary importance for further studies of Menzerathian regularities. As already shown, the general tendency for relative greater categorial abstractness of derivatives of each next step on the word-formational chain is modified by oscillations as a result of collaboration of two tendencies – the main tendency of the production of new words of relatively greater abstractness (for instance, in the course of derivational movement from nouns to adjectives), with a minor tendency of negative correlation between contiguous steps of derivation in relative quality (more abstract and more specific) of derivatives.

So, if at the zero step of the process we usually have an almost pure concrete word category (semantically objective nouns), the next (first) step of derivation should result in an overwhelming majority of non-nouns. The second step, according to the above-mentioned negative correlation of steps, should restore to some degree the categorial quality lost during the previous step of derivation (like the derivation of abstract nouns from adjectives: 'friendliness' from 'friendly'). Nevertheless, these backward and forward movements are realized within a more general tendency to the eventual relative abstractivization of word and morpheme categories. Seemingly, there is a general tendency present by a block consisting of every next pair of derivational steps. Each new block, on the average contains a more abstract word category and, correspondingly, a shorter suffix, than each previous block. Oscillations in this case may be considered as inner processes inside each such block. "Menzerath's Law" for word/morphemic relations is a mixed result of the action of three different, more elementary, local laws (affecting prefixal, root, and suffixal length differently), which can be integrated into a more complex dependence only taking into account each of them one-by-one. In the current study, we have attempted to integrate these regularities, in relation to suffixes and prefixes in the general pattern of positional dependence of their length. Roots still need a similar integrative effort. On this point, one important empirical observation has been made by Victor Kromer in 2002 (personal communication), which states that the root length may be organically integrated into the general morpheme sequence in the zero position of a word in the case where only half of an empirically given length of it is taken.

We would hope that the above considerations would ultimately lead to a general ontological and quantitative theory of length dependencies in human language, for the explanation of the specific shape of length distributions for units of various linguistic levels.

References

Altmann, G.
1980 "Prolegomena to Menzerath's Law." In: *Glottometrika 2*. Bochum. (1–10).

Altmann, G.; Schwibbe, M.H.
1989 *Das Menzerathsche Gesetz in informationsverarbeitenden Systemen. Mit Beiträgen von Werner Kaumanns, Reinchard Köhler und Joachim Wilde.* Hildesheim etc.

Fenk, A.; Fenk-Oczlon, G.
1993 "Menzerath's Law and the Constant Flow of Linguistic Information." In: R. Köhler; B.B. Rieger (eds.), *Contributions to Quantitative Linguistics.* Dordrecht (NL) etc. (11–32).

Gerlach, R.
1982 "Zur Überprüfung des Menzerath'schen Gesetzes im Bereich der Morphologie." In: *Glottometrika 4*. Bochum. (95–102).

Hřebíček, L.
1995 *Text Levels. Language Constructs, Constituents and the Menzerath-Altmann Law.* Trier.

Khmelev, D.V.; Polikarpov, A.A.
2000 "Regularities of Sign's Life Cycle as a Basis for System Modelling of Human Language Evolution." In: *Abstracts of papers for Qualico-2000.* Praha. [http://www.philol.msu.ru/~lex/khmelev/proceedings/qualico2000.html].

Köhler, R.
1986 *Zur linguistischen Synergetik: Struktur und Dynamik der Lexik.* Bochum.

Köhler, R.
1989 "Das Menzerathsche Gesetz als Resultat des Sprachverarbeitungs-Mechanismus." In: G. Altmann; M.H. Schwibbe (eds.), *Das Menzerathsche Gesetz in informationsverarbeitenden Systemen.* Hildesheim etc. (108–112).

Menzerath, P.
1954 *Die Architektonik des deutschen Wortschatzes.* Bonn.

Polikarpov, A.A.
1993 "On the Model of Word Life Cycle." In: R. Köhler, R.; B. Rieger (eds.), *Contributions to Quantitative Linguistics.* Dordrecht (NL). (53–66).

Polikarpov, A.A.
1998 *Cikličeskie processy v stanovlenii leksičeskoj sistemy jazyka. Modelirovanie i èksperiment. [=Cyclic Processes in the Emergence of Lexical System: Modelling and Experiments.* Moscow, Doctoral Thesis.

Polikarpov, A.A.
2000 "Menzerath's Law for Morphemic Structures of Words: A Hypothesis for the Evolutionary Mechanism of its Arising and its Testing." In: *Abstracts of papers for Qualico-2000.* Praha.

Polikarpov, A.A.
2000a "Chronological Morphemic and Word-Formational Dictionary of Russian: Some System Regularities for Morphemic Structures and Units." In: *Linguistische Arbeitsberichte; 75.* [Institut für Linguistik der Universität Leipzig. 3. Europäische Konferenz ≫Formale Beschreibung slavischer Sprachen, Leipzig 1999≪. Leipzig. (201–212). [http://www.philol.msu.ru/~lex/articles/fdsl.htm]

Polikarpov, A.A.
2000b "Zakonomernosti obrazovanija novykh slov. [= Regularities of New Word Formation]." In: *Jazyk. Glagol. Predloženie. Sbornik v čest' 70-letija G.G. Cil'nitskogo.* Smolensk. (211–226). [http://www.philol.msu.ru/~lex/articles/words_ex.htm].

Polikarpov, A.A.
2001 *Kognitivnoe modelirovanie cikličeskich processov v stanovlenii leksičeskoj sistemy jazyka. [= Cognitive Modelling of Cyclic Processes in the Emergence of Lexical System].* Kazan'. [= *Trudy Kazanskoj školy po komp'juternoj i kognitivnoj lingvistike. TEL-2001.* [http://www.philol.msu.ru/~lex/kogn/kogn_cont.htm].

Polikarpov, A.A.
2001a "Cognitive Model of Lexical System Evolution and its Verification." In: *Site of the Laboratory for General and Computer Lexicology and Lexicography (Faculty of Philology,*

Lomonosov Moscow State University). [`http://www.philol.msu.ru/~lex/articles/cogn_ev.htm`].

Polikarpov, A.A.; Bogdanov, V.V.; Krjukova, O.S.
1998 "Khronologičeskij morfemno-slovoobrazovatel'nyj slovar' russkogo jazyka: Sozdanie bazy dannykh i ee sistemno-kvantitativnyj analiz. [=Chronological Morphemic-Word-Formational Dictionary of Russian Language: Creation of a Database and its Systemic-Quantitative Analysis." In: *Questions of General, Historical and Comparative Linguistics. Issue 2.* Moskva. (172–184).

Appendix

M-Pos. =	Morpheme positions, i.e. ordinal numbers of morphemes (pref3,2,1, root, suf1,2,3,4,5,6,7) in a wordform
L =	Length of morphemes in a given position (for words with a given number of suffixes)
m.s =	absolute number of morphemes
l.s =	absolute number of letters

Table 10.4: Dependence of Lengths of Morphemes of Different Type on the Ordinal Number of their Positions in a Word (for words with a given number of suffixes)

M-Pos.		**Word length (in number of suffixes in them)**							
PREF		**0**		**1**		**2**		**3**	
3	**L**	**m.s**	**l.s**	**m.s**	**l.s**	**m.s**	**l.s**	**m.s**	**l.s**
	0	2815	0	5402		22728		15504	
	1		0	2	2	1	1	4	4
	2	5	10	3	6	9	18	5	10
	3		0	1	3	8	24	10	30
	4		0			9	36	3	12
	$\sum$	5	10	6	11	27	79	22	56
	$\bar{x}$	2.00		1.83		2.93		2.55	
		4		**5**		**6**		**7**	
	L	**m.s**	**l.s**	**m.s**	**l.s**	**m.s**	**l.s**	**m.s**	**l.s**
	0	3655		531		70		10	
	1	1							
	2	2	4	1	2				
	3	5	15	3	9				
	4								
	$\sum$	8	19	4	11				
	$\bar{x}$	2.38		2.75					

Table 10.4 (cont.)

PREF		0		1		2		3	
2	L	m.s	l.s	m.s	l.s	m.s	l.s	m.s	l.s
	0	2697		5241		21502		14761	
	1	44	44	35	35	221	221	153	153
	2	53	106	71	142	475	950	345	690
	3	22	66	57	171	485	1455	229	687
	4	4	16	4	16	72	288	38	152
	$\sum$	123	232	167	364	1253	2914	765	1682
	$\bar{x}$	1.89		2.18		2.33		2.20	
		4		**5**		**6**		**7**	
	L	**m.s**	**l.s**	**m.s**	**l.s**	**m.s**	**l.s**	**m.s**	**l.s**
	0	3430		499		59		6	
	1	53	53	10	10	5	5	2	2
	2	77	154	11	22	4	8	2	4
	3	87	261	11	33	2	6		0
	4	16	64	4	16		0		0
	$\sum$	233	532	36	81	11	19	4	6
	$\bar{x}$	2.28		2.25		1.73		1.50	

M-Pos.		Word length (in number of suffixes in them)							
PREF		0		1		2		3	
1	L	m.s	l.s	m.s	l.s	m.s	l.s	m.s	l.s
	0	1463		3115		8122		5085	
	1	265	265	481	481	3041	3041	2421	2421
	2	624	1248	1125	2250	7200	14400	5215	10430
	3	372	1116	630	1890	4208	12624	2699	8097
	4	95	380	55	220	179	716	101	404
	$\sum$	1356	3009	2291	4841	14628	30781	10436	21352
	$\bar{x}$	2.22		2.11		2.10		2.05	
		4		**5**		**6**		**7**	
	L	**m.s**	**l.s**	**m.s**	**l.s**	**m.s**	**l.s**	**m.s**	**l.s**
	0	1455		220		16			
	1	613	613	96	96	20	20	7	7
	2	1072	2144	151	302	20	40	1	2
	3	500	1500	60	180	9	27	1	3
	4	20	80	8	32	5	20	1	4
	$\sum$	2205	4337	315	610	54	107	10	16
	$\bar{x}$	1.97		1.94		1.98		1.60	

Table 10.4 (cont.)

ROOT		Word length (in number of suffixes in them)							
		0		1		2		3	
	L	m.s	l.s	m.s	l.s	m.s	l.s	m.s	l.s
	1	10	10	70	70	87	87	78	78
	2	89	178	608	1216	1821	3642	1866	3732
	3	976	2928	1977	5931	10171	30513	7262	21786
	4	793	3172	1511	6044	6527	26108	4245	16980
	5	531	2655	821	4105	3017	15085	1649	8245
	6	279	1674	310	1860	780	4680	321	1926
	7	92	644	82	574	288	2016	87	609
	8	32	256	26	208	62	496	16	128
	9	13	117	2	18	2	18	2	18
	10	3	30	1	10				
	12	1	12						
	15	1	15						
	$\sum$	2820	11691	5408	20036	22755	82645	15526	53502
	$\bar{x}$	4.15		3.70		3.63		3.45	
		4		5		6		7	
	L	m.s	l.s	m.s	l.s	m.s	l.s	m.s	l.s
	1	16	16	10	10	4	4	1	1
	2	530	1060	103	206	16	32	1	2
	3	1748	5244	271	813	32	96	8	24
	4	985	3940	111	444	18	72		
	5	273	1365	18	90				
	6	75	450	20	120				
	7	29	203	2	14				
	8	7	56						
	9								
	10								
	12								
	15								
	$\sum$	3663	12334	535	1697	70	204	10	27
	$\bar{x}$	3.37		3.17		2.91		2.70	

Table 10.4 (cont.)

M-Pos.		Word length (in number of suffixes in them)							
SUF		0		1		2		3	
1	L	m.s	l.s	m.s	l.s	m.s	l.s	m.s	l.s
	0	2820							
	1			1764	1764	12766	12766	8463	8463
	2			2545	5090	4427	8854	4195	8390
	3			783	2349	5041	15123	2639	7917
	4			268	1072	401	1604	171	684
	5			37	185	51	255	46	230
	6			11	66	68	408	12	72
	7					1	7		
	$\sum$			5408	10526	22755	39017	15526	25756
	$\bar{x}$			1.95		1.71		1.66	
		4		5		6		7	
	L	m.s	l.s	m.s	l.s	m.s	l.s	m.s	l.s
	1	2257	2257	374	374	57	57	10	10
	2	1187	2374	118	236	11	22		
	3	126	378	23	69	1	3		
	4	73	292	17	68	1	4		
	5	15	75	3	15				
	6	5	30						
	$\sum$	3663	5406	535	762	70	86	10	10
	$\bar{x}$	1.48		1.42		1.23		1.00	
SUF		0		1		2		3	
2	L	m.s	l.s	m.s	l.s	m.s	l.s	m.s	l.s
	0	2820		5408					
	1					4786	4786	4495	4495
	2					16256	32512	9153	18306
	3					313	939	1491	4473
	4					1294	5176	209	836
	5					100	500	147	735
	6					6	36	31	186
	$\sum$					22755	43949	15526	29031
	$\bar{x}$					1.93		1.87	

Table 10.4 (cont.)

M-Pos.		Word length (in number of suffixes in them)							
SUF		**4**		**5**		**6**		**7**	
2	**L**	**m.s**	**l.s**	**m.s**	**l.s**	**m.s**	**l.s**	**m.s**	**l.s**
(cont.)	**0**								
	1	1575	1575	191	191	17	17	2	2
	2	1015	2030	190	380	28	56	3	6
	3	480	1440	49	147	14	42		
	4	583	2332	99	396	11	44	5	20
	5	6	30	3	15				
	6	3	18	3	18				
	$\sum$	3662	7425	535	1147	70	159	10	28
	$\bar{x}$	2.03		2.14		2.27		2.80	
SUF		**0**		**1**		**2**		**3**	
3	**L**	**m.s**	**l.s**	**m.s**	**l.s**	**m.s**	**l.s**	**m.s**	**l.s**
	0	2820		5408		22755			
	1							3778	3778
	2							11075	22150
	3							91	273
	4							567	2268
	5							15	75
	$\sum$							15526	28544
	$\bar{x}$							1.84	
		4		**5**		**6**		**7**	
	L	**m.s**	**l.s**	**m.s**	**l.s**	**m.s**	**l.s**	**m.s**	**l.s**
	0								
	1	1373	1373	297	297	18	18	3	3
	2	1767	3534	150	300	25	50		
	3	418	1254	37	111	19	57	6	18
	4	76	304	45	180	7	28	1	4
	5	27	135	3	15				
	6	1	6	3	18	1	6		
	7	1	7						
	$\sum$	3663	6613	535	921	70	159	10	25
	$\bar{x}$	1.80		1.72		2.27		2.50	

Table 10.4 (cont.)

M-Pos.	Word length (in number of suffixes in them)								
SUF		0		1		2		3	
4	L	m.s	l.s	m.s	l.s	m.s	l.s	m.s	l.s
	0	2820		5408		22755		15526	
	1								
	2								
	$\sum$								
	$\bar{x}$								
		4		5		6		7	
	L	m.s	l.s	m.s	l.s	m.s	l.s	m.s	l.s
	0								
	1	941	941	171	171	43	43		
	2	2530	5060	278	556	18	36	7	14
	3	4	12	58	174	7	21	1	3
	4	188	752	23	92	2	8	2	8
	5			4	20				
	6			1	6				
	$\sum$	3662	7425	535	1147	70	159	10	28
	$\bar{x}$	1.85		1.90		1.54		2.50	
SUF		0		1		2		3	
5	L	m.s	l.s	m.s	l.s	m.s	l.s	m.s	l.s
	0	2820		5408		22755		15526	
	1								
	2								
	$\sum$								
	$\bar{x}$								
		4		5		6		7	
	L	m.s	l.s	m.s	l.s	m.s	l.s	m.s	l.s
	0	3663							
	1			196	196	17	17	9	9
	2			321	642	52	104	1	2
	3				0	1	3		0
	4			18	72		0		0
	$\sum$			535	910	70	124	10	11
	$\bar{x}$			1.70		1.77		1.10	

Table 10.4 (cont.)

M-Pos.		Word length (in number of suffixes in them)							
SUF		0		1		2		3	
6	L	m.s	l.s	m.s	l.s	m.s	l.s	m.s	l.s
	0	2820		5408		22755		15526	
	1								
	2								
	4								
	$\sum$								
	$\bar{x}$								
		4		5		6		7	
	L	m.s	l.s	m.s	l.s	m.s	l.s	m.s	l.s
	0	3663		535					
	1					19	19	1	1
	2					50	100	9	18
	4					1	4		0
	$\sum$					70	123	10	19
	$\bar{x}$					1.76		1.90	

M-Pos.		Word length (in number of suffixes in them)							
SUF		0		1		2		3	
7	L	m.s	l.s	m.s	l.s	m.s	l.s	m.s	l.s
	0	2820		5408		22755		15526	
	1								
	2								
	$\sum$								
	$\bar{x}$								
		4		5		6		7	
	L	m.s	l.s	m.s	l.s	m.s	l.s	m.s	l.s
	0	3663		535		70			
	1							6	6
	2							4	8
	$\sum$							10	14
	$\bar{x}$							1.40	

11

ASPECTS OF THE TYPOLOGY OF SLAVIC LANGUAGES

Exemplified on Word Length

Otto A. Rottmann

Traditional linguistic approaches are characterized by a generous use of the terms 'classification' and 'typology'; this can for example be found with Haarmann (1976: 13), who calls the classification of natural languages the aim of general language typology, Lehmann (1969: 58), who says that the classification of languages is the main target of each typology, as do Horne (1966: 4) and Serebrennikov (1972), where we find the term of 'typological classification'). So it seems the two terms are used as synonyms. Linguistic dictionaries published in the second half of the 20th century also reflect a state which can already be found in the 19th century. A good example of this is the dictionary by Rozental'/Telenkova; in their dictionary the entry ≪typological classification of languages≫ is followed by the definition: "morphological classification of languages" (1976: 487). The same holds for quite modern works, e.g. Siemund (2000), in which several contributors identify typology with plain classification. This definition can already be found at the beginning of any interest in typology. For the purpose of our study we have separated both terms. We call the traditional method of grouping languages a classification and reserve the term 'typology' for the study of mechanisms generating types, i.e. in our conception typology is identical with Hempel's ideal typology or theory. We would like to take a well-known example to show the reach of classification and thus demonstrate the differences.

The genealogical approach groups languages according to their development and their ancestors, so it is oriented merely diachronically and its main criterion for the allocation of languages to a class is their common, historically founded root. According to Schleicher's family tree, the Slavic languages form a big branch which in turn ramifies into three smaller branches: the West, East and South Slavic languages. The group of East Slavic languages comprises the Russian, Ukrainian and Belorussian languages. All three of them are in this

P. Gryzbek (ed.), Contributing in the Science of Text and Language, 241-258.

attractor is a basin, e.g. an ocean into which all rivers flow. You can also imagine attractors to be accumulation points, means, real forms, abstract forms and many other objects or entities. Biological species are attractors for the organization of individuals, geometrical forms attractors for artifacts. In language all '-eme'-s, e.g. phoneme, morpheme, lexeme etc., are attractors. Of course, we know that '-eme'-s stand for theoretical objects, but those terms reflect – more or less vaguely – an attractor. For example, in a human being's mouth there is the area of the palate exploited by the tongue for the production of sounds. The area for a specific sound, however, is slightly different with every individual, and it is always slightly different in each speech act, but as long as articulation is effected in the same area, i.e. attractor, the sound is identified as identical. An attractor permits variability – it depends on how it is shaped.

At the semantic level each term is an attractor. The term 'tree' or 'bird' evokes certain ideas; in psychology and psycholinguistics such ideas are called 'prototypes'. A semantic attractor is the special constellation of specific neurones in the brains which can permanently alter their shape by learning or communication. The traditional classification was characterized by the search for attractors, for example as they were called, classes, a search which was based on the assumption that fixed forms existed in the frames of which languages could form themselves. This is in no way different to biology, where just a limited number of species is found despite an endless combining capability of genes. Not everything is combined with everything, the number of known fit-for-life combinations is not infinite, however, it is high. Today we know that a language is just a combination of states of linguistic entities with entities just taking the values in a state space; those states are interlinked by self-regulation. Theoretically, all states are possible, but not all their combinations seem to be preferred or even allowed. Self-regulation depends on the human being's different needs (e.g. minimization of the work of the brain, minimization of the extent of coding, minimization of the extent of decoding etc., cf. Köhler 1986), a large part of which is governed by Zipf's principle of least effort. A linguistic type is a special case of an efficient attractor, however we define it. It is a state vector, whose elements represent the properties of data interlinked by control cycles. For classical typology it was important that the elements of that vector represented some less preferred values; the numerical taxonomy (as represented by Silnickij) already permitted an arbitrary number of combinations, because they multiplied due to the inductive approach. In our point of view we do not only look for linguistic attractors, because the theoretically most important job is to find self-regulation cycles interlinking all linguistic levels. As already said, an attractor then, is just a state vector of all linked properties. The two graphical depictions elucidate this: Figure 11.1 shows a controlled circuit of the four properties E1–E4, as they occur in synergetic linguistics. The arrows represent functions connecting the properties.

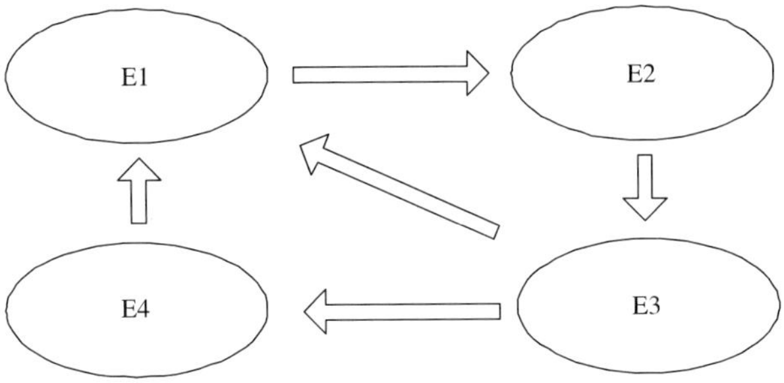

Figure 11.1: A Simple Control Cycle

If the relevant (observed) values of a property are inserted in a function, then the result is the values of all other properties linked with the initial one (elements of the vector). This is the way to build up a theory of language.

Our typological view, however, only considers the intrinsic shaping of a property, i.e. we examine the loops in control circuits (an example can be seen in Figure 11.2) and thus a branch of synergetic linguistics. A loop in the graph means that property E2 is controlled by an inherent dynamics having its own attractor.

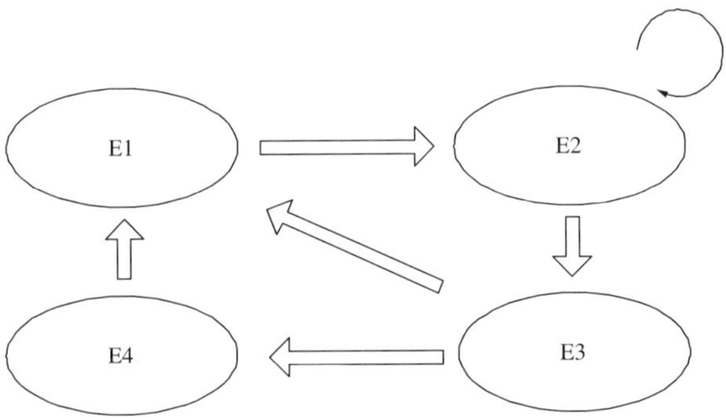

Figure 11.2: A Control Cycle With a Loop

To find such attractors, e.g. for word length, it is necessary to deductively set up (hypothetical) models and put individual languages to the test. Our models reflect the attractors. If a model is confirmed we say that an attractor is about to become or has already become dominant. The existence of attractors, in other words, the modelling capability of a property, is assumed automatically. Thus, it is not only possible to set up a theory of word length, but also group the languages according to the relevant attractor by which they are governed. This is a classification resulting from theory, i.e. an ideal typology as designed by Hempel. Just think of Mendeleev's classification of elements based on weight,

which has turned out to be a proven one, but today is based on fully different arguments. In analogy to that, linguists do not compare word length means, but search for common attractors. Thus, our view changes. We do not necessarily have a unique law (mechanism) moulding word length in the same way any more, but we can expect a mechanism sensitive to initial conditions and creating an attractor landscape. The initial conditions (genre, state of the author, audience, etc.) may decide which special attractor will be headed for. This means that we can expect several attractors for the given property. ≪We can expect≫ also includes the possibility that we find one attractor only, however, such a result would be surprising.
This immediately results in interesting questions like for example:

(a) How many attractors (models) exist in the Slavic languages for word length? Do Slavic languages even happen to have the same attractors?
(b) Does a historical development exist, i.e. a change from one attractor to another? We know that changes are set in motion on different grounds, e.g. contacts with other languages or socio-economic influences, tendencies to facilitate pronunciation to keep articulation efforts low or the tendency to limit the complex character of utterances, seemingly unexpected self-organization etc.
(c) How does this change materialize? Gradual change of parameters, modification of length classes (i.e. maintaining a model by adding ad hoc parameters), precipitous changes?
(d) Is the theory adequate or does it have to be modified?

Let's follow Hempel and thus his approach to modern scientific theory, we have to meet the following steps:

(1) Find hypotheses on the shaping of certain properties (e.g. word length). It is only of secondary character how these hypotheses come into being (cf. Bunge 1967: 243ff.), because the inception need not be identical with the reasoning, i.e. in the end those hypotheses must be deducible, testable and capable of being integrated into a system of hypotheses.
(2) Test the hypothesis/hypotheses given on many data. Observe that the data may incorporate other boundary conditions. Should a model not be suitable, provide for the following actions:
(3) (a) Check the data.
    (b) Check the computation.
    (c) Vary the parameters of the hypothesis either by using different point estimation or by iterative optimization.
    (d) Modify the hypothesis locally.

(e) Modify the hypothesis globally.
(f) Alter the basic assumptions of the hypothesis and derive a new model including minimum alterations to the basic assumptions.
(g) Generalize the basic model such that all its variants obtained so far become special cases.
(h) If all these measures do not help, search for other plausible hypotheses explaining most anomalies.

A warning has to be issued with respect to theories and models which attempt to explain everything, because a theory trying to explain everything undergoes the risk of explaining nothing. Just think that variability in languages is enormous, and even when we accept that everything in language is based on laws, we know that mechanisms only work in the same way when boundary conditions are identical and the *ceteris paribus* conditions are met. Thus we have to conclude that we have to derive a variety of models for one and the same phenomenon unless we are able to comprise all boundary conditions. This variety of models can be used for diachronic as well as synchronic purposes.

The reason for setting up a hypothesis and testing it in the area of word length is to obtain a theory in the form of an attractor landscape and, following therefrom, a typology in the Slavic languages. With respect to the construction of word length hypotheses, works by Grotjahn (1982), Wimmer et al. (1994), Wimmer/Altmann (1996, 2002) were taken as the sources for basic reflections. To come to a hypothesis on word length let us start with the general idea that the proportionality P_x P_{x-1} applies to the relationship between length classes. This proportionality is expressed by a function $g(x)$ which results in the basic assumption

$$P_x = g(x)P_{x-1} \tag{11.1}$$

$g(x)$ has an ordering function in the self-regulating system warranting redundancy, meeting different requirements (cf. Köhler 1986), braking excessive fluctuations etc.

A first hypothesis on word length distribution is found with Čebanov (1947) and independently with Fucks (1955). It is the 1–displaced Poisson distribution. Grotjahn (1982) adopts this model and gives evidence that it cannot be seen as an adequate model in general, which he shows by means of a word and syllable counting of German texts. Since Grotjahn assumes that the probability of word length also depends on influencing factors like context, change of subject etc., and therefore the probability of x syllables is not identical for each word, he generalizes the distribution by randomizing the parameter of the Poisson distribution. Using the gamma distribution, he obtains the negative binomial distribution which he proposes to be a good model after relevant tests in various languages.

In a later study, Altmann (1994) defines further $g(x)$ functions and adds some other distributions to Grotjahn's hypothesis on word length. Comprehensive studies in the course of the project at Göttingen University extended those results considerably. In order to obtain a general model comprising all Slavic languages, the proportionality function in (11.1) must be defined as

$$g(x) = 1 + a_0 + \frac{a_1}{(x + b_1)^{c_1}} \tag{11.2}$$

which is a special case of the "Unified Theory" presented by Wimmer and Altmann (2002). Inserting (11.2) into (11.1) we obtain

$$P_x = \left(1 + a_0 + \frac{a_1}{(x + b_1)^{c_1}}\right) P_{x-1} \tag{11.3}$$

representing the preliminary landscape of distributions of word length in Slavic languages. It has some pronounced centers with peripheries which signal the wandering from one center to another.

The basis for the testing performed were the living Slavic languages and the first known written Slavic language, Old Church Slavonic or Old Bulgarian. The decision as to what is to be considered a Slavic language was based on Panzer's classification (^{2}1996) despite the fact that it is for example vehemently different to the one presented by Rehder (^{3}1998), but Panzer's classification is next to the traditional one.

The number of texts analyzed was not identical in all languages; usually it amounted to thirty with the individual texts being randomly chosen. Half of them were fictional prose texts, half of them non-fictional texts with the actual kind of text being irrelevant. It was the aim of our work to come to statements on Russian, Polish, etc., and not on Russian press texts, Serbo-Croatian novel excerpts etc. It is, of course, self-evident that the Old Bulgarian language – due to its character – does not show any non-fictional texts. A number of texts slightly below or above 30 is as accidental as the choice of the texts itself.

Of course, we are conscious of the fact that an arbitrary number of texts would not be sufficient to characterize a language globally. Samples are used to draw conclusions representing the possibilities in a language. With respect to certain properties, texts could be assigned to a number of attractors which do not resemble a clearly limited landscape, but a jagged one, which, however, permits creativity and evolution and grants full adaptation to growing information needs.

We assume that the principle of randomly chosen texts applied to the choice of texts strengthens expressiveness. It is exactly this almost unlimited principle of randomly chosen objects (almost unlimited because of the only restriction by the division 50% fictional, 50% non-fictional texts) which is standard in other sciences as well. The metallurgical ASTM standard E112 (a text in a series of standards where quantitative examinations are used to assure quality) says in section 11.3:

> Fields should be chosen at random and without preference. Do not try to choose fields which look typical. Choose fields blindly and there choose different position on the polished surface.

We proceeded analogously when choosing the texts. Word length data were processed by means of the software Fitter. Word length was analyzed on the basis of syllables. The evaluation of the test results is mainly based on the criterion of P: If $P \geq 0.01$, the result can at least be called "satisfactory". Surely, this value does not have the character of a statistical law, but just a conventional decision. In many sciences, e.g. in the social sciences or in metallurgy, the threshold taken as the basis for decision is $P \geq 0.05$. In linguistics, however, the criterion could even be lowered, since the number of data processed is considerably high: it is a known fact that the χ^2 grows with the size of the sample. We will stick with the above convention. In those cases in which the value of P is not acceptable – e.g. the sample size is too great or the number of degrees of freedom is zero ($d.f. = 0$) –, another discrepancy criterion is used. In the software Fitter one finds $C = \chi^2/N$. C is satisfactory, if its value is $C \leq 0.01$. Values in the range $0.01 \leq C \leq 0.02$ are weak, but tolerable. C does not depend on degrees of freedom, it merely relativizes the observed discrepancy.

Word length, as it occurs in individual Slavic languages, has been the object of studies before and works we could refer to have been on word length in the Russian, Czech, Slovak, Slovene, modern Bulgarian and Old Bulgarian languages.

In our study counting was based on the following criteria:

(a) 'Word' is defined as an entity whose end is indicated orthographically by a subsequent blank or punctuation.

(b) Abbreviations occurring in the texts were dissolved and counted as if the text included the non-abbreviated form.

(c) Words were taken as we found them in the texts, not evaluated according to any differing correct spelling (a criterion which is especially important for Old Bulgarian where the written language reflects phonetic changes in the spoken language).

(d) Numbers, decimal numbers, years written in figures were counted as if written in full words in the texts.

(e) Headings and captions were counted, as in the case of word length, it is irrelevant if words are part of a full sentence, an ellipsis or a word combination.

(f) Quotations were only taken into consideration if they were worded in the same language as the text itself (e.g. an Old Russian quotation in a modern Russian text was not taken into consideration).

(g) Proper names were counted, if they were part of the language of the text.

(h) Initials of first names and patronymics were counted as one syllable.

(i) Abbreviated words were counted in compliance with the inflected word (e.g. ГУМ consists of one syllable, ГУМе comprises two and колхозе three syllables).

(j) Prepositions which like the modern Russian с do not include a vowel themselves were counted as one-syllable words.

As already mentioned, it was one of the aims of the study to find attractors (= types, frequently occupied states) which in the field of word length allow a typology of the Slavic languages. Within the scope of synergetic linguistics we only analyzed the internal dynamics (i.e. distributions) of lengths (i.e. the loops in the control circuit) and did not tackle the relation of length to other properties.

Those results are the boundary condition related realizations of a model within the meaning of the ideal typology when being systemized deductively. The allocation of attractors to languages, however, can be evaluated within the scope of classification. The first kind of evaluation is a theoretically constructed point of view, which under favorable conditions can also be understood as part of an evolution. Within the scope of ideal typology the entire range of models is presented as special cases, limiting cases or modifications of a general model, i.e. the movement is "from the top to the bottom". In case of a historical point of view the movement is "from the bottom to the top", i.e. analysis begins with the simplest models and is expanded gradually. It should be difficult to give evidence of the correspondence of the evolution based view with the real evolution, since multitudes and multitudes of data – and this includes a historical sequence – will have to be analyzed. The classificatory view is simply a status quo. The concrete form of this process is shown hereinafter with the partial results.

At first glance, the studies of the word lengths in the Slavic languages generally did not corroborate the hypothesis that word length is controlled by the 0-truncated negative binomial distribution, introduced by Grotjahn (1982); the evaluation of the control mechanism turned out to be a more complex problem. With respect to Old Church Slavonic – and this underlines a former result (Rottmann 1997) – the *1-displaced hyper-Poisson distribution* turned out to be a good model without restrictions. The formula for this distribution is:

$$P_x = \frac{a^{x-1}}{b^{(x-1)}\,{}_1F_1(1;b;a)}, \qquad x = 1, 2, 3, \ldots \tag{11.4}$$

with a and b being parameters; F is the hypergeometric function.

The *1-displaced Extended Positive Binomial distribution* turned out to be obviously dominant in the other Slavic languages. The formula for this distribution is:

$$P_x = \begin{cases} 1-\alpha, & x = 1 \\ \dfrac{\alpha \dbinom{n}{x-1} p^{x-1}\, q^{n-x+1}}{1-q^n}, & x = 2, 3, \ldots, n+1 \end{cases} \tag{11.5}$$

This distribution can be justified as follows: Originally in Slavic languages there were no zero-syllabic words; thus structurally every probability distribution concerning word length should be truncated at zero. However, after the fall of *jers* 0-syllabic words came into existence, e.g. some prepositions (in Russian с, к, в). Their number is, however, so small that the truncated distribution must be ad hoc modified (extended). This is the function of $1-\alpha$ in the above formula. According to our definition of ≪word≫ non-syllabic ones do not exist; we analyzed written texts and considered ≪word≫ to be a unit at orthographic level. Therefore Lehfeldt's opinion stated during discussions at our symposion in Graz according to which ≪word≫ must be defined as a phonetic entity (a point of view he borrowed from Mel'čuk and called "the best") is expressly rejected. In this way, equation (11.2) arises.

However, these two distributions could not be fitted in all cases. Like other scientists before, we had to exploit alternatives. Exactly those cases which are not exceptions within the meaning of grammatical rules, but have developed under unknown boundary conditions, compel us to find an embracing general model on condition the ideal-typological approach is chosen. We judge such cases, which cannot be integrated into the mainstream model as an attempt to leave the main attractor and import idiosyncratic forms into the text. In practice, the scientist sticks to a distribution as long as possible, e.g. by a suitable class pooling. If, however, that approach does not result in an unambiguous attractor, a model belonging to the hereinafter mentioned family is chosen. In our study (and in others known to us) the following distributions occurred: Extended Positive Binomial, Conway-Maxwell-Poisson, hyper-Pascal, hyper-Poisson, Positive Poisson, Cohen-Poisson, Positive Cohen-Poisson and their various modifications. To combine them in a kind of family we exploit a special case of the above mentioned Unified Theory

$$P_x = \left(1 + a_0 + \frac{a_1}{(x+b_1)^{c_1}}\right) P_{x-1} \tag{11.6}$$

whose solution leads to the main attractors (Binomial, Conway-Maxwell-Poisson, hyper-Pascal, hyper-Poisson, Poisson), which in turn by an a-posteriori modification lead to the remaining cases (Extended Positive Binomial, Positive Poisson, Cohen-Poisson, Positive Cohen-Poisson), and all cases found by Uhlířová (2001).

The basic reparametrizing operations of (11.1) are as follows:

Table 11.1: Reparametrizations of (11.1)

Binomial:	$1 + a_0 = -p/q, a_1 = (n+1)p/q, b_1 = 0, c_1 = 1$
Conway-Maxwell-Poisson:	$a_0 = -1, a_1 = a, b_1 = 0, c_1 = b$
Hyper-Pascal:	$-1 < a_0 < 0, 1 + a_0 = q,$ $a_1 = q(k-m), b_1 = m-1, c_1 = 1$
Hyper-Poisson:	$a_0 = -1, a_1 = a, b_1 = b-1, c_1 = 1$
Poisson:	$a_0 = -1, a_1 = a, b_1 = 0, c_1 = 1.$

For example, if we insert the reparametrization concerning the hyper-Pascal distribution into (11.3), we obtain

$$P_x = \left(q + \frac{q(k-m)}{x+m-1}\right) P_{x-1} \tag{11.7}$$

and by ordering the expression in the brackets, we obtain

$$P_x = \frac{q(x+m-1) + q(k-m)}{m+x-1} P_{x-1} = \frac{k+x-1}{m+x-1} q P_{x-1} \tag{11.8}$$

in which we recognize the recurrence formula of the hyper-Pascal distribution. Convergencies and special cases can be ascertained directly in the recurrence formulas. For example, if in the hyper-Pascal distribution $m = 1, k \to \infty, q \to 0, kq \to a$, then we obtain $P_x = \frac{a}{x} P_{x-1}$, i.e. the Poisson distribution, etc.

The interpretation of (11.3) is simple and elucidating (cf. Wimmer/Altmann 2002. The majority of linguistic laws have been derived on the assumption that the relative rate of change of the dependent variable is proportional to that of the independent one, i.e. the first step undertaken with continuous variables was

$$\frac{dy}{y} = \left(a + \frac{b}{x}\right) dx \tag{11.9}$$

which in discrete form is

$$\frac{\Delta P_{x-1}}{P_{x-1}} = a + \frac{b}{x} \tag{11.10}$$

Since the right hand side is, as a matter of fact, the beginning of an infinite series, it is sufficient to expand it to the necessary number of members and solve the pertinent equations. The further coefficients represent those factors which exert an influence only via the first independent variable and are relativized by certain powers of it. Thus different kinds of generalizations are obtained, from which it is sufficient ("sufficient" for our purposes) to take

$$\frac{\Delta P_{x-1}}{P_{x-1}} = a_0 + \frac{a_1}{(x+b_1)^{c_1}} + \frac{a_2}{(x+b_2)^{c_2}} + \ldots \tag{11.11}$$

Letting $a_2 = a_3 = \ldots = 0$ and by reordering, we obtain formula (11.3). All distributions mentioned above are shown in Table 11.2.

Table 11.2: Special Cases of (11.3)

Name	**g(x)**	**P$_x$**	**Modifications**
Poisson	$\frac{a}{x}$	$\frac{e^{-a}a^x}{x!}$	Cohen-Poisson
Positive Poisson	$\frac{a}{x}$	$\frac{e^{-a}a^x}{x!(1-e^{-a})}$	Pos. Cohen-Poisson
hyper-Poisson	$\frac{a}{b+x-1}$	$\frac{a^x}{b^{(x)}{}_1F_1(1;b;a)}$	
Conway-Max-well-Poisson	$\frac{a}{x^b}$	$\frac{a^x}{(x!)^b}P_0$	
Binomial	$\frac{n-x+1}{x}\frac{p}{q}$	$\binom{n}{x}p^x q^{n-x}$	Ext. Pos. Binomial
hyper-Pascal	$\frac{k+x-1}{m+x-1}q$	$\frac{\binom{k+x-1}{x}}{\binom{m+x-1}{x}}q^x P_0$	

All others used for modelling word length in Slavic languages originate from modifications of the binomial distribution [Extended Positive Binomial, Uhlıro̊va's´ cases (Uhlířová 2001)] and the Poisson distribution (Positive Poisson, Positive Cohen-Poisson, Cohen-Poisson).

All "plain" distributions are used in their 1-displaced forms, P_0 is the normalizing factor. The entire hierarchy then looks as follows (see Figure 11.3). The hierarchy includes the basic distribution, i.e. we do not make any difference between standard and displaced distributions; truncated distributions (called positive) are listed separately. The hierarchy in Figure 11.3 is not based on the number of parameters (simplicity), since modifications usually have more

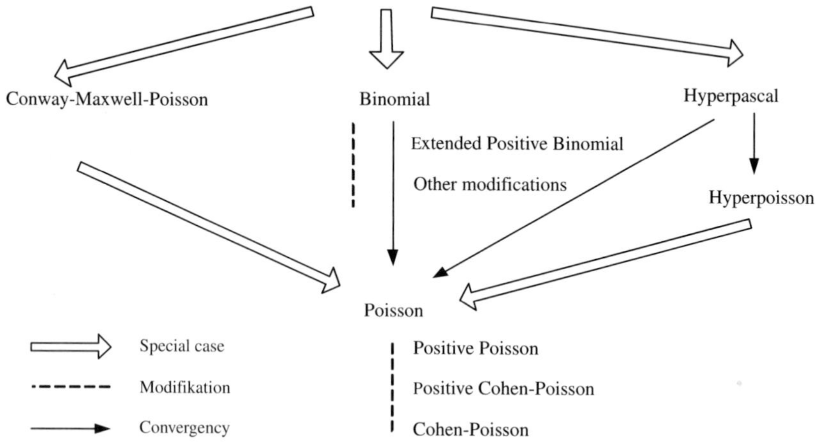

Figure 11.3: Hierarchy of word length distributions

parameters than the parent distribution. It is obvious that the range of Slavic languages is a rather narrow one and their positions are very close together. The allocation of the languages to those attractors is shown in Table 11.3 (the figures in brackets indicate the number of texts in our study).[1]

Table 11.3: Classification According to Evolutionary Tendencies

OCS	HYP(14)	EPB(1)	PCP(1)			
BG		EPB(31)				
MC		EPB(30)				
POL	EPB (30)					
RS	HYP(1)	EPB(30)				
SCR		EPB(59)	CP(1)			
SOR		EPB(21)		HPa(2)		
SK	HYP(1)	EPB(28)		HPa(1)	CMP (1)	PP(1)
SLO		EPB(29)			CMP(1)	
CZ		EPB(28)				ModBin (1)
UK	HYP(3)	EPB(26)				
BR	HYP(2)	EPB(28)				

[1] Abbreviations for distributions discussed in this paper: CMP = Conway–Maxwell–Poisson, CP = Cohen–Poisson, EPB = Extended Positive Binomial, HPa = Hyper-Pascal, HYP = Hyper-Poisson, ModBin = Modified Binomial, PCP = Positive Cohen–Poisson, PP = Positive Poisson

Table 11.3 is self-explaining. It shows the weight of an attractor (number in brackets) and the variation of the attractors, and it shows that the Slavic languages are all members of one word length family. Though the attractors give evidence of a strong gravitation, we find secondary attractors in nine out of twelve languages. This may be due to the evolutionary movement in the given language, other causes are: number of analyzed texts, size of the samples, kinds of texts etc.

A possibility to order languages and obtain a traditional, though not explanatory classification is a list including the number of attractors as the relevant criterion. Thus we obtain Table 11.4.[2]

Table 11.4: Classification According to Evolutionary Tendencies

Number of Attractors	*Languages*
1	BG, MC, POL
2	RS, SCR, SOR, SLO, CZ, UK, BR
3	OCS
5	SK

It can be assumed that studies on further texts in each Slavic language – most probably with the exception of the Old Church Slavonic language – will result in new attractors, the current representation, however, suggests the following interpretation: a language showing many attractors seems to be one governed by movement, i.e. alterations can be expected. With respect to the Old Church Slavonic language we can confirm that assumption: It was subjected to a movement evoking the *jer* modification and loss; the modern languages already stabilized after that modification. From a historical point of view those attractors are maintained, as the texts exist, but stabilization can be concluded from their occurrences.

With respect to history, Figure 11.3 can be turned around, and it can be assumed that evolutionary development starts with the simplest distribution, i.e. the Poisson distribution, and continues either by adding further parameters or extending the proportionality $g(x)$ or (after the solution of the difference equation, that is to say after the attractor comes into being) by local modifications of already existing distributions.

[2] Abbreviations for languages analyzed in this paper: BG = Bulgarian, BR = Belorussian, CZ = Czech, MC = Macedonian, OCS = Old Church Slavonic, POL = Polish, RS = Russian, SCR = Serbo–Croatian, SOR = Sorbian, SK = Slovak, SLO = Slovene, UK = Ukrainian

Table 11.2 clearly shows this development. The evolution based diagram for the Slavic languages can therefore be presented as in Figure 11.4.

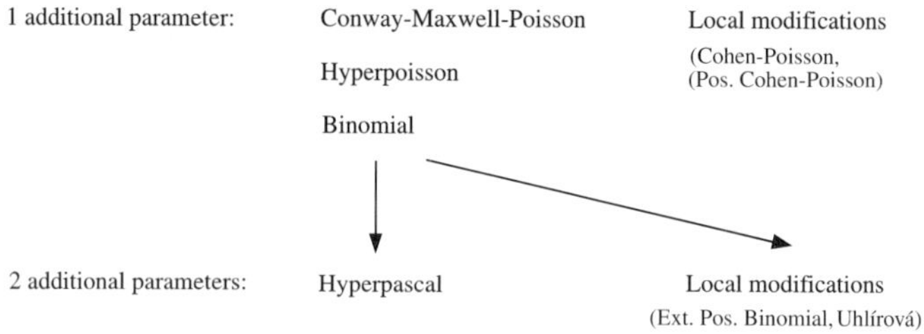

Figure 11.4: The History-Based Diagram of Attractors for Slavic Languages

This is, of course, merely a rational reconstruction of the evolution, not the real one. In order to ascertain the real development, texts from different historical epochs in all Slavic languages would have to be analyzed. This could easily turn out to be a task for a team of researchers. A preliminary historical reconstruction following from the allocation of the languages to the attractors in Table 11.3 is as follows: The primary model in the oldest stratum (*OCS*) was the hyper-Poisson distribution. The fall of the *jers* caused a shift in the landscape and all modern Slavic languages moved to the extended positive binomial distribution which was adequate to capture the complicated changes in syllable structurewhich in turn changed the word length. The hyper-Poisson distribution was almost completely eliminated. However, Slavic languages are not in absolute stasis, they begin to creatively search for new ways in the landscape. They already created six new attractors within the same family of distributions. Of course, a prediction is not possible.

A merely inductive classification based on attractors can be built as follows: Each language is represented as a vector whose elements are the proportions of texts belonging to individual attractors. Since we have eight attractors, the vector for word length (*WL*) will have the form

WL(Language) = [HYP, EPB, PCP, CP, HPa, CMP, PP, ModBin].

For example:

WL(OCS) = [14/16, 1/16, 1/16, 0, 0, 0, 0, 0] = [0.88, 0.06, 0.06, 0, 0, 0, 0, 0]

The vectors can be used to compute the concentration of a language in an attractor or to compute the similarity or dissimilarity of the languages to obtain a similarity or dissimilarity matrix. The latter is then taken as the basis for a standard taxonomy. Several softwares perform this task mechanically. With respect to Slavic languages such classifications have been elaborated for other properties several times; they were not practised in our study since they do not permit theoretical insight.

References

American Society for Testing and Materials (ASTM).
1996 *ASTM Standard E112: Standard Test Methods for Determining Average Grain Size.* West Conshocken.

Bunge, M.
1967 *Scientific research I. The search for system.* New York.

Bunge, M.
1983 *Treatise on basic philosophy. Vol. 5: Epistemology & Methodology I: Exploring the World.* Dordrecht.

Bunge, M.
1995 "Quality, quantity, pseudoquantity and measurement", in: *Journal of Quantitative Linguistics, 2*; 1–10.

Bunjakovskij, V.Ja.
1847 "O vozmoñosti vvedenija opredelitel'nych mer" doverija k" rezul'tatam" nekotorych" nauk" nabljudatel'nych", i preimuščestvenno statistiki." In: *Sovremennik, tom 3.* Sankt-peterburg. (36–49).

Carnap, R.
1969 *Einführung in die Philosophie der Naturwissenschaft.* München.

Čebanov, S.G.
1947 "O podčinenii rečevych ukladov indoevropejskoj gruppy zakonu Puassona." In: *Doklady Akademii Nauk SSSR, 55/2*; 103–106.

Essler, W.
1971 *Wissenschaftstheorie I–III.* Freiburg, 1971.

Fucks, W.
1955 *Mathematische Analyse von Sprachelementen, Sprachstil und Sprachen.* Köln.

Grotjahn, R.
1982 "Ein statistisches Modell für die Verteilung der Wortlänge", in: *Zeitschrift für Sprachwissenschaft, 1*; 44–75.

Haarmann, H.
1976 *Grundzüge der Sprachtypologie.* Stuttgart.

Horne, K.M.
1966 *Language Typology – 19th and 20th Century Views.* Washington.

Köhler, R.
1986 *Zur linguistischen Synergetik. Struktur und Dynamik der Lexik.* Bochum.

Lehmann, W.
1969 *Einführung in die historische Linguistik.* Heidelberg.

Nemcová, E.; Altmann, G.
1994 "Zur Wortlänge in slovakischen Texten", in: *Zeitschrift für empirische Textforschung, 1*; 40–43.

Panzer, B.
1996 *Die slavischen Sprachen in Gegenwart und Geschichte.* Frankfurt.

Papp, F.
1966 *Mathematical Linguistics in the Soviet Union.* The Hague.

Rehder, P.
1998 *Einführung in die slavischen Sprachen.* Darmstadt.

Rottmann, O.A.
1997 "Word Length Counting in Old Church Slavonic", in: *Journal of Quantitative Linguistics, 4*; 252–256.

Rozental', D.; Telenkova, M.
1972 *Spravočnik lingvističeskich terminov.* Moskva.

Serebrennikov, B.A.
1972 *Obščee jazykoznanie. Vnutrennjaja struktura jazyka.* Moskva.

Siemund, P. (ed.)
2000 *Methodology in Linguistic Typology. Sprachtypologie und Universalienforschung. Bd. 53, 1.*

More recent stylometric studies, however, usually have not concentrated on the specific impact of word length; rather, more than one textual characteristic has been included at a time – thus, observations as to various parameters (such as sentence length, word frequency, etc.) have been simultaneously combined, in the hope that this combination would lead to a maximum of information about the text under study; and to a certain degree, the same holds true for stylometric attempts as for text classification (not taking into account content-based approaches, here).

The systematic study of word length, along with the careful control of language-internal factors – such as authorship, or text type – possibly influencing word length, thus would yield precious insights for both quantitative linguistics and stylometry. Quantitative linguistics would not gain insight as to the question in how far its methodological apparatus is useful for the study of individual texts, too; also, it would learn in how far it is necessary to pay attention to such language-internal factors. Stylometry, in turn, would profit from realizing which linguistic factors contribute to what degree in analyzing questions of authorship, text attribution, etc.

In a way, the present case study attempts to combine both approaches: on the basis of word length analyses, multivariate analyses will be applied in order to test to what extent each individual text can be classified in one of three categories: literary prose, journalistic prose, and poetry. The study is based on 153 Slovenian texts: 51 of these texts are of a poetic nature, 102 texts are written in prose (52 of them represent literary prose, 50 journalistic prose).[1] Each text will be quantitatively described by a number of measures reflecting the moments of the distribution of its word length (mean value m_1, variance m_2, third moment m_3, and the quotients $I = m_2/m_1$ and $S = m_3/m_2$). Additionally, the number of syllables of the text will be defined as the $text\ length$. Our study was done within the framework of the Graz Project on Word Length (Frequencies) as described in Grzybek/Stadlober (2002) and is specifically based on the undergraduate thesis of Djuzelic (2002) considering the following approach. A collection of three categories of texts (literary prose, journalistic prose, and poetry) will be analyzed by means of discriminant analysis to give answers to the following questions. Is it possible to discriminate between the texts with the help of the measures mentioned above such that most of the texts can be assigned to the original category? Which measures are the most important ones for suitable discrimination and classification?

[1] Note that we use the same text base as the paper Antić et al. (2005), except one additional journalistic text in our data collection. The appendix of the paper mentioned contains details of these texts as to author, title, chapter, and year, as well as to statistical measures.

2. Quantitative Measures for the Analysis of Texts

The distribution of the word length of the texts are described by the four variables m_1, m_2, I and S, and the text length is characterized by the two variables TLS which is the length of text in syllables and its logarithm $\log(TLS)$. These two variables will act as *control variables* for our statistical procedures, because the texts were chosen from three groups which differ remarkably according their text length; e.g. the mean text length of literary texts is four times longer than the mean text length of journalistic texts, which again is four times longer than the mean text length of poetic texts (see Table 12.2). The definition of the variables used in our analysis are listed in Table 12.1.

Table 12.1: Six Statistical Measures Characterizing Slovenian Texts

m_1	average word length where word length is the number of syllables per word
m_2	empirical variance of the word length
$I = m_1/m_2$	first criterion of Ord (see Ord, 1967)
$S = m_3/m_2$	second criterion of Ord with m_3 the third moment
TLS	text length as number of syllables
$\log(TLS)$	natural logarithm of text length

Every text in our context is a statistical object carrying its information on $p = 6$ variables. In this way the quantitative description of text j from group i is given by an observation vector of dimension 6.

$$\mathbf{x}_{ij} = (TLS(i,j), m_1(i,j), m_2(i,j), \log(TLS)(i,j), I(i,j), S(i,j)) \\ \text{where} \quad j = 1, \ldots, n_i\,;\; i = 1,2,3. \tag{12.1}$$

For each group i the mean values of the six variables are collected to a mean vector of same dimension:

$$\overline{\mathbf{x}}_i = \left(\overline{TLS}(i), \overline{m_1}(i), \overline{m_2}(i), \overline{\log(TLS)}(i), \overline{I}(i), \overline{S}(i)\right)\ , \ i = 1,2,3\,. \tag{12.2}$$

An outline of the data with two texts of each category is given in Table 12.2.

2.1 Variance-Covariance Structure of the Variables

The variability of the data is measured by the symmetric variance-covariance matrix S of dimension 6×6. The diagonal elements s_{jj} of this matrix are the empirical variances of the variables and the non-diagonal elements s_{jk}, $j \neq k$, constitute the empirical co-variances between the variables j and k.

Table 12.2: Statistical Values of Two Slovenian Texts For Each Group

	Text category	TLS	m_1	m_2	$\log(TLS)$	I	S
1	literary prose	4943	1.89	1.02	8.51	0.54	0.95
2		2791	1.93	1.06	7.93	0.55	0.86
	$n_1 = 52, \bar{\mathbf{x}}_1 = ($	4000	1.84	0.96	8.05	0.52	0.90)
1	journalistic prose	1537	2.21	1.75	7.34	0.79	1.09
2		1200	2.31	1.62	7.09	0.70	0.74
	$n_2 = 50, \bar{\mathbf{x}}_2 = ($	1084	2.25	1.59	6.78	0.71	0.85)
1	poetry	312	1.81	0.72	5.74	0.40	0.50
2		402	1.75	0.91	6.00	0.52	1.27
	$n_3 = 51, \bar{\mathbf{x}}_3 = ($	270	1.74	0.68	5.41	0.39	0.69)

The elements r_{jk} of the correlation matrix R are obtained from the variance–covariance matrix by the standardization $r_{jk} = s_{jk}/\sqrt{s_{jj}s_{kk}}$. It follows that $-1 \leq r_{jk} \leq 1$ where values near ± 1 (high negative or high positive correlation) indicate a nearly linear relationship between the two variables, and values $r_{jk} \approx 0$ signify that the variables are uncorrelated. The variance-covariance matrix S_1 and the correlation matrix R_1 of the texts in group 1 (literary prose) are listed in Table 12.3. There are high correlations between the pairs *average word length* m_1 and quotient $I = m_2/m_1$ ($r = 0.98$), and moments m_1 and m_2 ($r = 0.92$). Rather low correlations appear between the second criterion of Ord (1967), $S = m_3/m_2$ and all other variables.

2.2 Statistical Distance and Linear Discriminant Function

Univariate Statistical Distance. The univariate statistical distance is an important measure for separating data of two different groups of text. It will be assumed that the texts are independent samples $(x_{11}, \ldots, x_{1n_1})$ and $(x_{21}, \ldots, x_{2n_2})$ of two distributions having possibly different theoretical means μ_i, but the same variance σ^2. The theoretical means are estimated by the arithmetic means $\bar{x}_i$ of the samples and the common variance can be estimated by pooling together the two empirical variances s_i^2 of the samples as

$$s_{pool}^2 = \frac{1}{n_1 + n_2 - 2}\left((n_1 - 1)s_1^2 + (n_2 - 1)s_2^2\right) . \tag{12.3}$$

Table 12.3: Variance-Covariance and Correlation Matrix For Text Category 1: Literary Prose

$$S_1 = \begin{pmatrix} & TLS & log(TLS) & m_1 & m_2 & I & S \\ TLS & 8664007.55 & 1961.689 & 80.350 & 75.170 & 18.007 & 27.434 \\ log(TLS) & 1961.69 & 0.504 & 0.019 & 0.017 & 0.004 & 0.005 \\ m_1 & 80.35 & 0.019 & 0.004 & 0.006 & 0.002 & 0.001 \\ m_2 & 75.17 & 0.017 & 0.006 & 0.009 & 0.003 & 0.003 \\ I & 18.01 & 0.004 & 0.002 & 0.003 & 0.001 & 0.001 \\ S & 27.43 & 0.005 & 0.001 & 0.003 & 0.001 & 0.007 \end{pmatrix}$$

$$R_1 = \begin{pmatrix} & TLS & log(TLS) & m_1 & m_2 & I & S \\ TLS & 1 & 0.94 & 0.41 & 0.27 & 0.17 & 0.11 \\ log(TLS) & 0.94 & 1 & 0.41 & 0.25 & 0.14 & 0.09 \\ m_1 & 0.41 & 0.41 & 1 & 0.92 & 0.82 & 0.17 \\ m_2 & 0.27 & 0.25 & 0.92 & 1 & 0.98 & 0.33 \\ I & 0.17 & 0.14 & 0.82 & 0.98 & 1 & 0.39 \\ S & 0.11 & 0.09 & 0.17 & 0.33 & 0.39 & 1 \end{pmatrix}$$

The univariate statistical distance D and the t-value $|t|$ are given as

$$D(\overline{x}_1, \overline{x}_2) = \frac{|\overline{x}_1 - \overline{x}_2|}{s_{pool}}, \quad |t| = \sqrt{\frac{n_1 n_2}{n_1 + n_2}}\, D(\overline{x}_1, \overline{x}_2)\,. \tag{12.4}$$

Tables 12.4, 12.5 and 12.6 contain the mean values, standard deviations and univariate statistical distances for all six variables giving the results of all pairwise comparisons according to the three categories of text.
The comparison of literary prose and journalistic prose in Table 12.4 shows the highest distance values $D \geq 3.6$ according the variables m_1 and I which are also highly correlated. However, the mean values of TLS differ at most, but the large empirical standard deviations keep the statistical distance between the two categories at a lower level.

The scatter plot in Figure 12.1(a) shows a very high correlation between m_1 and I for texts of type *literary prose* (lower part on the left) and also a high correlation for *journalistic texts* (upper part, right). However, the combination of these two variables results in a good discrimination of the two categories based on the larger values of both m_1 and I for journalistic texts.

Literary prose and *poetry* are discriminated best by the variable $\log(TLS)$ resulting in $D \approx 3.9$. Here a large difference of the mean values is combined with similar standard deviations having low order of magnitude compared to the means (see Table 12.5). Because of its better distributional properties, the variable $\log(TLS)$ is a more significant measure for discrimination than the untransformed text length TLS. According to this, the only possible discriminator

Table 12.4: Literary Prose and Journalistic Prose: Mean Values, Standard Deviations, Univariate Statistical Distances

Variable	Text type	$\bar{x}_j^{(1)} \vert \bar{x}_k^{(2)}$	$s_j^{(1)} \vert s_k^{(2)}$	$D(\bar{x}_j^{(1)}, \bar{x}_k^{(2)})$
TLS	literary prose	4000.00	2943.47	1.342
	journalistic prose	1084.20	784.47	
$\log(TLS)$	literary prose	8.05	0.71	1.869
	journalistic prose	6.78	0.64	
m_1	literary prose	1.84	0.07	**3.994**
	journalistic prose	2.25	0.13	
m_2	literary prose	0.96	0.96	0.900
	journalistic prose	1.59	0.20	
I	literary prose	0.52	0.04	**3.606**
	journalistic prose	0.71	0.06	
S	literary prose	0.90	0.09	0.328
	journalistic prose	0.85	0.22	

with respect to word length is the first criterion of Ord $I = m_1/m_2$ yielding $D \approx 2.1$.

The scatter plot of $\log(TLS)$ and I in Figure 12.1(b) illustrates the situation described above: the categories *literary prose* and *poetry* can be discriminated by $\log(TLS)$, but looking at the distribution of the variable I one can observe similar values in both text categories corresponding to a lower value of the statistical distance.

The most interesting results appear in the comparison of *journalistic prose* and *poetry*. Table 12.6 lists three measures of similar performance ($4.1 \leq D \leq 4.8$) for univariate discrimination where all three are based on word length variables: the variance m_2, the first criterion of Ord $I = m_1/m_2$ and the mean value m_1. For our comparison in Figure 12.1(c) we selected the most discriminating variables m_2 and I. The perfect linear relationship between these two variables is combined with a good discriminating power for the categories *journalistic prose* and *poetry*.

Multivariate Statistical Distance and Discriminant Function. In the following we will study multivariate observations looking at all $p = 6$ variables simultaneously. The theoretical background of discriminant analysis may be found in the books of Flury (1997) and Hand (1981). A distance measure be-

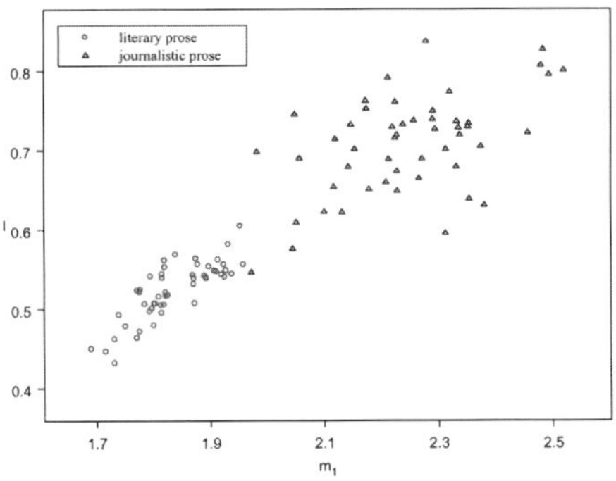

(a) Scatter Plot of the Pair (m_1, I) for Literary Prose and Journalistic Prose

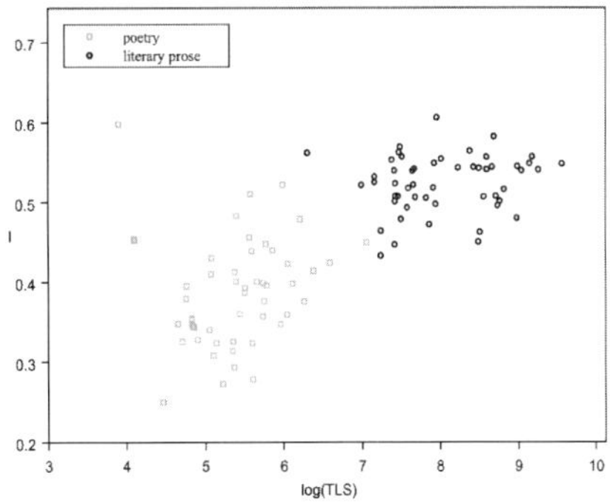

(b) Scatter Plot of the Pair $(\log(TLS), I)$ for Literary Prose and Poetry

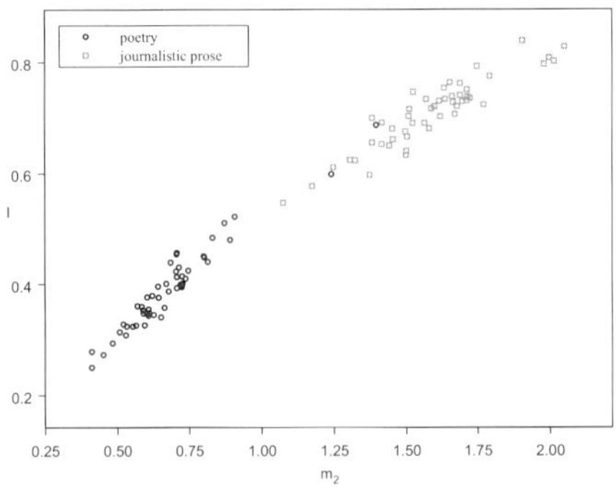

(c) Scatter Plot of the Pair (m_2, I) for Journalistic Prose and Poetry

Figure 12.1: Scatterplots

tween two groups of texts based on multivariate observations is a generalization of the univariate case given in (12.4). It will be assumed that the texts are independent samples of observation vectors $(\mathbf{x}_{j1}, \ldots, \mathbf{x}_{jn_j})$ and $(\mathbf{x}_{k1}, \ldots, \mathbf{x}_{kn_k})$ of two p–dimensional distributions having possibly different theoretical mean vectors $\boldsymbol{\mu}_j$ and $\boldsymbol{\mu}_k$ and the same $p \times p$ variance-covariance matrix Σ. The mean vectors are estimated by the vectors of the arithmetic means $\overline{\mathbf{x}}_j$ and $\overline{\mathbf{x}}_k$. The variance-covariance matrix Σ is estimated by the common empirical variance-covariance matrix S_{jk} obtained by pooling together the two variance-covariance matrices S_k and S_j of the groups as

$$S_{jk} = \frac{1}{n_j + n_k - 2} \cdot ((n_j - 1) \cdot S_j + (n_k - 1) \cdot S_k) \ . \qquad (12.5)$$

Table 12.5: Literary Prose and Poetry: Mean Values, Standard Deviations, Univariate Statistical Distances

Variable	Text type	$\bar{x}_j^{(1)} \vert \bar{x}_k^{(2)}$	$s_j^{(1)} \vert s_k^{(2)}$	$D(\bar{x}_j^{(1)}, \bar{x}_k^{(2)})$
TLS	literary prose	4000.0	2943.47	1.780
	poetry	269.86	1917.46	
$\log(TLS)$	literary prose	8.05	0.71	**3.943**
	poetry	5.41	0.62	
m_1	literary prose	1.84	0.07	1.045
	poetry	1.74	0.12	
m_2	literary prose	0.96	0.96	0.403
	poetry	0.68	0.17	
I	literary prose	0.52	0.04	**2.147**
	poetry	0.39	0.08	
S	literary prose	0.90	0.09	1.126
	poetry	0.69	0.25	

The multivariate statistical distance $D(\overline{\mathbf{x}}_j, \overline{\mathbf{x}}_k)$ between the mean vectors $\overline{\mathbf{x}}_j$ and $\overline{\mathbf{x}}_k$ is defined as

$$D_{jk} = D\left(\overline{\mathbf{x}}_j, \overline{\mathbf{x}}_k\right) = \sqrt{(\overline{\mathbf{x}}_j - \overline{\mathbf{x}}_k)' S_{jk}^{-1} (\overline{\mathbf{x}}_j - \overline{\mathbf{x}}_k)}\,, \tag{12.6}$$

where S_{jk}^{-1} is the inverse of matrix S_{jk} and $\mathbf{x}'$ the transposed vector of $\mathbf{x}$. So, the distance D_{jk} between two groups is defined as the distance between the group centers (means) standardized by the pooled variance-covariance structure. As numerical values of the distances we get

$$D_{12} = 5.5167\,, \quad D_{13} = 4.7661 \quad D_{23} = 5.4022 \tag{12.7}$$

which are remarkably higher than the maximal values 3.99, 3.94 and 4.80 of the corresponding univariate distances given in Tables 12.4–12.6. The variance-covariance matrices S_j, $j = 1, 2, 3$, and the pooled variance-covariance matrices S_{jk} may be found in Djuzelic (2002). The discrimination function Y_{jk} is introduced as a linear combination of the p-variables and can be calculated for each p-dimensional observation $\mathbf{x}_{lm}$ of the two groups as

$$Y_{jk}(\mathbf{x}_{lm}) = \mathbf{b}'_{ij}\mathbf{x}_{lm} \quad \text{with vector of coefficients} \quad \mathbf{b}_{ij} = S_{jk}^{-1}(\overline{\mathbf{x}}_j - \overline{\mathbf{x}}_k)\,. \tag{12.8}$$

Table 12.6: Journalistic Prose and Poetry: Mean Values, Standard Deviations, Univariate Statistical Distances

Variable	**Text type**	$\bar{x}_j^{(1)} \vert \bar{x}_k^{(2)}$	$s_j^{(1)} \vert s_k^{(2)}$	$D(\bar{x}_j^{(1)}, \bar{x}_k^{(2)})$
TLS	journalistic prose	1084.16	784.47	1.432
	poetry	269.86	191.75	
$\log(TLS)$	journalistic prose	6.78	0.64	2.173
	poetry	5.41	0.62	
m_1	journalistic prose	2.25	0.13	**4.149**
	poetry	1.74	0.12	
m_2	journalistic prose	1.59	0.20	**4.795**
	poetry	0.68	0.17	
I	journalistic prose	0.71	0.06	**4.417**
	poetry	0.39	0.08	
S	journalistic prose	0.85	0.22	0.660
	poetry	0.69	0.25	

The mean values $\overline{Y}_{jk}^{j}$, $\overline{Y}_{jk}^{k}$ of the groups, the center m_{jk} of the two groups, and the standardized discriminant function Z_{jk} are defined as

$$\begin{aligned} \overline{Y}_{jk}^{j} &= Y_{jk}(\overline{\mathbf{x}}_j)\,, \quad \overline{Y}_{jk}^{k} = Y_{jk}(\overline{\mathbf{x}}_k)\,, \\ m_{jk} &= \frac{1}{2}\left(\overline{Y}_{jk}^{j} + \overline{Y}_{jk}^{k}\right), \; Z_{jk}(\mathbf{x}_{lm}) = \left(Y_{jk}(\mathbf{x}_{lm}) - m_{jk}\right)/D_{jk}\,. \end{aligned} \tag{12.9}$$

Now each observation vector $\mathbf{x}_{lm}$ can be classified according to its value of Z_{jk}. For our data we get the following classification rules:

1. A text is classified as *literary prose* if $Z_{12} > 0$ and $Z_{13} > 0$.
2. A text is classified as *journalistic prose* if $Z_{12} < 0$ and $Z_{23} > 0$.
3. A text is classified as *poetry* if $Z_{13} < 0$ and $Z_{23} < 0$.

The specific situation is best explained by the histograms of the standardized discriminating variables Z_{12}, Z_{13} and Z_{23} exhibited as Figures 12.2(a), 12.2(b) and 12.2(c). With these graphical displays it is possible to judge the separation power of the discriminant functions. The cut point between two groups is zero as given above. The largest statistical distance $D_{12} = 5.5167$ appears between *journalistic prose* and *literary prose* resulting in a good discrimination by the variable Z_{12} (see Figure 12.2(a)). The lowest statistical distance of $D_{13} =$

4.7661 is between *poetry* and *literary prose* yielding a weaker potential of Z_{13} for separation – see Figure 12.2(b). A slightly better result is obtained in the comparison between *poetry* and *literary prose* where the rather large distance $D_{23} = 5.4022$ implies a good separation of these two groups as can be observed in Figure 12.2(c).

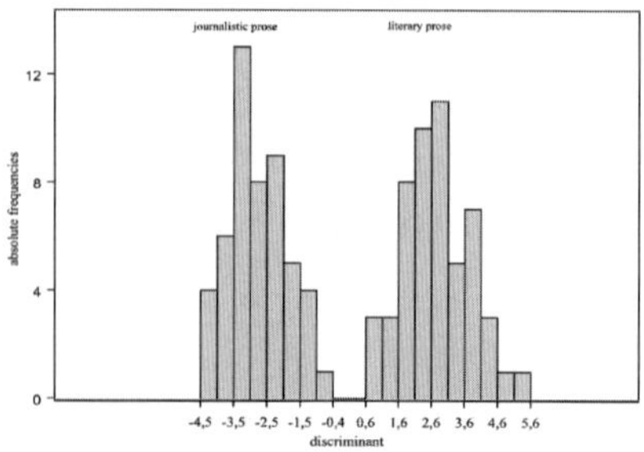

(a) Separation of journalistic prose and literary prose: histogram of the discriminant Z_{12} with multivariate statistical distance $D_{12} = 5.517$

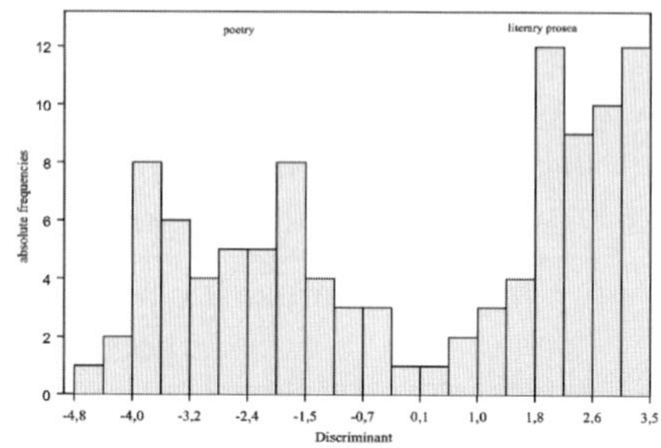

(b) Separation of poetry and literary prose: histogram of the discriminant Z_{13} with multivariate distance $D_{13} = 4.766$

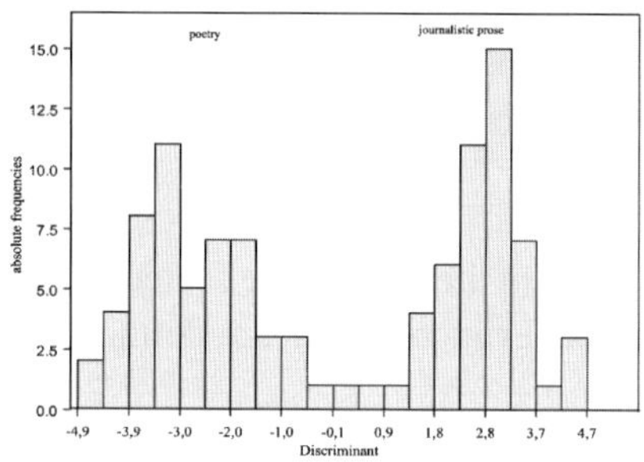

(c) Separation of poetry and journalist prose: histogram of the discriminant Z_{23} with multivariate statistical distance $D_{23} = 5.402$

Figure 12.2: Separations of Different Text Types

3. Relevant and Redundant Variables in Linear Discriminant Functions

The linear discriminant functions as defined in (12.8) are calculated as linear combinations of all $p = 6$ variables. However, there may be some redundancy because of the correlation structure of the variables. Some pairs of variables have high correlations as presented in the correlation matrix of Table 12.3 for literary prose. It is possible to locate redundant variables in the linear combination by testing the significance of each variable in a stepwise manner. Starting with the whole set of $p = 6$ variables, each variable in the set is tested by calculating the corresponding test statistic which is a Student t statistic with $n_k + n_j - p - 1$ degrees of freedom. If there is at least one redundant variable in the set, i.e. having value $|t| < 2$, then the variable with the smallest $|t|$ value (this is also the variable with the smallest reduction of the statistical distance) is removed from the set. In the next stage the same procedure is carried out on the reduced set with $p' = p - 1$ variables. The procedure terminates when all variables in the remaining set are relevant. This test procedure is demonstrated in Table 12.7 comparing *literary prose* with *journalistic prose* where the variables S and TLS are identified as redundant variables. Hence the set of 6 variables is reduced to a set of four relevant variables, and this reduction has no impact on the distance function (marginal reduction from 5.5167 to 5.5131).

Table 12.7: Redundant Variables S and TLS in Y_{12} (First Block), Redundant Variable TLS in $Y_{12}^{-\{S\}}$ (Second Block) and No Redundant Variable in $Y_{12}^{-\{S,TLS\}}$ (Third Block)

Variable	**coeff.** $b_{12(k)}$	**std.error** $se(b_{12(k)})$	**t-statistic** $t_{12(k)}$-values	**red.distance** $\hat{D}_{12(-k)}$
TLS	0.0002	0.0005	*0.3897*	*5.513*
$\log(TLS)$	4.0731	1.5774	2.5822	5.309
m_1	−117.3995	22.2230	−5.2828	4.757
m_2	129.0193	32.5310	3.9660	5.055
I	−314.3848	68.9248	−4.5613	4.926
S	0.6883	4.7043	**0.1463**	**5.516**
TLS	0.0002	0.0005	**0.3135**	**5.513**
$\log(TLS)$	4.1049	1.5533	2.6427	5.301
m_1	−118.0241	21.6579	−5.4495	4.724
m_2	128.8789	32.3504	3.9838	5.055
I	−312.4976	67.4393	−4.6338	4.914
$\log(TLS)$	4.5291	0.7755	5.8405	4.633
m_1	−116.3618	20.9648	−5.5759	4.697
m_2	126.8984	31.6495	4.0095	5.051
I	−308.8842	66.2722	−4.6608	4.911

In the following the reduced linear discriminant functions for all three pairwise combinations are listed. Each combination contains $\log(TLS)$ as relevant variable which was to be expected.

Literary Prose and Journalistic Prose:
Reduced Linear Discriminant Function With 4 Variables

$$Y_{12}^{red} = 4.5291 \cdot \log(TLS) - 116.3617 \cdot m_1 + 126.8984 \cdot m_2 - \\ - 308.8842 \cdot I$$

$$D_{12(red)} = 5.5131 \text{ vs. } D_{12} = 5.5167$$

Literary Prose and Poetry:
Reduced linear discriminant function with 3 variables

$$Y_{13}^{red} = -0.0014 \cdot TLS + 9.0437 \cdot \log(TLS) + 13.6011 \cdot m_2$$

$$D_{13(red)} = 4.7311 \text{ vs. } D_{13} = 4.7661$$

Journalistic Prose and Poetry:
Reduced linear discriminant function with 3 variables

$$Y_{23}^{red} = 3.0937 \cdot \log(TLS) + 22.9766 \cdot m_1 + 39.6065 \cdot I$$

$$D_{23(red)} = 5.3366 \text{ vs. } D_{23} = 5.4022$$

Figures 12.3(a), 12.3(b) and 12.3(c) demonstrate the importance of relevant variables for all pairs of categories by comparing the multivariate distances before and after removing the respective variable.

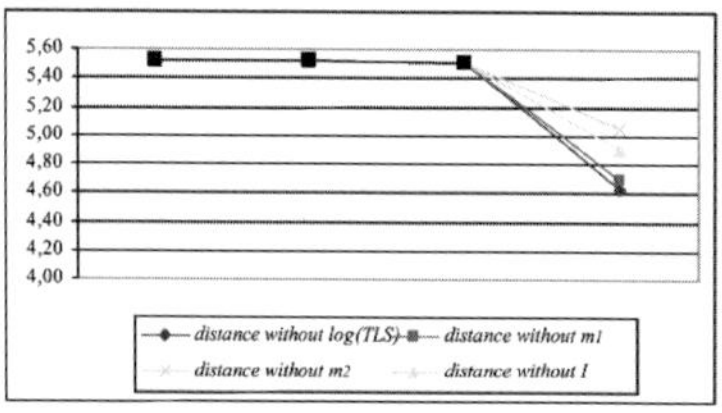

(a) Distances for Literary Prose and Journalistic Prose

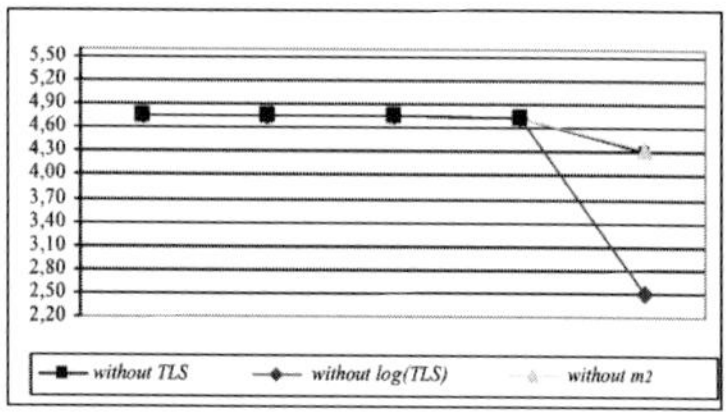

(b) Distances for Literary Prose and Poetry

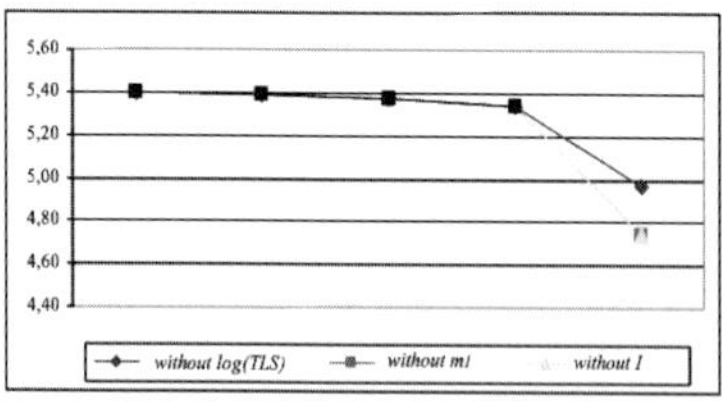

(c) Distances for Journalistic Prose and Poetry

Figure 12.3: Distances for Different Text Types

The pair *literary prose* and *journalistic prose* may be separated by the variables $\log(TLS)$ and m_1. *Literary prose* and *poetry* can not be discriminated without $\log(TLS)$; *Journalistic prose* and *poetry* differ at most with respect to the word length variables m_1 and I.

The scatter plots in Figures 12.4(a) and 12.4(b) show the values of the relevant variables $\log(TLS)$ and m_1 against the values of reduced discriminant functions (without the variable compared) for the categories *literary prose* and *journalistic prose*. The positive correlation in Figure 12.4(a) corresponds with a positive coefficient of $\log(TLS)$ in the discriminant function, i.e. the text lengths of the journalistic texts are rather shorter than the text lengths of the literary texts.

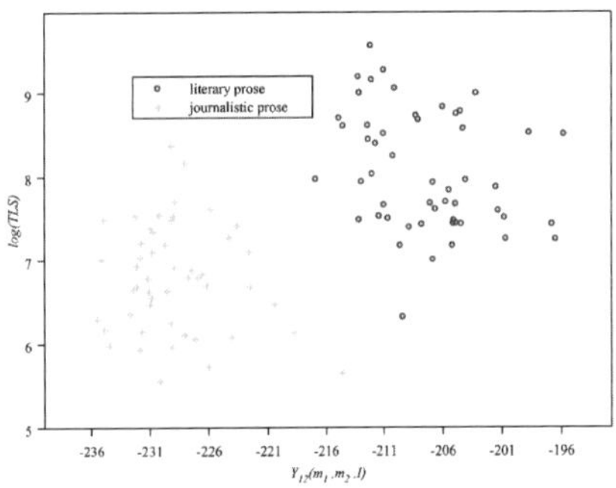

(a) Scatter plot of the relevant variable $\log(TLS)$ against the discriminant $Y_{12}(m_1, m_2, I)$

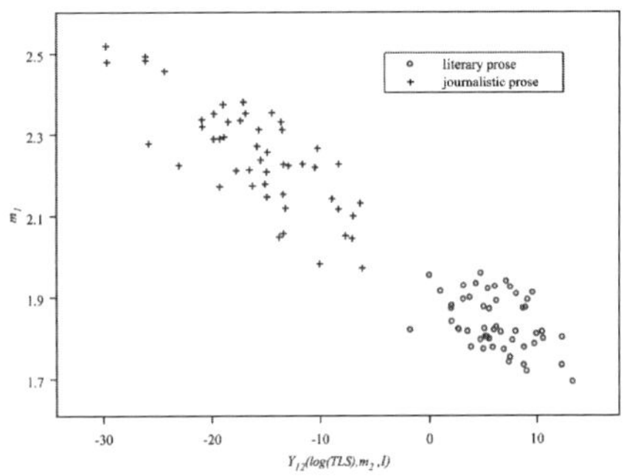

(b) Scatter plot of the relevant variable m_1 against the discriminant $Y_{12}(\log(TLS), m_2, I)$

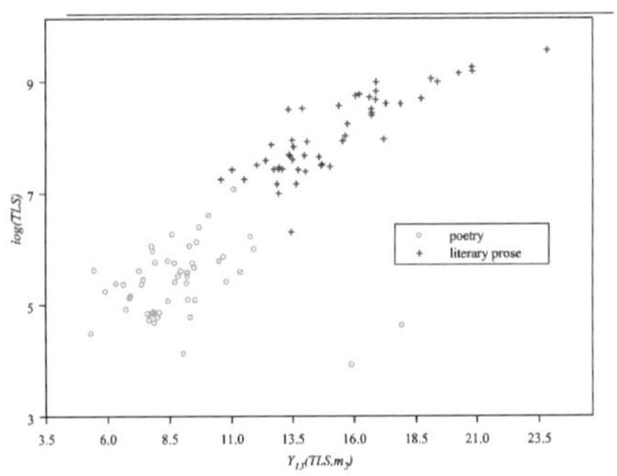

(c) Scatter plot of the relevant variable $\log(TLS)$ against the discriminant $Y_{13}(TLS, m_2)$

Figure 12.4: Scatter Plots of the Relevant Variables Against the Discriminants

Figure 12.4(b) exhibits strong negative correlation, i.e. the coefficient of m_1 in the discriminant function is negative, and the mean word length of journalistic texts is longer than the mean word length of literary texts.

The categories *poetry* and *literary prose* are compared in Figure 12.4(c) where $\log(TLS)$ is plotted against the reduced discriminant function. The positive correlation implies a positive coefficient for $\log(TLS)$ in the discriminant function. The scatter plot expresses the obvious fact that the poetic texts are shorter than the literary texts.

Figures 12.5(a) and 12.5(b) display the values of the relevant variables $\log(TLS)$ and m_1 against the values of the reduced discriminant functions in terms of *journalistic prose* and *poetry*. Positive correlation in Figure 12.5(a) is connected with a positive coefficient for $\log(TLS)$ in the discriminant function. However, more than 50% of the texts in both categories do not differ regarding text length. The effect of m_1 is also positive with a much better separation than before: all but two poetic texts have smaller values of m_1 than journalistic texts.

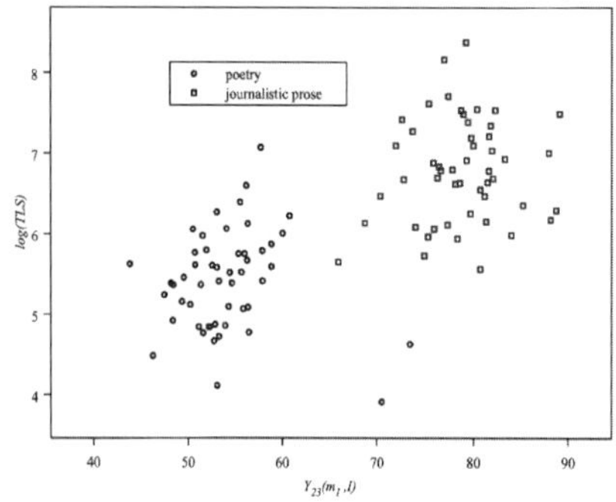

(a) Scatter plot of the relevant variable $\log(TLS)$ against the discriminant $Y_{23}(m_1, I)$

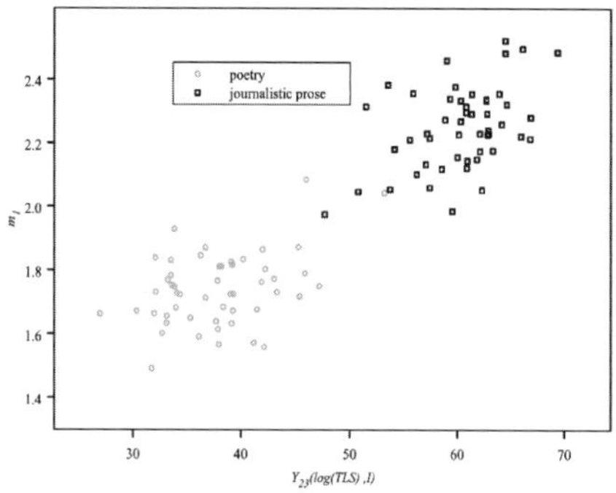

(b) Scatter plot of the relevant variable m_1 against the discriminant $Y_{23}(\log(TLS), I)$

Figure 12.5: Scatter Plots of the Relevant Variables Against the Discriminants

3.1 Canonical Discrimination

Our approach of comparing two categories of text can be generalized to a simultaneous comparison of all three categories of text. For this we used a so-called canonical discriminant analysis with the three variables $\log(TLS)$, m_1 and I establishing canonical discriminant functions Z_1 and Z_2. Details of this procedure, together with an SPLUS program may be found in Djuzelic (2002). For a description of statistics with SPLUS we refer to the book of Venables/Ripley (1999).

The first block in Table 12.8 lists the coefficients of the discriminant functions which are also the components of the eigenvectors of Z_1 and Z_2. The second block contains the mean values and variances of the discriminants Z_1 and Z_2 for each text category.

Table 12.8: Canonical Coefficients For Discriminants Z_1 and Z_2

Variable	Z_1	Z_2
$\log(TLS)$	0.33752	−1.40306
m_1	4.66734	4.47832
I	9.51989	−1.82010
text category	**group means I variances of Z_1 and Z_2**	
literary prose	16.25733 I 0.52973	−4.02454 I 0.83067
journalistic prose	19.49542 I 1.20942	−0.74287 I 1.09144
poetry	13.64796 I 1.27444	−0.51754 I 1.08310

The eigenvalues $\lambda_1 = 5.77386$ of Z_1 and $\lambda_2 = 2.64693$ of Z_2 express quotients of variances, i.e. the variance between the groups is 5.8 times, respectively 2.6 times higher than the variance within the groups. Hence, both variables Z_1 and Z_2 are good measures for the separation of the categories as can be observed in the scatter plot of Z_1 against Z_2 in Figure 12.6.

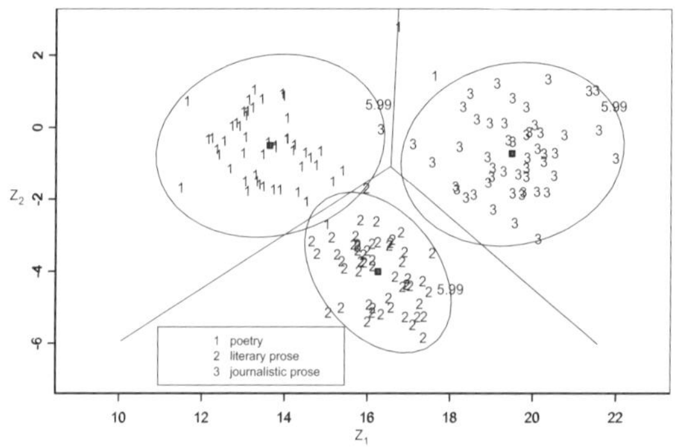

Figure 12.6: Canonical Discriminant Functions With Regions of Classification for the Three Text Types

The imposed lines partition the (Z_1, Z_2)-plane into the three regions of classification resulting in an excellent discrimination of the text categories: 150 of 153 texts (i.e., 98%) are classified correctly.

In detail we have the following. All 52 literary texts are classified correctly (category 3). One of the 50 journalistic texts (category 2) is assigned to category 1 (poetry). Only two of the 53 poetic texts are misclassified: one text is classified as journalistic text and one as literary text.

Figure 12.6 contains also three ellipses of concentration each defined by a quadratic distance of 5.99 from the corresponding group means given in Table 12.8.

4. Conclusions

Our case study on three categories of Slovenian texts was a first attempt to study the usefulness of discriminant analysis for the problem of text classification. The major results of our analysis may be summarized as follows.

1. In the univariate setting we calculated for all three pairwise comparisons the univariate statistical distances of six variables: two variables based on text length and four variables based on word length. This gave us the first hints of the overall order of discrimination and the order of influence of specific variables.
2. The corresponding analysis of multivariate distances and discrimination functions demonstrated that the correlation structure of the variables may change the role of the variables, e.g. comparing literary prose and poetry the univariate analysis listed variable I as important, but variable m_2 as unimportant. In the multivariate analysis we ended up with m_2 as relevant and I as redundant. (This special effect is caused by the high correlation of the variables.)
3. We established a linear discriminant function for the pair (literary prosel journalistic prose) with four relevant variables. For the two other pairs (literary prosel poetry) and (journalistic prosel poetry) only three relevant variables appear in each discriminant function.
4. Both types of variables were relevant for discrimination: variables for text length as well as variables for word length.
5. Canonical discrimination of all three text categories with the three variables $\log(TLS)$, m_1 and I was able to classify 98% of the texts correctly.
6. Our future research will be concentrated on the following considerations. Different categories of texts from various Slavic languages will be studied by classification methods to find combinations of discriminating variables based on word length only. For this we prepared a large collection of variables, i.e. statistical parameters describing word length. Our hope is to establish suitable classification rules for at least some interesting categories of texts.

References

Antić, G.; Kelih, E.; Grzybek, P.
2005 "Zero-syllable Words in Determining Word Length". [In the present volume]

Djuzelic, M.
2002 *Einflussfaktoren auf die Wortlänge und ihre Häufigkeitsverteilung am Beispiel von Texten slowenischer Sprache.* Diplomarbeit, Institut für Statistik, Technical University Graz. [`http://www.stat.tugraz.at/dthesis/djuz02.zip`]

Flury, B.
1997 *A First Course in Multivariate Statistics.* New York.

Grotjahn, R.; Altmann, G.
1993 "Modelling the Distribution of Word Length: Some Methodological Problems." In: Köhler, R.; Rieger, B. (eds.), *Contributions to Quantitative Linguistics.* Dordrecht, NL.

Grzybek, P.; Stadlober, E.
2002 "The Graz Project on Word Length (Frequencies)", in: *Journal of Quantitative Linguistics, 9(2)*; 187–192.

Hand, D.
1981 *Discrimination and Classification.* New York.

Ord, J.K.
1967 "On a System of Discrete Distributions", in: *Biometrika, 54*, 649–659.

Venables, W.N.; Ripley, B.D.
1999 *Modern Applied Statistics with S-Plus.* 3rd Edition, New York.

Wimmer, G.; Köhler, R.; Grotjahn, R.; Altmann, G.
1994 "Towards a theory of word length distribution", in: *Journal of Quantitative Linguistics, 1*; 98–106.

Wimmer, G.; Altmann, G.
1996 "The theory of word length: Some results and generalizations." In: *Glottometrika 15.* (112–133).

13

WORD LENGTH AND WORD FREQUENCY

Udo Strauss, Peter Grzybek, Gabriel Altmann

1. Stating the Problem

Since the appearance of Zipf's works, (esp. Zipf 1932, 1935), his hypothesis "that the magnitude of words tends, on the whole, to stand in an inverse (not necessarily proportionate) relationship to the number of occurrences" (1935: 25) has been generally accepted. Zipf illustrated the relation between word length and frequency of word occurrence using German data, namely the frequency dictionary of Kaeding (1897–98).

In the past century, Zipf's idea has been repeatedly taken up and examined with regard to specific problems. Surveying the pertinent work associated with this hypothesis, one cannot avoid the impression that there are quite a number of problems which have not been solved to date. Mainly, this seems to be due to the fact that the fundamentals of the different approaches involved have not been systematically scrutinized. Some of these unsolved problems can be captured in the following points:

i. *The direction of dependence.* Zipf himself discussed the relation between length and frequency of a word or word form – which in itself represents an insufficiently clarified problem – only in one direction, namely as the dependence of frequency on length. However, the question is whether frequency depends on length or vice versa. While scholars such as Miller, Newman, & Friedman (1958) favored the first direction, others, as for example, Köhler (1986), Arapov (1988) or Hammerl (1990), preferred the latter. As to a solution of this question, it seems reasonable to assume that it depends on the manner of embedding these variables in Köhler's control cycle.

ii. *Unit of measurement.* While some researchers – as, e.g., Hammerl (1990) – measured word length in terms of syllable numbers, others – as for example Baker (1951) or Miller, Newman & Friedman (1958) – used letters as the basic units to measure word length. Irrespective of the fact that a high correlation between these two units should seem likely be found, a systematic study of this basic pre-condition would be important with regard to different languages and writing systems.

P. Gryzbek (ed.), Contributing in the Science of Text and Language, 277-294.

iii. *Rank or frequency.* Again, while some researchers, as e.g., Köhler (1986), based his analysis on the absolute occurrence of words, others, such as Guiraud (1959), Belonogov (1962), Arapov (1988), or Hammerl (1990) who, in fact, examined both alternatives, considered the frequency rank of word forms. In principle, it might turn out to be irrelevant whether one examines the frequency or the rank, as long as the basic dependence remains the same, and one obtains the same function type with different parameters; still, relevant systematic examinations are missing.

iv. *The linguistic data.* A further decisive point is the fact that Zipf and his followers did not concentrate on individual texts, but on corpus data or frequency dictionaries. The general idea behind this approach has been the assumption, that assembling a broader text basis should result in more representative results, reflecting an alleged norm to be discovered by adequate analyses. However, this assumption raises a crucial question, as far as the quality of the data is concerned. Specifically, it is the problem of data homogeneity, which comes into play (cf. Altmann 1992), and it seems most obvious that any corpus, by principle, is inherently inhomogeneous. Moreover, it should be reasonable to assume that oscillations as observed by Köhler (1986), are the outcome of mixing heterogeneous texts: examining the German LIMAS corpus, Köhler (1986) and Zörnig et al. (1990) found not a monotonously decreasing relationship, but an oscillating course. The reason for this has not been found until today; additionally, no oscillation has been discovered in the corpus data examined by Hammerl (1990).

v. *Hypotheses and immanent aspects.* Finally, it should be noted that Zipf's original hypothesis implies four different aspects; these aspects should, theoretically speaking, be held apart, but, in practice, they tend to be intermingled:

   (a) *The textual aspect.* Within a given text, longer words tend to be used more rarely, short words more frequently. If word frequency is not taken into account, one obtains the well-known word length distribution. If, however, word frequency is additionally taken into account, then one can either study the dependence of length from frequency, or the two-dimensional length-frequency distribution. Ultimately, the length distribution is a marginal distribution of the two-dimensional one. In general, one accepts the dependence $L = f(F)$ or $L = f(R)$ [L = length, F = frequency, R = rank].

   (b) *The lexematic aspect.* The construction of words, i.e. their length in a given lexicon, depends both on the lexicon size in question and on the phoneme inventory, as well as on the frequential load of other polysemic words. Frequency here is a secondary factor, since it does not play any role in the generation of new words, but will only later result from the load of other words. This aspect cannot easily be embedded in the modeling process because the size of the lexicon is merely an empirical constant whose estimation is associated with great difficulties. It can at best play the role of *ceteris paribus*.

(c) Shortening through usage. This aspect, which concerns the shortening of frequently used words or phrases, has nothing to do with word construction or with the usage of words in texts; rather, the process of shortening, or shortening substitution, is concerned (e.g., references → refs).

(d) *The paradigmatic aspect.* The best examined aspect is the frequency of forms in a paradigm where the shorter forms are more frequent than the longer ones, or where the frequent forms are shorter. The results of this research can be found under headings such as 'markedness', 'iconism vs. economy', 'naturalness', etc. (cf. Fenk-Oczlon 1986, 1990, Haiman 1983, Manczak 1980). If the paradigmatic aspect is left apart, aspect (d) becomes a special case of aspect (a).

2. The Theoretical Approach

In this domain, quite a number of adequate and theoretically sound formulae have been proposed and empirically confirmed: more often than not, one has adhered to the "Zipfian relationship" also used in synergetic linguistics (cf. Herdan 1966, Guiter 1974, Köhler 1986, Hammerl 1990; Zörnig et al. 1990): consequently, one has started from a differential equation, in which the relative rate of change of mean word length (y) decreases proportionally to the relative rate of change of the frequency (Köhler 1986).

Since in most languages, zero-syllabic words either do not exist, or can be regarded as clitics, the mean length cannot take a value of less than 1. This is the reason why the corresponding function must have the asymptote 1. Finally, the equations get the form (13.1).

$$\frac{dy}{y-1} = -b\frac{dx}{x} \tag{13.1}$$

from which the well-known formula (13.2)

$$y = a \cdot x^{-b} + 1 \tag{13.2}$$

follows, with $a = e^C$ (C being the integration constant). Here, y is the mean length of words occurring x times in a given text. If one also counts words with length zero, the constant 1 must be eliminated, of course, and as a result, at least some of the values (depending on the number of 0-syllabic words) will be lower.

As compared to other approaches, the hypothesis represented by (13.2) has the advantage that the inverse relation yields the same formula, only with different parameters, i.e.

$$x = A \cdot (y-1)^{-B} \tag{13.3}$$

where $A = a^{1/b}$, $B = 1/b$. This means that the dependence of frequency on length can be captured in the same way as can that of length on frequency, only with transformed parameters.

In the present paper, we want to test hypothesis (13.2). We restrict ourselves exclusively to the textual aspect of the problem, assuming that, in a given text, word length is a variable depending on word frequency. Therefore, we concentrate on testing this relationship with regard to individual texts and not – as is usually done – with regard to corpus or (frequency) dictionary material. Though this kind of examination does not, at first sight, seem to yield new theoretical insights with regard to the original hypothesis itself, the focus on the variable text, which, thus far, has not been systematically studied, promises the clarification of at least some of the above-mentioned problems. Particularly, the phenomenon of oscillation as observed by Köhler (1986), might find an adequate solution when this variable is systematically controlled; yet, this particular issue will have to be the special object of a separate follow-up analysis (cf. Grzybek/Altmann 2003).

For the present study, word length has been counted in terms of the numbers of syllables per word, in order to submit the text under study to as few transformations as possible; further, every word form has been considered as a separate type, i.e., the text has not been lemmatized. Since our main objective is to test the validity of Zipf's approach for individual texts, we have chosen exclusively single texts

a) by different authors,
b) in different languages, and
c) of different text types.

Additionally, attention has been paid to the fact that the definition of 'text' itself possibly influences the results. Pragmatically speaking, a 'text' may easily be defined as the result of a unique production and/or reception process. Still, this rather vague definition allows for a relatively broad spectrum of what a concrete text might look like. Therefore, we have analyzed 'texts' of rather different profiles, in order to gain a more thorough insight into the homogeneity of the textual entity examined:

i. a complete novel, composed of chapters
ii. one complete book of a novel, consisting of several chapters
iii. individual chapters, either (a) as part of a book of a novel, or (b) of a whole novel

iv. dialogical vs. narrative sequences within a text.

It is immediately evident that our study primarily focuses the problem of homogeneity of data, inhomogeneity being the possible result of mixing various texts, different text types, heterogeneous parts of a complex text, etc. Thus, theoretically speaking, there are two possible kinds of data inhomogeneity:

(a) intertextual inhomogeneity

(b) intratextual inhomogeneity.

Whereas *intertextual inhomogeneity* thus can be understood as the result of combining ("mixing") different texts, *intratextual inhomogeneity* is due to the fact that a given text in itself does not consist of homogeneous elements. This aspect, which is of utmost importance for any kind of quantitative text analysis, has hardly ever been systematically studied. In addition to the above-mentioned fact that any text corpus is necessarily characterized by data inhomogeneity, one can now state that there is absolutely no reason to a priori assume that a text (in particular, a long text) is characterized by data homogeneity, per se. The crucial question thus is, under which conditions can we speak of a homogeneous 'text', when do we have to speak of mixed texts, and what may empirical studies contribute to a solution of these question?

3. Text Analyses in Different Languages

The results of our analyses are represented according to the scheme in Table 13.1, which contains exemplary data illustrating the procedure: The first column shows the absolute occurrence frequencies (x); the second, the number of words $f(x)$ with the given frequency x; the third, the mean length $L(x)$ of these words in syllables per word. Length classes were pooled, in case of $f(x) < 10$: in the example, classes $x = 8$ and $x = 9$ were pooled because they contain fewer than 10 cases per class. Since the mean values were not weighted, we obtained the new values $x = (8+9)/2 = 8.5$ and $L(x) = (1.5714+1.6667)/2 = 1.62$. This kind of smoothing yields more representative classes. In how far other smoothing procedures can lead to diverging results, will have to be analyzed in a separate study.

The following texts have been used for the analyses:

1. **L.N. Tolstoj: Anna Karenina** – This Russian novel appeared first in 1875; in 1877, Tolstoj prepared it for a separate edition, which was published in 1878. The novel consists of eight parts, subdivided into several chapters. Our analysis comprises (a) the first chapter of Part I, and (b) the whole of Part I consisting of 34 chapters.

Table 13.1: An illustrative example of data pooling

x	$f(x)$	$L(x)$	x'	L'
1	2301	27.432	1	27.432
2	354	22.090	2	22.090
3	93	20.645	3	20.645
4	39	19.487	4	19.487
5	29	13.793	5	13.793
6	23	16.087	6	16.087
7	11	11.818	7	11.818
8	7	15.714		
9	6	16.667	8.5	1.62
10	9	12.222		
11	2	10.000	10.5	1.11
...	...	...	...	...

2. **A.S. Puškin: Evgenij Onegin –** This Russian verse-novel consists of eight chapters. Chapter I first was published in 1825, periodically followed by further individual chapters; the novel as a whole appeared in 1833.
3. **F. Móra: Dióbél királykisasszony ["Nut kernel princess"] –** This short Hungarian children's story is taken from a children book, published in 1965.
4. **K.Š. Gjalski: Na badnjak ["On Christmas Evening"] –** This Croatian story was first published in 1886, in the volume Pod starimi krovovi. For our purposes, we have analyzed both the complete text, and dialogical and narrative parts separately.
5. **Karel & Josef Čapek: Zářivé hlubiny ["Shining depths"] –** This Czech story is a co-authored work by the two brothers Karel and Josef Čapek. The text appeared in 1913, for the first time, and was then published together with other stories in 1916, in a volume bearing the same title.
6. **Ivan Cankar: Hiša Marije Pomocnice ["The House of Charity"] –** This Slovenian novel was published in 1904. For our purposes, we analyzed the first chapter only.
7. **Janko Král: Zakliata panna vo Váhu a divný Janko ["The Enchanted Virgin in Váh and the Strange Janko"] –** This text is a Slovak poem, which was published in 1844.
8. **Hänsel und Gretel –** This is a famous German fairy tale, which was included in the well-known Kinder- und Hausmärchen by Jacob and Wilhelm Grimm (1812), under the title of "Little brother and little sister".

9. **Sjarif Amin: Di lembur kuring ["In my Village"] –** This story is written in Sundanese, a minority language of West Java; it was published in 1964. We have analyzed the first chapter of the story.
10. **Pak Ojik: Burung api ["The Fire Bird"] –** This fairy tale from Indonesia (in Bahasa Indonesia), which was published in 1971, is written in the traditional orthography (the preposition *di* being written separately).
11. **Henry James: Portrait of a lady –** This novel, written in 1881, consists of 55 individual chapters. We have analyzed both the whole novel, and the first chapter, only.

Table 13.2 represents the results of the analyses.[1] The first column contains the occurrence frequencies of word forms (x); the next two columns present the observed (y) and the computed (y) mean lengths of word forms having the corresponding frequency in the given individual texts. As described above, words having zero-length - such as for example the Russian preposition *k, s, v*, or the Hungarian *s* (from *és*) – have not been counted as a separate category, and have been considered as proclitics instead. In the last row of Table 13.2 one finds the values for the parameters a and b of (13.2), the text length N, and the determination coefficient R^2.
As can be seen from Table 13.2, hypothesis (13.2) can be accepted in all cases, since the fits yield R^2 values between 0.84 and 0.96, which can be considered very good – independently of language, author, text type, or text length.

[1] The English data for *Portrait of a Lady* have kindly been provided by John Constable; we would like to express our sincere gratitude for his co-operative generosity.– All other texts were analyzed in co-operation with the FWF research project #15485 ≫Word Length Frequency Distributions in Slavic Texts≪ at Graz University (cf. Grzybek/Stadlober 2002).

Table 13.2: Dependence of Word Form Length on Word Frequency

Russian *Anna Karenina* (ch. I)			Russian *Evgenij Onegin* (ch. I)			Hungarian *Dióbél királykisasszony*		
x	y	$\hat{y}$	x	y	$\hat{y}$	x	y	$\hat{y}$
1	2.92	3.03	1	2.66	2.70	1	2.52	2.57
2	2.14	2.04	2	2.13	1.99	2	2.00	1.88
3	2.05	1.70	3	1.78	1.71	3	1.56	1.62
4	1.50	1.53	4	1.42	1.57	4	1.57	1.49
5	1.33	1.43	5.50	1.36	1.45	6	1.33	1.35
6	1.50	1.36	7.50	1.30	1.35	14.66	1	1.17
7	1.67	1.31	11.50	1.35	1.25			
8	1	1.27	39.64	1.09	1.09			
9	1	1.24						
10	1	1.22						
13	1	1.17						
19	1	1.12						
20	1	1.11						
37	1	1.06						
$a = 2.0261, b = 0.9690$ $R^2 = 0.88, N = 3970$			$a = 1.7029, b = 0.7861$ $R^2 = 0.96, N = 1871$			$a = 1.5668, b = 0.8379$ $R^2 = 0.96, N = 234$		

Croatian *Na badnjak*			Czech *Zářivé hlubiny*			Slovenian *Hiša Marije P.* (ch. I)		
x	y	$\hat{y}$	x	y	$\hat{y}$	x	y	$\hat{y}$
1	2.83	2.95	1	2.69	2.76	1	2.71	2.80
2	2.44	2.37	2	2.20	2.17	2	2.35	2.36
3	2.22	2.12	3	2.15	1.92	3	2.23	2.16
4	2.18	1.96	4	1.74	1.77	4	2	2.03
5	1.63	1.86	5	1.74	1.68	5	2	1.94
6	1.76	1.79	6	1.58	1.61	6	2	1.87
7	1.87	1.73	7	1.33	1.55	7	1.86	1.82
8	1.69	1.68	9	1.51	1.48	8	2.14	1.78
9	1.57	1.64	36.23	1.16	1.21	9.5	1.50	1.73
10	1.67	1.61				18.25	1.22	1.56
16.11	1.49	1.48				89.13	1.25	1.30
32.91	1.14	1.33						
127	1	1.17						
$a = 1.9454, b = 0.5064$ $R^2 = 0.93, N = 2450$			$a = 1.7603, b = 0.5921$ $R^2 = 0.94, N = 1363$			$a = 1.7969, b = 0.4023$ $R^2 = 0.84, N = 1147$		

Table 13.2: (cont.)

Slovak *Zakliata panna*			German *Hänsel & Gretel*			Sundanese *Di lembur kuring*		
x	y	$\hat{y}$	x	y	$\hat{y}$	x	y	$\hat{y}$
1	2.41	2.48	1	2.12	2.17	1	2.79	2.86
2	2.05	1.92	2	1.79	1.82	2	2.38	2.31
3	1.55	1.69	3	1.73	1.67	3	2.05	2.06
4	1.85	1.57	4	1.71	1.58	4.5	1.13	1.86
5	1.50	1.49	5	1.55	1.52	6.5	1.58	1.72
6.50	1.39	1.41	6.5	1.56	1.45	13.29	1.33	1.50
10	1.07	1.30	8.5	1.49	1.40			
24.67	1.11	1.16	10.5	1.08	1.36			
			13.5	1.21	1.31			
			19.67	1.25	1.26			
			50.46	1.15	1.16			
$a = 1.1476, b = 0.675$ $R^2 = 0.88, N = 926$			$a = 1.1688, b = 0.5062$ $R^2 = 0.87, N = 803$			$a = 1.8609, b = 0.5110$ $R^2 = 0.91, N = 431$		

Indonesian *Burung api*			English *Portrait of a Lady* (ch. I)		
x	y	$\hat{y}$	x	y	$\hat{y}$
1	3.34	3.44	1	2.17	2.23
2	3.03	3.04	2	1.78	1.69
3	2.93	2.83	3	1.56	1.49
4	2.78	2.70	4	1.5	1.39
5	2.33	2.61	5	1.37	1.32
6	2.68	2.53	6	1	1.28
7	2.57	2.47	7	1.33	1.24
8	2.53	2.42	8.50	1.28	1.20
9	2.38	2.38	11	1	1.17
10	2.50	2.34	14.50	1.06	1.13
11	2.36	2.31	19.83	1.06	1.10
13	2.17	2.25	27.50	1.13	1.08
17	2	2.17	73.43	1	1.03
$a = 2.4353, b = 0.2587$ $R^2 = 0.92, N = 1393$			$a = 1.2293, b = 0.8314$ $R^2 = 0.89, N = 1104$		

By way of an example, Figure 13.1 illustrates the results of the first chapter of Tolstoj's *Anna Karenina*: the courses both of the observed data and the data computed according to (13.2), can be seen. On the abscissa, the occurrence frequencies from $x = 1$ to $x = 40$ are given, on the ordinate, the mean word lengths, measured in the average number of syllables per word. With a determination coefficient of $R^2 = 0.88$, the fit can be accepted to be satisfactory.

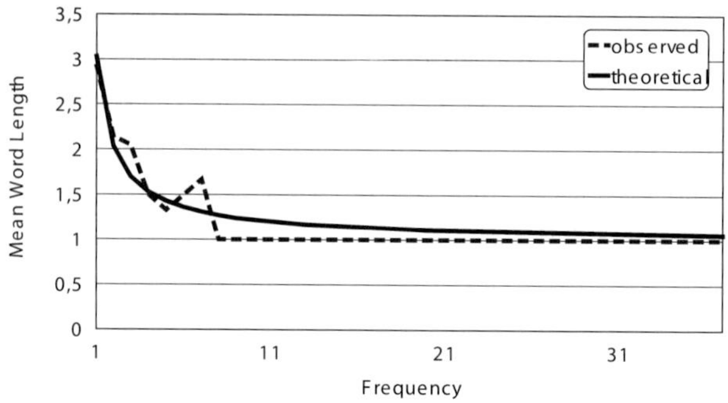

Figure 13.1: Observed and Computed Mean Lengths in *Anna Karenina* (I,1)

4. The Parameters

Since all results can be regarded to be good ($R^2 > .85$), or even very good ($R^2 > .95$), the question of a synthetical interpretation of these results quite naturally arises. First and foremost, a qualitative interpretation of the parameters a and b, as well as a possible relation between them, would be desirable.

Figure 13.2 represents the course of all theoretical curves, based on the parameters a and b given in Table 13.3.

Since the curves representing the individual texts intersect, it is to be assumed that no general judgment, holding true for all texts in all languages, is possible. In Table 13.3 the parameters and the length of the individual texts are summarized.

From Figure 13.3(a) it can easily be seen that there is no clear-cut relationship between the two parameters a and b.

The next question to be asked, quite logically concerns a possible relation between the parameters a and b, and the text length N; yet, the answer is negative, again. As can be seen in Figure 13.3(b), the relation rather seems to be relatively constant with a great dispersion; consequently, no interpretable curve can capture it.

It is evident that the fact of a missing relationship between the parameters a and b, and text length N, respectively, can be accounted for by the obvious data inhomogeneity: since the texts come from different languages and various text

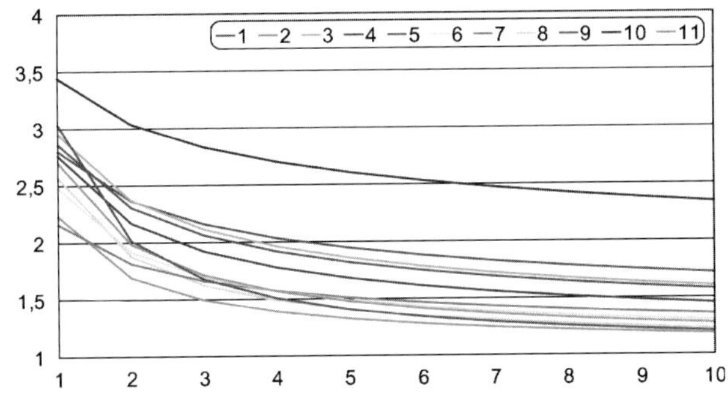

Figure 13.2: The Course of the Theoretical Curves (Dependence of Word Form Length on Frequency; cf. Table 13.2)

Table 13.3: Parameters and Text Length of Individual Texts

Text	**Language**	a	b	N
Anna Karenina (I,1)	Russian	2.03	0.97	397
Evgenij Onegin (I)	Russian	1.70	0.79	1871
Na badnjak	Croatian	1.95	0.51	2450
Zářivé hlubiny	Czech	1.76	0.59	1363
Hiša Marije Pomocnice (I)	Slovenian	1.80	0.40	1147
Zakliata panna	Slovak	1.48	0.69	926
Hänsel und Gretel	German	1.16	0.51	803
Fairy Tale by Móra	Hungarian	1.57	0.84	234
Di lembung kuring	Sundanese	1.86	0.51	431
Burung api	Indonesian	2.44	0.26	1393
Portrait of a Lady (I)	English	1.23	0.83	1104

types, the *ceteris paribus* condition is strongly violated, and the data in this mixture are not adequate for testing the hypothesis at stake.

5. The Homogeneity of a 'Text'

In order to avoid the encroachment caused by the different provenience of the texts, we will next examine the problem using texts whose linguistic and textual homogeneity can, at least hypothetically, a priori be taken for granted. However, even here, the problem of homogeneity is not ultimately solved.

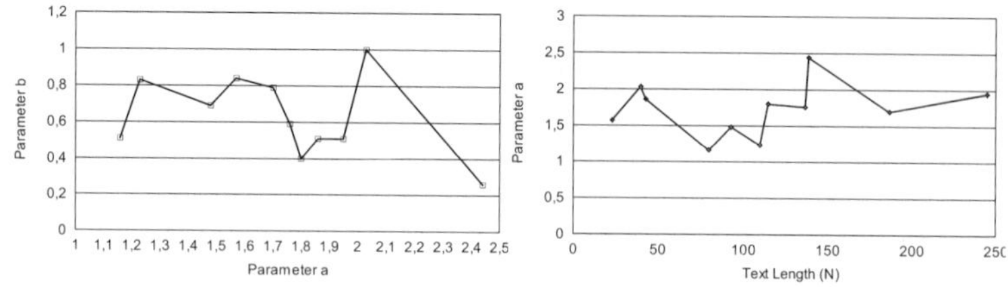

(a) Parameters a and b (b) Text Length N and Parameter a

Figure 13.3: Relationship Between Parameters a and b and Text Length N (cf. Table 13.3)

Let us therefore compare the results for Chapter I of Tolstoy's *Anna Karenina* with those for the complete Book I, consisting of 34 chapters, as represented in Table 13.4.

Table 13.4: The Length-Frequency Curves for Chapter I and the Complete Text of *Anna Karenina*

Chapter 1			Complete text					
x	y	$\hat{y}$	x	y	$\hat{y}$	x	y	$\hat{y}$
1	2.92	3.03	1	3.38	3.60	22	2.20	2.13
2	2.14	2.04	2	3.04	3.16	23	1.94	2.12
3	2.05	1.70	3	2.84	2.94	24.50	2.27	2.10
4	1.50	1.53	4	2.76	2.79	26.50	2.04	2.08
5	1.33	1.43	5	2.84	2.69	28.50	2.27	2.05
6	1.50	1.36	6	2.65	2.61	30.50	2.07	2.04
7	1.67	1.31	7	2.45	2.54	33.50	2.29	2.01
8	1	1.27	8	2.57	2.49	38	1.70	1.98
9	1	1.24	9	2.47	2.44	42.50	2.13	1.95
10	1	1.22	10	2.64	2.40	51.50	1.67	1.90
13	1	1.17	11	2.59	2.36	57.50	1.83	1.87
19	1	1.12	12	2.41	2.33	62	1.64	1.85
20	1	1.11	13	2.50	2.30	73.25	1.88	1.82
37	1	1.06	14	2.20	2.28	91.71	1.43	1.77
			15	2.43	2.25	106.86	1.33	1.74
			16.50	2.11	2.22	137.70	1.70	1.69
			18	2.35	2.19	229.11	1.28	1.60
			19.50	2.32	2.17	458.75	1.38	1.50
			21	2.20	2.14			

In Figure 13.4, the empirical data and the theoretical curve are presented for the sake of a graphical comparison. One can observe two facts:

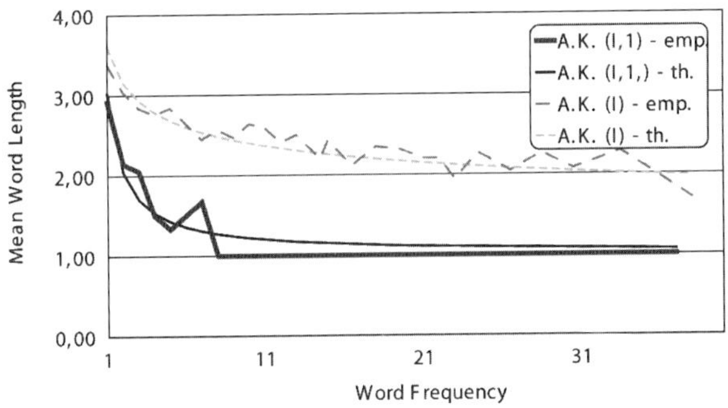

Figure 13.4: Comparison of *Anna Karenina*, chap. I and Book I

1. The empirical and, consequently, the theoretical values of the larger sample (i.e., Book I, 1-34), are located distinctly higher. For the theoretical curve this results in an increase of a and a decrease of b.
2. The fitting for the greater sample is still acceptable, but clearly worse ($R^2 = 0.86$) as compared to the smaller sample ($R^2 = 0.97$).

	A.K. (I,1)	**A.K. (I)**
Tokens	702	38226
Types	397	8661
a	2.03	2.60
b	0.97	0.27
R^2	0.97	0.86

The important finding, that a more comprehensive text unit leads to a worse result than a particular part of this 'text', can be demonstrated even more clearly, comparing the single chapter of a novel with the whole novel. Testing the complete novel *Portrait of a Lady* to this end, one obtains a determination coefficient of merely $R^2 = 0.58$, even after smoothing the data as described above. As compared to the first chapter of this novel taken separately, yielding a determination coefficient of $R^2 = 0.89$, (cf. Table 13.2), this is a dramatic decrease. In fact, an extremely drastic smoothing procedure is necessary in order to obtain an acceptable result (with $a = 1.34, b = 0.47; R^2 = 0.92$), as shown in Table 13.5 and Figure 13.5.

Thus, appropriate smoothing of the data turns out to be an additional problem. On the one hand, some kind of smoothing is necessary because the frequency class size should be "representative" enough, and on the other hand, the particular kind of smoothing is a further factor influencing the results.

Table 13.5: Results of Fitting Equation (13.2) to *Portrait of a Lady*, Using the Given Pooling of Values

Class lower limit	Class upper limit	x'	y	$\hat{y}$	Class lower limit	Class upper limit	x'	y	$\hat{y}$
1	10	1	2.22	2.34	601	700	70	1	1.18
11	20	2	1.92	1.97	701	800	80	1	1.17
21	30	3	1.84	1.80	801	900	90	1	1.16
31	40	4	1.81	1.70	901	1000	100	1	1.15
41	50	5	1.71	1.63	1001	2000	200	1.17	1.11
51	60	6	1.71	1.57	2001	4000	400	1	1.08
61	70	7	1.66	1.53	4001	5000	500	1	1.07
71	80	8	1.49	1.50	5001	6000	600	1	1.06
81	90	9	1.55	1.47	6001	7000	700	1	1.06
91	100	10	1.30	1.45	7001	8000	800	1	1.06
101	200	20	1.40	1.32	8001	9000	900	1	1.05
201	300	30	1.25	1.27					
301	400	40	1.40	1.23					
401	500	50	1.25	1.21					
501	600	60	1.18	1.19					

However, there is a clear tendency according to which the individual chapters of a novel abide by their own individual regimes organizing the length-frequency relation. This boils down to the assessment that even a seemingly homogeneous novel-text is an inhomogeneous text mixture, composed of diverging superpositions. As to an interpretation of this phenomenon, it seems most likely that after the end of a given chapter, a given ruling order ends, and a new order (of the

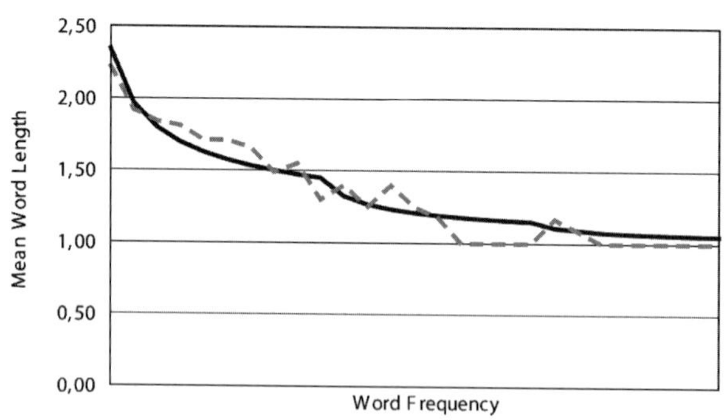

Figure 13.5: Fitting Equation (13.2) to *Portrait of a Lady* (cf. Table 13.5)

same organization principle) begins. The new order superposes the preceding, balances or destroys it. Theoretically speaking, one should start with as many components of $y = a_1x^{b_1} + a_2x^{b_2} + a_3x^{b_3} + \ldots$, as there are chapters in the text. Whether this is, in fact, a reasonable procedure, will have to be examined separately).

As a further consequence, one must even ask if one individual chapter of a novel, or a short story, etc. is a homogeneous text, or if we are concerned with text mixtures due to the combination of heterogeneous components. In order to at least draw attention to this problem, we have separately analyzed the narrative and the dialogical sequences in the Croatian story "Na badnjak". As a result, it turned out that the outcome is relatively similar under all circumstances: for the dialogue sequences we obtain the values $a = 1.61, b = 0.84, R^2 = 0.96$, for the narrative sequences $a = 1.93, b = 0.54$, and $R^2 = 0.91$ (as compared to $a = 1.95, b = 0.51, R^2 = 0.93$ for the story as a whole). It goes without saying, that more systematic examination is necessary to attain more reliable results.

While on the one hand, it turns out that a longer text does not necessarily yield better results, on the other hand, increasing text length need not necessarily yield worse results. By way of an example, this can be shown on the basis of cumulative processing of *Evgenij Onegin* and its eight chapters (i.e., chapter 1, then chapter 1+2, 1+2+3, etc.). In this way, one obtains the results shown in Table 13.6; the curves corresponding to the particular parts are displayed in Figure 13.6.

Table 13.6: Parameters of the Frequency-Length Relation in *Evgenij Onegin*

	Parameters		*Types*	*Tokens*	*Fit*
Chapter	a	b	N	M	R^2
1	1.703	0.786	1871	3209	0.96
1-2	1.838	0.691	2918	5546	0.88
1-3	1.921	0.574	3951	8359	0.88
1-4	1.967	0.525	4851	10936	0.92
1-5	1.954	0.476	5737	13376	0.94
1-6	1.968	0.52	6509	15978	0.94
1-7	2.031	0.425	7476	19061	0.86
1-8	2.049	0.399	8329	22482	0.88

As can be seen, the curves do not intersect under these circumstances. The displacement of the curve position with increasing text size can be explained

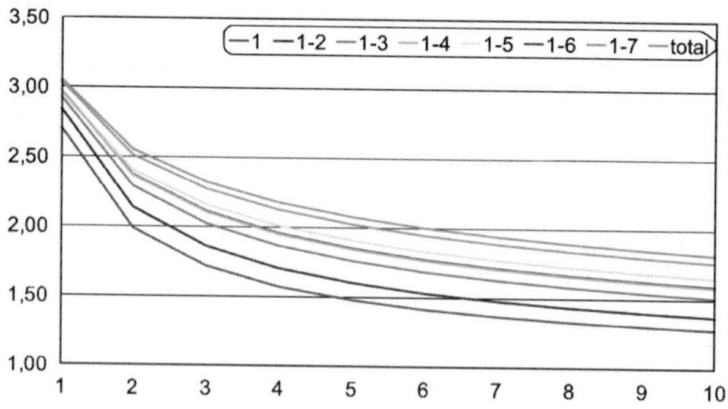

Figure 13.6: Fitting (13.2) to the text cumulation of *Evgenij Onegin*

by the fact that words from classes with low frequency wander to higher classes and are substituted by ever longer words. In Figure 13.7(a) the dependency between the parameters a and b is shown for the cumulative processing (b being represented by its absolute value).

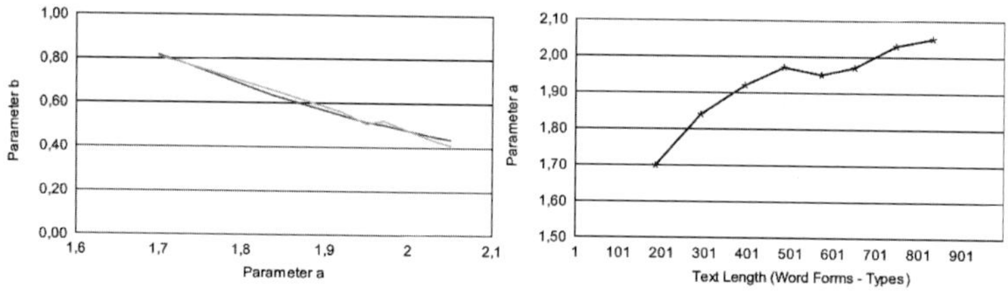

(a) Parameters a and b

(b) Text Length N and Parameter a

Figure 13.7: Relationship Between Parameters a and b and Text Length N in *Evgenij Onegin* (cf. Table 13.6)

Evidently, b depends on a. Although there seems to be a linear decline, the relation between a and b cannot, however, be linear, since b must remain greater than 0. The power curve $b = 4.9615a^{-3.3885}$ yields a good fit with $R^2 = 0.92$. In the same way, b depends on text length N. The same relationship yields $b = 21.4405N^{-0.4360}$ with $R^2 = 0.96$. The dependence of a on N can be computed by mere substitution in the second formula, yielding $a = 0.6493N^{0.1286}$ whose values are almost identical with the observed ones. It is irrelevant whether one considers types or tokens since they are strongly correlated ($r = 0.997$). Fig. 13.7(b) shows the relationship between text length N and parameter a.

It can thus be concluded that, in a homogeneous text, i.e., in a text in which one can reasonably assume the *ceteris paribus* condition to be fulfilled, the relationship between frequency and length remains intact: with an increasing text length, the curve is shifted upwards and becomes flatter. The parameters are joined in form of $a = f(N), b = g(a)$ or $b = h(N)$, respectively, f, g, h being functions of the same type.

6. Conclusion

Let us summarize the basic results of the present study. With regard to the leading question as to the relationship between frequency and length of words in texts, we have come to the following conclusions:

I. The above hypothesis (2) is corroborated in the given form by our data;

II. A homogeneous text does not interfere with linguistic laws, an inhomogeneous one can distort the textual reality;

III. Text mixtures can evoke phenomena which do not exist as such in individual texts: In text mixtures, the *ceteris paribus* condition does not hold; short texts have the disadvantage of not allowing a property to take appropriate shape; without smoothing, the dispersion can be too strong. Long texts contain mixed generating regimes superposing different layers. In text corpora, this may lead to “artificial” phenomena as, probably, oscillation. Since these phenomena do not occur in all corpora, it seems reasonable to consider them as a result of mixing.

IV. With increasing text size, the resulting curve of frequency-length relation is shifted upwards; this is caused by the fact that the number of words occurring only once increases up to a certain text length. If this assumption is correct, then b converges to zero, yielding the limit $y = a$.

References

Altmann, G.
1992 "Das Problem der Datenhomogenität." In: *Glottometrika 13*. Bochum. (287–298).

Arapov, M.V.
1988 *Kvantitativnaja lingvistika*. Moskva.

Baker, S.J.
1951 "A linguistic law of constancy: II", in: *The Journal of General Psychology, 44*; 113–120.

Belonogov, G.G.
1962 "O nekotorych statističeskich zakonomernostjach v russkoj pis'mennoj reči", in: *Voprosy jazykoznanija, 11(1)*; 100–101.

Fenk-Oczlon, G.
1990 "Ikonismus versus Ökonomieprinzip. Am Beispiel russischer Aspekt- und Kasusbildungen", in: *Papiere zur Linguistik, 42*; 49–68

Fenk-Oczlon, G.
1986 "Morphologische Natürlichkeit und Frequenz." Paper presented at the 19th Annual Meeting of Societas Linguistica Europae, Ohrid.

Grzybek, P.; Altmann, G.
2003 "Oscillation in the frequency-length relationship", in: *Glottometrics, 5*; 97–107.

Grzybek, P.; Stadlober, E.
2003 "The Graz Project on Word Length Frequency (Distributions)", in: *Journal of Quantitative Linguistics, 9(2)*; 187–192.

Guiraud, P.
1954 *Les caractères statistiques du vocabulaire. Essai de méthodologie*. Paris.

Guiter, H.
1977 "Les relations /fréquence – longueur – sens/ des mots (langues romanes et anglais)." In: *XIV Congresso Internazionale di linguistica e filologia romanza, Napoli, 15-20 aprile 1974*. Napoli/Amsterdam. (373–381).

Haiman, J.
1983 "Iconic and economic motivation", in: *Language, 59*; 781–819.

Hammerl, R.
1990 "Länge – Frequenz, Länge – Rangnummer: Überprüfung von zwei lexikalischen Modellen." In: *Glottometrika 12*. Bochum. (1–24).

Herdan, G.
1966 *The advanced theory of language as choice and chance*. Berlin.

Kaeding, F.W.
1897–98 *Häufigkeitswörterbuch der deutschen Sprache*. Steglitz.

Köhler, R.
1986 *Zur linguistischen Synergetik. Struktur und Dynamik der Lexik*. Bochum.

Manczak, W.
1980 "Frequenz und Sprachwandel." In: Lüdtke, H. (ed.), *Kommunikationstheoretische Grundlagen des Sprachwandels*. Berlin/New York. (37–79).

Miller, G.A.; Newman, E.B.; Friedman, E.A.
1958 "Length-frequency statistics for written English", in: *Information and Control, 1*; 370–389.

Zipf, G.K.
1932 *Selected studies of the principle of relative frequency in language*. Cambridge, Mass.

Zipf, G.K.
1935 *The psycho-biology of language: An introduction to dynamic philology*. Boston.

Zörnig, P.; Köhler, R.; Brinkmöller, R.
1990 "Differential equation models for the oscillation of the word length as a function of the frequency." In: *Glottometrika 12*. Bochum. (25–40).

14

DEVELOPING THE CROATIAN NATIONAL CORPUS AND BEYOND

Marko Tadić

1. The Croatian National Corpus – a Case Study

The Croatian National Corpus (HNK) has been collected since 1998 under grant # 130718 by the Ministry of Science and Technology of the Republic of Croatia. The theoretical foundations for such a corpus was laid down in Tadić (1996, 1998), where the need for a Croatian reference corpus (both synchronic and diachronic) was expressed. The tentative solution for its structure was suggested, its time-span and size as well as its availability over the WWW further elaborated. The overall structure of the HNK was divided on two constituents:

1. $30m$: a 30-million corpus of contemporary Croatian
2. HETA: Croatian Electronic Textual Archive

The $30m$ is collected with the purpose of representing a reference corpus for contemporary Croatian language. It encompasses texts from 1990 until today, from different domains and genres and tries to be balanced in that respect.

The HETA is, according to the blurred border between text-collections and third generation of corpora, intended to be a vast collection of texts older than 1990, or a complete series (sub-corpora) of publications which would mis-balance the $30m$.

Since for Croatian there has been no research on text production/reception or systematized data on text-flow in society, we were forced to use figures from book-stores about the most selling books, from libraries about books which are the most borrowed ones, and overall circulation figures for newspapers and magazines in order to select the text sources for the HNK. The literary critic's panoramic surveys on Croatian fiction were also consulted for the fictional types of texts.

The overall structure of $30m$ consists of:

- 74% Informative texts (Faction): newspaper, magazines, books (journalism, crafts, sciences, ...)
- 23% Imaginative texts (Fiction): prose (novels, stories, essays, diaries, ...)
- 3% Mixed texts

P. Gryzbek (ed.), Contributing in the Science of Text and Language, 295-300.

Several technical decisions were made at the beginning of corpus collecting: we wanted to avoid any typing and/or OCR-input of texts. This narrowed our sources to texts in the format of *e*-text, i.e. already digitally stored documents. On the grounds of these decisions we had no problems with the text quantity for newspapers, fiction, textbooks from social sciences and/or humanities, but we experienced severe lack of sources from the natural and technical sciences. Until now, more than 100 million words have been collected but it is not included in the corpus because it would disturb the planned balance. The copyright problem is another problem, which emerges in the process of corpus compilation since the copyrights have to be preserved. We are making agreements with text-suppliers on that issue.

The corpus is encoded in Corpus Encoding Standard (Ide, Bonhomme & Romary 2000), more precisely, its XML version called XCES. The idea to stick to standard data formats is very important because it allows us (and others as well) to apply different tools to the different data sets while maintaining the same data-format. The choice of XML as mark-up language in 1998 turned to be right as nowadays the majority of new corpora are being encoded with XML. Since XML is Unicode compatible, there are no problems with different scriptures (i.e., code-pages). The level of mark-up is XCES level 1, which includes the division on the level of document structure and on the level of individual paragraphs. For the mark-up at level 2, we have developed the tokenizer but it has been applied only experimentally on limited amounts of texts. The sentence delimitation is also being done with the system we have developed but the serious problem in Croatian are ordinal numbers written with Arabic numbers. The Croatian orthography prescribes the obligatory punctuation (a dot) which discerns between cardinal and ordinal numbers. The problem is that on average 28% of all ordinal numbers written with Arabic numbers and dot are at the same time the sentence endings. In those cases, the dot can also be a fullstop. For the moment this can not be solved in any other way other than with human inspection.

The tool 2XML was developed in order to speed the process of conversion from the original text format (RTF, HTML, DOC, QXD, WP, TXT etc.) to XML. The tool has a two-step procedure of conversion with the ability to apply user-defined script for fine-tuning the XML mark-up in the output. The conversion can be done in batch mode as well.

The HNK is available at the address `http://www.hnk.ffzg.hr` where a test version is freely available for searching. The results of the search are KWIC concordances with frequency information and possibility to turn each keyword in KWAL format.

The POS tagging of HNK is currently in its experimental phase right now. Since Croatian is an inflectionally rich language (7 cases, 2 numbers for nouns; 3 genders, 2 forms (definite/indefinite), 3 grades for adjectives; 7 cases, 2 numbers,

3 persons for pronouns; 7 cases for numbers; 2 numbers, 3 persons, 3 simple and 3 complex tenses etc. for verbs) there exists a serious complexity in that process. Bearing in mind that Croatian, like all other Slavic languages, is a relatively free-order language, it is obvious that the computational processing of inflection is a prerequisite for any computational syntactic analysis since the majority of intra-sentential relations is encoded by inflectional word-forms instead of word-order (like for example English).

Since there are no automatic inflectional analysers for Croatian, we took a different approach. Based on a Croatian word-forms generator (Tadić 1994), a Croatian Morphological Lexicon (HML) has been developed. It includes generated word-forms for 12,000 nouns, 7,700 verbs and 5,500 adjectives for now. It is fully conformant to the MULTEXT-East recommendations v2.0 (`http://nl.ijs.si/et/MTE`). The HML is freely searchable at `http://www.hnk.ffzg.hr/hml` and allows queries on lemmas as well as word-forms. The POS (and MSD) tagging of HNK will be performed by matching the corpus with the word-forms from HML thus giving us the opportunity to attach to each token in the corpus all possible morphosyntactical descriptions on unigram level. The reason for this is that we do not have any data on "morphosyntactical or POS homographical weight" of Croatian words and this presents a way of getting it. We will do the matching on a carefully selected 1 million corpus. After that we will disambiguate between all possible MSDs and select the right one for each token in the corpus. This will be done with the help of local regular grammars that will process the contexts of tokens, and with human inspection. What we expect is a large amount of "internal" homography (where all possible different MSDs of the same token belong to the same lemma) and relatively small amount of "external" homography (where possible different MSDs of the same token belong to different lemmas). The manually disambiguated 1 million corpus will be used as a training data for the POS-tagger. The thus trained POS-tagger will be used to tag the whole HNK with expected precision above 90%.

The new project proposals have been submitted recently to our Ministry of Science and Technology and we have proposed a new project: *Developing Croatian Language Resources* (2003-2005). Its primary goals would be the completion of the $30m$ corpus and its enlargement to $100m$. The inclusion of some kind of spoken corpus would be highly preferable as well as development of several parallel corpora with Croatian being one side of the pair. The new corpus manager (Manatee coupled with its client Bonito) is being considered as a basic corpus software platform.

2. Some Methodological Remarks

We have to look upon the corpora as the sources of our primary linguistic data. But what kind of data do we get from corpora exactly? We can assume that on the first level there are three basic types of data:

1. evidence: *is the linguistic unit we are looking for there?*
2. frequency: *if it is there, how often?*
3. relation: *if it is there more than once, is there any recognizable relationship with other units? Are there different relationships or only one?*

What do we count in corpora? This question should be spread over different linguistic levels:

- phonemes/graphemes (and their combinations, syllables)
- morphemes (and their combinations: words)
- words (and their combinations: syntagms)
- syntagms (and their combinations: clauses and sentences)
- meanings (?)

Let us concentrate on the level of words only. If we get the "bag of words" containing (*ženom, žene, ženu, ženom*), we can say that in it there are four tokens, three types, two lemmas and one lemma (two lemmas in the case of word-form *žene*, which is "externally" homographic). When we say "words", we must be precise and define to which possible types of words we are referring. Corpora start with tokens.

But in the case of Croatian even such a straightforward concept as the word can be is not always easy to grasp in real texts (corpora). Consider the examples:

(a) *nikoji*, pron. adjective = nijedan, nikakav (no one)

(b) *Ni u kojem se slučaju ne smiješ okrenuti*

(c) *oligo- i polisaharidi*

(d) *Ivan je Šikić radosno krenuo nizbrdo.*

where (a) is a citation from the Anić (1990) dictionary, (b) is a case of divided pronominal adjective, (c) a case of text compression, (d) a very frequent case of analytical (or complex) verbal tense where auxiliary can be almost anywhere in the clause. How many words do we have here? Is it a trivial question? How does the opposition between "graphic words", phonetic words, types and lemmas stand?

Measuring of word length implies (1) a definition of the word "word", and (2) a definition of the unit of measurement.

(1) Words can be defined as a graphic, phonetic, morphotactic, lexical (= listeme), syntactic or semantic word. Each of these possible definitions concentrates on different features of words.

(2) Units of measurement can be graphemes, phonemes, syllables, morphemes. It would be really interesting to see a whole corpus with words measured in all possible units of measurement.

What is the nature of linguistic investigation? It is always about the two sides of the same "piece of paper": form and meaning. Form is there to convey the meaning. Our meaning motivates the choice of the form on the level of lexical choice and syntactic constructions. What we do in a normal situation is that we choose the best forms we have at our disposal in the language we speak to convey the meaning. If we try to compare forms of different languages, we should have meaning under controlled conditions; meaning should be a neutral factor in our experiment. It would be best to have (more-or-less) the same meaning in both languages. Therefore, I plea for the use of parallel corpora for any purpose of this kind. The parallel corpora are original texts paired with their translations. This is the closest we can get in our attempt to keep the "same" meaning in two or more languages. This is the situation in which our comparison of forms between languages will yield the methodologically cleanest results.

Regarding purely quantitative approaches to language, there is a lot of ground for fruitful cooperation with corpus linguistics. Quantitative and corpus linguistic approaches are complementary. Corpus linguistics gives quantitative linguistics large amounts of systematized data, far more variables and the possibility to test and define parameters in quantitative approaches. On the other hand, quantitative linguistics gives corpus linguistics tools to discrete segmentation of text continuum which results in discrete classes and/or units. Quantitative and corpus linguistics should work in synergy.

References

Anić, V.
1990 *Rječnik hrvatskoga jezika.* Zagreb.

Ide, N.; Bonhomme, P.; Romary, L.
2000 "An XML-based Encoding Standard for Linguistic Corpora." In: *Proceedings of the Second International Language Resources and Evaluation Conference, vol. 2.* Athens. (825–830).

Rychlý, P.
2000 *Korpusové manažery a jejich efektivní implementace.* [= Corpus Managers and their effective implementation). Ph.D. thesis, University of Brno. [http://www.fi.muni.cz/~pary/disert.ps]

Tadić, M.
1994 *Računalna obradba morfologije hrvatskoga književnoga jezika.* Ph.D. thesis, University of Zagreb. [http://www.hnk.ffzg.hr/txts/mt_dr.pdf].

Tadić, M.
1996 "Računalna obradba hrvatskoga i nacionalni korpus," in: *Suvremena lingvistika, 41-42*; 603–611. [English: http://www.hnk.ffzg.hr/txts/mt4hnk_e.pdf].

Tadić, M.
1997 "Računalna obradba hrvatskih korpusa: povijest, stanje i perspektive," in: *Suvremena lingvistika, 43-44*; 387–394. [English: http://www.hnk.ffzg.hr/txts/mt4hnk3_e.pdf].

Tadić, M.
1998 "Raspon, opseg i sastav korpusa hrvatskoga suvremenog jezika," in: *Filologija, 30-31*; 337–347. [English: http://www.hnk.ffzg.hr/txts/mt4hnk2_e.pdf].

Tadić, M.
2002 "Building the Croatian National Corpus." In: *Proceedings of the Third International Language Resources and Evaluation Conference, vol. 2.* Paris. (441–446).

15

ABOUT WORD LENGTH COUNTING IN SERBIAN

Duško Vitas, Gordana Pavlović-Lažetić, Cvetana Krstev

1. Introduction

Text elements can be counted in several ways. Depending on the counting unit, different views of the structure of a text as well as of the structure of its parts such as words, may be obtained. In this paper, we present different distributions in counting words in Serbian, applied to samples chosen from a corpus developed by the Natural Language Processing Group at the Faculty of Mathematics, University of Belgrade.

This presentation is organized in four parts. The first part presents formal approximations of a word. These approximations partially normalize text in such a way that the influence of orthographic variations is neutralized in measuring specific parameters of texts. Text elements will be counted with respect to such approximations. The second part of the paper describes in brief some of the existing resources for Serbian language processing such as corpora and text archives. Part three presents the results of analysis of structure of word length in Serbian, while in part four, distributions of word frequencies in chosen texts are analyzed, as well as the role morphological, syntactic and lexical relations play in a revision of the results obtained in counting single words.

1.1 The Formal word

The digital form of a text is an approximation of the text as an object organized in a natural language. Text registered in such a way, as a raw material, appears in the form of character sequences. The first step in recognizing its natural language organizations consists of the identification of words as potential linguistic units. In order to identify words, it is necessary to notice the difference between a character sequence potentially representing a word, and the word itself, represented by the character sequence, and belonging to a specific language system.

Let Σ be a finite alphabet used for writing in a specific language system, and Δ a finite alphabet of separators used for separating records of words (alphabets Σ and Δ do not have to be disjointed in a natural language). Then a formal word is any contingent character string over the alphabet Σ. For example, if

P. Gryzbek (ed.), Contributing in the Science of Text and Language, 301-317.

$\Sigma = \{a, b\}$, then $aaabbb$ and $ababab$ are formal words over Σ, but the first one belongs to the language

$$L = \{a^n b^n | n \geq 0\}$$

while the second does not. If Δ={c, d} is an alphabet of separators, then in the string $aaabbbcabababdaabb$ there are three formal words over Σ, the first and the third of which being words from the language L, while the formal word $ababab$, enclosed with the separators c, d, is not a word from the language L. If, on the other side, the alphabet of separators is $\Delta = \{b, c\}$, i.e., $\Sigma \cap \Delta \neq \emptyset$, then the segmentation of the sequence $abacab$ into formal words is ambiguous. The necessity to differentiate a formal word from a word as a linguistic unit arises from the following example: let Σ be the Serbian language alphabet (no matter how it is defined). Even if we limit the contents of Σ so as to contain alphabet symbols only, the problem of identifying formal word is nontrivial. For example, in the string *PETAR I PETROVIĆ*, *I* has twofold interpretation (either as a Roman numeral or as a conjunction). Similarly, in the course of transliteration from Latin to Cyrillic and vice versa, formal words occur in a Serbian text that do not belong to Serbian language, or that have twofold interpretation. String *VILJEM* has two Cyrillic interpretations, string *PC* has different interpretations in Latin and Cyrillic, and the string *Xorx* in the Latin alphabet is a formal word resulting in transliteration from the Cyrillic alphabet (in the so-called *yuscii*-ordering) of the word *Džordž* etc.

Ambiguity may originate in orthographic rules. For example, the name of the flower *daninoć* (Latin *viola tricolor*) has, according to different orthographic variants, the following forms:

(1a) daninoć (cf. Jovanović/Atanacković (1980)
(1b) dan-i-noć (cf. Pešikan et al. (1993)
(1c) dan i noć (cf. Pešikan et al.(1993)

It is obvious that segmentation into formal words depends on whether the hyphen is an element of the separator set or not. Let us look at the following examples of strings over the Serbian language alphabet:

(2)	1%-procentni	*versus*	jednopostotni
	3,5 miliona evra	*versus*	tri i po miliona evra
		or	tri miliona i pet stotina hiljada evra
	21.06.2003.	*versus*	21. juni ove godine

If we constrain Σ to the alphabet character set, it is not possible to establish formal equality between the former strings. Extending the set Σ to digits, punctuation or special characters leads to ambiguity in interpreting and recognizing formal words.

For a more thorough discussion on the problem of defining and recognizing formal words, see Vitas (1993), Silberztein (1993).

1.2 The Simple and compound word

If we assume that $\Sigma \cap \Delta = \emptyset$, then it is possible to reduce the concept of a formal word to the concept of a simple word. By a simple word we assume a contingent string of alphabet characters (characters from the Σ set) between two consecutive separators. Then in example (1) only the form *daninoć* is a simple word. The other two forms are sequences of three simple words, since they contain separators. Simple words represent better approximation of lexical words (words as elements of a written text), than formal words. Still, a simple word does not have to be a word from the language, either. For example, *in džiju-džica* (Pešikan et al. (1993: t. 59a), segmentation to simple words gives two strings *džiju* and *džica* which by themselves do not exist in the Serbian language.

In some cases, simple words participating in a compound word cannot stand by themselves. For example, in contemporary Serbian the noun *koštac* occurs only in the phrase *uhvatiti se u koštac*.

Based on the notion of a simple word, a notion of a compound word is defined, as a sequence of simple words. The notion of a compound word has been introduced in Silberztein (1993), including different constraints necessary in order for a compound word to be differentiated from an **arbitrary** sequence of simple words. Let us compare the following sentences:

(3a) Radi dan i noć

(3b) Cveta dan i noć

At the level of automatic morphological analysis, segmentation to simple words is unambiguous and both examples contain four simple words, and in both sentences the same grammatical structure is recognized: $V\ N\ Conj\ N$. But, if a notion of a compound word is applied to the segmentation level, the segmentation becomes ambiguous. The string *dan i noć* in (3a) is a compound word (an adverbial), and the sentence (3a) then may consist of one simple and one compound word and have a form of *V Adv*. In example (3b), considering the meaning of the verb cvetati (to bloom), a twofold segmentation of the compound word *dan i noć* is possible: as an adverbial compound or as the name of a flower.

It follows that the notion of a word as a syntactic-semantic unit can be approximated in a written text in several different ways: as a formal or a simple word, including correction by means of a compound word. The way words are counted as well as the result of such a counting certainly depends on the accepted definition of a word. Ambiguity occurring in examples (3a) and (3b) offers an example of possibly different results in counting words as well as in counting morpho-syntactic categories.

1.3 Serbian Language Corpora

One of the resources for empirical investigation of the Serbian language are Serbianlanguage corpora in digital form.
In the broadest sense, significant resources of Serbian language are collections of texts collected without explicit linguistic criteria. One such collection is represented by the project Rastko (`www.rastko.org.yu`). This *website* contains several hundred integral texts. A different source is the *website* of Danko Šipka (`main.amu.edu.pl/\~{}sipkadan/`), which is a corpus of Serbo-Croatian language, representing a portal to collections of texts available through the *web*, regardless of the way texts are encoded and tagged. Pages of daily or weekly newspapers, as well as CD editions, can be considered as relevant material for quantitative language investigations.

If the notion of a corpus is constrained so that explicit criteria of structuring resources have to be applied in its construction, two corpora then exist: the diachronic corpus of Serbian / Serbo-Croatian language compiled by Đorđe Kostić, and the corpus of contemporary Serbian language developed at the Faculty of Mathematics, University of Belgrade.
The diachronic corpus compiled by Đorđe Kostić originated in the 1950s as a result of manual processing of samples of texts. It encompasses the period from the 12th century to the beginning of the 1950s. During the 1990s, this material was transformed into digital form, and insights into its structure and examples can be found at the URL: *www.serbian-corpus.edu.yu/*. This corpus contains about 11 million words and it is manually lemmatized and tagged. Although significant in size, it does not make explicit relationships between textual and lexical words, and the process of manual lemmatization applied cannot be reproduced on new texts.[1]

The corpus developed at the Faculty of Mathematics, University of Belgrade, contains Serbian literature of the 20th century, including translations published after 1960, different genres of newspaper texts (after 1995), textbooks and other types of texts (published after 1980), in integral form. Some parts of the corpus are publicly available through the *web* at `www.korpus.matf.bg.ac.yu/korpus/`. The total size of the corpus is over 100 million words, and only a smaller portion of it is available through the *web* for on-line retrieval. The corpus at the Faculty of mathematics has been partly automatically tagged and disambiguated using the electronic morphological dictionary system and the system Intex (Vitas 2001). Besides, parallel French-Serbian and English-Serbian corpora have been partially developed, consisting of literary and newspaper texts.

[1] For inconsistencies in traditional lexicography, see Vitas (2000).

1.4 Description of Texts

For the analysis of word length in Serbian, texts were chosen from the corpus of the contemporary Serbian language, developed at the Faculty of Mathematics in Belgrade. Texts are in ekavian, except for rare fragments. The sample consists of the following texts:

i. The *web*-editions of daily newspapers *Politika* (`www.politika.co.yu`) in the period from 5th to 10th of October 2000 (further referred to as *Poli*). These texts are a portion of a broader sample of the same newspaper (period from the 10th of September to the 20th of October 2000, referred to as *Politika*).

ii. The *web*-edition of the Serbian Orthodox Church journal *Pravoslavlje* [Orthodoxy](`www.spc.org.yu`) – numbers 741 to 828 from the period 1998–2001. This sub-sample will be referred to as *SPC*.

iii. Collection of tales entitled *Partija karata* [Card game], written by Rade Kuzmanović (Nolit, Belgrade, 1982). The text will be referred to as *Radek*.

iv. The novel *Treći sektor ili žena sama u tranziciji* [Third sector or a woman alone in transition] by Mirjana Đurđević (Žagor, Belgrade, 2001). This text will be referred to as *Romi*.

v. Translation of the novel *Bouvard and Pécuchet* by Gustave Flaubert (Nolit, Belgrade, 1964). The text will be referred to as *Buvar*.

Table 15.1 represents the way characters from the Serbian alphabet are encoded.

Table 15.1: Serbian Alphabet-Specific Characters Encoding

ć	**č**	**đ**	**dž**	**ž**	**š**	**lj**	**nj**
cx	cy	dx	dy	zx	sx	lx,lj	nx,nj

The length of the texts, in terms of total number of tokens (and different tokens), after initial preprocessing by INTEX, is given in Table 15.2. Any of the following three types of formal words are considered to be tokens: simple word, numeral (digits) and delimiters (string of separators).

2. Word Length in Text and Dictionary of Serbian

Considering the sub-samples described in table 15.2, let us examine word length distributions in Serbian, using different criteria for expressing word length.

Table 15.2: Length of Texts Expressed by the Total Number of Tokens and Different Tokens

source	tokens (diff.)	simple words	digits	delimiters
Politika	1736094 (107919)	1355785 (107867)	82135 (10)	298172 (42)
Poli	190664 (26921)	147913 (26884)	9079 (10)	33672 (27)
SPC	369541 (48987)	293460 (48940)	15505 (10)	60576 (37)
Romi	68389 (11131)	53271 (11101)	120 (10)	14998 (20)
Radek	101231 (16438)	88105 (16420)	67 (10)	13059 (8)
Buvar	96170 (21272)	79176 (21245)	129 (10)	16865 (17)

2.1 Word Length in Terms of Number of Characters

The length of a simple word may be expressed by the number of characters it consists of. In this sense, word length may be calculated by a function such as, for example, *strlen* in the programming language C, modified by the fact that characters have to be alphabetical (from the class [A–Z a–z]). Considering the method of encoding, since diacritic characters are encoded as digraphs (Table 15.1), the function for calculating simple word length treats digraphs from Table 15.1 as single characters. Results of such a calculation are given in Table 15.3, and graphically represented by Figure 15.1.

The local peak on the length 21 in the *SPC* sub-sample comes from the high frequency of different forms of the noun *Visokopreosvesxtenstvo* (71) and the instrumental singular of the adjective *zahumskohercegovacyki* (1). With this approach to calculating the length of a formal word, the word *foto-reporter* (in *Radek*) or *raško-prizrenski* (in *SPC*) are considered as two separate words.

2.2 Word Length in Terms of Number of Syllables

The length of a simple word may also be expressed by the number of syllables also. Calculation is based on the occurrence of characters corresponding to vowels and syllabic ‘r’ (where it is possible to automatically recognize its

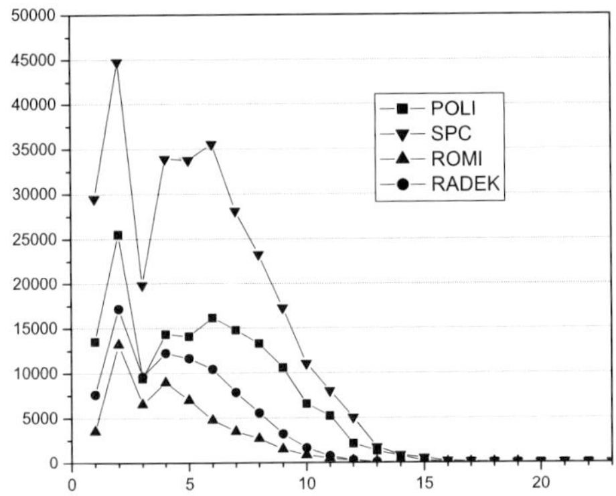

Figure 15.1: Differences Found in the Within-Sentence Distribution of Content and Function Words

occurrence). Word length in terms of the number of syllables is represented in Table 15.4, and graphically by Figure 15.2.

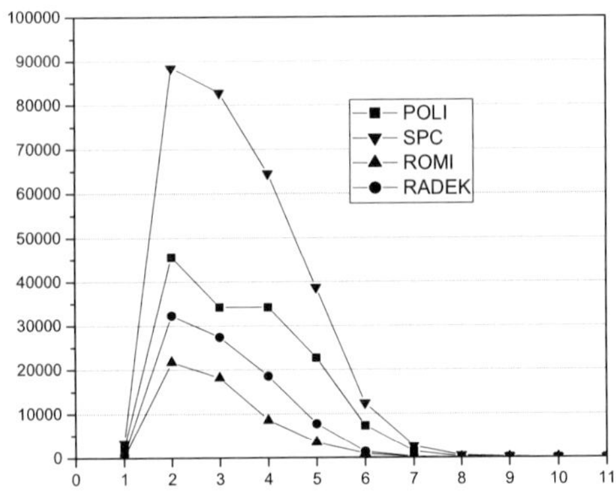

Figure 15.2: Word Length in Terms of Number of Syllables

Prepositions such as 's' [with], 'k' [toward], abbreviation such as 'g.' [Mr], 'sl.' [similar], etc., are considered as words with 0 syllables. As a side effect in calculating word length by the number of syllables, the vowel-consonant word structure in Serbian has been obtained. If we denote the position of a vowel in a word by **v**, and position of a consonant by **c**, then Tables 15.5 and 15.6 present

Table 15.3: Word Length in Terms of Number of Characters

length in characters	number of simple words *Poli*	*SPC*	*Romi*	*Radek*
1	13509	29496	3511	7630
2	25509	44756	13201	17142
3	9389	19813	6519	9602
4	14335	33926	8946	12242
5	14092	33766	6963	11638
6	16155	35554	4754	10435
7	14779	28093	3472	7846
8	13262	23235	2689	5535
9	10593	17218	1508	3197
10	6545	11022	834	1634
11	5223	8013	481	747
12	2131	5025	228	285
13	1307	1715	95	89
14	734	846	34	33
15	192	525	19	27
16	73	201	12	19
17	43	106	3	1
18	28	44	1	3
19	7	13	1	
20	4	7		
21	2	78		
22	1	7		
23		1		
$\sum$	147913	293460	53271	88105

frequencies of vowel-consonant structure for two literary texts analyzed, and respectively for newspaper texts. Along with each structure, the first occurrence of a simple word corresponding to the structure is given. Simple words consisting of open syllables have high frequencies. It can be seen that newspaper and literary texts show different distributions regarding vowel-consonant orderings in a simple word, although data about length of words in terms of number of characters or syllables do not show such differences. A detailed analysis of the consonant group structure in Serbo-Croatian is given in Krstev (1991).

The texts analyzed, both literary texts and newspapers, have an identical set of eight most frequent vowel-consonant word structures. It is rather interesting that among the literary as well as among the newspaper texts, the ordering of

Table 15.4: Word Length in Terms of Number of Syllables

length in syllables	number of simple words *Poli*	*SPC*	*Romi*	*Radek*
0	2295	3331	278	633
1	45570	88496	21708	32269
2	34215	82796	18112	27358
3	34196	64513	8544	18503
4	22660	38648	3519	7725
5	7277	12411	925	1378
6	1413	2618	152	217
7	229	471	24	18
8	52	163	9	4
9	5	12	0	0
10	1	1	0	0
$\sum$	147913	293460	53271	88105

these structures by frequency is identical too; between literary and newspaper texts there is, however, a noticeable difference in this ordering (consecutive structures in one are permuted in another), cf. Figure 15.3.

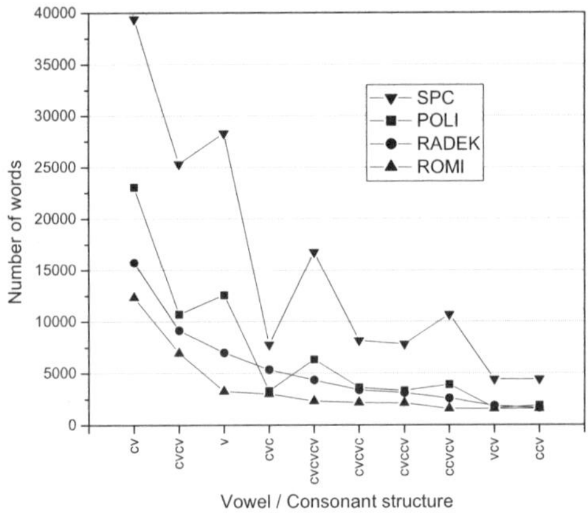

Figure 15.3: Top Frequencies of Vowel-Consonant Structures in Literary and Newspaper Texts

Table 15.5: Top Frequencies of Vowel-Consonant Structures For Two Literary Texts

Radek			*Romi*		
group	**frequ.**	**example**	**group**	**frequ.**	**example**
cv	15745	je	cv	12349	Ne
cvcv	9147	nebu	cvcv	6942	rada
v	6999	i	v	3260	I
cvc	5357	sam	cvc	3019	Josx
cvcvcv	4342	kucxice	cvcvcv	2315	dodusxe
cvcvc	3391	Taman	cvcvc	2152	jedan
cvccv	3097	Tesxko	cvccv	2127	Jeste
ccvcv	2587	svoje	ccv	1583	gde
vcv	1852	Ona	ccvcv	1577	vreme
ccv	1638	dva	vcv	1559	one
ccvcvcv	1621	sparina	vc	817	od
vc	1394	ih	cvcvcvcv	762	Terazije
cvcvcvcv	1374	nekoliko	ccvcvcv	721	primiti
cvccvcv	1337	putnika	cvccvcv	636	najmanxe
cvccvc	1260	zadnxem	vcvc	618	opet

2.3 Word length in a dictionary

Let us further examine the length of simple words in a dictionary, e.g., the *Sistematski rečnik srpskohrvatskog jezika* by Jovanović/Atanacković (1980). Simple words are reduced here to their lemma form, i.e., verbs to infinitive, nouns to nominative singular, etc. There are 7773 verbs and 38287 other simple words (nouns, adjectives, adverbs) in the dictionary. The distribution of their length in terms of number of characters (calculated in the manner described above) is depicted by the diagram in Figure 15.4. It is substantially different from the word distribution in a running text.

This distribution may be proved to be Gaussian normal distribution with parameters (8.58; 2.65), established by Kolmogorov χ^2-test with significance level α=0.01, number of intervals $n = 8$ and interval endpoints

$$5 < a_1 < 6 < a_2 < 7 < a_3 < 8 < a_4 < 9 < a_5 < 10 < a_6 < 11 < a_7 < 12.$$

2.4 Word frequency in text

The results of calculating simple word frequencies in samples from 1.4 confirm well-known results about the participation of functional words in a text. The

Table 15.6: Top Frequencies of Vowel-Consonant Structures For Two Newspaper Texts

Poli			*SPC*		
group	**frequ.**	**example**	**group**	**frequ.**	**example**
cv	23053	da	cv	39408	SA
v	12583	i	v	28304	U
cvcv	10717	SUDA	cvcv	25328	SAVA
cvcvcv	6330	godine	cvcvcv	16788	godine
ccvcv	3910	sceni	ccvcv	10676	SVETI
cvcvc	3635	danas	cvcvc	8164	kojoj
cvccv	3310	posle	cvccv	7826	CENTU
cvc	3294	sud	cvc	7773	nxih
cvcvcvcv	3140	politika	cvcvcvcv	6132	delovanxa
cvccvcv	2809	Tanjugu	cvccvcv	5259	poznate
ccvcvcv	2484	gradxana	ccvcvcv	5100	dvorani
vc	2209	od	ccv	4410	sve
vccvcv	2162	odnosi	vcv	4403	ove
cvcvccv	2133	ponisxti	vc	4254	od
ccv	1888	svi	ccvcvc	3859	Dragan

most frequent ten words coincide in all of the chosen samples (*a, da, i, je, na, ne, se, u, za*), with some insignificant deviations (the form *su* – 'are' in the

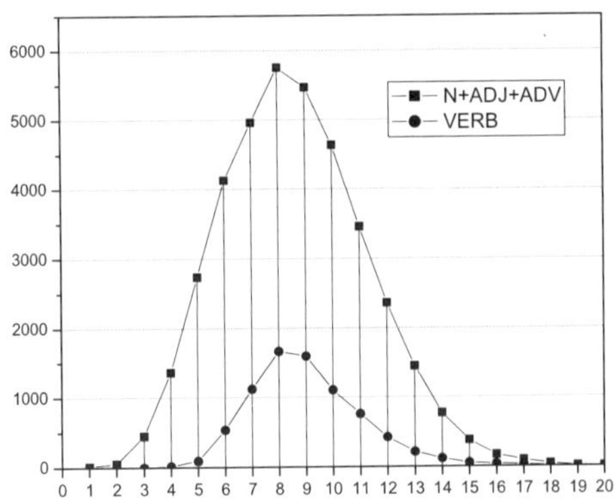

Figure 15.4: Word Length Distribution in a Dictionary

newspaper sample versus the form *sam* – 'am' in the literary sample), as shown in Table 15.7. Thus, underlined are words occurring in four out of five samples (e.g., od, sa), in underlined italic are those occurring in three samples (e.g., *iz*, *koji*, *su*), in italic – two (e.g., *cxe*, *kao*, *mi*, *o*, *sam*, *sxto*, *to*), in bold face – those occurring in one sample only, e.g., **ja**, **nije**, **s**, **ti**.

Table 15.7: Most Frequent Words

	Politika		*Poli*		*SPC*		*Radek*		*Romi*	
	frequ.	**word**	**frequ.**	**word**	**frequ.**	**word**	**frequ.**	**word**	**frequ.**	**word**
1.	53215	i	5507	i	15163	i	3838	i	2326	da
2.	46338	u	5077	je	9656	u	3202	da	1658	je
3.	43778	je	5174	u	8675	je	2643	se	1230	se
4.	34875	da	4196	da	5525	da	2392	u	1431	i
5.	20689	se	2340	se	4913	se	1906	je	1006	u
6.	19875	na	2087	na	3831	na	1569	*sam*	915	ne
7.	16093	za	1726	*su*	3138	*su*	1493	na	752	*sam*
8.	15596	*su*	1456	za	2167	za	807	ne	651	na
9.	8854	a	1070	a	1779	od	610	*mi*	470	a
10.	8263	od	1002	sa	1733	sa	598	**s**	422	**ja**
11.	8208	sa	844	od	1718	a	579	od	422	*mi*
12.	7200	*koji*	768	*cxe*	1544	*koji*	532	*sxto*	414	*to*
13.	6013	*cxe*	723	*koji*	1406	ne	515	za	384	sa
14.	5730	*iz*	599	*o*	1397	*kao*	498	*to*	383	za
15.	5480	*o*	592	*iz*	1131	*iz*	474	*kao*	361	**ti**
16.	5197	ne	566	ne	1016	sxto	422	a	326	**nije**

Table 15.8: Top Frequencies of Word Bigrams

	Radek		*Romi*		*Politika*		*SPC*	
	frequ.	**bigram**	**frequ.**	**bigram**	**frequ.**	**bigram**	**frequ.**	**bigram**
1.	286	**da se**	124	**da se**	297	**da se**	455	**da se**
2.	114	kao da	81	**da je**	274	**da je**	310	kao i
3.	90	**da je**	43	Ne znam	185	rekao je	279	**da je**
4.	29	i onda	37	da ne	181	da cxe	252	koji je
5.	28	ja sam	37	da mi	159	kao i	235	koji su
6.	28	i ja	33	ja sam	140	i da	158	je u
7.	28	da bih	32	Ja sam	135	koji je	152	Sxto je
8.	27	sxto se	32	i da	120	koji su	147	i u
9.	27	mislim da	31	a ne	109	u Beogradu	126	i da
10.	26	je u	29	ne znam	95	On je	120	koja je
11.	26	je bilo	27	to je	91	sxto je	118	To je
12.	25	mogu da	26	mi je	90	kako je	112	da bi
13.	24	mogao da	26	I sxta	90	rekao da	110	Nxegova Svetost
14.	24	da cxu	26	a ja	79	da su	109	pravoslavne crkve
15.	24	bih se	25	A i	73	izjavio je	102	da cxe

Still, a picture of the most frequent words will be significantly changed if, instead of calculating frequencies of single simple words, frequencies of contingent sequences of two or three simple words are calculated (Table 15.8).

Except for the strings *da je* and *da se*, the first 15 combinations of two simple words do not include any other common element. On the other hand, meaningful words such as verbs, nouns, adjectives, emerge in highly frequent levels. Frequency of the most frequent word bigrams is significantly lower than the frequency of single simple words, which points out the influence of syntactic conditions in combining simple words. When the same comparison with word trigrams is performed, the results represented in table 15.9 is obtained.

Among the high frequent combinations of three simple words, in our sub-samples there is no more common element. Participation of functional words in each of the sub-samples depends on a type of a sentence construction, or they are parts of compounds.

Table 15.9: Top Frequencies of Word Trigrams

	Radek		*Romi*		*Politika*		*SPC*	
	frequ.	**trigram**	**frequ.**	**trigram**	**frequ.**	**trigram**	**frequ.**	**trigram**
1.	28	kao da sam	17	ne mogu da	34	od nasxeg stalnog	41	Nxegova Svetost patrijarh
2.	27	u neku ruku	8	ne znam da	30	Demokratske opozicije Srbije	38	Kosovu i Metohiji
3.	25	cyinilo mi se	8	a ne samo	30	kako je rekao	34	Srpske pravoslavne crkve
4.	23	kao da je	7	sxta ti je	29	kazxe se u	28	na Kosovu i
5.	18	znao sam da	7	da mi je	29	navodi se u	27	Kao sxto je
6.	17	da tako kazxem	7	bojim se da	25	da cxe se	21	a to je
7.	16	po svoj prilici	6	da je to	22	kako bi se	20	i da se
8.	15	Tacyno je da	5	Ti si stvarno	22	kao i da	19	da bi se
9.	15	kao da se	5	Otkud ti znasx	20	i da se	18	Nxegova Svetost je
10.	14	u svakom slucyaju	5	Ne znam ni	18	i da je	17	bracxo i sestre

2.5 Morphological Problem in Counting Words

Results presented naturally raise questions about results that will be obtained if a simple word from text is substituted by its lemma and further on, by its part of speech. Results of such a substitution over texts *Radek* and *Romi*, considering the verb *znati* (to know) which occurred in both texts, are given in Table 15.10.

Table 15.10: Lemma Frequency – Example of the Verb *znati*

<znati>	*Total*	*Present tense*	*Participle*	*Infinitive*
Radek	121	80	40	1
Romi	218	186	29	3
Poli	77	62	8	3

In the *Poli* sample, *<znati>* appears in adverbial form (*znajući*, 2) and passive participle form (*znan*, 2). This suggests the conclusion that the distribution of word length will further change if lemmatization of word forms is performed. Note that among the word trigrams, phrases *po svoj prilici* (probably) and *u svakom slučaju* (anyway) can be found (*Radek*), representing adverbial compounds, as well as noun toponym *Kosovo i Metohija* (*SPC*).

The problem becomes more evident if a parallelized text is analyzed, as the example of the *Buvar* sample shows: in the original text string *Bouvard* occurs 635 times in total; in the Serbian translation, this string is separated into different forms of the proper name *Buvar* and its possessive adjective. Further considerations in this direction are given in Senellart (1999).

References

Jovanović, Ranko; Atanacković, Laza
1980 *Sistematski rečnik srpskohrvatskog jezika.* Novi Sad.

Krstev, Cvetana
1991 "Serbo-Croatian Hyphenation: a TEX point of view", in: *TUGboat*, 12_2; 215–223.

Pešikan, Mitar; Pižurica, Mato; Jerković, Jovan
1993 *Pravopis srpskoga jezika.* Novi Sad.

Senellart, Jean
1999 *Outils de reconnaissance d'expresions linguistiques complexes dans des grands corpus.* Université Paris VII: Thèse de doctorat.

Silberztein, Max D.
1993 *Le dictionnaire électronique et analyse automatique de textes: Le systeme INTEX.* Paris.

Vitas, Duško
1993 *Matematički model morfologije srpskohrvatskog jezika (imenska fleksija).* University of Belgrade: PhD. Thesis, Faculty of Mathematics.

Vitas, Duško; Krstev, Cvetana; Pavlović-Lažetić, Gordana
2000 "Recent Results in Serbian Computational Lexicography." In: Bokan, Neda (ed.), *Proceedings of the Symposium ≪Contemporary Mathematics≫.* Belgrade: University of Belgrade, Faculty of Mathematics. (113–130).

Vitas, Duško; Krstev, Cvetana; Pavlović-Lažetić, Gordana
2002 "The Flexible Entry." In: Zybatow, Gerhild; Junghanns, Uwe; Mehlhorn, Grit; Szucsich, Luka (eds.), *Current Issues in Formal Slavic Linguistics.* Frankfurt/M. (461–468).

16

WORD-LENGTH DISTRIBUTION IN PRESENT-DAY LOWER SORBIAN NEWSPAPER TEXTS

Andrew Wilson

1. Introduction

Lower Sorbian is a West Slavic language, spoken primarily in the south-eastern corner of the eastern German federal state of Brandenburg; the speech area also extends slightly further south into the state of Saxony.

Although the dialect geography of Sorbian is rather complex, Lower Sorbian is one of the two standard varieties of Sorbian, the other being Upper Sorbian, which is mainly used in Saxony.[1]

As a whole, Sorbian has fewer than 70,000 speakers, of whom only about 28% are speakers of Lower Sorbian. However, an understanding of both varieties of Sorbian is a key element in understanding the structure and history of the West Slavic language group as a whole, since Sorbian is generally recognized as constituting a separate sub-branch of West Slavic, alongside Lechithic (i.e. Polish and Cassubian) and Czecho-Slovak.[2]

This study is the first attempt to investigate word-length distribution in Sorbian texts, with a view to comparison with similar studies on other Slavic languages.

2. Background

The main task of quantitative linguistics is to attempt to explain, and express as general language laws, the underlying regularities of linguistic structure and usage. Until recently, this task has tended to be approached by way of normally unrelated individual studies, which has hindered the comparison of languages and language varieties owing to variations in methodology and data typology. Since 1993, however, Karl-Heinz Best at the University of Göttingen has been coordinating a systematic collaborative project, which, by means of comparable

1 For an overview of both varieties of Sorbian, see Stone (1993).

2 For a brief review of the arguments for this and for other, previously proposed groupings, see Stone (1972). It is, of course, important to analyse Sorbian for its own sake and not just for comparative purposes.

P. Gryzbek (ed.), Contributing in the Science of Text and Language, 319-327.

methodologies, makes it possible to obtain an overview of many languages and language varieties. The present investigation is a contribution to the Göttingen project.

Thë Gottingen project has so far been concerned especially with the distribution of word lengths in texts. The background to the project is discussed in detail by Best (1998, 1999), hence only the most important aspects are summarized here.

Proceeding from the suggestions of Wimmer and Altmann (1996), the project seeks to investigate the following general approach for the distribution of word lengths in texts:

$$P_x = g(x)P_{x-1} \tag{16.1}$$

where P_x is the probability of the word length x and P_{x-1} is the probability of the word length $x - 1$. It is thus conjectured that the frequency of words with length x is proportional to the frequency of words with length $x - 1$. It is, however, clear that this relationship is not constant, hence the element $g(x)$ must be a variable proportion. Wimmer and Altmann have proposed 21 specific variants of the above equation, depending on the nature of the element $g(x)$. The goal of the Göttingen project is thus, first of all, to test the conformance of different languages, dialects, language periods, and text types to this general equation, and, second, to identify the appropriate specific equation for each data type according to the nature of the element $g(x)$. Up to now, data from approximately 40 languages have been processed, which have shown that, so far, all languages support Wimmer and Altmann's theory, and, furthermore, that only a relatively small number of theoretical probability distributions are required to account for these (see, for example, Best 2001).

3. Data and Methodology

3.1 Data

In accordance with the principles of the Göttingen project[3], a study such as this needs to be carried out using homogeneous text, ideally between 100 and 2,000 words in length. It was therefore decided to use newspaper editorials (section "tak to wiźimy") from the Lower Sorbian weekly newspaper *Nowy Casnik*. These were available in sufficient quantity and were of an ideal length. Similar text types have also been used for investigations on other languages (cf. Riedemann 1996).

The following ten texts were analyzed, all dating from 2001:

[3] http://www.gwdg.de/~kbest/principl.htm

1	March, 3	Dolnoserbsko–engelski słownik – to jo wjelgin zajmna wěc
2	March, 31	Na škodu nimskeje rěcy?
3	April, 7	Tenraz 'olympiada' mimo Casnika
4	April, 14	Rědnje tak, Picański amt!
5	April, 21	PDS jo pšašała – z połnym pšawom
6	April, 28	Serbski powědaś – to jo za nas ważne
7	May, 5	Sud piwa za nejwušu maju
8	May, 26	Nic jano pla WITAJ serbski
9	June, 2	Pšawje tak, sakski a bramborski ministaŕ
10	June, 16	Ga bużo skońcnje zgromadna konferenca šołtow?

3.2 Count Principles

For each text analyzed, the number of words falling into each word-length class was counted. The word lengths were determined in accordance with the usual principles of the Göttingen project, i.e., in terms of the number of spoken syllables per orthographic word.

In counting word lengths, there are a number of special cases, which are regulated by the general guidelines of the project:

1. *Abbreviations* are counted as instances of the appropriate full form; thus, for example, *dr.* is counted as a two-syllable word (*doktor*).
2. *Acronyms* are counted as they are pronounced, e.g. *PDS* is counted as a single three-syllable word.
3. *Numerals* are counted according to the appropriate spelt-out (written) forms, e.g. *70* is treated as *sedymzaset* (a word with four syllables).

There is no general guideline for the treatment of hyphenated forms. In this study, hyphens are disregarded and treated as inter-word spaces, so that, for example *WITAJ-projektoju* is treated as two separate words.

A special problem in Lower Sorbian, as also in the other West Slavic languages, is the class of zero-syllabic prepositions. Previously, these have been treated as special cases within the Slavic language group and have been included in the frequency statistics (cf. the work of Uhlířová 1995). However, if one counts these prepositions as independent words, it is then necessary to fit rarer probability models to the data. Current practice is therefore to treat these zero-syllabic words as parts of the neighbouring words (i.e. as clitics), and, since they do not contain any vowels, they are thus simply disregarded (Best, personal communication). If treated in this way, then more regular probability distributions can normally be fitted.

The word-length frequency statistics for each text were run through the Altmann Fitter software[4] at Göttingen to determine which probability distribution was the most appropriate model. [5]

3.3 Statistics

The Altmann Fitter compares the empirical frequencies obtained in the data analysis with the theoretical frequencies generated by the various probability distributions (Wimmer and Altmann 1996; 1999). The degree of difference between the two sets of frequencies is measured by the chi-squared test and also by the discrepancy coefficient C; the latter is given by χ^2/N (where N is the total number of words counted) and is used especially where there is no degree of freedom.

A probability distribution is considered an appropriate model for the data if the difference between the empirical and theoretical frequencies is not significant, i.e., if $P(\chi^2) > 0.05$ and/or $C < 0.02$. The best distribution is that which shows the highest P and/or lowest C.

4. Results

In all cases, the 1-displaced hyper-Poisson distribution could be fitted to the texts with good P and/or C values. In some cases, however, it was necessary to combine length classes in order to obtain a good fit; this is indicated by vertical lines linking length classes in the individual results tables.

The 1-displaced hyper-Poisson distribution is given by equation (16.2), in which a and b are parameters and F is the hypergeometric function:

$$P_x = \frac{a^{(x-1)}}{b^{(x-1)}\,{}_1F_1(1;b;a)}, \qquad x = 1, 2, \ldots \tag{16.2}$$

The following tables present the individual results for the ten texts, where:

$x[i]$	number of syllables
$f[i]$	observed frequency of i-syllable words
$NP[i]$	theoretical frequency of i-syllable words
χ^2	chi-square
$d.f.$	degrees of freedom
$P[\chi^2]$	probability of the chi-square
C	discrepancy coefficient (χ^2/N)
a	parameter a in the above formula (16.2)
b	parameter b in the above formula (16.2)

[4] RST Rechner- und Softwaretechnik GmbH, Essen

[5] I am grateful to Karl-Heinz Best for running the data through the Altmann Fitter.

Text # 1	**March, 3**	
$x[i]$	$f[i]$	$NP[i]$
1	61	61.01
2	67	67.01
3	19	29.20
4	18	7.94
5	2	1.85
a	0.7223	
b	0.6576	
χ^2	0.0001	
$d.f.$	0	
C	< 0.0001	

Text # 2	**March, 31**	
$x[i]$	$f[i]$	$NP[i]$
1	71	75.17
2	76	66.64
3	25	32.61
4	13	11.02
5	2	2.84
6	1	0.59
7	1	0.12
a	1.0920	
b	1.2317	
χ^2	3.73	
$d.f.$	2	
$P[\chi^2]$	0.15	
C	0.0197	

Text # 3	**April, 7**	
$x[i]$	$f[i]$	$NP[i]$
1	68	67.58
2	54	51.74
3	23	27.82
4	14	11.53
5	4	3.88
6	1	1.45
a	1.8059	
b	2.3588	
χ^2	1.61	
$d.f.$	3	
$P[\chi^2]$	0.66	
C	0.0098	

Text # 4	**April, 14**	
$x[i]$	$f[i]$	$NP[i]$
1	56	55.42
2	49	52.70
3	32	33.68
4	25	16.21
5	5	9.00
a	1.9492	
b	2.0500	
χ^2	1.26	
$d.f.$	1	
$P[\chi^2]$	0.26	
C	0.0075	

Text # 5 April, 21

$x[i]$	$f[i]$	$NP[i]$
1	56	52.64
2	28	34.05
3	24	21.70
4	29	13.62]
5	6	21.00]
a	43.1085	
b	66.6484	
χ^2	1.54	
$d.f.$	1	
$P[\chi^2]$	0.22	
C	0.0108	

Text # 6 April, 28

$x[i]$	$f[i]$	$NP[i]$
1	68	66.97
2	44	43.33
3	21	24.46
4	20	12.24]
5	3	9.00]
a	4.4144	
b	6.8223	
χ^2	0.66	
$d.f.$	1	
$P[\chi^2]$	0.42	
C	0.0042	

Text # 7 May, 5

$x[i]$	$f[i]$	$NP[i]$
1	77	76.21
2	64	66.98
3	36	30.64
4	6	9.47
5	3	2.70
a	0.9540	
b	1.0856	
χ^2	2.39	
$d.f.$	2	
$P[\chi^2]$	0.30	
C	0.0128	

Text # 8 May, 26

$x[i]$	$f[i]$	$NP[i]$
1	51	50.05
2	62	55.56]
3	15	25.84]
4	12	7.60
5	1	1.96
a	0.8003	
b	0.7210	
χ^2	3.27	
$d.f.$	1	
$P[\chi^2]$	0.07	

Text # 9	June, 2		Text # 10	June, 16	
$x[i]$	$f[i]$	$NP[i]$	$x[i]$	$f[i]$	$NP[i]$
1	60	59.65	1	48	47.02
2	52	54.89	2	44	42.55
3	30	26.33	3	19	23.04
4	9	8.54	4	13	8.90
5	0	2.09	5	0	2.67
6	1	0.49			
a	1.0024		a	1.3479	
b	1.0893		b	1.4895	
χ^2	1.66		χ^2	4.45	
$d.f.$	2		$d.f.$	2	
$P[\chi^2]$	0.44		$P[\chi^2]$	0.11	
C	0.0109		C	0.0356	

5. Conclusions

Since one of the theoretical distributions suggested by Wimmer and Altmann can be fitted to the empirical data with a good degree of confidence, we may conclude that the Lower Sorbian language is no exception to the Wimmer-Altmann theory for the distribution of word lengths in texts.

It has also been found that the 1-displaced hyper-Poisson distribution is the most appropriate theoretical distribution to account for word lengths in present-day Lower Sorbian newspaper texts. However, this cannot yet be considered as a general distribution for the Lower Sorbian language as a whole, since text type and period can have an effect on word-length distribution.[6] Further studies are therefore necessary to investigate these variables for Lower Sorbian.

Direct comparisons with all the other Slavic languages are not yet possible, since most of the existing data were processed under earlier counting guidelines, i.e., with the inclusion of zero-syllabic words. Rarer variants of word-length probability distributions thus had to be fitted in these cases. However, Best (personal communication) has re-processed the data for a West Slavic language (Polish) and an East Slavic language (Russian) without zero-syllabic words. In both cases, the 1-displaced hyper-Poisson distribution gave the best results. It is thus possible that the 1-displaced hyper-Poisson distribution may prove to be

[6] For example, Wilson (2001) found that quantitative Latin verse showed a different distribution to that previously demonstrated for Latin prose and rhythmic verse; and Zuse (1996) demonstrated a different distribution for a genre of Early Modern English prose to that shown by Riedemann (1996) for a genre of present-day English prose.

a generally applicable distribution for the Slavic language group. However, this cannot yet be said with certainty: the processing of data without zero-syllabic words from the other West, East and South Slavic languages (including Upper Sorbian) is a pre-condition for such a claim. Different text types and periods in each language must also be examined.

References

Best, K.-H.
1998 "Results and perspectives of the Göttingen project on quantitative linguistics", in: *Journal of Quantitative Linguistics, 5*; 155–162.

Best, K.-H.
1999 "Quantitative Linguistik: Entwicklung, Stand und Perspektive", in: *Göttinger Beiträge zur Sprachwissenschaft, 2*; 7–23.

Best, K.-H. (ed.)
2001 *Häufigkeitsverteilungen in Texten.* Göttingen.

Riedemann, H.
1996 "Word-length distribution in English press texts", in: *Journal of Quantitative Linguistics, 3*; 265–271.

Stone, G.
1972 *The smallest Slavonic nation: the Sorbs of Lusatia.* London.

Stone, G.
1993 "Sorbian (Upper and Lower)." In: Comrie, B.; Corbett, G. (eds.), *The Slavonic languages.* London. (593–685).

Uhlířová, L.
1995 "On the generality of statistical laws and individuality of texts. A case of syllables, word forms, their length and frequencies", in: *Journal of Quantitative Linguistics, 2*; 238–247.

Wilson, A.
2001 "Word length distributions in classical Latin verse", in: *Prague Bulletin of Mathematical Linguistics, 75*; 69–84.

Wimmer, G.; Altmann, G.
1996 "The theory of word length: Some results and generalizations." In: *Glottometrika 15.* (112–133).

Wimmer G.; Altmann, G.
1999 *Thesaurus of univariate discrete probability distributions.* Essen.

Zuse, M.
1996 "Distribution of word length in Early Modern English letters of Sir Philip Sidney", in: *Journal of Quantitative Linguistics, 3*; 272–276.

17

TOWARDS A UNIFIED DERIVATION OF SOME LINGUISTIC LAWS*

Gejza Wimmer, Gabriel Altmann

1. Introduction

In any scientific discipline the research usually begins in the form of *membra disiecta* because there is no theory which would systematize the knowledge and from which hypotheses could be derived. The researchers themselves have different interests and observe at first narrow sectors of reality. Later on, one connects step by step disparate domains (cf., for example, the unified representation of all kinds of motion of the macro world by Newton's theory) and the old theories usually become special cases of the new one. One speaks about epistemic integration (Bunge 1983: 42):

> The integration of approaches, data, hypotheses, theories, and even entire fields of research is needed not only to account for things that interact strongly with their environment. Epistemic integration is needed everywhere because there are no perfectly isolated things, because every property is related to other properties, and because every thing is a system or a component of some system... Thus, just as the variety of reality requires a multitude of disciplines, so the integration of the latter is necessitated by the unity of reality.

In quantitative linguistics we stand at the beginning of such a development. There are already two "grand" integrating cross-border approaches like language synergetics (cf. Köhler 1986) or Hřebíček's (1997) text theory as well as "smaller" ones, joining fewer disparate phenomena out of which some can be mentioned as examples:

(a) Baayen (1989), Chitashvili and Baayen (1993), Zörnig and Boroda (1992), Balasubrahmanyan/Naranan (1997) show that rank distributions can be transformed in frequency distributions, announced already by Rapoport (1982) in a non-formal way.

(b) Altmann (1990) shows that Bühler's "theory" is merely a special case of Zipf's theory who saw the "principle of least effort" behind all human activities (1949).

* Supported by a grant from the Scientific Grant Agency of the Slovak Republic VEGA 1/7295/20

P. Gryzbek (ed.), Contributing in the Science of Text and Language, 329-337.

(c) More integrating is Menzerath's law whose effects can be noticed not only in different domains of language but also in molecular biology, sociology and psychology (Altmann/Schwibbe 1989); it is a parallel to the allometric law and can be found also in chaos theory (Hřebíček's 1997, Schroeder 1990), in self-organized criticality (Bak 1996), in music (Boroda/Altmann 1991) etc.

(d) Orlov, Boroda and Nadarejšvili (1982) searched for commonalities in language, music and fine arts where they found the effect of Zipf-Mandelbrot's law.

(e) Krylov, Naranan and Balasubrahmanyan, all physicists, came independently to the conclusion that the maximization of entropy results in a law fitting excellently frequency distributions of language entities.

One could continue this enumeration of unification of domains from a certain point of view ad libitum – here we have brought merely examples. In all cases one can see the common background that in the end leads to systems theory. All things are systems. We join two domains if we find isomorphies, parallelities, similarities between the respective systems or if we ascertain that they are special cases of a still more general system. From time to time one must perform such an integration in order to obtain ever more unified theories and to organize the knowledge about the object of investigation.

In this contribution we want to present an approach that unifies several well known linguistic hypotheses, is easy to be generalized and is very simple – even if simplicity does not belong to the necessary virtues of science (cf. Bunge 1963). It is a logical extension of the "synergetic" approach (cf. Wimmer et al. 1994; Wimmer/Altmann 1996; Altmann/Köhler 1996). The individual hypotheses belonging to this system have been set up earlier as empirical, well fitting curves or derived from different approaches.

2. Continuous Approach

In linguistics, continuous variables can be met mostly in phonetics but we are aware that "variable" is merely a construct of our mathematical apparatus with which we strive for capturing the grades of real properties transforming them from discrete to continuous (e.g., average) or vice versa (e.g., splitting a continuous range in intervals) as the need arises, which is nothing unusual in the sciences. Thus there is nothing wrong in modelling continuous phenomena using discrete models or the other way round. "Continuous" and "discrete" are properties of our concepts, the first approximations of our epistemic endeavor. Here we start from two assumptions which are widespread and accepted in linguistics, treating first the continuous case:

(i.) Let y be a continuous variable. The change of any linguistic variable, dy, is controlled directly by its actual size because every linguistic variable is finite and part of a self-regulating system, i.e., we can always use in modelling the relative rate of change dy/y.

(ii.) Every linguistic variable y is linked with at least one other variable (x) which shapes the behavior of y and that can be considered in the given case as independent. The independent variable influences the dependent variable y also by its rate of change, dx, which is itself in turn controlled by different powers of its own values that are associated with different factors, "forces" etc. We consider x, y as differently scaled and so these two assumptions can be expressed formally as

$$\frac{dy}{y-d} = \left(a_0 + \sum_{i=1}^{k_1} \frac{a_{1i}}{(x-b_{1i})^{c_1}} + \sum_{i=1}^{k_2} \frac{a_{2i}}{(x-b_{2i})^{c_2}} + \dots \right) dx \quad (17.1)$$

with $c_i \neq c_j, i \neq j$. (We note that for $k_s = 0$ is $\sum_{i=1}^{k_s} \frac{a_{si}}{(x-b_{si})^{c_s}} = 0$.)

The constants a_{ij} must be interpreted in every case differently; they represent properties, "forces", order parameters, system requirements etc. which actively participate in the linkage between x and y (cf. Köhler 1986, 1987, 1989, 1990) but remain constant because of the *ceteris paribus* condition. In the differential equation (17.1) the variables are already separated. The solution of (17.1) is (if $c_1 = 1$)

$$y = Ce^{a_0 x} \prod_{i=1}^{k_1} (x-b_{1i})^{a_{1i}} e^{\left(\sum_{j\geq 2} \sum_{i=1}^{kj} \frac{a_{ji}}{(1-c_j)(x-b_{ji})^{c_j-1}} \right)} + d \quad (17.2)$$

The most common solutions of this approach result in

(a) type-token curves
(b) Menzerath's law
(c) Piotrovskij-Bektaev-Piotrovskaja's law of vocabulary growth
(d) Naranan-Balasubrahmanyan's word frequency models
(e) Geršić-Altmann's distribution of vowel duration
(f) Job-Altmann's model of change compulsion of phonemes
(g) Tuldava's law of polysemy
(h) Uhlířová's dependence of nouns in a given position in sentence
(i) The continuous variant of Zipf-Mandelbrot's law and its special cases (Good, Woronczak, Orlov, Zörnig-Altmann)

3. Two-Dimensional Approach

This is of course not sufficient. In synergetic linguistics there is a number of interrelations that cannot be captured with the aid of only one variable, concealing the other ones under the "ceteris paribus" condition. They are frequently so strong that they must be explicitly taken into account.
Consider first a simple special case of formula (17.1)

$$\frac{dy}{y} = \left(a_0 + \frac{a_1}{x} + \frac{a_2}{x^2}\right) dx \tag{17.3}$$

whose solution yiels

$$y = Ce^{a_0 x} x^{a_1} e^{-a_2/x} \tag{17.4}$$

which represents e.g. Gěrśic-Altmann's model of vowel duration. In (17.3) we assume that all other factors (besides x) are weaker than x and can be considered as constants relativized by powers of x (e.g., $a_2/x^2, a_3/x^3$ etc.). But in synergetic linguistics this is not usual. In many models, the researchers (e.g. Köhler, Krott, Prün) show that a variable depends at the same time on several other variables which have a considerable influence. Now, we assume – as is usual in synergetic linguistics – that the dependent variable has the same relation to other variables as shown in (17.3). Thus we combine several approaches and obtain in the first step

$$\frac{\partial y}{\partial x} = y\left(a_0 + \frac{a_1}{x} + \frac{a_2}{x^2} + \ldots\right); \quad \frac{\partial y}{\partial z} = y\left(b_0 + \frac{b_1}{z} + \frac{b_2}{z^2} + \ldots\right) \tag{17.5}$$

which results in

$$y = Ce^{a_0 x + b_0 z} x^{a_1} z^{b_1} e^{\left(-\sum\limits_{i=1}^{\infty} \frac{a_{i+1}}{i x^i} - \sum\limits_{i=1}^{\infty} \frac{b_{i+1}}{i z^i}\right)} \tag{17.6}$$

The special cases of (17.6) are often found in synergetic linguistics where more than two variables are involved. This system can be generalized to any number of variables, can, as a matter of fact, encompass the whole synergetic linguistics and is applicable to very complex systems. Some well known cases from synergetic linguistics are

$$y = Cx^a z^b \tag{17.7}$$

$$y = Ce^{ax+bz} \tag{17.8}$$

$$y = Ce^{ax+bz} x^a z^b \tag{17.9}$$

etc.

4. Discrete Approach

If X is a discrete variable – being the usual case in linguistics – then we use instead of dx the difference $\Delta x = x - (x-1) = 1$. Since here one has to do mostly with (nonnegative discrete) probability distributions with probability mass functions $\{P_0, P_1, \ldots\}$ we set up the relative rate of change as

$$\frac{\Delta P_{x-1}}{P_{x-1}} = \frac{P_x - P_{x-1}}{P_{x-1}} \tag{17.10}$$

and obtain the discrete analog to (17.1) as

$$\frac{\Delta P_{x-1}}{P_{x-1}} = a_0 + \sum_{i=1}^{k_1} \frac{a_{1i}}{(x-b_{1i})^{c_i}} + \sum_{i=1}^{k_2} \frac{a_{2i}}{(x-b_{2i})^{c_2}} + \ldots \tag{17.11}$$

If $k_1 = k_2 = \ldots = 1, d = b_{11} = b_{21} = \ldots = 0, c_i = i, a_{i1} = a_i, i = 1, 2, \ldots$ the equivalent form of (17.11) is

$$P_x = \left(1 + a_0 + \frac{a_1}{x} + \frac{a_2}{x^2} + \ldots\right) P_{x-1}\,. \tag{17.12}$$

The system most used in linguistics is

$$P_x = \left(1 + a_0 + \frac{a_1}{x-b_1} + \frac{a_2}{x-b_2}\right) P_{x-1}, \tag{17.13}$$

whose solution for $x = 0, 1, 2, \ldots$ yields

$$P_x = \frac{(1+a_0)^x \binom{C-B+x}{x}\binom{D-B+x}{x}}{\binom{-b_1+x}{x}\binom{-b_2+x}{x}} \times {}_3F_2^{-1}(1, C-B+1, D-B+1; -b_1+1, -b_2+1; 1+a_o) \tag{17.14}$$

where

$B = \frac{b_1+b_2}{2}$

$C = \frac{a_1+a_2-\sqrt{2(1+a_0)^2(b_1-b_2)^2 - 2(1+a_0)(a_1-a_2)(b_1-b_2)+(a_1+a_2)^2}}{2(1+a_0)}$

$D = \frac{a_1+a_2+\sqrt{2(1+a_0)^2(b_1-b_2)^2 - 2(1+a_0)(a_1-a_2)(b_1-b_2)+(a_1+a_2)^2}}{2(1+a_0)}$

From the recurrence formulas (17.12) and (17.13) one can obtain many well known distributions used frequently in linguistics, e.g., the geometric distribution, the Katz family of distributions, different diversification distributions, rank-frequency distributions,, distribution of distances, the Poisson, negative binomial, binomial, hyper-Poisson, hyper-Pascal, Yule, Simon, Waring, Johnson-Kotz, negative hypergeometric, Conway-Maxwell-Poisson distributions etc. etc.

The laws contained in this system are e.g. Frumkina's law, different syllable, word and sentence length laws, some forms of Zipf's law, ranking laws, distributions of syntactic properties, Krylov's semantic law, etc. etc.

5. Discrete Two-Dimensional Approach

In the same way as with the continuous approach one can generalize the discrete approach to several variables. Since the number of examined cases in linguistics up to now is very small (an unyet published article by Wimmer and Uhlířová, an article on syllable structure by Zörnig/Altmann1993, and an article on semantic diversification by Beöthy/Altmann 1984), we merely show the method.
In the one-dimensional discrete approach we had a recurrence formula – e.g., (17.12) or (17.13) – that can be written as

$$P_x = g(x)P_{x-1} \tag{17.15}$$

where $g(x)$ was (a part of) an infinite series. Since now we have two variables, we can set up the model as follows

$$\begin{aligned} P_{i,j} &= g(i,j)P_{i,j-1} \\ P_{i,j} &= h(i,j)P_{i-1,j} \end{aligned} \tag{17.16}$$

where $g(i,j)$ and $h(i,j)$ are different functions of i and j. The equations must be solved simultaneously. The result depends on the given functions. Thus Wimmer and Uhlířová obtained the two dimensional binomial distribution, Zörnig and Altmann obtained the two-dimensional Conway-Maxwell-Poisson distribution and Beöthy and Altmann obtained the two-dimensional negative binomial distribution.

6. Conclusion

The fact that in this way one can systematize different hypotheses has several consequences:

(1) It shows that there is a unique mechanism – represented by (17.1), (17.5), (17.11), (17.16) – behind many language processes in which one can combine variables and "forces".

(2) Formulas (17.1), (17.5), (17.11), (17.16) represent systems in which also extra-systemic factors can be inserted.

(3) This approach allows to test inductively new, up to now unknown relations and systematize them in a theory by a correct interpretation of factors; this is usually not possible if one proceeds inductively. The explorative part of the work could therefore be speeded up with the appropriate software. One should not assume that one can explain everything in language using this approach but one can comfortably unify and interpret a posteriori many disparate phenomena.

References

Altmann, G.
1990 "Bühler or Zipf? A re-interpretation." In: Koch, W.A. (ed.), *Aspekte einer Kultursemiotik.* Bochum. (1–6).

Altmann, G.; Köhler, R.
1996 " 'Language Forces' and synergetic modelling of language phenomena", in: *Glottometrika, 15*; 62–76.

Altmann, G.; Schwibbe, M.H.
1989 *Das Menzerathsche Gesetz in informationsverarbeitenden Systemen.* Hildesheim.

Baayen, R.H.
1989 *A corpus-based approach to morphological productivity.* Amsterdam: Centrum voor Wiskunde en Informatica.

Bak, P.
1996 *How nature works. The science of self-organized criticality.* New York.

Balasubrahmanyan, V.K.; Naranan, S.
1997 "Quantitative linguistics and complex system studies", in: *Journal of Quantitative Linguistics, 3*; 177–228.

Beöthy, E.; Altmann, G.
1984 "Semantic diversification of Hungarian verbal prefices. III. 'föl-', 'el-', 'be-'." In: *Glottometrika 7.* (73–100).

Boroda, M.G.; Altmann, G.
1991 "Menzerath's law in musical texts." In: *Musikometrika 3.* (1–13).

Bunge, M.
1963 *The myth of simplicity.* Englewood Cliffs, N.J.

Bunge, M.
1983 *Understanding the world.* Dordrecht, NL.

Chitashvili, R.J.; Baayen, R.H.
1993 "Word frequency distributions of texts and corpora as large number of rare event distributions." In: Hřebíček, L.; Altmann, G. (eds.), *Quantitative Text Analysis.* Trier. (54–135).

Geršić, S.; Altmann, G.
1988 "Ein Modell für die Variabilität der Vokaldauer." In: *Glottometrika 9.* (49–58).

Hřebíček, L.
1997 *Lectures on text theory.* Prague: Oriental Institute.

Köhler, R.
1986 *Zur linguistischen Synergetik. Struktur und Dynamik der Lexik.* Bochum.

Köhler, R.
1987 "Systems theoretical linguistics", in: *Theoretical Linguistics, 14*; 241–257.

Köhler, R.
1989 "Linguistische Analyseebenen, Hierarchisierung und Erklärung im Modell der sprachlichen Selbstregulation." In: *Glottometrika 11.* (1–18).

Köhler, R.
1990 "Elemente der synergetischen Linguistik." In: *Glottometrika 12.* (179–187).

Orlov, Ju.K.; Boroda, M.G.; Nadarejšvili, I.Š.
1982 *Sprache, Text, Kunst. Quantitative Analysen.* Bochum.

Rapoport, A.
1982 "Zipf's law re-visited." In: Guiter, H.; Arapov, M.V. (eds.), *Studies on Zipf's Law.* Bochum. (1–28).

Schroeder, M.
1990 *Fractals, chaos, power laws. Minutes from an infinite paradise.* New York.

Wimmer, G.; Köhler, R.; Grotjahn, R.; Altmann, G.
1994 "Towards a theory of word length distribution", in: *Journal of Quantitative Linguistics, 1*; 98–106.

Wimmer, G.; Altmann, G.
1996 "The theory of word length: Some results and generalizations." In: *Glottometrika 15.* (112–133).

Zipf, G.K.
1949 *Human behavior and the principle of least effort.* Reading, Mass.
Zörnig, P.; Altmann, G.
1993 "A model for the distribution of syllable types." In: *Glottometrika 14.* (190-196).
Zörnig, P.; Boroda, M.G.
1992 "The Zipf-Mandelbrot law and the interdependencies between frequency structure and frequency distribution in coherent texts." In: *Glottometrika 13.* (205–218).

Contributing Authors

Gabriel Altmann, Stüttinghauer Ringstraße 44, D-58515 Lüdenscheid, Germany.
e-mail: ram-verlag@t-online.de

Simone Andersen, Textpsychologisches Institut, Graf-Recke-Straße 38, D-40239 Düsseldorf, Germany.
e-mail: andersensc@aol.com

Gordana Antić, Technische Universität Graz, Institut für Statistik, Steyrergasse 17/IV , A-8010 Graz, Austria.
e-mail: djuras@stat.tu-graz.ac.at

Mario Djuzelic, Atronic International, Seering 13-14, A-8141 Unterpremstätten, Austria.
e-mail: mdjuzelic@atronic.com

August Fenk, Universität Klagenfurt, Institut für Medien- und Kommunikationswissenschaft, Universitätsstraße 65-67, A-9020 Klagenfurt, Austria.
e-mail: august.fenk@uni-klu.ac.at

Gertraud Fenk-Oczlon, Universität Klagenfurt, Institut für Sprachwissenschaft und Computerlinguistik, Universitätsstraße 65-67, A-9020 Klagenfurt, Austria.
e-mail: gertraud.fenk@uni-klu.ac.at

Peter Grzybek, Karl-Franzens-Universität Graz, Institut für Slawistik, Merangasse 70, A-8010 Graz, Austria.
e-mail: peter.grzybek@uni-graz.at

Primož Jakopin, Laboratorij za korpus slovenskega jezika, Inštitut za slovenski jezik Frana Ramovša ZRC SAZU Gosposka 13, SLO-1000 Ljubljana, Slovenia.
e-mail: primoz.jakopin@uni-lj.si

Emmerich Kelih, Karl-Franzens-Universität Graz, Institut für Slawistik, Merangasse 70, A-8010 Graz, Austria.
e-mail: emmerich.kelih@uni-graz.at

Reinhard Köhler, Universität Trier, Linguistische Datenverarbeitung / Computerlinguistik, Universitätsring 15, D-54286 Trier.
e-mail: koehler@uni-trier.de

Victor V. Kromer, Novosibirskij gosudarstvennyj pedagogičeskij universitet, fakul'tet inostrannych jazykov, ul. Vilujskaja 28, RUS-630126 Novosibirsk-126, Russia.
e-mail: kromer@newmail.ru

Cvetana Krstev, Filološki fakultet, Studentski trg 3, CS-11000 Beograd, Serbia and Montenegro.
e-mail: cvetana@matf.bg.ac.yu

Werner Lehfeldt, Georg-August Universität, Seminar für Slavische Philologie, Humboldtallee 19, D-37073 Göttingen, Germany.
e-mail: wlehfel@gwdg.de

Gordana Pavlović-Lažetić, Matematički fakultet, Studentski trg 16, CS-11000 Beograd, Serbia and Montenegro.
e-mail: gordana@matf.bg.ac.yu

Anatolij A. Polikarpov, Proezd Karamzina, kv. 204, dom 9-1, RUS-117463 Moskva, Russia.
e-mail: anatolp@philol.msu.ru

Otto A. Rottmann, Behrensstraße 19, D-58099 Hagen, Germany.
e-mail: otto.rottmann@t-online.de

Ernst Stadlober, Technische Universität, Institut für Statistik, Steyrergasse 17/IV, A-8010 Graz, Austria.
e-mail: stadlober@stat.tu-graz.ac.at

Udo Strauss, AIS, Schuckerstraße 25-27, D-48712 Gescher, Germany.
e-mail: strauss@a-i-s-gmbh.de

Marko Tadić, Odsjek za lingvistiku, Filozofski fakultet Sveučilišta u Zagrebu. Ivana Lučića 3, HR-10000 Zagreb, Croatia.
e-mail: marko.tadic@ffzg.hr

Duško Vitas, Matematički fakultet, Studentski trg 16, CS-11000 Beograd, Serbia and Montenegro.
e-mail: vitas@matf.bg.ac.yu

Andrew Wilson, Lancaster University, Linguistics Department, Lancaster LA1 4YT, Great Britain.
email: eiaaw@exchange.lancs.ac.uk

Gejza Wimmer, Slovenská akadémia vied, Matematický ústav Štefánikova 49, SK-81438 Bratislava, Slovakia.
e-mail: wimmer@mat.savba.sk

Author Index

Subject Index

M

N

O

P

U

W

Y

Z